◆ What do present assumptions about the structure of long-term memory
imply for the successful storage and use of knowledge? ___ ___ ___ ___ ___ important
◆ What unique types of knowledge of knowledge in different
that teachers evaluate various types of knowledge for students to
◆ When is it appropriate and inappropriate for students to
about their own learning?
◆ How do external educational tasks influence internal
◆ What basic changes in classroom experience are reco
els of instruction emphasizing active learning? How can
to encourage active learning?

ACTIVE
COOPERATION
THEME-BASED
INTEGRATED
VERSATILE
EVALUATION

You will find that much of the theoretical rationale
vironments is presented in this chapter. Look for t
margins.

COGNITIVE MODELS OF LEA

A cognitive perspective

As you read about the instructional strateg
book, you will note that we frequently spec
fluences a learner's mental activities. We
classroom experiences influence mental
decisions teachers make about using tech
to understand the mental behaviors in
sents a *cognitive perspective*.

Cognitive models emphasize h

Why learn how students accomplish academic tasks?

skills, solve problems, and engage in
and mathematical reasoning. Un
plished, the barriers to be overcom
help you recognize differences in
your students' instructional en
different learning tasks encou
can help you assign more effe
ing environment for your stu

Understanding how students learn and think

One way to understand
a processor of information
information is represente
cognitive system. It will
stored (storage); how
whole system is guide

MENTAL TOOLS: DOING THE WORK OF THINKING AND LEARNING

Something very important is still missing in our consideration of what is necessary for learning. Thinking and learning are active. Students acquire information from the world around them and generate personal knowledge. They
solve problems. They create new ideas and new things. The cognitive system
we have described to this point just sits there. If teachers want to search for
more effective learning experiences for their students, they will need to have
some general ideas about the mental actions that productive learning experiences should encourage.

The basic actions of the information-processing system are often referred
to as *processes*. Instead of an extended discussion of the volumes of research
on cognitive processes, permit the substitution of a simplifying idea based on
this research: that of a *mental tool*. Assume that students have at their disposal
mental tools they can use to accomplish a variety of cognitive tasks. We will
attempt to describe some tools to help you understand this idea. Here are four
general hypothetical tool categories:

1. Attend to: Maintains certain ideas in consciousness for an extended period of time.

ACTIVE
C
T
I
V
E

(From Chapter 2)

Active learning, collaboration, and technology

THE PAINTED LADY PROJECT AND MEANINGFUL LEARNING

What is going on in this classroom? You probably realize from earlier chapters
that these students are working on a hypermedia project as part of a science
unit. Why should teachers add hypermedia projects as part of a science
experiences they provide students? How does involvement in such projects
help students learn in a generative way? How do students go about putting a
project together? In this chapter we provide some answers to these questions
by exploring the topic of knowledge as design, by discussing several multimedia
basic principles of multimedia design, and by describing several multimedia
projects. We will return to Pam's classroom to follow her and her second-
grade class as they develop several new projects. One of these projects will be
presented in considerable detail so you will have a better understanding of
what both a teacher and students do over the course of developing a theme-
based project. You will learn how active learning, student collaboration, and
technology come together as students prepare for and craft their project.

ACTIVE
COOPERATION
THEME-BASED
INTEGRATED
VERSATILE
EVALUATION

Useful knowledge

As we describe how students prepare for and craft their project,
areas, we will try to instill one important perspective relevant to many content
the result of a student's personal cognitive process of design: meaningful learning as
can be considered a design (Perkins, 1986). *Useful knowledge*
learning experiences around the concept that useful knowledge is purposefully generated by learners could have important implications for your classroom. The more traditional concept of design may also be important. One
way to actively involve students is by challenging them with a design project.
Designing a tangible product appears to facilitate the design of personal
knowledge. As we proceed, we will explore both the design of products and
the design of knowledge as well as possible connections between these two
types of tasks.

KNOWLEDGE AS DESIGN

Knowledge as information

How we think about knowledge can strongly influence our behavior as teachers and learners (Perkins, 1986). At least two perspectives are possible. The
first views knowledge as information. Information is basically factual knowledge; that is, ideas that are accumulated from various academic and life experiences and that are known for the sake of knowing. Information is stored
assuming that it will eventually prove useful. The perspective of knowledge as
information is consistent with the metaphor of learning as transmission. A
more knowledgeable person passes knowledge on to a less knowledgeable
person.

Knowledge as design

In contrast, **knowledge as design** is knowledge adapted to a purpose. In
the context of the model of active learning used throughout this book, knowl-

ogy an
sider th
rest of
classr
activities that have
of information will be discussed

Integrating Technology for Meaningful Learning

Second Edition

MARK GRABE

University of North Dakota

CINDY GRABE

Technology Facilitator, Grand Forks Schools

HOUGHTON MIFFLIN COMPANY

BOSTON   NEW YORK   TORONTO

SENIOR SPONSORING EDITOR: Loretta Wolozin

ASSOCIATE EDITOR: Lisa Mafrici

PROJECT EDITOR: Nicole Ng/Rebecca Bennett

SENIOR PRODUCTION/DESIGN COORDINATOR: Jennifer Waddell

SENIOR MANUFACTURING COORDINATOR: Priscilla Bailey

COVER DESIGNER: Tony Saizon

COVER IMAGE: Howard Hodgkin, Small Durand Gardens, 1974. Anthony d'Offay Gallery, London

LINE ART: Maria Di Paolo, NuGraphic Design

Printed in the U.S.A.

Library of Congress Catalog Number: 97-72476

ISBN: 0-395-87136-0

23456789—MV—01 00 99 98

Acknowledgment is made to the following sources for permission to reprint selections from copyrighted material:

Preface figure: Copyright © 1993 and published by Weekly Reader Corporation. All rights reserved. Used by permission. **Table 1.1:** Adapted by permission from Brown, "Changes in Classroom Philosophy," *Journal of the Learning Sciences*, 2 (2). **Figure 1.2:** Reprinted by permission. **Figures 2.1, 7.2:** Used by permission of North Dakota Game & Fish. **Figures 3.1, 3.2:** Copyright © 1993 MagicQuest, Inc., a Sanctuary Woods Company. All rights reserved. **Figures 3.3, 3.4:** Reprinted by permission of Scholastic, Inc. **Figures 3.5, 3.6:** Screen displays used by permission of Methods & Solutions/Mindplay, 160 West Fort Lowell Road, Tucson, Arizona. **Figure 3.7:** Reproduced from MICROTYPE: THE WONDERFUL WORLD OF PAWS with the permission of South-Western Educational Publishing, a division of International Thomson Publishing Inc. Copyright © 1992 by South-Western Educational Publishing. All rights reserved.

Copyright page continues on page 451.

Dedication

Allow me to tell a brief story. I remember a trip my wife and I took to my parents' home during the later stages of Cindy's and my education as graduate students. I happened to awake about six in the morning and went down to the kitchen of our old farm house because I was thirsty and needed a drink of water. When I walked into the kitchen, I was surprised to see that the lights were already on and my mother was busy working at the kitchen table preparing her lessons for the day. For some reason, the image has always stayed with me. My mother had taught Home Economics since I was in junior high school, and although I was also preparing for a career in education I had never really thought much about her dedication to what she did. My mother used hardware and software too. She had a shallow tray containing a substance that looked like Jell-O, and with this equipment and typed or hand-drawn spirit masters she would turn out dittoed pages about nutrition, sewing, childcare, or whatever she was intending to discuss. It was a slow process. First, the master had to be pressed against the "Jell-O" for a few minutes. It was important to align the master carefully or the final product would be crooked. Then, blank sheets of paper were individually pressed against the Jell-O-like material and carefully peeled away to create the handouts. Try to keep my mom's use of technology in mind as you read about the techniques we describe in this book. The contrast is amazing and provides just one indication of the tremendous change that has occurred in a relatively brief period of time. This story is intended to get you to think about more than the pace of change in our world. While Cindy and I believe strongly that technology can have a profound impact on our schools, our confidence in technology is justified only in classrooms led by dedicated and skillful teachers. We should be amazed and excited by the power of modern technology, but we should remain impressed by the teachers who begin work at six because last year's lesson may not be good enough. This book is dedicated to Frances Grabe and to all teachers like her.

Brief Contents

Contents

 *Preface*

Sophisticated technology has become so pervasive and intertwined with so many aspects of our private and professional lives that we seldom even notice it. You may not realize that your car is controlled by complex microelectronics that monitor and adjust the engine's functioning. You listen to music on CD-ROMS and view the video images captured by a camcorder without being amazed by the technology or feeling intimidated by the equipment that makes these experiences possible. You may become annoyed when the person stopped at the light in front of you is so intent on his cellular phone conversation that he fails to notice that the light has turned to green, but you have probably come to accept this as part of driving in city traffic. Video games, ATM machines, fax machines, cellular phones, caller ID, voice mail, personal satellite dishes, microwave ovens—the list of technological innovations we have accepted into our daily lives goes on and on.

TECHNOLOGY IN CLASSROOMS

We wrote this book because technology seldom plays the same natural role in classrooms that it does in other areas of our daily lives. There is a tremendous need for practical, understandable information about integrating technology in K–12 classroom instruction. We realize that some teachers are uncertain and anxious about computer hardware, software selection, and the learning activities that are likely to be useful and productive. If you feel that way, we hope the information and suggestions we provide in this book will move you from apprehension to excitement.

THIS TEXT'S GOALS AND PERSPECTIVE

You will find that this book is about technology *and* about teaching and learning. We feel it is important to consider and discuss both areas together. Our primary goals are the following:

◆ to present the different roles technology might play in your classroom;
◆ to provide specific examples of each type of role;
◆ to inform you of a few technical ins and outs of some applications you might use in implementing each role;
◆ to suggest how to initiate particular applications with your students; and
◆ to promote your thinking and reflection about the best uses of technology.

As you think about this information, we hope that you will also consider why you and your future students should spend time using technology in the ways we propose. As a teacher, you play the important role of decision maker. The discussion of classroom learning and how learning is influenced by the classroom tasks and activities students experience should help you make decisions about whether to devote precious school time to a given activity.

We also hope that as you read this book, you will not assume that school experiences as you know them must remain fixed, with technology somehow finding a way to fit within the existing framework. Some educational leaders are urging both a restructuring of schools and serious consideration of what schools do. Criticism of public education is not new, of course, and whether or not massive changes ever occur, continual scrutiny of educational practice should be encouraged.

Technology is functioning as a catalyst in some of these considerations, and it may serve the same role for you. As you think about how to use technology in your classroom, you will likely find yourself examining broad educational issues. Just remember: in most cases effective teaching with technology is effective teaching by any means. Criticisms of the way technology has been used may also alert you to more traditional practices that should also be criticized. For example, if many experts put down drill and practice computer software, what do you think these same experts might say about the heavy use of traditional worksheets? If some advocates of technology suggest that teachers use technology to encourage a more active and personal form of learning, why not examine how active student learning is under traditional circumstances? We want you to think carefully about the many different issues that will determine how you and your students use technology.

THE COGNITIVE LEARNING APPROACH IN THIS BOOK

Our intent is to emphasize technology-facilitated classroom activities in an active learning environment—one that strongly engages the thinking and reasoning behaviors of students. We use the term *cognitive* to refer to these behaviors. To implement effective classroom activities, it is critical that teachers understand the connection between learning tasks and the mental activities of students.

Chapter 2, "Cognitive Learning and Technology Tools," establishes the foundation for this connection, as its title indicates. As later chapters familiarize you with various software applications and strategies for classroom use, we continually extend key concepts that were introduced in Chapter 2. Several of these later chapters focus on computer tools that allow students to create multimedia projects and culminate in Chapter 10, "Learning from Student Projects: Knowledge as Design and the Design of Hypermedia." That chapter integrates strategies for effective learning and technology skills while placing special emphasis on using technology in support of content-area instruction in the design of cooperative student multimedia projects. These projects and many other original student projects included throughout the book provide good examples of tasks that encourage meaningful learning.

Moreover, throughout this entire text we put our emphasis on integrating technology for meaningful *learning* within actual classroom contexts. To help you try out and use key teaching and learning principles, we identify several characteristics of technology-supported learning experiences in ways that you will find easy to remember. We label this collection of characteristics the ACTIVE learning environment.

A CTIVE
C OOPERATION
T HEME-BASED
I NTEGRATED
V ERSATILE
E VALUATION

ACTIVE is an acronym for experiences that encourage *active* mental behaviors. Often these experiences are based in *cooperative* and *theme-based* tasks that are *integrated* into content area instruction. We emphasize the use of technology tools that are *versatile* so any technology skills students acquire can be used repeatedly and efficiently. We also emphasize activities resulting in products that can be used to *evaluate* understanding and skill. As you read, you will see the ACTIVE icon in the margin to alert you to a discussion of one or more of these characteristics.

THE AUTHORS' COMPLEMENTARY EXPERIENCES

The topics and orientation of this book are a blend of the orientations, experiences, and individual interests of the two authors. Mark Grabe's background is in educational psychology—he is a professor and chair of the Psychology Department at the University of North Dakota. He brings to this collaboration the theoretical perspectives and research experiences more typical of a university faculty member. Mark has been developing microcomputer courseware for approximately twelve years in support of his own research activities and has done some programming and courseware design as a consultant. Mark has been conducting in-service workshops for practicing teachers since the Apple II⁺ came with only 48K of memory and users were loading programs from cassette tapes. For those of you completely unfamiliar with the brief history of K–12 applications of computer technology, this means he has been working with computers in schools basically since there first were computers in schools. Mark's professional career began as a teacher of high school biology; he currently works with the North Dakota Department of Game and Fish to bring information about the biology of the northern prairies to students and the general public through the Internet.

Cindy Grabe's original certification was as an elementary teacher; she later earned a master's degree as a learning disabilities specialist. After she had worked for many years as a reading specialist, her interest in technology led her to a full-time position as a technology facilitator for the Grand Forks, North Dakota, school district. Her position requires that she review software and hardware for district purchase and negotiate purchase agreements with vendors; provide training to district teachers, administrators, and staff members; serve as a resource person for district curriculum committees; and conduct demonstration activities with students. She is heavily involved in providing continuing education experiences for teachers from many area schools, and she consults with regional schools regarding issues related to technology. Cindy deals directly and continuously with the very practical circumstances of integrating technology in classrooms. In addition to her more general role in writing this book, she has generated most of the lists of ideas for implementation provided here. Her own work with students and her association with many gifted classroom teachers also afforded numerous samples of student work for inclusion. Cindy was recently recognized as an Apple Distinguished Educator by the Apple Computer Corporation.

FEATURES OF THE REVISION

It seems that the printer has barely had a chance to cool down from running off drafts of the original version of *Integrating Technology for Meaningful Learning* and here we are finishing the second edition. The rapid transition from one edition to the next was a necessary consequence of the rapid pace of development and change in technology and some new possibilities for how technology can be applied in classrooms. However, do not interpret this to mean that what you learn here about the applications of technology has no permanence. The second edition is based on the same principal themes as the first. New advances in hardware and software just provide additional opportunities for implementing these ideas in classrooms.

Following is a summary of some of the changes in the second edition:

a) The most obvious change in the second edition is a much heavier emphasis on the World Wide Web and other Internet tools. Chapter 6, "Learning with Internet Tools," is now devoted exclusively to a discussion of Internet tools and related classroom applications. It addresses questions about how course-relevant World Wide Web resources can be found and how teachers can structure e-mail activities and Web projects to engage students in meaningful learning. We emphasize student Web authoring as an option for student content area projects in Chapter 10. An Internet Web site supplementing the content of this book is available at http://www.hmco.com/college/ and will provide updates, as well as many teaching and learning resources. You will also find that we cite Web sources in most chapters to provide the most current information possible. The addition of this new material has not required that we alter our basic philosophy. We see the problems and the promise of the Internet as an educational resource to be remarkably consistent with the classroom challenges we first set out to address. The student's main goal is still to build personal understanding from whatever information resources are available. Technology can provide access to some of these new sources of information and can also provide tools for manipulating and exploring these resources in ways that are personally meaningful.

b) All chapters have been upgraded to include new examples of software and more recent references.

c) A new feature, "Emerging Technology," has been added to several chapters. It allows us to acquaint educators with new products that are available but that have yet to be widely implemented. We believe we have identified products with the potential to make a contribution in many classrooms.

OUR APPROACH IS ANCHORED IN EVERYDAY LIFE

You should know one more thing about this book's development. We wanted to be able to assure you that what we propose here would be practical for you to implement. As we worked through the early drafts of many of the chapters, we made a conscious commitment to rely heavily on our own experiences with our local school district. We decided it would be unfair to present a picture of technology use painted with scenes from various high tech demonstration sites scattered around the country. What we describe here, then, are projects undertaken in classrooms by teachers we know personally.

We both work and live in Grand Forks, North Dakota. We anticipate that many of you may have only a vague understanding of where that is. What might be more relevant is that the technology present in our local schools is there because of the investment of local taxpayers and the applications of technology we describe result from the decision making of the school board, local administrators, and teachers. What exists here is not a demonstration site for any vendor or a research center associated with a major university. Local resources for technology are above average, but certainly are not at the extreme level that might identify special demonstration sites. What we have done is draw examples from some of the more involved and creative teachers we know. We do not claim that these teachers are typical, but rather, that they work in fairly typical schools under typical circumstances.

LEARNING FEATURES OF THE TEXT

Embedded in the chapter content are special features to help you better understand important concepts and move toward using ideas and approaches you find useful in your own classroom.

Scenes from Real Classrooms

Detailed descriptions of classroom events can provide a powerful way to "see" in action many of the ideas we present. Several chapters begin with a classroom example to provide a context for what you will read. Other chapters have stories and interviews embedded as demonstrations of teacher or student behavior. We have tried to remain true to the stories teachers and students actually related to us.

Screen Images and Program Examples

The graphics in this book are mostly images captured as they appear on the computer screen and examples of student work. These resources will help you understand what the programs we describe are like and how students use them.

Focus Boxes

"Focus" boxes provide technological information or extend discussions of important people, instructional issues, or instructional strategies. They allow the reader to consider this information independently. If we were presenting this material using hypermedia, we could use some great techniques for linking the presentation of the more central ideas to interesting details. Focus boxes are the next best thing.

Emerging Technology Features

New to this edition, the "Emerging Technology" features that appear in many chapters allow us to explore innovations that are available but that have yet to be widely implemented. If our description of the innovation and potential application should intrigue you, you will find the information necessary to learn more about or obtain the product.

Spotlight on Assessment Boxes

Assessment practices represent a powerful yet largely invisible barrier to change in educational practice. Many interesting ideas for things students might do or skills they should learn end up being ignored because we are uncomfortable with how we might assess knowledge and skills. The answers to assessment questions are not easy, and we are not even sure there are always good answers, but we do think it tremendously important to realize the limitations a narrow view of assessment imposes and to constantly try to broaden our awareness of assessment alternatives. We hope putting the spotlight on assessment will bring some of the issues and possibilities to your attention.

Activities and Projects for Your Classroom Boxes

We have included a large number of application ideas in this book, but we also recognize that teachers work in many disciplines with students of different ages. Writing activity boxes allowed us to list variations of applications that might be more discipline- or age-specific. The combination of the extended examples and the variations provided within the activity boxes is a reasonable way to acquaint you with classroom applications.

Keeping Current Boxes

Writing a book about technology is daunting. Software, hardware, and ideas for how to apply technology are constantly changing. We have tried to prepare you for "life after this book" by providing you with sources of information that are likely to further address educational issues we have raised or to provide a periodical review of software, hardware, and applications.

End of Chapter Activities

Each chapter ends with several activities. We considered listing specific tasks requiring the use of technology. We have decided against a strong emphasis on this approach because the resources available to our readers will vary a great deal. Instead, we found other ways to involve you in actively thinking about key ideas. We do believe that reading about the application of technology will not be enough to prepare you to use ideas in your classroom. We trust that this book will not be the only resource at your disposal and that you will also learn a great deal from teachers and colleagues.

End of Chapter Resources to Expand Your Knowledge Base

Each chapter ends with annotated lists of resources that offer further information about, and investigations of, the topics covered in the chapter. These sources include: books, journals, Web sites, and addresses for hardware and software companies.

ACKNOWLEDGMENTS

No book originates in the minds of the authors alone, and this book is no exception. We owe many individuals our gratitude for helping to bring you this book. Loretta Wolozin, senior sponsoring editor at Houghton Mifflin, saw in our original proposal the germ of a unique idea and made the trip to North Dakota to talk with us and examine student projects. Putting students in control of powerful tools was and is not typical, and yet Loretta has supported our belief that this theme should be at the core of what teachers learn about the classroom applications of technology. We have had the opportunity to work with several developmental editors in completing the two editions of this textbook: Lisa Mafrici, Susan Yanchus, and Janet Edmonds. All were patient and helpful as we explored what we wanted to say and how we should say it. We hope you will find our arguments and explanations clear and our style friendly. Nicole Ng, production editor, was responsible for the tedious tasks associated with polishing our prose, making certain there was a citation for each of our references, and handling many of the other details of a textbook that you as a reader take for granted and we as writers are never quite careful enough to guarantee. We were also assisted in the developmental process by the guidance and feedback of some very knowledgeable reviewers including

Marcus D. Childress, Emporia State University
Don E. Decey, Mankato State University
Laura Diggs, University of Missouri
Edwin J. George, State University of New York, Cortland
Gail Lilly Hill, University of Mary Hardin-Baylor
Janette R. Hill, University of Northern Colorado
Patricia L. Leonard, Rider University
Lonell Moeller, South Dakota State University
Debra Sprague, George Mason University
Kim E. Zahniser, Mesa State College

Finally, we owe a giant debt to the many teachers and students who provided the authentic examples we have included. The individuals identified throughout this book represent a wider circle of individuals who have influenced our thinking about teaching and instructional applications of technology. Because she represents this group, we would like to recognize the special contribution of Pam Carlson. Pam was a second grade teacher and is now a graduate student with whom we worked closely in developing our early ideas. In our interactions we taught Pam a few things about technology and she taught us many things about helping students become active and excited learners.

ONE FINAL WORD

It is not always possible to determine where ideas originate, but we know exactly how we began working with student-authored multimedia. Several years ago we were preparing for a workshop in which Cindy planned to introduce Kid Pix to a group of teachers. We were just learning the program ourselves and were searching for something that would get the teachers excited. Our daughter Kim (then in first grade, now in middle school) had been studying dinosaurs, so we scanned a picture of a dinosaur. We asked Kim to use Kid Pix to color the picture and then record a song she had learned about dinosaurs. We were pleased with the result and decided to use the product as part of our presentation. As we continued to work on other parts of the workshop, Kim remained at the computer, singing the dinosaur song over and over. It turned out she was singing as she typed in the lyrics. We saved her picture (see below). Since we have thanked many people in this preface, we should also thank Kim, who has been very tolerant of the work habits of her parents. Her own creative talents and her enthusiasm for learning have served to inspire us for what has now been quite a few years. We know students enjoy working in the ways we describe because we have been able to watch and work with them.

Kim's Original Multimedia Project (Converted to Gray Scale)

my name is stagasurus i'm a funny looking disasaur
for on my back are meny boney platse and
on my tail there,s more

PART ONE

A Teaching and Learning Framework for Integrating Technology in Classrooms

Part One *introduces you to the roles technology now plays in education and the roles it is likely to play in the future. The opening chapters introduce you to this text's major themes, including the "tools approach," activity-based approaches to learning, active roles for students, integrated or multidisciplinary approaches to learning, cooperative learning, and the role of teachers as facilitators. You will also explore some major ideas about meaningful learning and find out how educational technology fits among these ideas.*

Chapter 1

Key Themes and Issues for Using Technology in Your Classroom

ORIENTATION

In new fields of study, there should always be opportunities to demonstrate vision and encourage optimism, to dream about, imagine, and even predict the future. Thinking about the future is important for educators. And preparing students for that future requires some consideration of skills students will need and the rapidly evolving role of technology in educational practice. As educators, you will participate in shaping an era of dramatic change. We open this chapter with a description of a multimedia project that highlights some of the themes and applications that figure prominently throughout this book. As you read, look for answers to the following questions:

FOCUS QUESTIONS

♦ How does the role of the teacher as facilitator differ from more traditional teachers' roles?
♦ What are the most common inequities in computer use?
♦ Why are students not actively involved with the technology already in schools?
♦ What are the characteristics of activity-based approaches to learning?

USES OF TECHNOLOGY IN TEACHING AND LEARNING

Although we have written this book as a well-balanced introduction to the many uses of technology in teaching and learning, there are several themes and suggested applications that will play more prominent roles than others. The following project illustrates some of our priorities.

Ocean Project: An Introductory Example of Technology in the Classroom

Pam Carlson is an experienced second grade teacher. She is strongly committed to involving her students in projects that are challenging, require student initiative, and often are not based on prepackaged instructional materials. When she introduced the project we are about to describe, her background in technology was limited to a few in-service workshops after school or on Saturday mornings. She was excited by what she had been exposed to. In general, she finds new ideas exciting, but she can hardly be called a "techie"; in this respect, she is no different from thousands of other teachers.

Pam's goal was to involve her class in a science unit on ocean life. Her original instructional strategy was to expose students to a variety of written documents (such as poetry, magazine articles, fictional stories, and factual resource books) related to ocean life. In the initial activities, the students and Pam examined a single document (a resource book, for example), and Pam wrote key concepts and terms on chart paper as both she and her students identified them. They added information to the chart as more documents (such as poems) were considered. Later, Pam asked the students to write a paragraph summarizing the information they had gathered. After working through examples as a group, under Pam's guidance, students later completed the activity on their own with new documents.

As Pam began collecting materials for the unit, one of her colleagues showed her a collection of **shareware** clip art depicting different marine organisms. Clip art is graphic material prepared for another person's use. It usually consists of pictures of individual objects with no background (see Figure 1.1). Pam's original intent was to use the clip art herself to add interest to materials prepared for the students. However, before she started the unit, she saw demonstrations of HyperCard and Kid Pix and decided to see what her students could do using these tools. (Don't worry if you don't understand all of these terms right now. We will discuss them in more depth later, and all the boldface terms are in the Glossary.) Both Pam and her students learned to use the computer hardware and software as the ocean project evolved.

To begin the computer portion of the project, black-and-white images of fish were printed on individual sheets of paper and posted on the classroom bulletin board. First, all of the students used resource books to identify each fish. When students thought they could identify one of the pictures, they penciled the fish's name on the picture. At times, images ended up with more than one label; additional research and class discussion resolved what each fish was called. When all the fish were identified, each student chose one to research. In examining the various sources of information that Pam provided, the students used research skills they had practiced earlier. Then they used the computers in the school's lab to enter notes and create a written report. Working in pairs, students edited each other's work and made suggestions for improvements: Does the report make sense? Could more information be added? Are words spelled correctly?

As the students worked on their reports, Pam learned the basics of operating her classroom computer and some related **peripheral devices**, external to the computer. One of the first peripherals with which she became familiar was a **hand-held scanner**. A scanner allows an image on paper, such as a diagram or photo, to be copied to the screen and memory of a computer. Pam used the scanner to generate a computer image of each student by scanning each student's school picture. Each student's picture was added to the computer image of the fish the student had selected, so that the student's picture appeared in an upper corner of the screen when the composite picture was displayed. At this point, students were introduced to Kid Pix, an inexpensive color **paint program** designed for children. After exploring the program's capabilities, the students **loaded** their fish pictures into the computer. Each student found a color picture of his or her fish in a resource book and attempted to paint the fish and background as realistically as possible.

FIGURE 1.1 A Sample of Original Clip Art

As it turned out, Kid Pix allowed the students to do more than add color and text to their pictures. They could use a small microphone connected to the computer to attach short segments of sound to the pictures. The students were fascinated with Kid Pix's capacity to record their voices and store this information on disk and they decided to prepare the information they had gathered about each fish as thirty-second oral reports. In preparing to actually use the computer to store their reports, the students practiced giving their presentations to each other. They worked together to critique each other's reading speed, enunciation, and report length. Some students were told to speak more slowly; others, to speak louder; still others, to say more. The students then used the computer's built-in microphone to attach their oral reports to the stored picture files.

A more computer-experienced colleague helped Pam put the final touches on the class's ocean project. They used a simple multimedia program called HyperCard to display the students' work. The finished HyperCard **stack** presented several introductory screens complete with musical accompaniment and each student's image and oral report, followed by several concluding screens with the actual sound of a mother blue whale calling to her baby as musical background. See Figure 1.2 for an example of one of these screens (unfortunately, without the sound or the color!). The completed program presented the entire sequence of graphics, music, and messages in about ten minutes.

FIGURE 1.2 Completed Graphic for Ocean Project

Lane's Hammerhead Shark Report

These strange looking sharks are easy to recognize. Their hammer like heads have a thick lobe sticking out on each side. This is where the eyes and the nostrils are found. The eyes are wide apart as much as three feet in a fifteen foot shark.

Understanding the project's effect

Although this brief description should provide some insights into the teacher and student activities and the actual multimedia product that they developed, it is more difficult to convey the overall effect. Students were clearly motivated by the process. They demonstrated persistence and cooperation.

What was your response?

Did this example of a multimedia project surprise you? If you *have* thought about how students in an elementary school classroom would be likely to use computers, is this the kind of thing you assumed they would be doing? Was this because you wouldn't expect this level of work from second graders or because you weren't familiar with the capabilities of the technology itself? How would you assess each student's work on such a project? For some ideas about assessment, see Spotlight on Assessment on page 7.

THEMES OF TECHNOLOGY USE IN THE CLASSROOM

To be truthful, the ocean project example is not quite as typical of technology in the classroom as advocates would like. Students don't yet make the extensive use of technology that this example might imply, but there are many themes in the example that strongly recommend the way Pam Carlson chose to use technology. Here are some of those themes.

Technology Integrated into Content-Area Instruction

Two points might be raised here. First, the students in this example are learning about marine animals. Whatever they learn about how to operate the hardware and software systems is secondary. Although the lack of student experience with technology probably requires that they learn a great deal about technology, many of the skills associated with hardware and software manip-

Applying skills and extending learning goals

ulation can be applied to new content very efficiently. Second, the technology fits comfortably with the teacher's instructional plans and philosophy and represents more an extension of them than an alternative or addition to them.

A Tools Approach

Technology can play various instructional roles. A tools approach assumes that general-purpose software, such as word processing or paint programs or

Spotlight on Assessment

Relating Learning and Assessment

In practice, learning and assessment end up being interrelated in complex ways. Assessment methods do more than provide information on the quantity and quality of learning. Student experiences with assessment methods carry over into new learning situations, and the types of assessment anticipated appear to influence how and what they learn. You probably know this from your own experiences. Do you study differently when anticipating a multiple-choice or an essay examination? Do you review information differently when intending to demonstrate your understanding through a paper in contrast to an examination? If you are a typical student, the way you think about course content is likely to be heavily influenced by how you think your learning will be assessed (Crooks, 1988). Some researchers have claimed that the quickest way to change how students learn is to change the way learning is assessed (Elton and Laurillard, 1979). Others have cautioned instructors that students will be more influenced by the method of assessment than by classroom experiences and stated instructional goals (Snyder, 1971).

So, what does the research on assessment and learning suggest that teachers should do? The answer, but not necessarily its implementation, is fairly simple. Teachers should think carefully about the knowledge and skills they would like students to develop and make certain that knowledge and those skills are emphasized in the evaluation process. The research would suggest that, although some learning outcomes may seem difficult to evaluate, it is very important that we strive to find ways to evaluate them (Crooks, 1988). We hope that this text will acquaint you with techniques targeting some of the more evasive learning goals. ✳

Applying software tools to learn

an Internet World Wide Web browser, can be flexibly applied by the learner to various topics. This approach can be contrasted with the use of software developed specifically to teach a particular topic.

An Active Role for Students

The word *active* as used here does not refer directly to the physical activity of the learner, as might be involved in coloring the fish pictures. Rather, *active* describes the mental behavior of the students. In the example, the information to be learned was not presented to students in some kind of final, distilled form. Students had to dig for what they learned. They had to pull together bits and pieces of information from several sources, generate personal summaries, and make decisions. In later chapters, you will see this type of student activity described as "constructive learning" or "learning by design."

Students' constructive mental behavior

A Facilitative Role for the Teacher

When students play a more active role in their own learning, what happens to the teacher's role? One possible shift is a change in role, from "dispenser of knowledge" to "facilitator of learning." One assumption behind such a shift is that learning is accomplished by the student, and that teachers' role is to consider how they might assist their students. A second assumption is that academic work extends beyond the mere storage of information.

Why take a cognitive approach?

This book takes a cognitive approach because the cognitive perspective fits so well with assumptions like these. The focus in a cognitive approach is on mental activity. Consider for a moment the challenge of teaching a behavior that cannot be directly viewed. How would you explain to a child how to "comprehend" what he or she is reading about a mako shark? One promising approach might be to externalize your own thinking and use the externalized product as a way to interact with your students. You get a brief glimpse of such behavior when you see Pam Carlson offering her own suggestions for important ideas to remember. You will also note that she uses a chart to make the process more observable. Note also that, after demonstrating the skill, Pam gradually gives control of the process over to her students. First, the process is practiced with the charts and under supervision. However, the students eventually perform the process on their own, without concrete external aids. The introduction of the technique, the monitoring of early performance, and the eventual shift to independent functioning have all been facilitated by the teacher.

An Integrated or Multidisciplinary Approach

Using a wide range of skills with multimedia projects

It would be difficult to say that this example project fell within one content area and inappropriate to claim that the project had a single objective. The multimedia product that the students generated described sea life but required that the students use reading, writing, speaking, artistic expression, and library research skills. Even the materials they examined to gather information for the report crossed several genres and could hardly be described as typical fare for science instruction. The factual knowledge the students learned was not isolated, but could be related to multiple, varied contexts.

Cooperative Learning

Technology can enhance interaction among students

One charge consistently leveled against the rising academic interest in technology has been that it isolates students from each other and from the teacher. Nothing could be further from the truth. Technology is a tool and has no inherent or required mode of application. The role of technology in education is always under the control of the teacher and is isolating only if teachers require that students work on projects or assignments alone. In some cases, independent work is appropriate, and in other cases, cooperative work is desirable. As the example illustrates, technology can enhance interaction.

Blaming technology for isolating students or engaging them in passive activity is like blaming heavy reliance on worksheets on the No. 2 pencil.

You will encounter many of these themes again and again in this book. For now, focus on understanding how they relate to the example you have just read.

WHERE IS TECHNOLOGY IN TODAY'S CLASSROOM?

What use of technology is typical today?

If you are already a teacher or plan to become one, you are probably interested in what typical schools and classrooms are like. What technological resources — hardware and software — are available to teachers? How does the typical student use technology at the grade level or within the subject area you plan to teach, and how much time out of a day or week does the student spend learning this way? If you already teach, you are probably interested in how common your own experiences are. The media sometimes focus on glamorous but atypical examples, and it is easy to assume that things are different from your own experiences in other schools or other states. In addition to examining the current state of affairs, it is intriguing to speculate about the future. Will classrooms change drastically during the next ten years because of technology, or will interest in technology wane?

What data are available?

Let us warn you of several limitations before we continue. You will find that the most recent and reliable data are available for questions that can be answered from existing school records, for example, how many computers have schools purchased in the past year? Data that are more judgmental and require the sampling of input from many individuals are gathered much less frequently and are also less reliable, for example, how much time do typical secondary science students spend on different types of computer activities (Office of Technology Assessment, 1995)? We are using very commonly cited sources, but we want you to recognize that describing trends in a rapidly changing area is difficult.

You will also find that the material that follows focuses almost exclusively on computers and computer software. We take this focus for two reasons. First, whereas certain forms of educational technology (videodiscs, television) do not involve the computer, the computer is involved in most applications of technology presented in this book. Second, the use of computers in schools has been studied extensively, and the thoroughness of these analyses allows us to consider broader educational questions. Often, the same detailed statistics or interpretive analyses are not available for other types of equipment.

We want to get beyond questions of what technology is available and into the meatier issue of whether or not technology is being used effectively. In

*How can schools'
experiences have
relevance for life?*

some cases, the gap between how computers have been used and how some educators would like to see computers used makes a useful focus for basic questions, such as what we really want students to learn in school and how students should learn so that school experiences have the greatest relevance for life. As you will see, there are a variety of opinions on the extent to which technology is influencing today's classrooms. The sentiments expressed range from discouragement and frustration to optimism. Some of the more nega-

*Moving toward
optimism*

tive views are expressed because of missed opportunities rather than because advocates have been unable to demonstrate benefits. In most of this book you will encounter the optimistic perspective, but there is also some value in confronting the opinions of critics. Teachers interested in technology must understand that some of their colleagues and others with whom they may interact will not always share their enthusiasm. It is useful to understand some of the limitations and concerns. It is also valuable to make your own decisions about those situations in which technology has been criticized in ways that are unfair.

STUDENTS' ACCESS TO TECHNOLOGY

*Increasing number of
computers in schools*

The number of computers in schools is increasing rapidly. The trend for the twelve-year span ending in 1996 saw the ratio of students to computers change from 125:1 to 10:1. Growth is also evident in computer-related products (videodisc players, CD-ROM players, local area networks) and computer-independent forms of technology (cable TV access was added in nearly 20 percent of schools in three years — 76 percent of all U.S. school districts have cable) (Quality Educational Data, 1996). Clearly, schools are investing heavily in computer technology. The per pupil expenditure for technology at the beginning of the decade was approaching $60 (Anderson, 1993) and by 1996 the expenditures were nearly $90. About 63 percent of this money goes toward the purchase of hardware, 12 percent toward the purchase of software, 3 percent for online service, and only 5 percent for staff development and training (Quality Educational Data, 1996).

One problem with statistics like these is that they may create false assumptions about what can be done in classrooms or what any given classroom may look like. Schools have been investing in computers for approximately 15 years and the computers available over this time period differ drastically in capability. Many schools still have a large number of older computers. In 1994, it was estimated that nearly 50 percent of school computers were still Apple IIs (Schurman, 1994). When a distinction is made between any computer and "multimedia computers" (Macintosh or computer with a 386 or higher processor), the student-to-computer ratio changes from 10:1 to 35:1. Many of the applications discussed in this book would not be possible unless students had access to the more powerful kinds of computer. The data

Different views of the potential of technology

may also create false assumptions about what any given school may look like. At the level of individual states, the student-to-computer ratio for high-end machines varies from 16:1 to 74:1. Individual school districts would be even more variable (Quality Educational Data, 1996). Teachers working in schools at the extremes of this range would likely view the potential of technology for their classrooms very differently.

As we attempt to understand the circumstances that exist in classrooms, it is important to recognize that the availability of equipment influences, but does not totally determine, whether students actually work with the equipment. It is possible that equipment could sit unused in the back of the classroom or computer laboratory. Let's approach this matter in the following way. Considering only those students who actually use computers, how much time do students typically spend using the computer per week? When computer coordinators and teachers estimate the amount of time, the average is 1.75 hours at the elementary level, 2 hours at the middle school level, and 3 hours at the secondary level. Student estimates for the same grade levels were 24 minutes, 38 minutes, and 61 minutes. One explanation for the large discrepancy in the estimates provided by students and teachers is that students may only count the time in which they as individuals were actually working at the keyboard while teachers used the time involved for computer-based projects possibly involving several individuals per machine (Office of Technology Assessment, 1995).

How much time do students spend with computers?

WHAT STUDENTS DO WITH COMPUTERS

Computers can play a variety of roles in school. They can be used to teach, to facilitate the study of traditional content-area topics, to provide opportunities for students to learn how to use technology, or to give students general-purpose tools for performing academic tasks more efficiently (Becker, 1991a).

The tutor, tool, tutee model

These distinctions are similar to what was originally called the tutor, tool, tutee model (Taylor, 1980). In the role of *tutor,* a computer application could be designed specifically to teach the student (for example, a tutorial program explains how to use a photospectrometer, and a drill-and-practice program helps an elementary school student become more proficient with number facts). Computer *tools* are more general-purpose applications designed to help the user function more productively. Such tools include word processing programs used to write reports and database programs used to organize and search for information about all the students in an elementary school. Applications that allow students to search for information on the Internet would also be considered tools. When functioning in the *tutee* role, the student programs (or teaches) the computer.

The situation in secondary schools

In secondary schools, most students use tool applications (word processing, spreadsheets, World Wide Web browsers, and databases), and this emphasis seems to be increasing. Elementary school students spend more time than secondary students working with tutorial applications, but the emphasis on tool applications, particularly word processing, is also increasing rapidly (Office of Technology Assessment, 1995). Given the description of computer tools provided here, there is some danger that you might misinterpret what students actually do. Much of the time students spend working with computer tools, they are actually learning to use them, not using them to do academic work in other areas. For example, students may learn to use the various features of a word processing program as part of a computer literacy class, but then not write their English themes or history papers using the computer. Becker (1991a) estimates that secondary school students spend only 25 percent of their computer time doing what he defines as "productive work." Productive work includes learning course content directly from the computer, using the computer to rehearse or practice content skills, or using the computer to complete course assignments such as writing papers. These specific estimates are now outdated, but the concern about the extent to which students actually learn with technology persists (Mehlinger, 1996). Learning about the computer and learning to use the computer are important. However, the message is clear: Technology is not yet well integrated into secondary school content-area instruction.

The situation in elementary schools

The situation in elementary schools is a bit different. Younger students spend more of their time using applications that teach typical content-area material. Math and language arts receive the most attention. With the recent interest in tool applications, however, students now also spend time learning to use computer tools (Becker, 1991a). Computer coordinators estimate that elementary students spend the largest proportion of computer time learning keyboarding skills and using word processing programs (Office of Technology Assessment, 1995).

How teachers can integrate technology in content areas

Finally, there are several ways teachers can integrate technology in content-area instruction. As we just mentioned, students can use computer tools to do work related to their courses. Students can also learn with the assistance of the computer. A distinction often applied to computer-based learning is whether the computer experience focuses on factual knowledge and basic skills or on higher-level problem solving and critical thinking. For a variety of reasons, experiences focused on the mastery of factual knowledge and basic skills have dominated early computer applications. One of the reasons why elementary school teachers spend proportionately more time with content-area software is that these teachers involve students in drill-and-practice activities and factual tutorial programs more often than high school teachers. Among elementary school teachers using a single type of instructional application more than five times during the year, the most frequent application was drill (56 percent of teachers). Drill activities are also used frequently by high school teachers and still represent the most frequent single category of use for most disciplines: 25 percent of science and math teachers

(Becker, 1991a). Even within related disciplines, such as the sciences, use of drill activities varies a great deal. Biology teachers are more likely to use drill software than are physics teachers (Baird, 1989).

Data on the use of drill-and-practice software are usually cited to support complaints. However, it is a bit unfair to link complaints about excessive drill with the use of technology. The tendency to stress factual knowledge and drill activities, such as worksheets, exists in most of the situations just described — whether or not technology was present in the classrooms (Grabe, 1986). The factual orientation is pervasive in education. Although such mastery of basic skills and facts is important, there is nevertheless a concern that more attention is not given to other forms of learning. We give this issue more attention later in the chapter.

INEQUITIES IN TECHNOLOGY USE

Not all students have the same access to technology. We tend to be most concerned with inequities when differences in school opportunities compound existing disadvantages, such as low socioeconomic status, and when differences in student experiences within the same school are associated with a student characteristic (gender, for example) that we feel should not influence educational opportunities. We are alerting you to inequities at this point to provide a foundation for some of the recommendations that follow. The topic of inequities is discussed in greater detail in Chapter 11 and both the nature of inequities and possible remedies will be considered in greater detail at that point.

SOCIOECONOMIC STATUS

Recognizing differences in experiences and opportunities

As you might expect, students attending schools in poorer neighborhoods have fewer opportunities to use computers and other forms of technology in their homes. Although educators cannot control such differences in experience, it is important to recognize that such differences exist. Learning is not confined to the classroom, and differences in knowledge and experience in any environment can affect classroom performance.

You may have heard that a particular school qualified for Chapter 1 funds. Schools receive Chapter 1 funds when a relatively high number of their students come from low-income families. The money is used to make additional educational services and materials available to the students. In many cases now, some of this money goes toward purchasing technology and software. However, as new technologies come into schools, the schools with less money tend to be slower to take advantage of the new opportunities. Funding is constantly being shifted to cover new problem areas. At present, access to the Internet represents one important area in which low-income schools are seriously behind.

Even when additional resources are provided, it appears that school experiences are still not equivalent. Students in Chapter 1 schools or in schools that have been classified in some other way as less affluent are more likely to work with fact-oriented drill programs and are less likely to have experiences programming or engaging in special technology projects. This situation seems to be based on the belief that students from what are considered poorer academic backgrounds need greater exposure to "the basics" or to lower-level skills before they can learn higher-order skills. A different kind of consequence associated with this orientation is that students in less-affluent schools will have fewer opportunities to control technology or to use it creatively (Sutton, 1991). Students will find themselves spending most of the time they interact with technology merely responding to what the technology requests them to do. Because the technology ends up being used in different ways, some have argued that the particular applications of computers have only reinforced and extended existing inequalities (Laboratory of Comparative Human Cognition, 1989).

Challenging assumptions about the skills students need

Computer tasks can provide meaningful learning activities for all students. Here a diverse group works with a computer and CD-ROM. (© Michael Zide)

GENDER DIFFERENCES

A number of surveys have reported that female students are less involved with technology than males. Becker (1991a) found no gender difference in planned classroom activities, but greater male involvement in unscheduled computer activities (before- and after-school use of computers, elective programming, and game playing). In the middle-school years, males spend three more hours per week using computers outside of school (FIND/SVC, 1995). Stereotypes of the typical computer user are sometimes given as an explanation for gender differences. Popular journalism shows such a bias in its image of the potential computer user. Illustrations used in computer magazines include fewer women and tend to depict women in less active roles (Sutton, 1991).

The role of stereotypes

ABILITY DIFFERENCES

More-able students enjoy greater access to technology at all grade levels. Less-able students have about the same level of access as average students at the elementary and middle-school levels, but less involvement in high school. The activity of less-able students tends to be more focused on factual knowledge and drill activities (Hill, 1993). The probable explanation for the different experiences of different ability groups is the same as that given for differential treatment of different socioeconomic groups. There is an assumption that less-able students lack the basics, and that these skills must be developed before more advanced tasks will be possible.

Biased assumptions about less-able students

These inequities are disturbing because they seem to represent missed opportunities for students needing positive experiences. We believe that the general approach and the related activities we emphasize in the following chapters offer solutions to many of the existing problems.

ACCEPTING THE INFORMATION AGE: A DIFFERENT ARGUMENT FOR CHANGE

One perspective urging change in the way we function as educators is based on the belief that students will encounter a rapidly changing world and will need different intellectual tools and skills to function effectively in this new environment. Several characteristics of the future are particularly relevant to educational planning.

Tools and skills for a changing world

LEARNING TO THINK AND LEARNING TO LEARN

Why tomorrow's employees must learn to learn

We are told that employees of the future will change professions more frequently than in the past. It has been estimated that the students of today will experience four to five different occupations during their lifetimes. Since students cannot presently hope to learn the specific skills required for all these occupations — assuming that the occupations even exist now — it seems most appropriate to alter the orientation of education somewhat, so that more attention is paid to helping students learn how to think and learn how to learn. Naisbitt (1984) claims that we will have to move away from the training of specialists who are soon obsolete to the development of generalists who can adapt. To be successful, people will have to have periods of learning and work that are less differentiated as distinct time periods in life. Adults will spend more time learning, and much of this learning will occur outside the traditional classroom. Although instruction will be available in new forms, learners must be more self-reliant to profit from these opportunities.

THE GROWING BODY OF INFORMATION

The amount of available information

Another characteristic of the future that already seems to be taking place is that learners will face an ever increasing body of information. Futurists (Naisbitt, 1984; Toffler, 1980) delight in startling us with just how much information is available and how the pace of information generation is accelerating. Six to seven thousand scientific articles are authored daily in this country alone. The amount of information available in the world doubles every 5.5 years. The World Wide Web, an Internet application we feel offers tremendous potential for learning (see Chapter 6), is beginning to make a contribution to the information glut. As a very conservative estimate, one indexing service presently reviews the contents of 145,166 Web servers offering information resources of varying quality — and the number of servers and the amount of information available is increasing at an ever accelerating rate (WebCrawler Team, 1996). So what do statistics like these have to do with the task of the average classroom teacher? It would seem that the increasing amount of information would make the teacher's job much more stressful. How can students be expected to learn more and more material in the same amount of time?

The Internet adds new information resources

Why learning huge amounts of information is unnecessary

A possible approach to the problem of more and more information is to realize that attempting to learn huge amounts of information may be unnecessary and unwise. Learning more information is unnecessary because it is becoming increasingly possible to retrieve specific information when needed. Procedures for searching huge bodies of information are becoming both more powerful and more readily available. Libraries are increasingly turning to technology to allow the location of material specifically related to a patron's interests. The Internet allows access to an ever expanding array of information resources, and services are available to anyone with a computer and a modem. Making productive use of these new resources requires that we all learn new skills.

The point is that students can substitute learning to *find* what they need to know for the impossible task of *learning* everything they may need to know. Second, attempting to learn huge amounts of information may be un-

Focus

The Big Six Research Process

The Big Six process was developed as a practical approach to the instruction of the interrelated skills required in using information to solve problems. At one time such skills might have been called library skills, but with ready access to online resources such as the World Wide Web this description seems too narrow; information-processing skills might now be a more accurate description of what is actually involved.

The six interrelated information-processing skills include:

◆ Task definition — define the problem and identify information resources needed to solve the problem
◆ Information-seeking strategies — identify the range of possible information resources and prioritize resources for investigation
◆ Location and access — find the information sources and the relevant information within sources
◆ Use of information — process (read, view) the information and extract relevant ideas
◆ Synthesis — organize and create a product (e.g., decision, paper) from ideas
◆ Evaluation — consider the product and the effectiveness of the problem-solving process.

The Big Six skills can also be expressed as a series of questions: What needs to be done? What can I use to find what I need? Where can I find what I need? What information can I use? How can I put my information together? How will I know if I did my job well (Jansen & Culpepper, 1996)?

You might already have some personal experience in applying such skills at your college library and in many of your college classes. How would you find a book that might contain information about the possible relationship between the destruction of the rain forests and global warming? How would you use this information as part of a paper advocating international subsidies for alternative economic ventures in countries likely to resort to massive deforestation? Would you be able to find this same information if you were asked to use the World Wide Web instead of your local library? Would you be able to create a multimedia product as a way to present your point of view on this topic? Although developing "information skills" has always been part of a solid education, technology provides new opportunities for access, manipulation, and expression that should increase the attention paid to these skills and broaden how educators think about them. ✴

Source: Adapted from Eisenberg & Berkowitz, 1990. Reprinted by permission of the publisher.

Students can learn to find information

wise. Information is not the same as useful knowledge, and the time spent accumulating huge amounts of factual information might be better spent working with information to generate knowledge of personal significance. New skills are necessary.

RESTRUCTURING SCHOOLS

Changing the learning environment

Educators are talking more and more about the need to restructure schools. Although restructuring means a lot of different things to different people, the basic challenge is to think carefully about what we want schools to actually do and then to consider how we might most successfully accomplish these goals. Those who are strong advocates of restructuring are concerned either that schools are stressing the wrong things or that the methods schools employ are ineffective. We explain some of their concerns in more detail in Chapter 2. Many of the nontraditional learning activities we suggest turn out to be good examples of the type of learning experiences that advocates of restructuring recommend. Table 1.1 (based on Brown, 1992) provides an introduction to some of the main differences between traditional and restructured educational settings. You will learn more about many of these distinctions as we

TABLE 1.1

Comparison of Traditional and Restructured Schools

	TRADITIONAL SETTING	**RESTRUCTURED SETTING**
STUDENT ROLE	STORE INFORMATION	CREATE KNOWLEDGE
TEACHER ROLE	Present information Manage classroom	Guide student discovery Model active learning
CONTENT	Basic literacy with higher-level skills building on lower-level skills	Emphasis on thinking skills and application
CURRICULUM CHARACTERISTICS	Breadth Fact retention Fragmented knowledge and disciplinary separation	Depth Multidisciplinary themes Knowledge integration and application
SOCIAL CHARACTERISTICS	Independent learning	Collaborative learning
ROLE FOR TECHNOLOGY	Drill and practice Direct instruction Programming	Facilitate exploration and collaboration
ASSESSMENT	Fact retention Traditional tests	Knowledge application Performance Projects Portfolio

Providing student-centered learning experiences

proceed. At this time, we take a moderate position on the issue of restructuring. We value providing more student-centered learning experiences than tend to be commonly available, but we do not see such experiences completely dominating the day-to-day routine in classrooms.

CHANGING THE WAY TECHNOLOGY IS USED IN SCHOOLS

Although the 1980s were a time of rapid technological growth when many computers were brought into the schools, for most of this time there were too few computers in most schools to effect drastic change. There still is not much equipment available in many schools. What about the schools fortunate enough to have more technological resources? If technology is going to produce drastic differences in what or how students learn, these trends should be more evident in schools that allow teachers and students greater access to technology.

A need to focus on higher-order thinking and problem solving

Many schools with greater access to technology have changed very little in their basic approach to instruction. Students rarely use computers either for content-area learning tasks in general or for a large portion of the time spent on any single learning task. When used in content-area instruction, technology is likely to be focused on the acquisition of factual information rather than on higher-order thinking and problem-solving. When computer-using teachers were asked to classify how their students used technology, they were more likely to describe these applications as enrichment or remediation rather than as regular instruction. Skills in using technology are developed (originally keyboarding, basic computer operations, sending e-mail, searching the World Wide Web), but students spend little time applying these skills to meaningful projects.

If resources are becoming less and less of a problem, what seems to be limiting the involvement of technology in content-area instruction? The following sections present some answers to this question.

TEACHER PREPARATION AND TEACHER TRAINING

The title "Why schools of education are still sending you staff you'll have to train in technology" appeared in a prominent technology publication (Barksdale, 1996). This is not a unique complaint (e.g., Spotts & Bowman, 1995) — the title just happens to be a very direct way of raising the teacher-training problem. The basic concern is that colleges of education have not been responsive to the expectation that new teachers will come into K-12 classrooms prepared to use the resources the schools have purchased. Approximately 50 percent of teacher-education graduates surveyed felt they either were not

Fifty percent of new teachers feel unprepared to use technology

College faculty make limited use of technology

prepared or were poorly prepared to use technology. The analysis of causes for this poor preparation included: (a) the frequent situation, in which colleges of education are less well equipped than the elementary schools where their graduates will work; (b) the large number of college faculty members unable to make appropriate use of technology in their own classrooms and unwilling to try because of anxiety or lack of interest; and (c) the common teacher preparation curriculum in which most experiences with technology are focused in a single course that concentrates on learning to use the technology rather than on learning how to facilitate learning *with* technology. You will find that we deal with many of these same issues throughout this book, but our focus is on how teachers in elementary and secondary schools can do a better job using technology with their own students. It is ironic that the educators of educators persist in employing practices and modeling attitudes that many consider barriers to the effective use of technology in elementary and secondary classrooms. There is probably a positive message for all of us in recognizing this irony, and this message is clearly not limited to the use of technology. Change at any level of education does not come easily, but starts with each of us.

The challenge of keeping current

Changing how teachers are trained will not have an immediate impact on school practice. It will take years to place a majority of teachers with extensive college-based technology training into the work force. Even if teachers have had a college technology course within the past year or so, the field advances very rapidly and new equipment, programs, and ideas for classroom practice are always emerging. There are many practicing teachers who may have had some exposure to computers but who have not worked with videodiscs, high-speed modems and direct connections to the Internet, CD-ROMs, or video-capture products (we will discuss all of these products in later chapters). The World Wide Web emerged as a powerful and widely used Internet application in an extremely short period of time. While some may find this situation discouraging, we think it is exciting. The tools of many professions are changing at an incredible rate. Why would we as teachers want to be excluded from this progress?

How teachers respond to new technology

It is easy to be glib about the excitement of new opportunities. It is another matter to deal with the uncertainty created by sophisticated equipment suddenly left in your classroom. Teachers are used to being in control of their environments and in command of the content they teach. It is not uncommon to find them nervous and reluctant to learn how to use technology — particularly when they might be expected to work on it with their students before they feel secure in their own mastery. As we mentioned in the Preface, one of us is involved full-time in helping classroom teachers learn to use technology. During a session designed to introduce teachers to the four new computers that had just been installed in their classrooms, one of the teachers asked if it would be possible to exchange her four computers for a piano. What do you say to a question like that? Once teachers actually work with the equipment and experience different applications, however, their enthusiasm usually grows, and they begin to find ideas of their own that they can implement with the new resources. Probably not all teachers would get to this stage if they had to work completely on their own. This is why ongoing training of teachers already working in classrooms is so important (see Focus: The Emerging Importance of the Computer Coordinator).

We also try to encourage teachers to recognize that technology can represent a unique situation in which they can learn with their students. New

Focus

The Emerging Importance of the Computer Coordinator

Do you remember the party scene in *The Graduate* in which Dustin Hoffman receives advice about future vocational opportunities as a single word — *plastics?* We have similar advice for you — computer coordinator. Schools are hiring staff members to assist teachers, administrators, and sometimes students in making use of technology resources. Initially, some administrators assumed that coordinators would work themselves out of their jobs once teachers were trained and began making heavy use of technology. This assumption now seems silly. Technology is a moving target and it is not cost-effective for teachers to try to keep up on their own. If anything, there are now more opportunities as staff members in larger districts specialize as network administrators, elementary or secondary specialists, and others who might work with the business and recordkeeping applications that provide administrative support to schools. Sometimes, such an individual has a primary background as an educator and sometimes not. Even computer coordinators — who usually need to have education backgrounds because of the importance of curriculum awareness and fa-

miliarity with the realities of classroom work — can have very different preparatory experiences. The coordinator job might require graduate training, or some specialized undergraduate training might be sufficient. Some coordinators work full-time as support staff and some split time between regular classroom teaching assignments and staff development activities. Their job may require certification of some type, but sometimes employment is merely a matter of convincing an administrator that you can do the job. While circumstances presently vary greatly from location to location, there are employment opportunities here that may appeal to you now or in the future. We see the ideal computer coordinator as an individual with fairly advanced technical skills who can find ways to use these skills in service of instructional and learning needs. An understanding of curriculum issues is essential. It is important that the priority be on the curriculum needs and not on the technology. Finally, working as a computer coordinator requires advanced social skills. Knowledge of technology and curriculum is of little value unless the coordinator is capable of motivating and supporting teachers as they move out of their "comfort zones" to try integrating technology into the classroom routine.✹

Technology offers unique opportunities

equipment and software will show up in your classroom. What a tremendous opportunity to model problem solving, persistence when things go wrong, and the joy of developing a new skill! So, what do you say when someone wants to trade in computers for a piano? How about, "No, I think you and your students will really enjoy working with these computers once you learn a little more about them"? In the case of this particular teacher, this turned out to be true.

SCHEDULING DIFFICULTIES

Gaining access to computers

There is more equipment and software in schools now than there was in the recent past, but teachers still perceive working with it as cumbersome. In part, this perception may stem from traditional beliefs that all students should be doing the same thing at the same time. Computer labs allow whole-group instruction or simultaneous participation in a common activity, but laboratory access often must be coordinated with many other classes. Spontaneous access can be difficult. Unfortunately, if you end up with a free hour on Friday afternoon, you can't just take the class down to the lab to work on a project you already have underway. Having a few computers in the classroom also can require a different mindset. If most of the day is taken up with group work and you feel uncomfortable releasing individual students to work at the computers, the computers may go unused much of the time. In those times when students are free to work on the computers, competition for the computers will be fierce, and the time available to individual students will be very limited (Loveless, 1996).

The fundamental issue

In a way, these challenges are all secondary to a more fundamental issue. For change to occur, teachers must want to integrate technology into content-area instruction and to use it for more than transmitting factual knowledge. For this motivation to be present, teachers must value forms of learning other than the acquisition of factual knowledge and feel confident that they have sound and efficient classroom strategies for facilitating the development of both basic knowledge and more advanced thinking and problem-solving skills. This book has been written to be particularly sensitive to these two issues, as well as to the related concern that students be given more experiences in which they must gather, understand, and manipulate information.

Developing basic knowledge and more advanced thinking skills

THE ACTIVE LEARNING ENVIRONMENT

It is sometimes helpful to propose a simple structure learners can use to organize and carefully examine a large amount of information. We call the organizational structure we apply in this book the ACTIVE learning environment (see Figure 1.3). The word ACTIVE is an acronym for the characteristics of technology-facilitated learning environments we feel are most beneficial to students. We want to promote classroom tasks that are:

Active — tasks require cognitive behaviors that emphasize the transformation of information into personal knowledge

Cooperative — tasks require meaningful interaction among students

Theme-based — tasks are flexible and multidisciplinary based on an organizing theme

Integrated — tasks emphasize content area knowledge and use technology tools to encourage learning this content in ways that are meaningful

Versatile — tasks make efficient use of technology skills and develop those that can be applied repeatedly

Evaluative — tasks allow the assessment of the student's ability to use the knowledge and skills we want them to learn.

FIGURE 1.3 ACTIVE Acronym

We will greatly expand these ideas and provide examples of their application in the following chapters.

While we have written much of this book to encourage teachers to consider the characteristics of ACTIVE learning environments, we also recognize the dangers in committing to a convenient organizational structure or to a single model of instruction. Effective educational practice is much too complicated to be characterized by any recipe and the types of learning students must accomplish cannot be addressed in any one way. What we are trying to do is increase the probability that certain productive classroom practices involving technology be employed. Students should experience ACTIVE learning environments more frequently.

A balanced approach

The classroom project we used to introduce this chapter is an excellent example of students learning in an ACTIVE environment. Review the description and see if you can pick out the ACTIVE components. Including student-centered design projects among more traditional classroom activities is one very effective way to offer students productive opportunities for learning.

THE ACTIVITY-BASED OR DESIGN MODEL OF TECHNOLOGY USE

The approach to educational technology use that we believe can meet this rather demanding set of goals has been described in a number of ways: activity-based learning (Laboratory of Comparative Human Cognition, 1989); the project approach (Katz and Chard, 1989); using computer activities as mindtools (Jonassen, 1996); and design projects (Carver et al., 1992; Perkins, 1986).

EARLY USE OF ACTIVITY-BASED APPROACHES

Activity-based approaches were introduced in the 1960s as a way to reform science and math education (Laboratory of Comparative Human Cognition, 1989). At the time, most learning and instruction was based in larger groups and was dominated by teacher presentations. The activity-based approach recommended that at least part of the time available for instruction be shifted to hands-on, student-centered activities and that students collaborate in small groups to work on these projects. The teacher was responsible for the following:

Hands-on, student-centered activities

◆ Selecting the activity and providing the materials
◆ Introducing the activity so that the students' task was set in a meaningful context and had clear goals
◆ Facilitating the students' work as it proceeded
◆ Helping the students see the connections between their observations and associated principles or theory.

The teacher's role

Without carefully considering what the teacher actually must accomplish in this approach, it might appear that the teacher just presents the assignment and then sits at his or her desk until the students are ready to turn in their work. As you might expect, this is not at all what was intended. The teacher moves from group to group, participating, probing, and suggesting. A fundamental goal is to help students shift back and forth between theory, principles, and their own observations and experiences. Many kinds of questions are possible. Is what the students have read about what they are observing? What is a good way to explain why this happened?

Positive attitudes and better understanding

Evaluations of activity-based learning were impressive. Students had more positive attitudes toward science, demonstrated better understanding of the concepts, and were more advanced in using creative and higher-level thinking skills. However, more than twenty years later, still fewer than 10 percent of science classrooms use what was demonstrated to be a motivating and effective curriculum model. This may not seem very logical to you, but there is an explanation. Understanding the explanation is a good lesson in some of the realities of implementing change in schools.

Early efforts at activity-based learning

Activity-based learning was not a movement that arose out of the schools themselves. Early efforts were often supported by federal funding and implemented by highly motivated classroom teachers. In many cases, additional classroom materials and travel funds were provided to the schools for use in the projects. Projects were often able to draw on outside personnel (community members appropriate to the projects) and researchers to help implement them. As the federal support was withdrawn, even teachers previously involved in the projects found it difficult to generate the level of effort and to find materials to substitute for those that were no longer available. Without training, teachers who had not been involved in the original efforts had an even more difficult time implementing some of the ideas. Many of the early implementations of student-centered, small-group projects have gradually languished.

TODAY'S USE OF ACTIVITY-BASED APPROACHES AND TECHNOLOGY

The role of technology in activity-based learning

Technology may represent the critical element in reintroducing these ideas in a sustainable way and in allowing activity-based learning to play a more prominent role in K–12 education. The hardware and software already present in many schools, or available at a reasonable cost, can be used to involve students in motivating and active learning tasks focused on many of the same topics students would otherwise encounter by listening to teacher presentations or reading textbooks. The activity-based or project-centered approach that this book explores makes heavy use of what we earlier described as computer tools.

Tool applications

The tool applications we will consider include word processing, graphics programs, database programs, spreadsheets, telecommunications software, sound capture and editing software, hardware and software for capturing images and video segments from a variety of sources, and software for authoring hypermedia. Each of these tools was designed to increase the productivity of users attempting to perform a certain general type of task. For example, word processing applications were designed to help users write more effectively, and telecommunications software was designed so that users could exchange information inexpensively across great distances. The purpose of the writing and the type of information exchanged are not determined by the application software itself. Most tools on this list were not intended uniquely for education. They were designed to increase productivity in a variety of work settings.

The value of tools

The value of these tools for education is that your applying them to carefully selected tasks encourages the active mental behaviors so necessary for meaningful learning and critical thinking. The same tool can be applied

ACTIVE
C
T
I
VERSATILE
E

Using software tools in student projects

over and over in new ways and in the processing of new information. It is this flexibility and reusability that overcomes some of the preparation difficulties inherent in the activity-based approach of the 1960s. Both teachers and students become adept at using the tools, and projects become easier to implement.

WAYS TO USE COMPUTER TOOLS

The variety of ways in which software tools can be used in student projects is endless, and new ideas seem to emerge daily. Just to get you started thinking about the possibilities, consider the following categories of use.

Authoring

From simple text documents to complex hypermedia

◆ Students author presentations to inform or persuade others. Presentations can be based on academic information or skills that are already emphasized in existing coursework. For example, the presentation described at the beginning of this chapter applied knowledge of marine life, library research skills, and writing skills. Presentations can range from simple text documents to complex hypermedia. The audience for the presentation may consist of classmates or, if the presentation is created in the form of World Wide Web pages, anyone in the world with access to the Internet. The development of presentations requires students to locate relevant information, evaluate and organize the information, and communicate it effectively. If the presentation is a group project, it also involves a number of social skills.

Telecommunications

What teachers can use telecommunications for

◆ Students communicate with others at distant sites. The process of communication can be used to obtain information, to develop communication skills, or as an incentive to encourage some other type of academic work. Consider each of these applications. Telecommunications can be used to learn about lifestyles or daily experiences very different from your own. A common application is to set up regular interaction with another class in a different part of the country or even in another country. This interaction may even occur in "real time" and unlike a telephone conversation can include video images. Imagine the experiences that can be shared as students from a farming country discuss their daily lives with students in a major metropolitan area. In addition, consider what students might learn about the French language by corresponding with a "key pal" in Quebec or France. Finally, telecommunications can be used to encourage other academic activity. For example, students might exchange book reviews as a way to encourage more free reading.

Data Organization and Manipulation

Organizing and manipulating information

◆ Tools such as spreadsheets and databases can be used to organize and manipulate quantitative and factual data. For example, a spreadsheet can be used to record and perform simple statistics on data obtained from science experiments. A database could be used to categorize library books along a number of dimensions (author, topic, literary style); store a short description of each book; serve as a way for the readers generating the summary data to think about what they have read; and allow readers to search for new books that might appeal to them.

COMPUTER TOOLS AND STUDENT PROJECTS AS A SOLUTION

Teachers can use the basic project approach outlined above to solve some of the problems inherent in many current applications of technology.

Integration of Technology into the Curriculum

A
C
T
INTEGRATED
V
E

The primary focus of this book is on helping teachers improve student learning opportunities in the traditional content areas. Projects are appropriate in all content areas and such projects can provide the opportunity to use technology more extensively.

More Effective Use of Existing Resources

A
COOPERATION
T
I
VERSATILE
E

The goal in all educational settings is to get the most from existing resources. Technology can be applied creatively to a nearly unlimited number of projects. Group-based activities make efficient use of available, reasonably priced software. Students also do not and probably should not work on projects only when they have access to the technology. A great deal of the planning, information acquisition, and information interpretation can be done "off-line." Constructing a technology-based product, such as a hypermedia presentation, or engaging in a technology-facilitated experience, such as a telecommunications link with another classroom, serves to direct, encourage, and organize these other learning experiences. Students can make minimal or extensive use of technology depending on what is available.

More Active Learning

ACTIVE
C
T
I
V
E

Existing applications of technology have often focused on fact acquisition and rote memory-oriented learning tasks. Activity-oriented uses of technology emphasize other important learning goals and thus expand the variety of uses of technology and the variety of experiences for students. The emphasis in activity-based learning shifts from the transmission of information to an emphasis on asking critical questions, finding goal-relevant information, evaluating and integrating information to create personal knowledge, and communicating effectively.

Greater Equity of Involvement

Drawing girls and disadvantaged students toward math and the sciences

Using technology as the focal point of group projects puts technology in a somewhat different role and seems to involve students who in the past have been less interested in the tasks to which technology has traditionally been assigned. When technology is used to provide opportunities for collaboration and to address self-selected problems in math and science, female and disadvantaged students are more likely to be drawn toward these content areas (Laboratory of Comparative Human Cognition, 1989).

Motivating students

Here is an example of how a collaborative group project can motivate and benefit students of differing abilities. Pam Carlson, the second grade teacher you read about at the beginning of this chapter, has involved her students in a study of the planets. After an introduction, she asks the students to write their names and the name of a planet they would like to learn more about on a piece of paper. She collects the papers and divides the class into three-person groups based on the planet of interest. Each group learns as much as it can about its planet so that the group members will be able to write a report from which the rest of the class may learn. The reports will be produced using the one computer in their classroom. To make the projects a little more interesting, Pam provides each group with a scanned color picture of the planet they have selected. The color picture and the information that each group finds will be integrated using a program called The Writing Center. By using large-size fonts and a color printer, each group will be able to create a very attractive product for display in the classroom.

Making projects interesting

In the early phases of research, group members often work in isolation. Depending on their ability and sometimes on their perseverance, different members of the group accumulate different amounts of information to contribute to the final report. As you might expect, nearly all of the material located by some of the students of lower ability is redundant with material located by the more-able students. Pam wants each student to feel that he or she has made a real contribution to the final product. So, as she works with each group, she asks the student with the least amount of material to open The Writing Center and enter his or her information. The next student then comes to the computer, reads what the first student has entered, and adds any unique material he or she has to offer. The third student does the same thing. As you might expect, reports written in this fashion are not very well organized; even second graders are aware that the reports can be improved. Because the students are inexperienced with word processing, a more concrete technique is used: the report is printed for them. The students then take scissors, cut the report apart, and try different ways of rearranging what they have written. Next, the teacher demonstrates how to use the cut and paste features on the computer, and the students work together to rearrange the computer version of their report to match what they have done by hand. At last, the final version, complete with color picture, is printed for display (see Figure 1.4).

All students make contributions

FIGURE 1.4 First Student's Report and Final Group Report

First Student's Report

Saturn is the six planet from the sun. It is the second largest planet. Saturn is mostly made out of gases. The rings are made of rocks and ice. No one is sure why Saturn has rings. Saturn has the most rings in the solar system.

Text of Final Report

Saturn has been a fascinating planet for a long, long time. Saturn is the sixth planet. Saturn is an outer-planet. Saturn is slightly smaller than Jupiter.

Saturn is the most beautiful planet in the solar system. The rings are brightly colored. The rings around Saturn are made of ice. Some pieces are as big as a house. Some are smaller than grains of sand.

Saturn spins quickly. It takes the planet $19\frac{1}{2}$ years to revolve around the sun. It is 887 million miles away from the sun.

Saturn has inner moons and outer moons. Its number of moons is possibly 27. Until 7 years ago, Saturn was thought to have only 10 moons. Mimas, one of Saturn's moons, is one ninth the size of our moon. Titan is the most interesting moon.

There is no life on Saturn. Saturn is made of gas. Saturn's gases are lighter than water.

The diameter of Saturn is 74,000 miles. The gravity on its surface is 1.2 times that of Earth's. At the center of Saturn is a core as big as Earth. One Saturn year is 29 Earth years. A day on Saturn is 10 hours, 39 minutes, and 24 seconds long.

SUMMARY

Classroom use of technology is growing and may be changing in its orientation. Many schools are investing in new equipment, purchasing new software, and encouraging faculty participation in training and innovation.

The situation is not without limitations and concerns. Growth and enthusiasm are not universal. Schools differ drastically in what they have made available to teachers and students, and teachers differ in their own interests, skills, and beliefs. Technology is expensive, and schools have to carefully consider how resources are to be spent.

Many of the applications briefly discussed in this introductory chapter make very efficient use of technology. Technology is proposed as a focal point for activities that engage students actively in collaborative, multidisciplinary learning projects in traditional areas of instruction.

While the individual teacher can have only an indirect impact on the amount of technology available, the teacher *can* determine how technology is applied. There are concerns here, too. The applications present in classrooms appear to have created some gender, grade-level, and socioeconomic inequities and have overemphasized fact-oriented learning. The focus on fact-based learning may relate to the more obvious availability of this type of software and the widely held belief that basic skill learning must be accomplished before higher-order skills can be attempted. The latter argument is most evident in instructional applications with younger children and with disadvantaged students. This chapter presents counterarguments to the reasons given for heavy reliance on applications focused on knowledge transmission. General-purpose tool software is widely available, relatively inexpensive because of its reusability, and easily applied in the context of content-area tasks. Tool applications are especially well suited to the gathering, understanding, and application of information. A more holistic approach, in which the learning context motivates and anchors the learning of factual knowledge and basic skills within meaningful tasks, is one alternative. The more holistic approach also seems an effective way to involve all students on a more equal basis.

REFLECTING ON CHAPTER 1

Activities

◆ You can personally investigate some of the equity issues discussed in this chapter. Check out a general-purpose computer magazine from the library, and make a tally sheet to evaluate the advertisements. How many white males appear in the ads? How many women? How many members of minority groups? You may also be able to classify the role played by each person in the ads. Is one group consistently more active or more in control than others?

◆ There are other simple observations you can make. If your college or university has computer labs, take a stroll through a lab and observe who is doing what. If game playing or activities such as sending electronic mail or exploring the Internet are allowed, do you notice any group more heavily involved in these activities?

◆ Consider how technology has influenced you as a college student. Have you used technology as a tutor, tool, or tutee? Have you used technology at all? If technology is going to begin to play a larger role in education, do you imagine the change coming from the top down (college students first and then elementary and secondary school students) or from the bottom up (elementary and secondary school students before college students)?

◆ Think of a course you have taken recently that seems especially well suited to preparing you for the Information Age. What specific skills were stressed in this course?

Key Terms

hand-held scanner   *(p. 4)*

load   *(p. 4)*

paint program   *(p. 4)*

peripheral devices   *(p. 4)*

shareware   *(p. 3)*

stack   *(p. 5)*

Resources to Expand Your Knowledge Base

Many of the topics in this introductory chapter will be expanded in later chapters, and additional readings will be provided at those points. If you find the idea that technology may change the basic nature of education exciting, you may want to examine the following sources:

Jones, B., & Maloy, R. (1996). *Schools for an information age.* Westport, CT: Praeger.

Means, B., ed. (1994). *Technology and education reform: The reality behind the promise.* San Francisco: Jossey-Bass.

Computer magazines for educators do not limit themselves to discussing hardware and software; they also include articles focused on more general educational issues. *Electronic Learning,* a popular and long-running magazine for K–12 educators, now subtitles its publication *The Magazine for Technology and School Change.* A list of magazines and journals focused on educational applications of technology appears in Resources to Expand Your Knowledge Base at the end of Chapter 3.

Chapter **2**

Cognitive Learning and Technology Tools

ORIENTATION

This chapter summarizes some key ideas about school learning. Our intent is to help you develop a deeper understanding of how and what students learn and to examine the role various applications of technology might play in facilitating or inhibiting desirable outcomes. To achieve these goals, it is essential to focus on the mental activities of students. It is these activities that are responsible for the success or failure of learning and thinking. Discussing mental behavior is challenging because we must describe something we cannot really see or sense. One productive approach makes use of models that have been developed to represent mental behavior. These models identify important components of mental behavior and describe how these components work. This chapter will present several models that have been persuasive and have influenced educational practice.

Our emphasis on the mental behaviors of the learner in no way diminishes the importance of teachers or learning tasks. Teachers must provide students with the best possible environment for learning. Teachers must consider the kinds of learning outcomes that are useful and the experiences most likely to encourage the learner to engage in the mental behaviors consistent with these outcomes. Certain experiences help students learn more effectively, apply what they have learned, and become more excited about the process of learning. We believe technology can play a prominent role in providing these productive experiences. As you read, look for answers to the following questions:

FOCUS QUESTIONS

◆ When is it useful to learn a skill to the point of being able to perform it without thinking?

◆ What do present assumptions about the structure of long-term memory imply for the successful storage and use of knowledge?

◆ What unique types of knowledge do we acquire, and why is it important that teachers evaluate various types of knowledge in different ways?

◆ When is it appropriate and inappropriate for students to make decisions about their own learning?

◆ How do external educational tasks influence internal mental behaviors?

◆ What basic changes in classroom experience are recommended by models of instruction emphasizing active learning? How can technology be used to encourage active learning?

ACTIVE
COOPERATION
THEME-BASED
INTEGRATED
VERSATILE
EVALUATION

You will find that much of the theoretical rationale for ACTIVE learning environments is presented in this chapter. Look for the ACTIVE symbol in the margins.

COGNITIVE MODELS OF LEARNING

A cognitive perspective

As you read about the instructional strategies and learning activities in this book, you will note that we frequently speculate about how an experience influences a learner's mental activities. We believe that understanding how classroom experiences influence mental behaviors can be invaluable to the decisions teachers make about using technology in the classroom. Attempting to understand the mental behaviors involved in thinking and learning represents a *cognitive perspective.*

Why learn how students accomplish academic tasks?

Cognitive models emphasize how students acquire information and skills, solve problems, and engage in such academic tasks as reading, writing, and mathematical reasoning. Understanding how such tasks are accomplished, the barriers to be overcome, and sources of individual variability can help you recognize differences in performance and propose modifications to your students' instructional environment. In addition, understanding how different learning tasks encourage or discourage specific mental behaviors can help you assign more effective tasks and create a more productive learning environment for your students.

Understanding how students learn and think

One way to understand learning and thinking is to think of the student as a processor of information. This perspective will help you understand how information is represented and manipulated as it moves within the student's cognitive system. It will also help you think about issues of how knowledge is stored (storage); how knowledge is manipulated (processing); and how the whole system is guided (control mechanisms).

TWO APPROACHES TO DESCRIBING LEARNING AND THINKING ACTIVITIES

In this chapter we take two approaches to describing learning and thinking activities. The first approach explores some of the fundamental properties of mental activity. The second approach explores important issues of school learning at a more conceptual level.

How these two approaches differ

The major distinction between these approaches is in the amount of specificity they use to describe learning and thinking activities. Our analysis of fundamental properties of mental activity is much more detailed and complete. The more conceptual approach, on the other hand, glosses over details to describe behavior in terms of larger units. Breaking conceptual accounts of behavior into more fundamental elements can be unwieldy and unnecessary. Because teachers are most likely to communicate with students and with each other by describing behaviors at the conceptual level, much of the discussion in this chapter analyzes learning and thinking behavior on this level.

However, we believe that considering some of the fundamental details of how thinking and learning work is also interesting and enlightening. If nothing else, a more detailed understanding of how the mind works is useful in justifying some of the general conceptual principles that guide instruction. We hope the ideas we present about what students must do in order to learn and think productively will provide you with some important principles to consider and some ideas about how you might apply them to classroom uses of technology.

WHY LEARN ABOUT LEARNING?

We present this discussion of school learning because we want you to examine how applications of technology might influence student thinking and learning. You will revisit many of these principles in later chapters as we discuss specific applications of technology and describe strategies for using them in your classroom. We encourage you to consider the material in this and the

Take an active approach to this chapter

following chapters actively. Discuss the assumptions and proposals with your classmates and instructor. Perhaps you will disagree with some of the ideas and values presented here. But whether you accept or reject them, they are important to consider. As we point out in the pages ahead, it is the active, personal work of mental behavior that turns information into useful knowledge. We want you to work with these ideas actively because we do not want this information to end up tucked away as inert bits of academic trivia. Your personal understanding is important, for you will determine how the students of the future experience technology.

FUNDAMENTAL PROPERTIES OF MENTAL ACTIVITY

Implications of characteristics of mental behavior

Learning and thinking activities can be described in terms of multiple *memory stores,* the *processes* or mental actions that we use as we think and learn, and some *executive mechanisms* that oversee and control the processes and determine whether or not the processes have accomplished what we as learners have intended. We will not spend a great deal of time attempting to describe classroom learning and thinking at the most fundamental level. However, we do want to familiarize you with some of the most important characteristics of mental behavior and show you some important implications of these characteristics for specific classroom situations involving technology.

MEMORY STORES

Two memory stores

Memory stores function within the cognitive system to hold information. Once information is taken in through our sensory receptors (e.g., eyes, ears) memory stores come into play. This discussion will consider two memory stores: short- and long-term memory.

Short-Term Memory

The most effective way to describe **short-term memory** (**STM**) is as consciousness — the thoughts, ideas, and images of which a person is aware at any point in time. A moment of reflection will give you some insight into the contents of your short-term memory right now. What ideas are you aware of? These ideas are available in your short-term memory, and we hope they include the ideas presented here.

Working memory

Short-term memory is also frequently called **working memory**. Learning and thinking activities occur in working memory. Again, a bit of reflection will suggest some important characteristics of working memory. Experience should suggest that working memory operates within time and capacity lim-

Time and capacity limits

its. That is, there is a limit to how much information we can be aware of and how much mental activity we can engage in at any one time. There is also a limit to how long information will be maintained in working memory without continued attention. How often have you found yourself repeating something or concentrating on it to keep the thought available? Mental rehearsal is a way we all attempt to respond to the time limits of working memory.

Many of the characteristics of working memory have implications for explaining learning or thinking difficulties and, as a result, how specific task performance might be improved. Using what you now know about the characteristics of working memory, think about the following classroom scenario:

Jack and his seventh grade classmates have been receiving keyboarding instruction for several years. Jack can find most of the keys without looking, and he uses the computer to type papers he has already hand-written. However, he is not an accomplished typist. His English teacher has assigned an in-class theme and decides it is important for students to learn to compose at the keyboard. The teacher takes the class to the computer lab and tells the students they must complete their papers by the end of the class period. Jack has great difficulty with this task. Although his typing proficiency clearly limits how quickly he can work, his problems go beyond his ability to get his ideas down on paper. He has an unusual amount of difficulty thinking of what he wants to say and how he wants to organize his paper. The paper he writes is atypically poor.

What does short-term or working memory have to do with Jack's poor English paper? One very likely explanation for Jack's writing problems involves the time and capacity limitations of working memory. If Jack must think to recall the keyboard position of individual letters, the thinking behavior he must employ in order to type competes for working memory capacity with the various thinking behaviors required to write the paper. The slow speed at which he works only makes matters worse. He is forced to expend limited cognitive resources to keep thoughts active for a longer period of time.

There are some ways this situation can be improved. An improvement in typing proficiency is a long-term solution, but it has little immediate value. If the teacher insists that the paper be typed in class, Jack might improve his performance by first generating an outline of his ideas and referring to this outline as he works. In this manner, Jack would decrease what he has to accomplish and retain in working memory.

The teacher might also want to think carefully about the goals of the assignment. There may be other ways to accomplish the same ends. If developing writing skills and composing at the computer are both important, imposing a severe time limitation is probably not a good idea for novice typists. Either less-demanding assignments should be given, or students should have an extended period of time to complete the assignment.

The relationship between word processing and writing is one example of a situation in which the student uses technology as a tool to perform some other academic task. It is helpful for teachers to recognize that in situations like this, an inexperienced student really faces several cognitive tasks. First, the student needs to learn to use a particular computer program. Second, the student needs to perform some academic task using the technology. Composing at the keyboard involves both the motor skills of typing and the thinking and problem-solving skills involved in writing.

Under certain circumstances, the combination of these tasks can strain working memory. The story about Jack provides a worst-case scenario of a student who is still an unskilled typist trying to complete a difficult writing assignment. Both the use of the technology and the academic task are difficult for him and compete for his limited working memory resources.

The need for well-developed computer skills

This story also illustrates that challenging classroom assignments become unnecessarily difficult when the computer skills needed to perform them are not well developed. Teachers may fail to see that the opposite relationship between classroom tasks and technology also holds. Students may have difficulty learning to take full advantage of the power of computer programs when they apply the programs only to challenging classroom problems. When the task to be accomplished is difficult or must be completed under time pressure, the student is less likely to explore the potential of the technology and, as a consequence, never gets beyond using the technology in the most mundane fashion. We propose that students need to be able to operate the technology with ease to perform challenging assignments.

A play phase

The same logic may be applied to learning how to use the technology. To ease the burden of learning to use new programs, students might first be asked to apply programs to very easy or familiar tasks. In other words, it is often useful to allow for a *play phase*. A play phase is valuable because it allows students to explore the capabilities of new software in low-stress settings with low-stress tasks. For example, when students are first learning the features of a word processing program, they should write on a topic such as their families or themselves. This kind of topic allows information to flow freely while the student focuses on features such as fonts, cutting and pasting, and saving the document to disk. Hurrying the process of learning a new program is not always the best long-term solution.

Recognizing when drill and practice are appropriate

In Chapter 3 we will discuss a type of computer software called *drill and practice*. Drill and practice activities are relevant when certain skills (such as typing) need to be learned to the point that executing them takes little working memory capacity so attention can be devoted to other mental tasks (such as writing).

Long-Term Memory

Permanent store of knowledge and skills

Long-term memory (**LTM**) contains a person's permanent store of knowledge and skills. It includes all the stored products of learning, whether those products result from formal education or from everyday experiences. A full discussion of theories about biological and psychological properties of LTM,

Activities and Projects for Your Classroom

Introducing Students to Computer Programs

Teachers are often concerned that students will find new programs difficult to learn and that they will be unable to remember the steps required to complete an assignment. Won't students become frustrated and balk at our new expectations? These concerns are usually unwarranted. Many students are familiar with technology and have grown up programming VCRs and playing video games. The hesitancy that adults first bring to a computer task is seldom evident when students are confronted with an interesting challenge. Students seem to enjoy learning new computer skills. This does not mean that acquiring the skills takes no work or time. You can use a variety of approaches when introducing the students to an assignment they will complete on the computer. Here are a few ideas:

◆ Students first need a demonstration of what they will be doing in order to set the background and establish motivation for the assignment. You can then go step by step through the process needed to complete the project. When all students hear detailed instructions, they become resources for each other. After the demonstration, you can ask for a couple of volunteers to be the first to attempt the skills required by the assignment. If these students are successful, they can begin to supervise the efforts of other students. You will find that you have many computer experts in your own classroom!

◆ You can give small assignments that use a particular function of a program. For example, you may want students to learn to use the feature of a word processing program that checks for spelling errors. An elementary school teacher might use this as a way to have students practice their spelling words for the week. Students can work together in groups of two, one dictating the spelling list while the other types the words. When the list has been completed, the spell checker can be used to search for errors.

◆ Teachers can easily prepare instructional handouts explaining the key features of a program. Using screen capture (a technique for saving a picture of the screen for later use in another program; see Chapter 9, pages 318-324), you can create illustrated step-by-step instructions for more complicated techniques.

◆ Instructional videos can be used when it is desirable for students to learn independently. Commercial videotapes are available to teach the ins and outs of some of the higher-end programs. Schools might consider creating their own videotapes for programs used by large numbers of students. If the hardware available in the school allows "video-out," instructional tapes are easy to create. Video-out is a feature that converts the image viewed on the computer monitor into a form that can be displayed on a television monitor. Video-out can be used to present the screen image on a large monitor, which can be a useful instructional technique. The same signal can also be recorded on videotape by connecting the cable to a VCR instead of to a television monitor. In this case, the teacher would slowly execute the steps needed to complete a desired procedure, and all actions visible on the computer screen would be recorded to tape. If learning a program involves learning which buttons to press or which commands to type, this information can be reviewed by watching the recording. ✷

how storage is accomplished, and what exactly is stored would far exceed the scope of this book. What is important here is to consider some basic properties of LTM. Knowledge of these properties should inform the learning experiences we provide students and the types of cognitive activities we encourage them to engage in on their own.

Contents of Long-Term Memory.   Since we all have some sense of what we know, we all have some insight into what LTM contains. How would you describe all the different things you have learned? Different theorists (Anderson, 1983; Gagne and Glaser, 1987) categorize the contents of LTM in different ways. The memory components we will discuss here include imagery, episodic memory, and declarative and procedural knowledge.

Memory components

Imagery

◆ Experience tells us that we have the capacity to store **imagery** of different types (smells, sounds, visual representations). We are capable of recalling very specific smells (Mom's kitchen when she made chicken dinner on Sundays) or visual images (the house you grew up in) from long ago. Researchers, working mostly with visual images, have demonstrated just how remarkable our long-term storage really is. In one very creative experiment, researchers (Read and Barnsley, 1977) presented pages from elementary school reading textbooks to adults. The adults, who had not seen these books for as long as thirty years, viewed entire pages, the text portions of pages, or just the illustrations originally on the pages. The adults could recognize all versions above the level of chance and were most accurate when a picture was included.

Remembering textbooks thirty years later

Episodic Memory

◆ An **episodic memory** is a stored representation of something you have experienced (Tulving, 1972). Specific experiences might include a film-strip on butterflies viewed in an elementary school science class, a marketing field trip to a local shopping mall to view store window displays, or a conversation with a friend about today's lunch. Episodic memories are very rich in detail, much of which may be of no great significance. They can also be related to a particular time and place. In fact, we often use time and place to help us recall the details of a specific event we have experienced. For example, during a quiz, a student may attempt to recall last Thursday's lecture to locate information relevant to a particular question.

Examples of episodic memories

In education, episodic memories can be a mixed blessing. Certainly, it is important for students to have a rich store of experiences to draw on. In some circumstances, we want students to use experiences from their lives either to discover principles or as a route to richer understanding of the principles we present as teachers. For example, a psychology instructor might ask, "Did your mother ever tell you that you couldn't have dessert until you'd finished your vegetables? Why do you think she said that?" The instructor hopes that you have had an experience like this and that recalling it might help you understand psychological concepts such as contingency and reinforcement. Instructors do have to recognize that relying on student experience involves making assumptions about student backgrounds. The assumption that students have shared certain experiences is not always valid and using the recollection of these experiences as part of an instructional activity can present problems for some students. "Life stories" play a very important role in thinking and problem solving outside of schools. We often also use such stories, rather than more abstract principles or rules, to convey knowledge to our daily acquaintances. The recollection of what we or someone else did in a particular situation can be recalled and adapted as a solution to a new problem (McLellan, 1996).

Encouraging students to create knowledge

It is also very important, however, for teachers to appreciate the limitations of episodic representations. Teachers also do not usually want students to store their academic experiences as episodes. They may want students to think about a lecture and store the major ideas rather than the verbatim comments. The key issue here is how to encourage the student to work at generating and storing a personally meaningful representation of what was experienced. Much of what we present in this book is focused on this issue: *How do teachers get students to create knowledge and not be satisfied with simply storing information?* Students need to take an active role in working with the information they receive. As we get more and more into the discussion of classroom technology applications, you will note that we frequently consider whether the application puts a student in the role of passive recipient of information or active generator of knowledge. We think that certain uses of technology can be very useful in helping students generate personal meaning.

Technology and generating personal meaning

Declarative and Procedural Knowledge

◆ Many memory theorists have drawn a distinction between verbally based factual knowledge and know-how (Anderson, 1976, 1983; Gagne, 1985). This distinction is often described as the difference between knowing *that* something is the case and knowing *how* to perform a certain cognitive process or action. **Declarative knowledge** represents our factual knowledge base, and **procedural knowledge** represents the stored methods we use to do things.

Much of school learning has to do with the storage of declarative knowledge. We learn the names of things, significant dates, terms, definitions, number facts, theories of this and that, and many similar categories of facts and concepts. We are also taught to do things. We learn to tie our shoes and button our coat, to add and subtract, to write, to solve algebra problems, and to argue for a position. In reality, most accomplishments require both declarative and procedural knowledge. It is, for example, difficult to write without having something to say. To engage in an argument, we need the skills of logic and effective communication, as well as factual knowledge.

One final point of clarification: procedural knowledge is not the same as a verbal account of how to do something. Procedural knowledge is demonstrated by actual performance, not by a description of how something should be done. The stored description of where the letter *Q* appears on a keyboard is declarative knowledge. Pressing the Q key when desired is procedural knowledge.

A Network Model of Long-Term Memory.   Most academic and life tasks require the use of several categories of memory contents. Consequently, the various elements of memory are most likely meaningfully organized — not isolated by category of memory unit. Effective educational experiences must result, then, in both the accumulation *and* the organization of memory units. We call this organized structure of memory units a **network**.

Applying several categories of memory contents

The network is a useful way to conceptualize how what we know (our memory) is stored and the ways memory works. **Network models** represent memory in terms of **nodes**, which are cognitive units, and **links**, which establish the relationships among nodes (Anderson, 1983; Collins and Quillian, 1969; Gagne, 1985; Gagne, Yekovich, and Yekovich, 1993).

Nodes and links

Figure 2.1 is a graphic representation of what such models attempt to describe. This representation portrays a small part of a high school biology student's knowledge. Included are examples of the four categories of LTM contents: (1) imagery (recollections of animals the student has seen), (2) episodic knowledge (the recollection of a hunting trip), (3) declarative knowledge (conceptual knowledge about pheasants and grouse), and (4) procedural knowledge (the stored strategy for identifying particular game birds). As you can see from the figure, these elements are linked in meaningful ways. For example, the image of a male pheasant is connected with the concept "male" and "pheasant." (What would you guess is one way to distinguish a female pheasant from a sharp-tailed grouse? One difference is whether the leg is feathered or unfeathered.)

Meaningful links

The network-like structure of memory explains an important characteristic of human thought. We seldom recall isolated thoughts. One idea seems to make us aware of other ideas, images, or stored experiences. The related nodes that are first activated or brought into our awareness are those that are the most directly linked. Many important kinds of mental performance depend on more than whether relevant ideas, images, events, and procedures exist in LTM. Performance may depend instead on *how* individual nodes of memory are linked or organized. Organized elements of memory are more likely to be available to our awareness at any given point than are unorganized elements. Certainly we create new information when information does not exist, and we can also search out additional relevant elements of memory

Organized and unorganized elements of memory

FIGURE 2.1 A Network of Biological Knowledge Stored in LTM

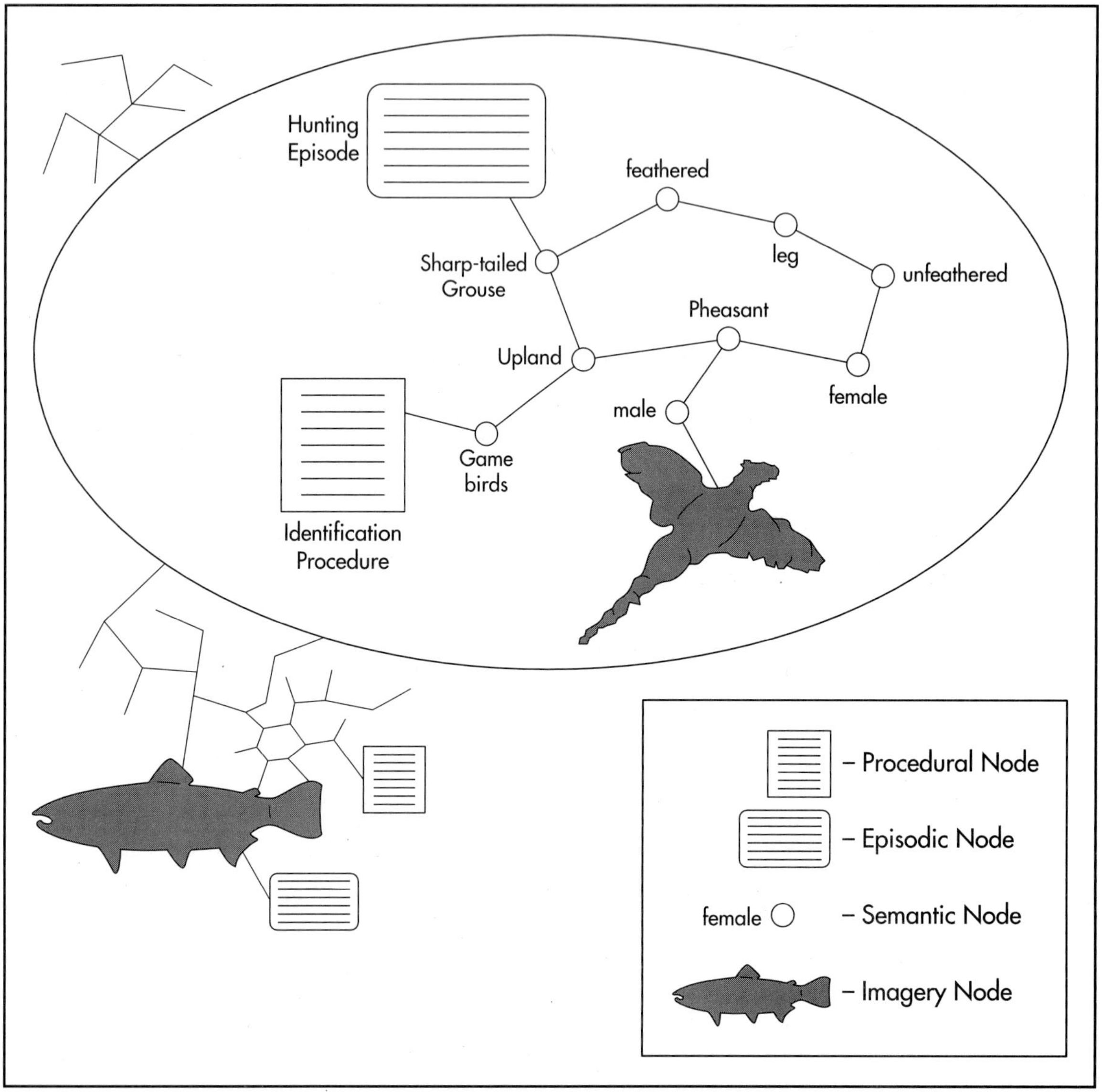

when the existing organization does not make the relevant elements immediately available to us. Some external experiences provided by a teacher or by instructional materials may also cause us to activate unrelated memory units. Whether internally or externally initiated, however, such mental work takes time and effort, both of which are limited resources within working memory. Mental tasks will go much more successfully when the elements required to accomplish a particular task already exist in memory and are well organized.

If LTM consists of a network of nodes, then a major goal of education is to construct and modify this network. One important way to modify the network is to add new nodes (ideas, events, images, or procedures). However, it is also important to organize nodes by adding new links and possibly eliminating other, inappropriate links. The least valuable learning experiences add few nodes or add nodes linked to few existing nodes. The most valuable learning experiences encourage students to create rich interconnections among stored elements of knowledge. Creating links is not an automatic process. Students must activate stored experiences and find appropriate connections with new ideas. How all this happens is not fully understood, but we will provide further insights as we discuss cognitive processes.

A major goal of education

As teachers make decisions about how they want students to use technology and about general classroom assignments and activities, they should consider the way the tasks involve students in learning. We will devote most of the rest of this chapter to the characteristics of active learners and to introducing classroom activities that encourage active learning. Technology-supported activities that have the potential for engaging students in the active processing of information will be discussed throughout this book.

Valuable learning experiences

MENTAL TOOLS: DOING THE WORK OF THINKING AND LEARNING

Something very important is still missing in our consideration of what is necessary for learning. Thinking and learning are active. Students acquire information from the world around them and generate personal knowledge. They solve problems. They create new ideas and new things. The cognitive system we have described to this point just sits there. If teachers want to search for more effective learning experiences for their students, they will need to have some general ideas about the mental actions that productive learning experiences should encourage.

The basic actions of the information-processing system are often referred to as *processes.* Instead of an extended discussion of the volumes of research on cognitive processes, permit the substitution of a simplifying idea based on this research: that of a *mental tool.* Assume that students have at their disposal mental tools they can use to accomplish a variety of cognitive tasks. We will attempt to describe some tools to help you understand this idea. Here are four general hypothetical tool categories:

1. Attend to: Maintains certain ideas in consciousness for an extended period of time.

Tool categories

2. Link/Associate/Organize: Establishes connections between information units stored in LTM or active in working memory.

3. Elaborate/Extend/Exemplify/Infer: Creates or discovers new knowledge from the logical and purposeful combination of active or stored memory components.

4. Test/Evaluate/Question: Determines whether a situation is as desired or expected.

We have organized the descriptive verbs in groups to indicate that all verbs in a group describe similar functions. Certainly it would be possible to propose more tools or to explain these phenomena in different terms. The point is, within the cognitive system, there seem to exist mechanisms — mental tools — for operating on the raw information fed into the system from the world and for managing and continually modifying what the system has stored previously. These tools accomplish the work of cognitive activity.

METACOGNITION

Knowing how to use mental tools

In evaluating the utility of the mental tool metaphor, Paris and Winograd (1990) note that having a collection of tools is not enough. A good craftsperson is a person who knows how to use the appropriate tools wisely and independently to complete desired projects. The same is true of effective learners. Effective tool use requires insights into task demands, awareness of personal strengths and weaknesses, and ongoing analysis of whether progress on the task is proceeding well or poorly. The skilled learner can plan to avoid difficulties or compensate for problems. Perhaps a different tool must be used. Perhaps the action of a tool already employed must be repeated until the desired outcome is achieved.

Metacognition and strategic use of cognitive tools

Any model of reading, writing, problem solving, or general study must propose some mechanism to account for the adaptive and strategic nature of actual student thinking and learning behavior. What prominent researchers and theorists have come up with to account for strategic behavior is the admittedly fuzzy and rather poorly operationalized construct of **metacognition** (Brown, 1981, 1987; Flavell, 1987; Garner, 1987; Paris and Winograd, 1990). Metacognition is responsible for guiding cognitive behavior. It accounts for the strategic use of cognitive tools and for our ability to evaluate the success of our mental behaviors. Metacognition is usually described in terms of a combination of *metacognitive knowledge* and *metacognitive control functions*.

Metacognitive Knowledge

Metacognitive knowledge consists of personal insights into how cognitive tasks such as memory or writing are accomplished, about what makes particular tasks difficult or easy, and about personal cognitive characteristics and capabilities. We all have such knowledge, accurate or not. Students may real-

What metacognitive knowledge consists of

ize, for instance, that information stored in an organized fashion is easier to retrieve than information stored haphazardly. They may realize that when they can't remember something, they should try to think of related things.

Metacognitive knowledge covers the skills of both academic and professional life. In some cases, this knowledge is the intended result of direct instruction. We are expected to learn strategies for figuring out the meaning of an unfamiliar word, to learn how to research and write a position paper, and to learn how to study for an essay examination. Other metacognitive knowledge is picked up less directly. Some students may realize that math is a particularly difficult subject for them. Students may also figure out that instructors are more likely to ask examination questions on topics covered in class than on textbook topics that were not discussed.

Metacognitive Control Functions

Metacognitive control functions are demonstrated in planning, regulating, and evaluating behaviors (Paris and Lindauer, 1982). Planning concerns decision making before beginning a project; regulating involves adjustments made while working on the task; and evaluating has to do with decisions made once the project has been initially completed.

Educational significance of metacognitive control functions

Metacognitive control functions have great educational significance. Consider the roles of planning, evaluating, and regulating as they might apply to some of the research and writing tasks involved in a student's preparation of a paper for a history class. The student might begin by outlining a rough set of issues to investigate and by identifying some sources of information about these issues. As the student examines the sources, he or she must locate specific information about the issues and determine if enough information is available to attempt writing the paper. If no information turns up related to some key issue, the student may decide to find additional sources, modify the initial topic of the paper, or abandon the original idea entirely. As the student writes the actual paper, he or she must determine whether the text meets acceptable standards for spelling and grammar. The student must also determine whether the intended ideas are being presented in an organized and persuasive manner.

Metacognitive control functions and self-directed learning

Metacognitive control functions also play a major role in self-directed learning. Thomas and Rohwer (1986) describe study behavior as effortful, private, self-managed activities, often operating with little in the way of external guidance regarding what is to be accomplished or what level of mastery is required. If you think carefully about what is (or was) expected of you as a college student, you will note just how much responsibility advanced students must accept. Usually much more material is presented than would be practical to master. Consequently, you must decide what is essential to master and what you can cover more superficially. The nature of future examinations is also vague, and you must make decisions about how your understanding will likely be evaluated. Finally, as you prepare for these examinations, there are few or no concrete ways for you to judge how adequately you have prepared. Do I understand this chapter well enough to go on to the next? Will I be able to solve this type of problem if it appears on the test? You must develop study plans, evaluate the adequacy of your understanding, and continually regulate study methods and your allocation of time and attention.

As you can see, it is relatively easy to provide examples of the many ways students use metacognitive control functions and demonstrate metacognitive knowledge. You can also see that metacognitive knowledge and metacognitive control functions interact to influence student behavior. Knowledge of the self and the task to be accomplished make important contributions to the planning process. Knowledge of what the teacher expects or what is considered acceptable performance are used as standards in evaluating work in progress. Knowledge of personal weaknesses may direct the learner to study some subject areas longer than others.

Improving study behavior

Metacognitive skills related to academic performance often need improvement. Study behavior, for example, is often passive (rereading textbook assignments) and relies on less powerful systems for organizing and emphasizing important content (note taking and highlighting). Students frequently use the same study approach, even though course material and evaluation procedures may vary considerably. Regulatory functions are also suspect. Students frequently are unaware of failures in their comprehension of material they have read (Baker, 1985; Markman and Gorin, 1981). They also seem unable to predict accurately how they will do on tests covering the material they are studying (Pressley et al., 1987). When students are unable to detect comprehension failures or test preparation difficulties, remediation strategies — even simple activities such as rereading or asking the teacher or a classmate for assistance — are unlikely to be used.

Using Technology to Improve Metacognitive Skills

Using technology to encourage active learning

How can technology help? As students progress through school, they are expected to take more and more responsibility for their own learning. Many of them are unprepared to function productively in this role. Perhaps teachers concentrate too heavily on the transmission of subject matter knowledge and either do not teach students how to learn or do not engage them in learning tasks in ways that allow them to develop more sophisticated learning and thinking skills. In addition to reviewing traditional applications of technology to education, this book explores ideas for using technology that place students in a different kind of relationship to teachers, other students, and academic content. These ideas emphasize the use of technology in projects that require students to play more active roles in their own learning. We will discuss some of the basic principles of this orientation toward education in the final section of this chapter.

Technology may offer several ways to address metacognitive weakness. As the following example illustrates, which of these approaches is to be preferred is controversial. When technology is used for the presentation of course content, it is possible that certain decisions about learning can be made either by the learner or by the computer. Either the computer or the learner can make decisions about pacing, the sequence of instruction, and the specific content to be covered (Milheim and Martin, 1991).

One form of traditional computer-based instruction called a tutorial makes heavy use of questions. Students are presented with several screens of information and then are asked questions about the information just covered. If the student does poorly on the questions, a program using computer control might automatically move the student into some material attempting to explain the same information in a different way. A program allowing learner control would likely allow the learner the option of selecting the review material or continuing to the next section. Empirical studies of computer-based instruction frequently demonstrate an advantage for computer control over learner control (Milheim and Martin, 1991; Steinberg, 1989). Such findings are frustrating to those who advocate the supposed motivational and learning advantages of allowing the learner to fine-tune instruction to personal needs. However, allowing the learner a great deal of control does not seem to work in practice.

Traditional computer-based instruction

There may be a productive compromise. Learner control with advisement is a technique that allows the student to make decisions after considering information or suggestions provided by the computer. In a study evaluating the effectiveness of computer advisement (Tennyson, 1980), students were learning the physics concepts of force, power, velocity, and speed. College students first learned formal definitions for each concept. The students were then provided with examples and asked to determine which of the four concepts would explain each example. In the learner control condition, students worked with the examples until they felt prepared for the posttest. In the computer control condition, the computer made decisions about how many examples were required, using a mathematical model based on pretest performance and performance on the examples. In the third condition, the learner made the actual decision to take the posttest but was provided with the same information used in the computer control condition. This study and others have demonstrated that learner control with advisement is superior to unaided learner control (Tennyson, 1980; Tennyson and Buttrey, 1980). Without advisement, students tended to terminate study of the lessons more quickly, possibly indicating that they had overestimated their level of mastery.

Learner control with advisement

A possible advantage of learner control with advisement is that this combination of computer monitoring and learner decision making potentially allows for the development of metacognitive and "learning-to-learn" skills. Students are put in the situation of thinking about the decisions they make *as they attempt to master* the assigned material. This situation is clearly different from the more common situation, in which feedback follows instruction and is likely to be perceived by the student as useful only for determining the

Developing metacognitive skills

grade. Heightened sensitivity to the processes and the successes and failures of learning may allow the student to develop new planning, regulating, and evaluating skills.

A SUMMARY AND TRANSITION

Let us make a transition of sorts. The way students think about their own behaviors and the way teachers tend to discuss student behaviors are not likely to rely on the fundamental language or concepts of information processing. Classroom concepts of mental behavior tend to involve a more global level of description. We will adopt this global level of analysis as we consider the general topic of active learning.

We do not want to launch into a discussion of active learning without providing ways to connect to what you now know about the fundamentals of how learners process information. We also want to summarize some of the central ideas covered in the first part of this chapter. Figure 2.2 is a diagram that addresses both of these needs. The portion of the diagram labeled "the student" depicts the important components of the information-processing system and identifies some of the more important cognitive activities involving these components. This combination of components and basic cognitive activities represents a simple summary of what is addressed by fundamental models of cognitive behavior. Our discussion of conceptual models will focus much more heavily on how effective teachers tend to interact with students and how they involve students in valuable learning activities. Of course, the activities we emphasize in this book involve technology. The diagram is intended to suggest that the mental activities a student engages in are strongly influenced by interactions with the classroom teacher and with the learning environment the teacher establishes. You will note that in this diagram the information a student encounters is not shown in a dominant position. The conceptual models you will encounter next suggest that active learning concerns what students do with information, not with how much information the teacher and learning environment can provide.

Following is a brief review of cognitive information processing. Thinking and learning are represented as the movement and generation of information within short- and long-term memory. The concept of cognitive tools is a useful way to represent how the actions of thinking and learning are accomplished. Many of the cognitive tools we identified are included in the diagram as arrows. Depending on the task, individual students use these tools in a variety of ways and with varying degrees of success. A good teacher and an effective learning environment will increase the probability that more desirable outcomes will occur, but the teacher and the environment can only provide information to the learner (see diagram). Once information about what to know or how to think has been taken in by the student, what actually happens

Linking the fundamental and conceptual models of thinking

to this information and the content information to which this advice applies are the responsibility of the student. This is where issues of skill, motivation, and existing knowledge are involved. Metacognition, the capacity of a student

FIGURE 2.2 Connections Among the Teacher, Learning Environment, and Student

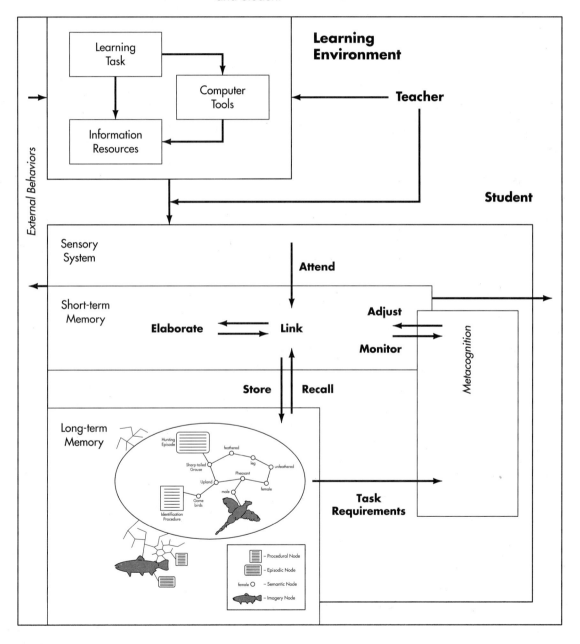

to evaluate and adjust personal behaviors, also plays an important role in adapting thinking and learning behaviors for success.

How technology can play a role

How is technology involved in this diagram? First, technology can present information to students. Mostly this information will be ideas or concepts the student is to master or perhaps experiences the student is to think about to produce learning. Second, students may use computers and other forms of technology to complete learning tasks. In that case, technology is not a direct source of information. Instead, the student manipulates information using technology as a tool, and the experiences resulting from this manipulation are what the student thinks about and learns from.

Teacher, student, and learning tasks interact

There are two arrows in the diagram that are easy to overlook but that are very important — the arrows leading back from the student to the teacher and to the learning environment. For effective learning, all of these components are intended to be interactive. The student can produce a product — perhaps something as simple as the answer to a question or as complex as a multimedia project — for the teacher to evaluate. The teacher's response becomes new information for the student to process. The student also acts on the learning environment. In a simple form of action, the student might select an option within a computer-learning activity and the computer might then inform the student whether the response was correct. In a more complex action, the results of student thinking behavior may take form in the paper being created on a classroom computer. This half-written composition then becomes another information resource for the student to think about. Does this paper make sense? Will I convince a future reader of my point of view?

While the details of mental behavior can be related to classroom practice, you will find only an occasional mention of memory stores and cognitive tools in the chapters that follow. The depth allowed by such an analysis is only necessary in certain situations. For the most part, our discussion of effective classroom use of technology will rely on conceptual models of learning and thinking.

CONCEPTUAL MODELS OF ACTIVE LEARNING

Three conceptual models

Several useful models of school learning outline instructional goals, preferred instructional practices, and ideal student behaviors. These models provide some challenging ideas to consider. We will use three of these models — meaningful learning, generative learning, and constructivism — both to evaluate some common uses of technology and to advocate some new ideas about classroom instruction that take advantage of technology. At a basic level, these theories share one very important feature. They all argue that educators must be equally as concerned with what learners do cognitively with information as they are with what information learners receive. The role of the teacher and instructional materials is to engage each learner in ways that will encourage the active integration of new ideas or skills into the existing knowledge of the learner.

Theories differ in focus

While they share a common base, these theories are unique and worth considering individually. Because theories arise in different historical periods, from different philosophical perspectives, or out of different research traditions, they concentrate on somewhat different issues. As each theory is presented, some of the specific concerns and recommendations related to educational practice associated with that theory will also be considered. There is no reason you must value one theory over the others because each might apply in different situations. We hope these models and the issues they raise will provide a background you can use to consider the specific practical ideas throughout the rest of this book. In the end, you will make the final decisions about how you will use technology in your classroom. Our goal is to provide background to help you make well-informed decisions.

MEANINGFUL LEARNING

Meaningful learning occurs when new information is related to an image, experience, concept, or proposition already existing in the learner's cognitive structure (Ausubel, 1963).

Meaningful Learning Versus Rote Learning

What is rote learning?

Meaningful learning can be contrasted with **rote learning**, which Ausubel describes as the learning of a sequence of words with little attention to meaning. Meaningful learning assumes that students are willing to do the mental work required to establish relationships and that the material to be learned is potentially meaningful; that is, that stored information is available to which the new information can be linked. Instruction can contribute to the establishment of effective links by helping the student activate relevant existing structures (ideas, events, images, procedures) or even by adding content to memory so that links are possible.

What is meaningful learning?

Motivation to learn meaningfully is also important. Ausubel points out that it can be subverted by a reward structure emphasizing rote learning, by a lack of confidence in the ability to learn meaningfully, or by disinterest. Consider the responsibilities of the teacher and the student in this model. Clearly, the student bears ultimate responsibility for meaningful learning. The student must expend mental effort to learn and to establish links among ideas. The teacher must provide an optimal environment that makes the student feel capable. The teacher should also help each student think of existing ideas or experiences that will help him or her understand the new material. If the topic is such that most students can find few related experiences, the teacher needs to provide new experiences or perhaps begin instruction at a more appropriate point. Finally, the student should feel there is some payoff for

Spotlight on Assessment

Performance Assessment

Students usually take tests alone, under intense time pressure. Unlike classroom tests, many of the problems of life are complex, requiring collaboration with colleagues and coordination of a variety of resources and tools over an extended period of time. Inconsistencies between the way we ask students to use their knowledge and skills in class and the way we believe they will use the same knowledge and skills outside of our classrooms trouble many educators and have led to the search for alternative approaches. Many educators have begun to consider performance assessment methods as ways to assess knowledge and skills more authentically.

Performance assessment relies on a variety of methods, all of which require students to demonstrate what they know or can do by creating an answer or a product (Office of Technology Assessment, 1992). One situation in which educators have traditionally relied on performance assessment is the culminating task in graduate education: a thesis or dissertation. The thesis or dissertation is a formal written presentation of the graduate student's original research. Students must use what they have learned throughout their graduate education to plan and implement a research project, to interpret and communicate the results of their research as a written product, and to defend the written interpretation of their findings in a public forum. Graduate education is intended to prepare advanced students to function as independent scholars; the production and defense of a scholarly product assesses their ability to perform in this capacity.

Performance assessment covers a contin-uum of tasks, ranging from essay examinations to collections of work accumulated over time. You are probably already familiar with essay examinations and have had the opportunity to write descriptions, analyses, or summaries to demonstrate your understanding. Research and writing tasks conducted outside class represent a further step along the continuum. Original research and a related exhibition closely resemble the thesis model used with advanced students. A science fair project is a good example. Exhibitions are culminating experiences in which the knowledge or skill gained over many hours of work are displayed. The public nature of the exhibition requires careful consideration of how best to communicate what has been learned; this additional processing has other cognitive benefits. Portfolios anchor the end of the continuum that reflects more inclusive summaries of student performance. You are probably familiar with the term *portfolio* as the collection an artist or architect might put together to demonstrate his or her skills. Student portfolios are similar, containing samples of the student's best work collected over time. Unlike the portfolio of an artist, the items in a student portfolio, such as writing samples, are intended to document improvement.

Technology-supported activities can provide many opportunities for performance assessment. Throughout this book you will find examples and ideas demonstrating how students can use technology as a tool both to learn and to demonstrate what they have learned. The final products are ideal for performance assessment. Thinking of technology in this way is not the most common perspective, but it is clearly one that is gaining attention and credibility. ✳

meaningful learning. At a practical level, this might mean that assessment should reward understanding and application as well as recall.

Reception Learning Versus Discovery Learning

In addition to differentiating meaningful and rote learning, Ausubel (1963) felt it was important to differentiate reception and discovery learning. In **reception learning**, the ideas to be learned are presented to the student directly and in a relatively complete form. In **discovery learning**, the student must work to uncover, or discover, what is to be learned. Ausubel suggests that a large proportion of what is learned in school is acquired through reception learning and much of what is learned through everyday living is acquired through discovery learning.

Educators should not equate reception learning with rote learning, and meaningful learning with discovery learning (Ausubel, 1963). The activities connected with discovery are more concerned with generating the ideas to be learned and not with relating these ideas to existing mental structures. Rote discovery learning is quite possible and is probably best exemplified in cookbook laboratory activities. In such activities, a student follows a detailed set of instructions to complete an experiment or task. Because the student makes few decisions and does not have to understand the processes involved to move from one step of the activity to the next, meaningful learning may not occur.

If this seems unlikely to you, consider the similarity between baking a cake and conducting a chemistry experiment with detailed instructions. It is probably fair to suggest that baking is in fact chemistry in action, and yet little about chemistry is ever meaningfully learned from "experiments" conducted in the kitchen. The baker is seldom invested in understanding the chemical changes undergone by the ingredients and has little opportunity to gain this information from the baking activity. The baker is interested in carefully following the instructions to achieve the desired outcome. Even if the recipe provided additional information about important chemical reactions, as is often the case in academic chemistry experiments, the baker could complete the baking experiment without carefully attending to this added information. Processing this additional information would actually represent reception learning anyway. The baker thus may learn techniques of baking in a meaningful way and still acquire little meaningful knowledge of chemistry.

Various instructional applications of technology (for examples, see Chapter 3) fit nicely within this same framework. In a computer **tutorial,** technology presents the critical concepts and rules to be learned in a direct manner, and students working with it are involved in reception learning. In a **computer simulation,** the student attempts to identify key concepts or rules by interacting with a simulated responsive environment presented by the

What is reception learning?

What is discovery learning?

Activities connected with discovery

How technology applications fit in this framework

computer. The student has to discover the concepts or rules from the experiences that environment provides.

The dual dimensions of rote-meaningful learning and reception-discovery learning provide an informative framework for categorizing school learning experiences of all types (see Figure 2.3). The classification of learning activities in this figure requires assumptions about how the typical student will respond to the activities. It is always possible that students will react to any given learning task in very different ways. The school tasks not involving technology are positioned as proposed by Ausubel (1963). We have added technology-related activities, in brackets, based on our own perceptions of how these activities engage the learner. You may want to test your understanding of this figure by considering where other learning activities would be located. We feel that thinking about tasks and their relationship to student mental behavior is important. You might wonder whether there are some learning activities that should be avoided. The issue is probably more complicated than this, and all types of learning may be appropriate under some circumstances. Concern would probably be appropriate if rote learning were overemphasized or if an instructional activity resulted in a different type of

A framework for categorizing

FIGURE 2.3 Classification of Learning Tasks Using Ausubel's Dimensions of Meaningful-Rote and Reception-Discovery

Dimensions of Meaningful-Rote and Reception-Discovery

Meaningful Learning

Scientific Research
Original Art or Music

(Jasper Adventures)

(LOGO Programming)

(Good Simulations)

(Well designed Tutorials)

Lecture and Textbook Material

School Laboratories

(Drill and Practice)   Apply Formulas   Trial and Error
Math Facts   to Solve Problems   Puzzles

Rote Learning

Reception Learning   **Discovery Learning**

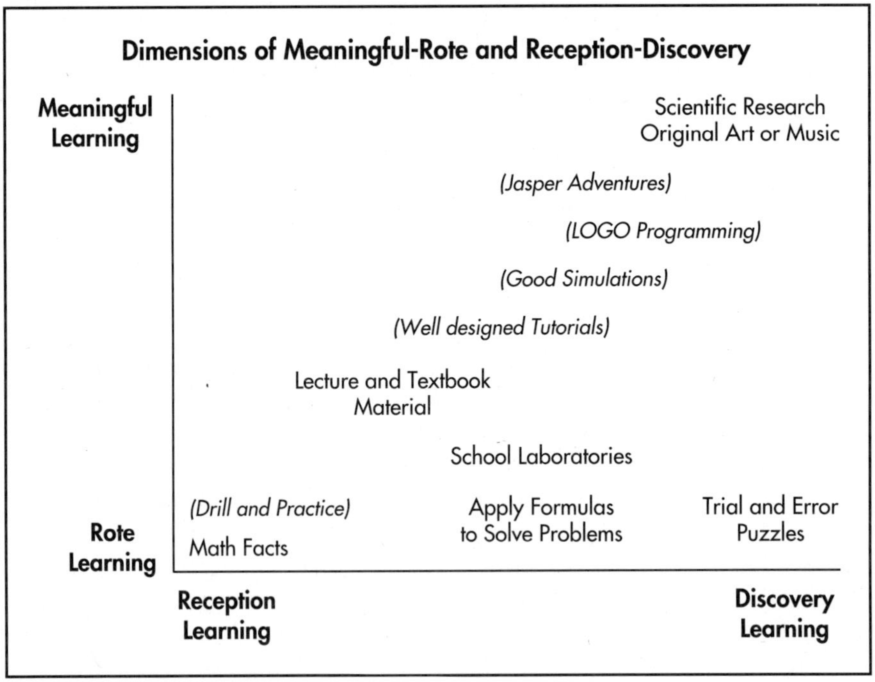

learning experience than was intended. For example, rote learning may be a reasonable way to approach the learning of basic number facts, but not the historical antecedents of World War II. It is also unlikely that school science laboratories are intended as rote-discovery experiences, and if students are in fact responding to laboratory experiences in a mindless fashion, then this is cause for concern. So part of the task in decision making is to determine what types of mental activities are desired in specific learning situations, and another part is to determine if learning activities used to produce these mental behaviors do result in the intended behaviors.

When to Use Discovery Techniques

Discovery techniques are most appropriate when reception methods are unlikely to bring about a high degree of cognitive involvement (Howe, 1972). Such situations include work with younger children and with concepts that are abstract because of unfamiliarity.

Motivation to learn

Motivation can be highly individual. An experienced computer programmer might prefer that a reference book simply explain a new technique or command. Working through a tutorial to learn about the technique may be unnecessary and distracting. Students less interested in programming would likely find a book listing command after command very boring. These students might become quite involved, however, if the book involved them in using the commands to create an interesting product. The difference here is motivation to perform the necessary mental work. The programmer is already motivated to learn and will process the new information meaningfully as soon as the ideas have been received. The student may need to be motivated by some exciting task before processing the information. When students are motivated and have adequate background knowledge, reception learning can be quite adequate for meaningful learning.

GENERATIVE LEARNING

Generative learning occurs when a student actively creates knowledge by selectively attending to events and generating meaning for these experiences either by interpreting experiences in terms of existing knowledge or by drawing inferences (Wittrock, 1974a, 1974b, 1989, 1992).

Generating relationships or links

Learning should be understood as generating relationships or links, not storing isolated elements of information. The active learner creates a model or explanation to account for new experiences and existing knowledge. In some cases, old ideas can assist a student in interpreting new experiences. In other cases, new experiences require the student to modify existing beliefs. In either situation, the process of linking ideas is distinct from simple storage. The generative model of learning assumes a commitment from the student.

External tasks

Generative activities require that the student assume responsibility for expending the effort necessary to construct meaning.

Although the generative activity Wittrock describes is mental and internal, it appears that useful thinking and learning activities can also be encouraged through external tasks. Many examples of the use of generative activities to improve academic performance can be found in the area of reading comprehension (Wittrock, 1989). Students can be asked, as they read, to engage in tasks assumed to require generative activity. Such tasks include writing paragraph summaries, creating paragraph headings, drawing pictures, or creating analogies or metaphors to encourage interpretation, organization, and storage. Generative activities applied in a nontrivial way have been consistently found to improve comprehension and retention.

Relating new experiences to existing knowledge

Although the generative model of learning emphasizes learning processes and learner control, Jonassen (1986) notes that the generative model should also emphasize students' control over the content to be learned. Because the generative model assumes that the ability to relate new experiences to existing knowledge is essential for understanding, it follows that effective learning environments should permit students to select content that allows them to establish these relationships. Usually, all students receive exactly the same content (for example, a common textbook, video, or classroom presentation), but with a standard presentation, some students may be unable to find connections to their existing knowledge. They may misunderstand some key terminology or lack some specific elements of background knowledge or some general organizing framework. As you will see in Chapter 7, technology can provide the necessary flexibility to individualize the learning experience. An exploratory learning environment such as hypermedia allows students to control the specific information they are studying. If a particular topic is especially interesting or difficult to understand, hypermedia allows the student to seek additional examples and alternative explanations, definitions, and other extensions of the information than would be presented in a more static format.

ACTIVE LEARNING AND EXTERNAL ACTIVITIES

A CTIVE
C OOPERATION
T HEME-BASED
I NTEGRATED
V ERSATILE
E VALUATION

What can teachers do when students seem unable or unwilling to employ internal cognitive tools to think or learn? How can teachers help students become more strategic in their learning and study behavior? Advocates of the theories of meaningful and generative learning offer concrete suggestions. One approach is to engage students in external activities that increase the probability that desired mental behaviors will become active. Some examples include:

Questions

While reading from a textbook or the computer screen, a student should attend most carefully to the important ideas. Most students are capable of doing this without help. However, some are not. In such cases, **interspersed questions** may be used to activate and direct the "attend to" mental tool (Rothkopf, 1970). Interspersed questions are questions embedded in reading material. You are probably most familiar with the variation of interspersed questions in which questions appear at the end of a lesson. However, you also may have read a textbook (including this one) or worked with a computer program in which questions were mixed in with the information presented. If the student cannot answer a question focused on an important idea, he or she can attempt to locate information related to the question for further study. If this happens, the external activity (in this case, the question) has resulted in the engagement of the "attend to" tool: desirable student behavior has been activated. Answering questions can also be very useful in activating existing knowledge that is relevant to new topics being considered. One way to increase the probability that you will find connections between new concepts and your past experiences would be to ask you to provide an example. Your classroom teachers probably use this technique frequently.

Interspersed questions

Students often operate according to the principle of least effort (Andre, 1979). The concern is that students store information acquired in an episodic form and do not process the information to a procedural level. That is, students often memorize key ideas and do not think about what this information means. The proposed solution for this common concern is to ask students higher-level questions. Higher-level questions are composed in such a way that the student must understand basic principles and related applications in order to provide answers. Students cannot find the answers in a word-for-word form. In answering these questions, students must generate a personally meaningful representation of the original information. Once generated, this representation can be stored as an alternative to the episodic representation.

Higher-level questions

Questions can also help with an important study and comprehension skill: the student's ability to evaluate how well things are going. Did I understand what I just read? Am I ready for tomorrow's test? These internal skills are manifestations of metacognition. Obviously, unless the student can evaluate areas of success and failure, it is impossible to take effective remedial action, such as rereading, studying some more, or asking for help. Many students seem unable to evaluate the success of their own learning activities. Again, questions can help. Researchers (Pressley et al., 1987) have demonstrated that allowing students to answer questions related to what they are studying helps improve how accurately they can predict later test performance. Teachers might call this "giving a practice quiz." The quiz is an external activity that helps students make decisions about the internal level of their

Metacognitive questions

understanding. Computer-based tutorials (see Chapter 3) make heavy use of questions in all of these roles.

Writing

Writing to encourage active learning

Writing is an example of an external activity that may not occur to you. Writing (termed *writing across the curriculum,* or *writing to learn;* McGinley, 1992; Zinsser, 1988) has been proposed as a general technique to encourage active learning. It is commonly believed that you will understand a topic better after writing about it. Skills involved in structuring ideas, clarifying meaning, searching for examples, and generating logical arguments are necessary in producing a written product and also contribute to thinking and learning. Many different types of writing can be helpful. Examples go far beyond the typical themes and term papers. Journals, for example, are an application of writing frequently recommended to encourage reflection. Student teachers are often asked to keep a journal of their daily experiences. You may have already done this or have it to look forward to. As student teachers write about their encounters with students, they have an opportunity to consider what has happened and why.

Computer Tools and Thinking Behavior

Technology and active learning

Computer tools such as word processors, spreadsheets, databases, and multimedia authoring programs may help students activate desirable thinking behaviors. Computer tools were designed to facilitate certain activities or to create certain products, and these activities or the construction of these products have great potential for generating meaningful learning. Daiute (1983; Daiute and Taylor, 1981) makes such a proposal in discussing the impact of a computer-based word processing environment on the process of learning to write.

Certain word processor features and the way a word processor stores and manipulates text (easy insertion or deletion, moving blocks of text with cut-and-paste functions, alternative edits without time-consuming rewrites) encourage students to revise and thus lead to the development of writing skills. It does appear that technology seems to encourage students to write more and to revise more frequently (Pea and Kurland, 1987). If you have written using word processing software, this claim may ring true to you. Did you rewrite more frequently and try out several approaches rather than attempt to get by with a single, painfully constructed final draft? If the revision power of the computer encouraged you to write differently, perhaps to experiment with different ways of saying something, then it might be said that the external tool (the computer and word processing software) influenced the thinking processes you employed while you wrote. Perkins (1985) describes this second potential value of many computer tools in terms of the "opportunities get taken" hypothesis. His argument is that powerful tools encourage thinking and exploration because learners are presented with realistic opportunities that involve minimal risks. (Chapter 5 presents a more complete discussion of word processing and learning to write.)

Hypermedia

We devote a substantial portion of this book to the proposal that students can benefit from projects incorporating the production of hypermedia. A hypermedia product might be thought of as a computer-based presentation potentially involving some combination of text, pictures, sound, and video. Developing this kind of presentation involves generating the elements of information (text segments, pictures) and creating meaningful links among the *Writing not the only* elements. Hypermedia authoring offers many of the same benefits as writing *form of authoring* to learn. In fact, it has been argued that writing has a privileged status in education that is not entirely deserved and that other means of representation or combinations of representational systems might be better suited to the content of some disciplines (Smagorinsky, 1995). This would certainly seem possible when the content emphasizes visual elements (e.g., biology, art), quantitative forms of representation (e.g., mathematics), or sounds (e.g., music).

We believe that the construction of a hypermedia product and associated activities (research, collaborative interaction with others working on the same product) encourage many of the desirable learning processes presented in this chapter. If we concentrate just on the processes involved in creating a hypermedia product, students will represent what they have learned in multiple formats (images, text), and organize information and establish links to demonstrate relationships of various types. To produce a hypermedia product, students must understand what they are presenting and think about how they can best represent these ideas to others. Creating the hypermedia product involves several external behaviors that require internal behaviors conducive to meaningful learning. You will encounter strategies for involving students in the creation of content-area hypermedia projects in the later chapters of this book.

It has even been claimed (Jonassen, 1986) that hypermedia may represent a superior learning environment because it is similar in structure to human memory (nonlinear presentation of ideas, multiple linkages among ideas, po*Similarities between* tential to represent ideas using several different formats). A variation on this *LTM and hypermedia* theme suggests that having students create hypermedia materials requires them to relate images, ideas, and units of meaning similarly to the actual organization of LTM. In other words, the creation of hypermedia is also a useful

way to encourage students to search out appropriate relationships among the units of information they are studying.

THE CONSTRUCTIVIST MODEL

The constructivist model

As presented here, the constructivist model of learning extends some of the ideas presented in our discussions of meaningful learning and generative learning. There is no single, official constructivist model, but a number of common ideas do surface repeatedly. The most basic principles of constructivism concern fundamental philosophical assumptions about knowledge and learning. The first, more generally accepted principle is that what a person "knows" is not passively received, but actively assembled by the learner (Jonassen, 1991; Wheatley, 1991). This is a general principle of most cognitive models and is certainly consistent with the models of meaningful and generative learning.

Learning is the storage of useful personal knowledge

The second principle is that learning serves an adaptive function. That is, the role of learning is to help the individual operate within his or her personal world. Learning is not the storage of "truths," but of *useful* personal knowledge. This principle leads to a couple of important implications. The first is the importance of the context of learning. Context has a lot to do with what is perceived as useful knowledge and how what is learned is integrated with existing knowledge. Does the learner perceive and use connections between the part of his or her world identified as "school" and what some of us from time to time refer to as "real life"?

The second implication of the principle that learning is an adaptive function challenges the assumption that education is about acquiring universal truths. Since each person has different experiences and constructs an individual account of these experiences, each person's reality is slightly different. New experiences are interpreted within the context of these individual realities, implying that each person "knows" a particular thing in a slightly different way. The lack of a focus on "truth" may concern some educators. But if they think about their own disciplines, most will be able to find examples of basic beliefs that have changed because of new discoveries. Ideas that worked for some time had to be modified to handle new findings. Even what experts regard as truth can change when a way of thinking that is more adaptive comes along. Perhaps educators could be convinced to substitute the acquisition of useful knowledge for finding the truth as they think about the goals of learning and instruction.

Constructivists have more to offer than these insightful generalities. They have both raised some concerns about existing educational practices and proposed some new efforts schools can make to encourage more effective learning. We will begin with a discussion of some of their concerns and then move to some of their solutions.

LEARNING FOR THE REAL WORLD — A DISCUSSION OF CONCERNS AND SOLUTIONS

Schools do not accomplish everything that everyone expects of them. Theories of learning are sometimes useful in evaluating why certain educational expectations have not been achieved and even in suggesting changes in instruction or experiences so that limitations might be overcome.

The challenge of relevance

One of the more demanding challenges in education is how to make learning relevant. Relevance is a broad topic, but at a basic level it assumes that what a student learns in one situation will improve his or her performance in another situation. Math skills should apply in physics class. Math skills should also be useful in determining how much lumber it will take to add a new deck to the back of the house. One component of relevance concerns what is learned: has the necessary knowledge been acquired? Certainly, curriculum committees must consider issues of relevance in recommending the content to be taught.

The challenge of application

A second demanding challenge is that of application: potentially appropriate knowledge and skills have been acquired but remain unapplied. It is this second problem that we will address here. As will become evident, the "usefulness" of education may depend not only on what is taught, but also on whether the content has been acquired in a way that encourages application.

We will consider two different perspectives on the problem of application. The first addresses the issue of why existing knowledge does not come to mind when the learner encounters potential opportunities for application. The second recognizes that we cannot learn specific solutions for every potential problem and considers how students can learn to adapt what they know to solve unique problems.

INERT KNOWLEDGE

What is inert knowledge?

Inert knowledge is knowledge that students have learned but fail to use (Whitehead, 1929). More exactly, it is knowledge available in a restricted set of contexts rather than in all of the contexts in which it might apply. Often, the restricted context is extremely narrow. Students may activate knowledge for classroom examinations and then fail to recognize the valuable role that the same knowledge could play in other situations. In a classic example (James, 1912, 150), a school visitor observing an elementary school science lesson asked the students, "What would you find if you were to dig a deep hole into the earth?" The students were stumped and had nothing to say. The teacher eventually became uneasy and told the visitor that he had asked the wrong question. The teacher then turned to the students and asked, "What is the state of the center of the earth?" In unison, the students responded, "Igneous fusion." The students had stored what they had learned in a way that allowed the knowledge to be activated only under specific circumstances, such as the way knowledge was likely to be used in their classroom. Teachers, frequently frustrated by the narrow, or inert, knowledge of their students, may wonder why knowledge from other classes is not available in theirs.

Another example of inert knowledge can be found in naive science conceptions. We all function somewhat like scientists in our everyday lives. People develop a wealth of knowledge from their unsystematic and uncontrolled daily observations of the world around them (Glover, Ronning, and Bruning, 1990). Here are some examples. Each time a student throws a baseball or snowball, the student observes how forces act on an object. Each time a student plugs in a lamp or hair dryer, the student is involved with electrical circuits. Each classroom experience we have as teachers or students provides an opportunity to form opinions about learning and motivation. These experiences do result in learning, and we form opinions, or **naive theories**, about all kinds of things, based on our observation of daily phenomena. Sometimes these naive theories are incorrect and contradict more appropriate theories learned through formal instruction. What may at first seem surprising is that, in these situations, incompatible academic and naive theories can *both* be maintained and utilized (Champagne, Gunstone, and Klopfer, 1985; Champagne, Klopfer, and Anderson, 1980; Clement, 1983; McCloskey, 1983). The academic theories seem to be applied in the classroom, and the naive theories, in the real world. This is disturbing because the knowledge gained in the classroom seems not to exist when it would be most relevant. The presence of incompatible knowledge would seem to require that, at any given time, one knowledge source or the other must be inert.

Naive theories

An Example of a Naive Theory

Here is an example of the type of problem used to test for naive theories. In this case, the example is from physics and the laws of motion (McCloskey, 1983; Striley, 1988). Imagine that a football is kicked directly forward from a cliff. What is the path the ball will follow in falling (see Figure 2.4)?

The correct answer is A. When a problem of this type was presented to students in an introductory college psychology class, 22 percent answered incorrectly (McCloskey, 1983). Although students in this group who had taken high school and college physics courses were more likely to answer correctly than students who had no formal training in physics, even students who had taken physics made mistakes. To some it seemed logical that the ball would fly forward until it ran out of energy and then fall nearly straight down. For those who remain fans of Saturday morning cartoons, alternative B is called the "roadrunner model" (Striley, 1988).

Changing Naive Theories with Technology

Students are unlikely to abandon beliefs based on life experiences unless they are convinced that models proposed in school make more sense and are more useful (Osborne and Freyberg, 1985). For change to occur, students need to

FIGURE 2.4   Alternate Depictions of Motion

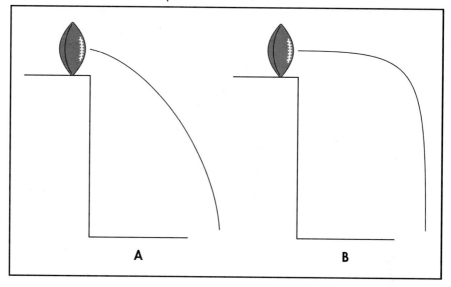

A   B

confront the discrepancies between their naive theories and school models of the world and appreciate the advantage of the school models. To confront a discrepancy in your own thinking, you must be made aware of both ideas at the same time. Hands-on activities conducted in the school environment seem a powerful way to activate both naive theories and school models (Shipstone, 1988). Hands-on activities provide an element of realism that prevents the student from escaping to a purely hypothetical way of thinking.

Computer simulations   Computer simulations provide practical alternatives to certain hands-on activities requiring expensive equipment, dangerous materials, trips outside the school, or time-consuming processes. Simulations also have the advantage of eliminating unnecessary elements and focusing students on manipulating and observing critical variables (Carlsen and Andre, 1992). They allow students to experience situations efficiently and can be structured so that existing ideas are activated before the simulation reveals consequences. For example, students have many naive ideas about the properties of current in electrical circuits. Some believe that a single wire connecting a battery and a light bulb will allow the light to go on. Some believe that current leaves from both poles of a battery, meets, and is used up in the bulb. Carlsen and Andre (1992) created a computer-based simulation that allowed students to build

Simulations and   and test electrical circuits. Using this simulation, if a student constructs a cir-
changing naive theories   cuit to achieve a specific goal, the student is in the situation of predicting that a certain outcome will occur. If the student throws the switch — in either a real or a simulated way — and the light does not go on, the student is in the position of having to determine why the circuit did not function as predicted.

The simulation allows the student to rapidly construct circuits involving many different electrical components and then predict and verify various properties of circuits. Because the simulation functions according to the actual properties governing the flow of current, naive preconceptions result in erroneous predictions and unanticipated consequences. Experience with simulations can activate and modify original naive beliefs. You will find an extended discussion of computer simulations in Chapter 3.

INFLEXIBLE KNOWLEDGE

Applying knowledge

There are other reasons why students do not apply school knowledge. Sometimes school tasks stop short of what is needed to prepare students to function outside the classroom setting. There may be levels or stages of expertise, and traditional classroom experiences may not get students past the lower levels (Spiro et al., 1991). A simple distinction might be made between the novice stage of basic knowledge and skill acquisition and the expert stage, at which knowledge can be applied in complex and somewhat inconsistent situations. The mental skills and the learning experiences associated with each stage are different. In the initial stage of learning, it is appropriate to use drill and practice to assure fact availability and to apply generative procedures to interrelate basic knowledge. Such activities help the student build a stable representation in memory and create rich connections among ideas so that knowledge is easy to retrieve. However, knowledge at this level may not be very useful in solving real problems. More advanced functioning often requires much more than the retrieval of intact knowledge. For advanced functioning in complex settings, experts need to be cognitively flexible. They need to assemble useful approaches from more basic ideas stored in memory.

Here is an example of inflexible knowledge in physics and engineering (Spiro et al., 1991). The basic principles of physics can be identified, isolated, and taught in an organized fashion. Whereas the basic ideas of physics may be intellectually difficult, the ideas are stable. The use of physics in the context of building a bridge is a different matter. Every situation in applied engineering is likely to be somewhat different; it is nearly impossible to know exactly what to do before the situation is encountered and the many situational variables are considered. The knowledge applied to the construction of a bridge has to be fabricated rather than retrieved.

Preparing students to use knowledge flexibly

Students can be prepared to use knowledge flexibly. However, teachers must recognize that this preparation requires more than mastery of a knowledge base. Students need to have opportunities to work with the knowledge they have acquired — for different purposes, at different times, and under different circumstances. The training of future physicians is a good example (Spiro et al., 1991). Over time, medical students come into contact with a number of cases exemplifying a particular medical condition. All the cases may deal with a certain type of heart condition, but the specifics (laboratory test data, symptoms, patients' physical characteristics) will vary. The variability that medical students encounter forces them to apply their knowledge base flexibly.

Technology is now being used to make this process more efficient. Hypermedia environments are being used to allow students to explore stored representations of many cases multiple times from multiple perspectives. The stored case summaries can be searched to find examples of a particular medical condition, a certain type of EKG test result, or a specific symptom (see Chapter 7 for an extended discussion of hypermedia and applications). Hypermedia may offer this same advantage for your classroom situation as well. Certainly, more information can be put at your students' fingertips to be searched quickly and flexibly. Students may be able to find many examples when they want and not be limited to the one or two examples provided by traditional sources.

WHAT DO CONSTRUCTIVISTS SUGGEST TO TEACHERS?

Recommendations for appropriate learning experiences

Advocates of constructivism make recommendations regarding appropriate learning experiences and appropriate classroom practices. Consider the following general suggestions (Duffy and Bednar, 1991):

1. The emphasis in learning should be on *reflective thinking* and *productivity*. The fundamental goal should be the ability to perform relevant tasks and not the accumulation of specific facts. Not every student will perform the tasks in exactly the same way or acquire the same task-relevant skills.
2. Students need rich contexts for learning. Learning should focus on *authentic activities,* allow *student collaboration* to explore alternate perspectives and evaluate ideas, and provide learning experiences that encourage communication and access to real-world examples.
3. Students should have *access to domain experts* who model the skills appropriate to the domain. Ideally, students should work with these experts within the context of an *apprenticeship* relationship.

While some advocates of constructivism can be quite radical and believe that schools need drastic restructuring before meaningful improvements in education can occur, there are still ways to apply constructivist principles without resorting to extremes. We have isolated some of the important ideas of constructivism for more detailed consideration below.

Authentic Activities

What are **authentic activities**, really? They are the ordinary practices of a culture (Brown, Collins, and Duguid, 1989). The term *culture* here means what you might consider the trappings of ordinary people doing ordinary things — readers or writers, biologists, users of mathematics, or speakers of Spanish. In a way, the ordinary people who define a given culture are experts because they perform in an accomplished way to complete tasks that are important to that group.

Again, language makes a good example. Expert users of a language apply their knowledge as a tool to complete tasks within their everyday environment. By this definition, most of us qualify as expert users of language.

Whereas experts define what is an authentic activity within their culture, one does not have to be an expert to perform within the culture or to learn the skills of the culture. An individual earning a living as an engineer, for instance, uses knowledge of mathematics and physics to solve problems and communicate within the culture of the engineer. Most of us do not qualify as expert users of mathematics and physics within the culture of the engineer, but we can nevertheless learn the skills. A young child has not mastered language but still uses language in attempts to communicate. The skill level may be lower, but the child nonetheless communicates. Young mathematicians and scientists can also be immersed in situations in which math and problem-solving skills are used to solve realistic dilemmas confronting the student (Cognition and Technology Group, 1991, 1996; Goldman, et. al, 1996). An example of these technology-based activities, *The Adventures of Jasper Woodbury*, is discussed in Chapter 3 (pages 105-106). Technology can often be very helpful in putting students in contexts in which they can apply emerging skills to meaningful problems.

Technology can help students apply new skills

Searching for authentic activities in classrooms reveals an interesting insight. There turns out to be a recognizable classroom culture and identifiable authentic activities. The problem is that authentic classroom tasks may not be what teachers really intend. The goals, values, and activities of the school culture and the subject matter domain culture can be very different (Brown, Collins, and Duguid, 1989). The person functioning in the culture of the biologist uses knowledge to solve problems relevant to that domain (for example, improving the habitat to increase the number of ducks). The student functioning in the school environment uses knowledge to solve problems relevant to the school domain (such as getting the most points possible on the next quiz, or pleasing the teacher). Both improving habitats for ducks and getting the most points on the next quiz are authentic activities. Both the culture of the biologist and the culture of the student may involve knowledge of ducks, habitat variables, and wildlife conservation. However, the way in which this knowledge has been stored and organized and the specific inferences that have been drawn may depend on what the student intends to do with the knowledge. It is easy to see how students can become confused and frustrated.

A
C OOPERATION
T
I
V
E

Collaborative Learning

Much of what goes on in classrooms is social. Classroom social interactions can influence individual students' mental behaviors in powerful ways. Group projects provide opportunities for more experienced and skilled individuals to demonstrate how they think and learn. Group projects also provide opportunities for students to use knowledge and newly acquired thinking skills. Such **collaborative learning** can take many forms. The following applications present several techniques through which students and sometimes students and teachers learn together.

Cognitive Apprenticeship.   Dolores Durkin (1978–1979) once did a study in which she observed how elementary teachers taught reading comprehension. She found that the teachers spent about 1 percent of reading class time involved in comprehension instruction. If you find this result shocking, consider for a moment what it means to teach someone how to comprehend. How do you explain a complex mental skill to someone else — particularly a young child? Do you know how *you* comprehend? Durkin observed that teachers spent a lot of time asking students questions. The questions may have helped the students evaluate whether or not they understood the material, but the questions did not teach students how to improve their comprehension.

Teaching students to comprehend

Reciprocal teaching, a frequently cited example of **cognitive apprenticeship**, was designed to teach students how to comprehend (Palincsar and Brown, 1984). In this approach, the teacher works with a small number of students. Initially, the teacher takes the most active role and models important cognitive behaviors. Because the actual behaviors are internal and cannot be observed, important behaviors are operationalized and expressed in the form of an external behavior. Specific external behaviors used in developing comprehension included asking questions about important content, summarizing content, identifying and clarifying difficulties, and making predictions (using external activities to activate internal tools was discussed earlier in this chapter, on pages 56-60).

The reciprocal teaching model

In the Palincsar and Brown method, the group reads a paragraph together. The teacher then models the external behaviors: asks the students a question, comments about something that seemed difficult to understand, and makes a prediction. Gradually, individual students in the group attempt these activities under teacher supervision. The same cycle of read, question, evaluate, summarize, and predict takes place with individual students attempting the different activities. Eventually, the individual student is expected to get to the point of performing all external behaviors and then eventually only the internal equivalents. As students become more experienced readers, mental processes likely to improve understanding and retention no longer depend on the support of external supplemental tasks.

What makes this an apprenticeship? Brown, Collins, and Duguid (1989)

Modeling, coaching, and fading

define an apprenticeship as enculturating a novice into authentic practices through activity and social interaction. Apprenticeship also suggests the use of situated modeling, coaching, and fading. Instructional activities are set, or situated, in the same context in which the skills to be learned are to be

Focus

Lev Vygotsky

Lev Vygotsky, a Russian developmental psychologist working in the early 1900s, is a classic example of a scholar whose ideas were much more influential after his death than during his lifetime. Following is a brief summary of Vygotsky's central theories (Harley, 1996; Vygotsky, 1978).

Private Speech

We have all seen children and even adults talk to themselves as they perform a difficult task. Vygotsky believed this externalized speech was quite functional as an "external" guidance mechanism. Vygotsky also proposed that learners use the speech of others as they solve problems. Gradually these forms of guidance become internalized as silent inner or **private speech.**

Zone of Proximal Development

Think of a set of related educational tasks positioned along a continuum. At one end of the continuum are tasks the learner can perform with ease. At the other end are tasks that are far beyond the capability of the learner. Between these areas are tasks that the learner can perform with the proper assistance. This area, called the **zone of proximal development,** defines the tasks for which instruction is likely to be most productive. Support usually implies adult guidance or even the cooperation of a

more experienced peer. There may be other forms of support that allow learners to achieve success. With experience, learners become capable of independent functioning.

Scaffolding

Scaffolding is doing some of the work for students until they develop the capability or capacity to do it for themselves. Such mechanisms might include reminders, pronouncing or explaining words students don't understand, clear step-by-step instructions, and demonstrations of tasks to be performed. Unlike behavioral approaches, which help less skilled learners by creating a simplified version of the task, scaffolding instead proposes simplifying the learner's role in accomplishing the actual task.

Reciprocal teaching is regarded as a good example of the application of Vygotsky's ideas. We did not mention private speech, the zone of proximal development, or scaffolding in our discussion of reciprocal teaching. See if you can pick out aspects of reciprocal teaching that would illustrate what each of these terms implies. Vygotsky's theoretical ideas are also illustrated in several other theories emphasized in this book. Some of these would include emphasizing the teacher's role as supporting learning rather than dispensing knowledge, the value of learning in cooperative groups, and the importance of engaging students with authentic tasks. ✳

applied. (Situating cognitive behaviors makes learning and applying behaviors much easier.) The teacher in our reading example interacts with the students first as model, then as coach, and then gradually withdraws, or fades, to the position of observer. The group setting allows the skills of reading to be distributed across the entire group so that the demands on individual students are reduced until they become more skilled. The group setting also provides for the expression of different views and perspectives. New insights and better understanding come from this diversity of ideas.

Often, technology provides students and teachers with an authentic opportunity for cognitive apprenticeship. Technology changes quickly, and teachers and students can explore a new videodisc, develop a database, try a new HyperCard technique, or send e-mail to another school together. Too often, teachers fear a situation in which they may not know exactly what should be done. Instead, such situations should be viewed as opportunities for teaching students *how* to learn. Share ideas with students as you consider them. Explain why ideas are rejected. Consider and discuss the ideas students offer. Explain your own thinking so that students will have something concrete from which to learn.

Technology provides many opportunities for cooperative learning

Cooperative Learning.   In **cooperative learning,** students work together to accomplish an instructional task. The nature of the task can vary from helping each other prepare for an examination to completing a project. Classroom applications of technology offer many opportunities for such group projects. Groups of students can work together to create a classroom newspaper, develop a hypermedia representation of the factors that caused the North and the South to enter into the Civil War, or complete a LOGO programming project.

Cooperative projects offer some valuable opportunities for active learning. The cooperative project becomes "an object to think with" (Kafai and Harel, 1991). As students work together on a project, they have to talk about course content related to the project. Not only do students acquire knowledge from each other, they also learn from the process of trying to put their ideas into words in order to allow someone else to understand them. Often understanding is not achieved. Others in the group may see a problem differently or have a different explanation in mind for some phenomenon. Without the cognitive conflict created by group interaction, it is very possible some of these ideas would remain unchallenged.

Think back to the example of Pam Carlson's lesson on marine life described in Chapter 1. Pam taped black-and-white illustrations of marine organisms on the blackboard and invited her students to use various books to identify the pictures. When a student felt able to identify a fish, he or she was allowed to pencil the fish's name on the picture. Several pictures ended up with several different labels. The teacher could have stepped in and resolved all disputes, but she felt it was more productive to allow the students to justify

Cooperative multimedia projects require students to work together to explain content area topics. (© Michael Zide)

the labels they had assigned. Students explained their thinking, often making use of information from reference materials. The class considered the arguments and made the final decisions. This group process provided some unique opportunities for thinking and decision making that would not have been present if students had worked in isolation — certainly not if the teacher had simply labeled the fish for them.

Planning and training for successful cooperation

Successful cooperation does not occur without some planning and training. Teachers must do more than form groups and tell students to work together. They must teach social skills. Some group members may take advantage of the group and look for a free ride. Others may try to dominate the group. Groups may run into conflicts and not know how to resolve them and move ahead.

Three activities for mastering social skills

Like other skills, social skills can be learned. Experts in classroom cooperation (Johnson and Johnson, 1989; Johnson, Johnson, and Holubec, 1991) suggest that three activities be involved in mastering social skills. First, teachers need to help students understand what the skill would look or sound like. The teacher or students can suggest examples. The teacher may explain that a basic principle of working together is learning to criticize ideas and not people, but the students still need to see and hear how this might be done. Would you say, "Sam, you're stupid. The picture you put in our program is not a picture of a Siamese fighting fish"? No, you wouldn't want to talk to someone in your group like that. To criticize the idea, you might say, "I can see that you thought it was a fighting fish because of the long dorsal fin. But look at the picture again. The fish we are looking for has bulging eyes, and a fighting fish does not."

Second, students need to practice the skill. Role playing is an effective way to learn social skills. Create scenarios for students and have them take turns practicing how they might respond in these situations.

Finally, students need to reflect on their use of the skill. Students engaged in a group activity need to discuss how well the targeted skills are being implemented in their group. If the matter of working through group conflicts was the issue, the teacher might attempt to generate discussion focused on this matter. Did the group encounter conflicts as they worked on their project during the past week? How did the group members respond? Were anyone's feelings hurt? Could something different have been said to solve the problem without criticizing individual group members?

The interaction among students in cooperative learning involves a variety of external behaviors that require desirable mental behaviors. Students are required to present their ideas to each other and to work through differences of opinion. They are actively involved in thinking about course content. Contrary to the myth that technology isolates students from each other, technology in fact offers a variety of opportunities for cooperative learning. This topic will surface in several of the following chapters. Specific cooperative methods are discussed in some detail in Chapter 10.

Activities and Projects for Your Classroom

Ideas for Content-Area Projects

We want to make sure that you understand that using technology in content-area instruction can mean something other than learning from the computer in the same way that a student might learn from a book. The student can use the computer to learn by doing. Here are just a few examples to get you thinking about using the computer in this role.

◆ Second grade students create alphabet books based on a space theme.

◆ Junior high school programmers write a LOGO program to draw a dream catcher. (A Native American dream catcher is a hoop enclosing an intricate, weblike pattern. The dream catcher is intended to keep bad dreams away from infants. Dream catchers are worn as jewelry or given as presents to new parents.)

◆ High school students develop a multimedia presentation to display wildflowers they observed and videotaped during a nature walk. Special attention is given to a discussion of the specific habitat within which each species was observed. ✷

A
C
T
I NTEGRATED
V
E

Project-Based Learning. Student projects provide a practical method for combining many of the elements of authentic activities and collaborative learning (see "Activities and Projects for Your Classroom: Ideas for Content-Area Projects"). Technology provides many opportunities for classroom projects. Examples of projects and descriptions of how they were developed appear throughout this book. Here are a few examples just to give you the idea. In all cases, small groups of students used some combination of the computer, printer, various programs, and computer peripherals, such as a scanner or video digitizer, to complete the project. In most cases, field or library research was also required.

Project-based learning is based on tasks, groups, and sharing (Wheatley, 1991). The ideal task should confront each student with a problem for which that student has no immediate solution. The task should also be chosen to focus on key concepts from the desired domain of study. The idea is to engage students in an activity requiring them to work with course content that might otherwise be treated more passively. For example, the general curriculum might specify that students should acquire a basic vocabulary associated with space, learn programming techniques, and observe plants during a field trip. The projects described on page 71 are intended to allow groups of students to meet these general goals in ways that are mentally challenging and motivating. In addition, good projects should (1) encourage students to make decisions; (2) encourage "what-if" questions; (3) require discussion and communication; (4) allow a final product or solution; and (5) be extendible.

Projects seem to be an ideal setting for cooperative approaches. Working with others requires greater attention to understanding. When students work together, they confront the ideas of others and are forced to voice and defend their own beliefs. Trying to explain what you know to someone else, perhaps in several different ways, is a very active way to think through important ideas.

Finally, Wheatley (1991) believes that teachers must allocate time for students to present their ideas, methods, and products. This is important not only at the conclusion of a project, but also as the project evolves. Presenting your work is an authentic activity that provides an important source of motivation. Presentation also allows groups to gather ideas from other groups and have their own work critiqued. Initial presentations are likely to be made before the teacher and classmates. Later presentations might be made to students from other classes, parents, and even the general public.

SUMMARY

Effective classroom decision making should include some insights into how thinking and learning behaviors function and how external activities and experiences influence these behaviors. The ways that technology can engage students in active learning and productive thinking are of greatest concern.

This book takes a cognitive perspective in discussing learning, thinking, and problem-solving behavior. The cognitive approach is concerned with describing how knowledge is stored (memory stores), how knowledge is manipulated (cognitive processes, or mental tools), and how the whole system is guided (control mechanisms, or metacognition).

Information exists in working memory (also described as short-term memory, STM) or in long-term memory (LTM). Working memory can be thought of as the contents of consciousness or awareness and as the location of mental activity. Working memory is limited in both storage capacity and duration. These limits have important educational implications, because performance breaks down when either limit is exceeded.

LTM can be described as a network linking images, episodes, and elements of declarative and procedural knowledge. There are many important educational implications related to the nature of these storage units, the organization of links among the units, and the quantity and quality of what has been stored.

We describe cognitive processes as mental tools that perform the work of moving and transforming information. The teacher or the instructional materials are assumed to operate indirectly to influence cognitive activity.

The cognitive system is adaptable and self-monitoring. These control functions are the responsibility of metacognition. To learn and think effectively, students must develop knowledge of task requirements and personal capabilities. They must also develop competence in planning, evaluating, and regulating their academic behavior.

This chapter presented three models of learning with many overlapping features. Both meaningful and generative learning stress the active role of the learner in creating personal knowledge by establishing links between new ideas and what is already known, respectively. Current constructivist models also place the learner in the role of creating a personal understanding of experience.

These general comments regarding instruction and learning are important when considering technology. Technology can be used in so many ways. Some applications present primarily information, some drill students on skills that need to be overlearned, and some allow students to create some externally visible project. When the purpose is learning with understanding, the technology must engage the student in active mental work.

REFLECTING ON CHAPTER 2

Activities

◆   Cognitive models of learning tend to emphasize problem-solving and thinking skills. Generate a list of situations in which you feel rote learning and learning through repetition are important. For each item on your list, explain which rote techniques are most appropriate for the type of knowledge or skill you have identified.

◆   Identify classroom situations you have experienced in which you feel the assessment was inconsistent with the type of skill or knowledge that was the focus of instruction. Propose a more appropriate assessment task for each situation.

◆   Provide a personal example of inert knowledge. What knowledge or skill was involved? Under what circumstances was this knowledge or skill available, and when was it not available? Propose learning activities that you feel would have improved your ability to transfer what you learned to more situations.

Key Terms

authentic activities   *(p. 65)*
cognitive apprenticeship   *(p. 67)*
collaborative learning   *(p. 67)*
computer simulation   *(p. 53)*
cooperative learning   *(p. 69)*
declarative knowledge   *(p. 40)*
discovery learning   *(p. 53)*
episodic memory   *(p. 39)*
generative learning   *(p. 55)*
imagery   *(p. 39)*
inert knowledge   *(p. 61)*
interspersed questions   *(p. 57)*
links   *(p. 41)*
long-term memory (LTM)   *(p. 37)*
meaningful learning   *(p. 51)*
metacognition   *(p. 44)*
metacognitive control functions
  (p. 45)

metacognitive knowledge   *(p. 44)*
naive theories   *(p. 62)*
network   *(p. 41)*
network models   *(p. 41)*
nodes   *(p. 41)*
performance assessment   *(p. 52)*
private speech   *(p. 68)*
procedural knowledge   *(p. 40)*
reception learning   *(p. 53)*
rote learning   *(p. 51)*
scaffolding   *(p. 68)*
short-term memory (STM)   *(p. 35)*
tutorial   *(p. 53)*
working memory   *(p. 35)*
zone of proximal development
  (p. 68)

Resources to Expand Your Knowledge Base

Students in undergraduate teacher education programs are also likely to encounter many of the topics covered in this chapter in an educational psychology course whose textbooks are likely to consider them in greater detail.

Some of the ideas presented in this chapter are probably new to our readers and certainly not part of their own previous experiences as students. The opportunity to see what some of these ideas might look like in the classroom should be helpful. The Computers as Learning Partners project at the University of California-Berkeley illustrates the application of cooperative learning, computer simulations, technology-supported scaffolding, externalization of expert thinking, project-based learning, and portfolio assessment within a single curriculum project focused on middle school physical science instruction. A World Wide Web site presents the theoretical background of the project, a description of project activities, and a presentation of research findings related to the project. A demonstration of the simulation software and the student lab book in action can be downloaded. The URL is http://www.clp.berkeley.edu/CLP.html.

Learning How to Integrate Technology with Your Teaching

Part Two *introduces you to categories of software, the most frequently applied computer tool applications (word processors, databases, spreadsheets, e-mail and World Wide Web browsers), multimedia tools, and the ways these applications support students in meaningful learning. You will learn about educational benefits associated with teaching students to program and how to take advantage of the potential of the Internet. You will also look at the advantages of hypermedia and multimedia and how they support students in meaningful learning. We will discuss types of multimedia projects you can have your students create and some of the tools and techniques used to produce the sounds and images described in multimedia applications throughout the book. Finally you will explore the concept of design and the learning opportunities students have when designing and presenting projects.*

Chapter 3

Using Instructional Software for Content-Area Learning

ORIENTATION

This chapter will acquaint you with computer applications used in an instructional role. First, we will consider what instruction is and look at how traditional instructional activities are being challenged. Then we will present a system for categorizing instructional software. Once you understand this system, you should be able to classify new programs that you encounter and understand how each category of software involves learners. For example, you will learn how to determine whether software presents new ideas and develops new skills, helps students become more proficient with skills learned elsewhere, or both presents new skills and provides opportunities for practice. In short, you will learn how to evaluate software and to evaluate how software is used. As you read, look for answers to the following questions:

FOCUS QUESTIONS

◆ What are the four stages of a complete instructional experience? Which of the stages of instruction do computer-based tutorials, simulations, drill-and-practice software, educational games, and exploratory environments address?

◆ Why would teachers want students to experience a computer-based simulation rather than the "real thing"?

◆ How are simulation fidelity, speed of learning, and likelihood of transfer interrelated?

◆ When are drill-and-practice activities used inappropriately?

◆ What are the characteristics of an exploratory learning environment, and what role should teachers play to help students learn from exploratory environments?
◆ What factors might teachers consider in evaluating software for potential adoption?

An Example of Learning from the Computer

A teacher and an elementary school student work with an activity called the Eco-Simulator. The Eco-Simulator is an example of a simulation, one of several categories of instructional software you will encounter in this chapter. As you read this dialogue, consider how the simulation and the teacher involve the student. Does this experience qualify as what Chapter 2 describes as meaningful learning?

Teacher: What's an herbivore?

Student: [*no response*]

Teacher: What do herbivores eat?

Student: They eat herbs.

Teacher: Okay, what's a carnivore?

Student: It has something to do with cars.

Teacher: Do you know what a food chain is?

Student: It starts with something little and then something eats that. [*crouches to demonstrate*] Some little fish eat something that lives in the water — little plants or something. [*pretends to engulf small plants with two-hand overhand motion*] Then bigger fish eat the little fish. Then bigger fish still eat those fish. [*stands a little more out of crouch with increasing size of fish*] Then [*arm over head for fin, then begins two-arm scissors motion and* Jaws *theme — daaa-duh, daa-duh, da-duh, da-duh*] a shark eats them all!

Teacher: Is that the only kind of food chain?

Student: No, people can be in a food chain, too. We eat other animals and plants.

Teacher: Let me show you how to work with this computer program.

Student: It looks like you get to draw pictures or something.

Teacher: Well, in a way you do. First, you click on one of these small pictures to select a biome. What do you think this one is?

Student: It's kind of small. I don't know.

Teacher: What does it say here? [*points to field above picture*]

Student: "Salt Water."

Teacher: Do you know what that means?

Student: Sure, it would be like the ocean.

Teacher: Do you remember telling me about the food chain? If I remember correctly, you told me about plants and fish that live in the ocean. Let me show you how to put plants and animals in the ocean. You just use the mouse to drag them into the picture. [*demonstrates how to use the mouse to drag object*] What would you put in the ocean?

Student: [*drags in algae, small fish, and a shark; see Figure 3.1*]

Teacher: How will this food chain work?

Student: The little fish will eat the plants, and the shark will eat the little fish.

FIGURE 3.1   Screen Display from Eco-Simulator

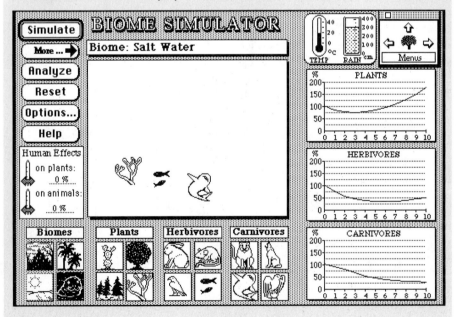

Teacher: Let me show you something. Click on this button [*points to "Simulate" button*] and watch these graphs.

Teacher: These graphs show how the number of plants and animals changes. Some of the plants and fish get eaten. Herbivores are fish or animals that eat plants. Carnivores are fish or animals that eat other fish or animals. The number of fish grows when they have baby fish. New plants may also grow. If the line on the graph goes up, there are more. If the line goes down, there are less. Why does the line for the little fish go down?

Student: Sharks eat them.

Teacher: Why does the line for the sharks go down?

Student: [*pause*] Probably get killed in boating accidents?

Teacher: What do you think happens when the sharks have few little fish left to eat?

Student: Oh, they die, too. The line would go down.

Teacher: Why would the line for the plants go up?

Student: Maybe it wasn't the right kind of plants for the fish to eat. Oh, there are less fish to eat them.

Teacher: How could you fix it so we end up with more sharks by the end of the graph?

Student: Put in more fish, but they'll need more plants to eat.

[*Now has a total of one shark, five sets of little fish, and five plants. Clicks "Simulate" button to produce graphs marked B in Figure 3.2.*]

Teacher: What happened?

Student: It still didn't work right. The plants went down too fast. I'm going to take out some of the little fish. [*Removes two sets of little fish. Now has five plants, three sets of little fish, and one shark. Clicks "Simulate" button to produce graphs marked C in Figure 3.2.*] There. Is that what you wanted me to do?

Teacher: Yes, there are more sharks at the end. [*points to graph*] Why do you have to start with more little fish than sharks?

Student: Because the shark could never live on just a few little fish — it's a lot bigger and it has to eat lots of little fish.

FIGURE 3.2 Screen Display Showing Graphs After Three Simulations

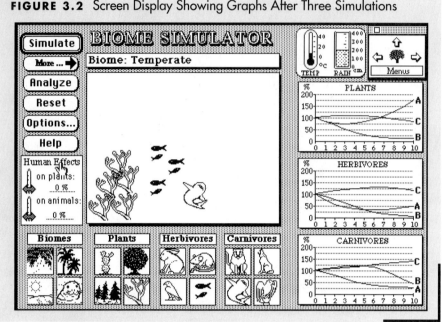

COMPUTER-BASED INSTRUCTION

Applications of technology to instruction are often called **computer-based instruction** (**CBI**) or **computer-assisted instruction** (**CAI**). If we were to categorize these applications using the traditional tutor, tool, tutee model (Taylor, 1980) introduced in Chapter 1 (pages 11 through 13), the applications we discuss here would best fit within the category of computer as tutor.

CBI and CAI

You might remember that the terms *tutor, tool,* and *tutee* refer to the role played by the computer. As a tutor, the computer is directly responsible for instruction. As a tool, the computer makes academic tasks such as writing and calculating easier. In the role of tutee, the student instructs the computer by writing programs. We will save our discussion of computer tools and programming for later chapters.

Technology in the role of tutor

In the role of tutor, technology exerts a high degree of control over the information to which students are exposed and over how students interact with this material. It is expected that students will acquire knowledge or skill directly from interacting with the activities provided by the computer. As a teacher or student, you are no doubt familiar with such instructional activities. You have been exposed to them all of your academic life. The general characteristics of control we just described for technology-based activities could just as easily apply to textbooks, workbooks, and teachers' presentations.

Each type of instruction presents information and engages students in specific activities to promote understanding, retention, or skill mastery.

This chapter presents the most traditional view of the purposes of education and the roles of educators and students. This traditional view argues that technology simply provides the means for educators and students to play their roles more effectively. Other advocates of instructional technology argue for drastic reform in both the purposes of education and how these purposes are accomplished; we discuss some of these views in greater detail in other chapters in this book. From this latter perspective, the increasing availability of new and powerful technologies provides both the opportunity and the means to accomplish rather drastic changes in schools.

Traditional views and drastic reform

Some of these changes have been captured in Papert's (1993) distinction between **instructionism** and **constructionism.** Instructivist approaches seek to convey knowledge and skill as effectively as possible and argue that the route to better learning is through the improvement of instruction. The constructionist position holds that students will benefit most by finding and generating their own knowledge. The teacher's primary responsibility is to support students in these tasks. Whereas some (Papert, 1993) have urged educators to take a bold step and move strongly toward a more constructionist model of education, we feel that a more productive approach, and the model most likely to be implemented in current school settings, will involve students in a combination of teacher-centered (here also used to mean instruction-oriented) and student-centered learning experiences. We also would argue that the distinction between learning activities seeking to instruct students and learning activities requiring students to take more responsibility for what and how they learn is not necessarily the same as the distinction between passive and active learning. High-quality technology-based learning experiences of any type should engage the learner in the active cognitive behaviors we identified in Chapter 2.

Instructionism and constructionism

A MODEL OF INSTRUCTION

A complete instructional experience takes students through four stages: (1) presentation of information or learning experiences; (2) initial guidance as the student struggles to understand the information or execute the skill to be learned; (3) extended practice to provide fluency or speed or to ensure retention; and (4) assessment of student learning (Alessi & Trollip, 1991). This model is intended as a general description of the components of instruction and not a model specific to instruction delivered with technology. If it can be accepted that all four stages should always be present in some form, awareness of the stages of instruction can serve several useful purposes. Here, we use an awareness of the four stages primarily to identify and differentiate the purposes of different categories of instructional software.

Four stages of instructions

Insight, from awareness of the four stages

Some of the more important insights you may gain from analyses of this type will be the recognition of important instructional experiences *not* provided by specific learning tasks. Some of the more common criticisms of instructional technology can be understood in this manner. In some cases, the criticism is fair, and the technology-based learning experiences either do not cover the stages of instruction as advertised or provide poor-quality experiences. For example, a program may claim to help students understand the blood flow within the circulatory system. What the program may actually do is present information about the circulatory system. Students very seldom learn all that is expected with a single exposure and some type of interactive process is required to locate and correct misunderstandings or oversights (Alessi & Trollip, 1991). If the program does not provide opportunities for the student to use factual knowledge or procedural skills, or does not adequately identify and respond to difficulties in understanding, the program has not met the requirements of the second stage of instruction. In this case, the claims made by the developers of the instructional materials would be inappropriate. Under different circumstances, the same instructional material might be used productively because the classroom teacher would take responsibility for helping students understand the information provided.

Not all criticisms of instructional materials are fairly directed toward the materials or the developers. In some cases, classroom teachers make assumptions or take liberties that are inappropriate. A common mistake of this type is to use materials designed for the third, or practice, stage as an initial instructional activity. Practice activities provide feedback on the quality of student performance, but this feedback is often not adequate to teach new skills to students with little understanding of the task. Simple feedback when basic principles are poorly understood is not very helpful.

CATEGORIES OF INSTRUCTIONAL SOFTWARE

In this section, you will learn the characteristics of five different categories of instructional software: tutorials, simulations, drill-and-practice applications, educational games, and exploratory environments. You will become familiar with the stages of instruction each type of software most frequently covers and see that some categories of learning activities offer students more control and flexibility than others. Once you have completed this section, you should be able to identify some of the strengths and weaknesses of each software category, in theory and in practice. When you reach the final section of this chapter, you can apply your understanding when we discuss teachers' selecting software to use in their classrooms.

Five categories of instructional software

TUTORIALS

High-quality **tutorials** should present information and guide learning — the first two stages of the instructional model (Alessi and Trollip, 1991). We usually think of tutoring as a form of instruction involving a teacher and one or two students. The individual nature of the interaction between tutor and student is assumed to offer certain advantages. In comparison to group-based instruction, tutorials can more precisely tailor the rate of progress and the content of presentations to the needs of the individual student, immediate adaptations in instruction can be made, and students can interact with the tutor. The more individual nature of the tutorial approach is frequently proposed as an advantage of computer-based tutorials.

Tutorials adapt instruction to individual students

How Tutorials Function

The human tutor usually begins by presenting a small segment of information or demonstrating a specific skill. Then the tutor requires some type of activity on the student's part. Depending on the content being taught, the tutor might ask the student to respond to a question or to demonstrate the skill just presented. The student's performance allows the tutor to judge how well the student has mastered the newly acquired content or skill. This appraisal allows the tutor to do two things. The tutor can provide motivational feedback ("You're doing very well" or "I think we need to work on this a little more") or use the quality of the student's performance to determine what to do next. Perhaps the student is having no difficulties, in which case it makes sense to move on. Perhaps the student has misunderstood something, in which case the tutor needs to explain a specific concept again.

Students can take an active role in tutorials

In a tutorial relationship, the student can take an active role by asking for clarification or requesting that the tutor repeat an explanation. Of course, the student can also just ask questions that come to mind. If the questions are relevant to the topic, the tutor can interact with the student to explore the topic, using the student's own curiosity and background knowledge.

High-quality computer tutorials are capable of imitating some of these elements of instruction. Even relatively inexpensive computers can present information using text, sound, animation, illustrations, and video. The powerful presentation capabilities of the computer, or the computer in combination with such devices as a CD-ROM or videodisc player, provide a fairly satisfactory solution to the requirements of the first stage of instruction. A CD or a videodisc offers tremendous storage capacity and can make a great deal of information available to the student. The more subtle and dynamic instructional elements present in guiding student learning are more difficult to mimic. Computers can certainly gather information about student understanding or skill mastery by frequently asking questions or requiring that students perform assigned tasks. However, computers' information-gathering and interpretation skills are crude in comparison to those of human tutors.

If you think about typical student behavior for a moment, you can probably anticipate the challenges involved in developing programs that do a good job of judging student responses. Students often spell words incorrectly or use a different term than was anticipated. Even sophisticated programs, which expect multiple responses and are capable of forgiving some spelling errors, can fail to credit acceptable answers and sometimes judge unacceptable answers as correct. Errors of this nature are fairly infrequent but can frustrate students. Alternate-response items such as multiple-choice questions also have limitations. Such items are easier to construct to assess factual knowledge than to assess understanding or application. If authors do not work to generate items sensitive to deeper understanding, student thinking at deeper levels will not be assessed or encouraged.

Linear tutorials and branching tutorials

Simply communicating to a student that he or she has missed key ideas in the lesson or has not developed important skills does not satisfy the expectations of guidance. Tutorials attempt to provide additional guidance through hints and remedial explanations. In **linear tutorials**, all students work their way through the same body of information. Students performing poorly may be cycled through a particular segment of instruction a second time. In **branching tutorials**, students having difficulty receive a different instructional approach rather than returning to material that has already proved difficult to understand. Branching decisions can also be made based on pretest information. Questions may reveal that some students already know some of the things a particular tutorial was designed to teach. Rather than sending these students through an unnecessary sequence of instruction, students can be routed to the material they need to learn. Branching programs are more complex than linear programs but allow for greater individualization of instruction.

Evaluating Tutorials

A fair question for you to ask when evaluating the instructional potential of computer-based tutorials is: What type of instruction represents a fair comparison? Although computer-based tutorials attempt to model some key behaviors of human tutors, they cannot duplicate all of these behaviors. The human tutor can evaluate student behavior in more sophisticated ways and can respond to student needs more flexibly. Classroom teachers, however, may often be unable to function as tutors because there are too many students and too many different responsibilities in classrooms. It is very possible there are some situations in which a less-than-perfect computer-based tutor can productively augment or provide an alternative to what the classroom teacher and traditional instructional materials are able to accomplish. It is neither necessary nor desirable to totally eliminate the teacher's involvement when some instructional functions are provided by technology. It may be possible for teachers to monitor student work as the student interacts with tutorials and to respond to student questions after the learning session has been completed. The most fundamental questions in evaluating tutorials concern the clarity, efficiency, and appeal with which important information is presented.

SIMULATIONS

Controlled learning environments

Simulations provide controlled learning environments that replicate key elements of real-world environments. A simulation's focus on a limited number of key elements provides a simplified version of the real world that allows the student to learn a topic or skill very efficiently. A simulation is designed so that actions a student takes within the simulated environment produce results similar to those that would occur in the actual environment. The student acts, and the simulated environment reacts.

Simulations can be used to learn about properties of physical or biological objects or the principles by which a variety of physical, social, and biological phenomena function. You may already have some personal experiences with simulations. Role-playing experiences, for example, are a type of simulation. Before student teachers go into elementary or secondary schools to work with real students, they commonly role-play such skills as leading a discussion, giving a short lecture, asking questions and providing feedback, and

Teachers should continually monitor student activity when students work with simulations, tutorials, or other CAI tasks. (© Charles Abel)

Role-playing is a kind of simulation

working with a misbehaving student. Instead of dealing with the complexities present in an actual classroom, role-playing experiences tend to focus on a particular skill, such as leading a discussion. Computer-based simulations attempt to meet similar instructional objectives.

In a way, the purpose of a simulation is to have students discover or come to understand the set of rules or the formula that determines how the simulation will respond. Why not just present students with the list of rules or the formula driving a particular simulation and have the students deal with this information directly? It is impossible to have a definitive answer to this question, because the answer depends on how students would react. If students respond to the direct presentation of information in a way that results in meaningful learning, there would be little advantage to the simulation. However, many students would probably memorize the rules or the formulas and make little attempt to understand the information or relate it to what they already know. If you are starting to flash back to some of the ideas in Chapter 2,

Active learning, inert knowledge, and learning in context

that is good. Topics such as active learning, inert knowledge, and learning in context are easy to apply in arguing the potential benefits of simulations. Because simulations embed principles or concepts within a fairly realistic environment, there is a good chance that students mastering these principles or concepts will also contextualize them. The context of the simulation provides at least one purpose or application for the information. The properties of effective simulations seem quite consistent with constructivist recommendations.

The active manipulation of a simulation does not avoid all learning problems, however. A common difficulty is that students simply manipulate the simulation through trial and error until they obtain an acceptable result; they never really determine the rules, relationships, or principles producing that result. This problem is similar to the problem of rote discovery we discussed

Applying knowledge

in Chapter 2 (page 51). The teacher can play a valuable role in encouraging students to take a thoughtful approach to simulations. Ask students to explain their "theories" about how the simulation works. Have students predict how the principles might apply to a new situation. If the simulation deals with setting the price of lemonade for a sidewalk lemonade stand, have students discuss how what they have learned might apply to selling cars.

A CTIVE
C OOPERATION
T HEME-BASED
I NTEGRATED
V ERSATILE
E VALUATION

Simulations can be used before the formal presentation of new material to pique students' interest, to activate what students already know about the topic, and to provide a concrete example to relate to the more general discussion that follows. Simulations can also be used after students have been ex-

What can simulations be used for?

posed to a new topic. In this approach, the simulation allows students to attempt to transfer what they have learned to an actual application and perhaps to reveal misconceptions. Research (Brant, Hooper, and Sugrue, 1991) suggests that using a simulation prior to formal instruction is particularly effective. Simulations can be used for all four stages of instruction: presentation, guidance, practice, and assessment (Alessi & Trollip, 1991). Although this does not mean that every simulation is intended to provide a stand-alone educational experience, it does imply that simulations are the most versatile of the different categories of computer-assisted instruction.

Operation: Frog — An Example of a Simulation

Simulating the dissection of a frog

Do you remember dissecting a frog in high school biology? Do you remember your reaction and the reaction of some of your classmates when your teacher explained that, before you could begin the dissection, you would have to "pith" your frog? (To pith a frog, you use a dissection needle to destroy the connection between the brain and body so that body organs such as the heart will still be functioning and can be observed during the dissection.) Operation: Frog is a computer program designed to allow students to simulate the dissection of a frog. And, no, you don't have to pith the frog before you begin! The program presents students with a set of dissection tools, a dissection tray complete with specimen, and an examination tray for organizing and examining organs removed from the frog (Figure 3.3).

Text, graphics, and photographs

The simulation proceeds something like this. The student initially uses the probe to locate the points on the intact frog where a cut should be made. The probe is moved over the frog, and when a desired "snip point" is located, a small spot of color appears. Attempts to use the scissors at any other location will produce no effect. When the student has located and cut all of the snip points, the first of three layers of internal organs is revealed. The student

FIGURE 3.3   Screen Display from Operation: Frog — Dissection Pan and Examination Tray

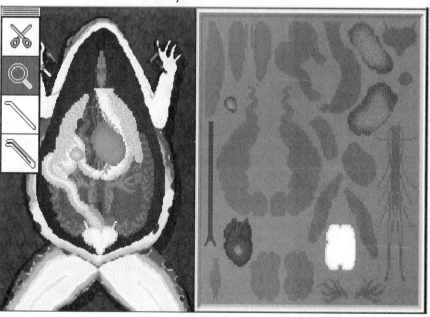

can again use the probe to reveal snip points or to reveal the names of the organs making up that layer. Here, too, the student is allowed to use the scissors only at designated spots. Once an organ has been freed with the scissors, it is moved to the examination tray with the forceps. The magnifying glass can be applied to any organ on the examination tray to reveal several types of additional information. Informative text, labeled graphics (see Figure 3.4), and digitized photographs from an actual dissection are available for each organ. Occasional animations (for instance, of blood flow) or QuickTime movies are also provided.

Operation: Frog exemplifies some of the features of simulations. Simulations tend to present a simplified version of the real thing and attempt to focus learners on key ideas, skills, or components. In contrast to the clumsiness and messiness involved in an actual dissection of a frog, work with the simulated frog involves simpler procedures and reveals simplified information. When simulated incisions are made at the proper locations, the skin magically disappears. Attempted incisions at other points are ignored. In fact, it is impossible to cut at an inappropriate point or to move a body part that the simulation does not intend the student to move. Developing the physical dexterity necessary to utilize dissection instruments is not a target behavior, so there is no attempt to involve these skills. The organs to be removed at a particular stage of the simulation are designated by color to make them easier to find. There is no need to separate the skin from other tissues or to remove abdominal muscles. Learning about the frog's musculature is not an objective of the simulation, so the abdominal muscles are just not present in the simulation. Based on the original description of Operation: Frog, you may be able to list several other ways in which the simulation has been simplified. The

Learners focus on key ideas, skills, and components

FIGURE 3.4   Exported Graphic from Operation: Frog

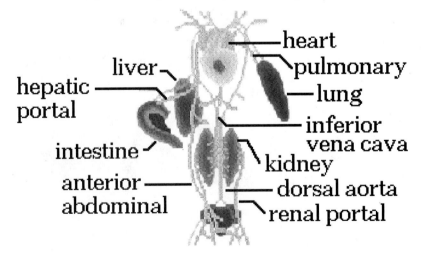

simulated dissection clearly focuses the student on the location of specific organs within the body of the frog.

Attributes of Simulations, Learning, and Transfer

The extent to which a simulation mimics reality is called **fidelity** (Alessi, 1988). When you make decisions about instruction or selecting instructional materials, an important issue to consider is how fidelity relates to learning and application. When looked at beside an actual dissected frog, the various forms of simplification identified in Operation: Frog do result in lower fidelity. Your initial reaction might be that if it is practical, experience with the real thing is always the best. But consider, for example, learning to fly an airplane. Would it be ideal to expose a novice to experiences in an actual plane?

Fidelity

Focus

Instructional Software on the World Wide Web

While the Internet and the World Wide Web (see Chapter 6) have captured the imagination of many educators, most of the resources presently available are best described as sources of information rather than instructional applications. The better Web sites do a great job of presenting information, but typically do not engage learners in any other components of instruction. There are exceptions, of course, and a few Web sites do engage students in ways that are similar to the techniques used by the instructional software presented in this chapter (Kinzie et al., 1996). In fact, several award-winning Web pages simulate frog dissection. The information necessary to reach these Web sites is provided at the end of this chapter.

Why aren't many instructional applications available on the Web? A number of factors are probably involved. First, the speed of Internet connections available in many schools is slow and may make certain experiences too tedious. The transitions from one view of the frog to another that are nearly instantaneous in Operation: Frog may take 30 seconds or more in a Web-based dissection. Second, Web applications are very good at serving information on request, but are typically poor at accepting, interpreting, and storing the many sources of information learners might provide as they work. Even the most basic tutorial programs keep a record of learner responses to provide feedback to the learner and to make decisions about when he or she should go on to new material. This would be an uncommon feature in a Web application. Finally, commercial uses of the Internet are emerging slowly. Instructional software is readily available because it can be sold to schools. Most examples of instructional applications on the Web are demonstration projects developed by a university or company.

Although the present offerings are limited, the long-term perspective is positive. Ways to overcome the limitations will likely emerge soon and the Internet will become a source of powerful instructional applications. ✳

Even if the issues of cost and safety were ignored or somehow taken care of, the situation of highest fidelity is still not necessarily the best learning situation. The student would be too anxious and the situation too confusing to allow much learning (Alessi and Trollip, 1991). Similar situations may happen in classroom settings more familiar to you. In presenting new concepts or principles, most experienced instructors initially ignore the exceptions and complications that might just confuse and increase the anxiety of students. The initial presentation describes concepts and principles with less than perfect fidelity. It appears that a moderate degree of fidelity is best for initial learning.

Applying or transferring knowledge

Now, consider the student's ability to apply or transfer what he or she has learned. (The relationship between learning, the context of learning, and transfer was discussed in Chapter 2.) Transfer depends on the degree of learning and on the extent to which a student has contextualized what has been learned or related what has been learned to the situations in which the skills or knowledge are to be applied. Here we confront a dilemma: extremely high fidelity would appear to reduce learning, but increase transfer. At the extremes, the problems of high and low fidelity are obvious. With no learning, there is nothing that can be transferred, no matter how similar the learning environment is to the eventual application environment. The example of the novice pilot in an actual airplane fits this case. It is also possible to represent situations at the other extreme. The problem of inert knowledge (see Chapter 2, page 61) describes situations in which learning has occurred but the experiences surrounding learning make it unlikely the knowledge will be used. Under more moderate circumstances, learning and transfer occur, but are both somewhat inefficient. A level of fidelity could very likely be identified that would confuse but not totally baffle the student. The realism of the learning environment increases the likelihood that the student, after an initial struggle to overcome the confusion, will be able to apply what has been learned.

Teachers should know what specific role the simulation is to play

This discussion should encourage one other insight. It may often make more sense to consider a combination of instructional experiences than to expose students to a single experience. Consider Operation: Frog one more time. The developers of this simulation really allow students working with the simulation to function on several levels of fidelity. There is the less realistic level at which the student manipulates organs within the actual simulation and the more realistic level at which the student can view digitized photographs from an actual dissection. To be useful to the student, a simulation does not have to provide a complete instructional experience, but the teacher should be aware of the specific role the simulation is to play and ensure that other necessary experiences are also available. This statement echoes the earlier claim that simulations can be used in all stages of instruction, but a specific simulation rarely provides the experiences required in all stages. In some cases, a teacher might decide that a particular simulation is a good way to introduce an area of study. In another situation, the teacher might introduce the topic and establish key principles before having students work on the simulation. A simulation can also be used after more thorough traditional instruction, to practice key skills or to evaluate students' ability to apply what they have learned.

Advantages of Simulations

Why use simulations?

Why should educators use simulations instead of allowing students to experience the real world? Simulations have several potential advantages. We have already considered how the simplification allowed by simulations can help learners focus on critical information or skills and make learning easier. Simulations can also allow students to observe phenomena that are not normally visible, to control processes that are not normally controllable, or to participate in activities that would normally be too expensive or too dangerous. Simulations make certain experiences practical and other experiences possible. There are other advantages, too.

Concreteness. Consider first that many things students study cannot really be observed. Think back to high school or to some of your college courses. You probably learned about the relative positions of the planets revolving around the sun, how electrons flow in electrical circuits, the movement of glaciers, continental drift, economic principles of supply and demand, how a signal is passed along and between neurons, and the interrelatedness of populations in a food chain. Clearly, certain phenomena are difficult or impossible to observe.

Putting objects and phenomena in observable form

Simulations dealing with these types of phenomena offer a great deal of variety. Sometimes the object of study has to be made larger (the neuron) and sometimes smaller (the solar system or continents). Sometimes the phenomena have to be speeded up (movement of glaciers and continents; the passage of generations of plants and animals) and sometimes slowed down (movement of electrons within electrical circuits). Sometimes what you view in the real world has to be put in a different form for you to observe it at all. The biome simulation we used to introduce this chapter and simulations of different economic principles often represent the relationships among several factors, graphically, as with the economic principles of supply and demand or the biological interdependence of predator and prey. Whether the technique involves making the object of study smaller or larger, the phenomena faster or slower, or just providing a way to visualize complex relationships, simulations give students concrete representations to ponder.

Control. A second valuable characteristic of simulations is the opportunity they provide for students to make decisions with logical consequences. Simulations put students in control of situations with which they would seldom be allowed to experiment under any other circumstance.

Allowing students to control certain aspects of a simulation encourages

Students build their own explanations

them to actively create and test hypotheses and, as a consequence, to build their own explanations of why the simulation works the way it does. Internally, many simulations are driven by sets of rules or mathematical formulas. For example, a simple business simulation might be based on mathematical expressions that define the relationship among such variables as money spent on advertising, the price the customer has to pay for the product, the number of items sold, and profit. As they work with this simulation, students might try to maximize profit and control both the price and the cost of advertising. The numerical values the students enter for advertising costs and price would be used in calculations performed by the computer. The computer would inform the student of the number of items sold and the profit earned. If you think about this set of variables for a bit, you can probably predict some of the things that will happen in the simulation. As advertising increases and price decreases, customers will buy more of the product. However, total profit will not necessarily increase, because of increased expenses (advertising) and a lower profit on each item sold. The ideal solution to the simulation will depend on how the simulation's designers have weighted the value of spending a certain amount of money on advertising and how they have decided changes in price will influence the number of items sold.

Cost Effectiveness.   Sadly, educators have to be constantly aware of how much money educational experiences cost. This reality applies to decisions regarding the purchase of hardware and software, but it also applies to the experiences or materials that simulations might replace. Taking the biology class on a field trip to a local pond probably requires that the school cover the cost of a bus and driver. The biome simulation described earlier costs considerably less than a single trip and will last for years.

Simulations can save money

The components needed for physics students to assemble electrical circuits are costly. Certain components, such as transistors, can easily be ruined if students make mistakes in the way they assemble circuits. A computer program allowing students to simulate the assembly of circuits does not require that additional components be purchased when students make errors. In certain situations, simulations provide quality experiences at a reasonable cost.

Safety.   There are some things students should learn that would be dangerous for them to experience directly. Some experiments in chemistry or projects exploring how electrical devices work may be too dangerous for elementary or secondary school students. The use of simulators in pilot training is an example of the value of simulation in increasing the safety of training experiences.

DRILL AND PRACTICE

You probably take your mastery of basic number facts for granted. You add, subtract, multiply, and divide without thinking much about your actions or

Learning basic skills

expending much effort. Of course, this was not always the case. Back in early elementary school, you spent a good deal of time developing arithmetic skills. Maybe you learned arithmetic skills effortlessly. Maybe arithmetic was a struggle and the source of anxiety and a few tears. Do you remember what you did to learn math skills? You probably completed a lot of worksheets. It is very likely you also used flash cards. The teacher probably had a complete set, and you could check them out so that you could practice alone or with a friend. Perhaps the flash cards were used to play Around the World or a similar competitive game. Around the World is played by seating a number of students in a circle. Two students stand, and the teacher shows them a flash card. Both students attempt to respond with the correct answer. The quickest student remains standing, and the other student must sit down. The next student in the circle then stands and competes. The goal is to see if any student is able to make it around the world. As you might guess or perhaps remember, the same students tend to win time after time.

If you have not experienced computer-based drill, you may want to consider the following example and imagine how a student's experience with this software would contrast with math worksheets or flash cards.

Math Magic is an addition and subtraction drill in an arcade game format. The purpose of the game is to help Wizrow free the enchanted dragons from the dungeon of the evil Doomlord. To free the dragons, the student must use a magic wand to rebound a ball against the brick wall to destroy the bricks and answer math problems (see Figure 3.5). Knocking down the wall

FIGURE 3.5   Screen Display from Math Magic

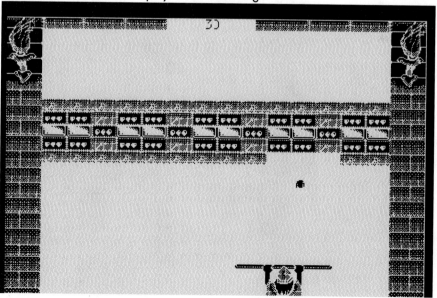

A math drill-and-practice program

has some obvious relationship to freeing the trapped dragons. On the other hand, the logical role of the math problems is never established. Maybe kids don't really care. Answering problems correctly does increase the student's score, however, and getting a high score allows the student to add his or her name to the Top Ten List.

The game begins in the dungeon with the student attempting to break through the brick wall. From time to time, the game automatically switches away from the dungeon to present math problems (see Figure 3.6). Game controls allow the number of problems presented in each dungeon level to be set between 0 and 9. An issue that sometimes comes up with software using gamelike features to motivate or involve students is how much practice the students actually receive. This might be described as the *instructional efficiency* of the software. To estimate the efficiency of this software, an elementary school student was asked to play the game for several ten-minute intervals. The problem frequency was set at the highest level. The number of problems the student received under "game conditions" ranged from fourteen to eighteen. Thus, it is very likely that Math Magic is less efficient than traditional worksheets or flash cards.

The issue of efficiency

The issue of efficiency is important. However, be careful not to jump to a quick conclusion. Whereas worksheets and the independent use of flash cards probably provide more intense practice, consider the experience of individual students playing Around the World. How many questions do you think one of the twenty students in the circle would answer in ten minutes? While some students not directly involved in the competition might silently rehearse an-

FIGURE 3.6 Presentation of Math Problem in Math Magic

swers to problems, many students sit passively until their turn comes. Students also seem to find Math Magic captivating and are willing to work independently with the activity. They may not complete as many problems per minute, but at least some students seem willing to spend considerably more time with the computer drill.

Clearly, personal motivation is emphasized in Math Magic. A fantasy situation creates interest in the student. Time spent playing keeps the student involved, and there are a number of sources of informative and encouraging feedback. If it has occurred to you that Around the World may also be motivating because of the competition involved, you are correct. However, the competition in this group activity is totally focused on performing faster and more accurately than one's classmates. Some students would seldom experience success in this setting. The Top Ten List has some of the same elements of peer competition, but most of the challenge in the computer activity is in competing with the activity itself or with improving your own best score. If you have played arcade games, you probably understand the temptation to play "just one more game" to see if you can improve your score. Normally, this urge would cost you another quarter. Here, the next game is free, and you get to practice a few math problems as well. There are also some potential disadvantages of this computer drill. Are the students even thinking carefully about the math problems they encounter? Without a teacher watching their work (or play), will the students pay attention to mistakes they have made? Is the time spent on the game part of the activity really necessary, or should students be expected to apply themselves to their school activities without such incentives? These comments should raise a few questions in your mind as you consider the following discussion of computer-based drill and practice.

The importance of motivation

Applications of Drill-and-Practice Software

Providing extended practice

Drill-and-practice software is developed to meet the needs of the third stage of instruction: extended practice. Students' initial exposure to academic facts or skills is seldom sufficient for an adequate level of mastery. Extended study is required before the facts or skills can be considered learned. The exact proficiency students should develop varies with the type of content. For factual information, the expectation is that students will be able to effortlessly retrieve the information from memory. Students are expected to be able to recall the product of 2 x 2, the capital of West Virginia, and thousands of similar facts. With procedural skills, the expectation is that students will be able to perform quickly, smoothly, and with few errors. Students are expected to complete long division problems with accuracy, to type 40 words per minute, and to perform many other tasks that require mastery of a routine. You will typically hear drill-and-practice software discussed as if it were a single category. Actually, drill activities can be differentiated from practice activities (Price, 1991). The distinction is the difference just described above — **drill** concerns factual memorization, and **practice** concerns the development of skill fluency. Since we are not considering instructional software in great detail, we follow the tradition of treating drill-and-practice software as a single category.

Consider an activity designed to develop skill fluency. Microtype (see Figure 3.7) is a popular practice activity for developing touch-typing skills. Students progress through a series of lessons. Each lesson begins with a review of skills from previous lessons and a brief tutorial introducing the skills or letters for the current lesson (such as *f* and *b*). The tutorial reminds the student of proper posture and hand position and explains the finger movement necessary to strike the new keys to be practiced in the lesson. The lesson begins with practice on the individual letters and simple letter combinations *(f b bf bf fib)*, advances to simple phrases *(to fib; or rob)*, and then moves to timed lines (see Figure 3.7) and timed paragraphs. Each lesson concludes with a simple game in which the student types lines of text to reveal parts of a picture. The program reports typing speed after each activity and provides a summary of line, paragraph, and game typing speeds at the end of the lesson.

Drill and practice to develop typing skills

Typing is a skill we want students to be able to perform accurately, swiftly, and automatically. **Automaticity** frees some of the limited capacity of short-term memory for other uses (see Chapter 2, pages 35–37). Usually, it is desirable that students *not* think about their finger placement or the location of the letters as they type. If they are writing, students need to watch the computer screen and think about what they are trying to say. Extended practice is about the only way to accomplish automaticity.

FIGURE 3.7 Screen Display from Microtype Practice Activity

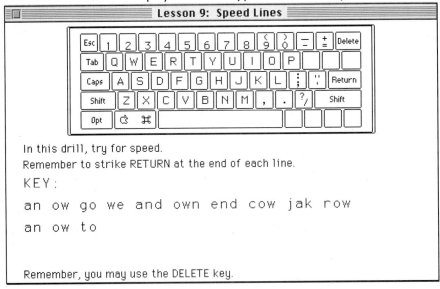

Focus of Drill and Practice

When should drill-and-practice software be used?

Whereas other types of instructional software may be used for several of the phases of instruction, drill-and-practice software has a more limited focus. This is an important point to remember. As we mentioned when the four stages of instruction were initially presented, drill-and-practice software should not be used to introduce new areas, as it has a narrow approach not suited to helping students understand new material. Drill-and-practice activities are appropriate after students have advanced past the guidance phase of instruction.

The mere mention of drill-and-practice activities is often sufficient to generate negative response in some educators. Educators who feel this way often use the word *drill* as a derogatory term and may apply the term in a more general way than it has been used here. Tutorials are sometimes erroneously labeled drill activities. It is true that a great deal of drill software is produced; it is easier to develop drill activities than other forms of instructional software. Actually, quite a lot is known about designing effective drill activities (Salisbury, 1990). Although most commercial software does not really take advantage of some of the techniques that could be used to make drill software even more effective, this is not really the concern of the critics. The problem is that drill activities emphasize fact and skill learning, and some feel that this type of learning is emphasized at the expense of developing higher-order thinking skills. Although this concern is justified, an emphasis on fact retention is an endemic educational problem not limited to computer applications (Grabe, 1985). Again, teachers need to be aware of this concern and emphasize drill and practice when fact availability and skill fluency are appropriate goals.

EDUCATIONAL GAMES

When are instructional activities categorized as games?

Instructional activities are categorized as **games** when the activities emphasize competition and entertainment. If the activity has a winner or a loser or focuses the student on competing against established records or standards, the activity has gamelike qualities. Games also employ fantasy, action, uncertainty, and similar features to make the activity interesting for the players. You will probably recognize that many of these same features were present in the activities already described as examples of other CAI categories. Commercial instructional software often combines elements of several different categories of software. Software developers also frequently attempt to incorporate gamelike features in instructional software to increase student involvement with the software. Some researchers (Lepper and Malone, 1987; Malone, 1981; Rieber, 1996) have even analyzed games to determine what makes them enjoyable, in order to suggest how software developers might improve their instructional products. If software is to be labeled, it is often necessary to

Edutainment?

subjectively determine the degree to which certain characteristics are present. Is some entertainment used to motivate learning, or does some learning result as a by-product of play? Some have begun describing some game activities as **edutainment.**

Examples of Educational Games

The Oregon Trail

Certain educational games have been popular for a long time and seem to embody characteristics teachers find of value. *The Oregon Trail* and *Where in the World Is Carmen Sandiego?* fall into this category. *The Oregon Trail* was first released in 1978 in a text-only format. For microcomputer software for the classroom, this is about as far back as you can go. Both games have been upgraded to take advantage of recent advances in technology, and both are now available in enhanced versions on CD-ROM.

The Oregon Trail takes the student on a covered wagon journey from Independence, Missouri, to Oregon in 1865. The game puts the student in the role of expedition leader, and the outcome of the journey depends to some degree on the decisions he or she makes along the way. What items should be purchased to outfit the wagon as the trip begins? How far should the wagon attempt to travel in a day? Should the wagon stop at a fort for supplies? Stops at landmarks, forts, and towns engage the leader in "conversations" that can be useful in revealing obstacles that are likely to be encountered and in suggesting ways to survive these difficulties. The leader may learn how to cross the river or when to hunt for food. We categorize *The Oregon Trail* as a game rather than as an authentic simulation because of its emphasis on entertainment and the general nature of its historical experiences. The game does provide a feel for the experiences of the early pioneers and may be a useful way to generate interest in a unit about this time period. Educators have taken to supplementing the game activity in a number of ways. One approach is to have students keep notes as they play the game and then write a diary compatible with their notes. Because different students make different decisions and because the experiences of the game are somewhat influenced by chance factors, students enjoy comparing their diary accounts. *The Oregon Trail* is so popular that World Wide Web sites have been developed or located to accompany the game. Such sites may provide current scenes along the route of the trail, related historical information, or the perspective of Native Americans from the region.

The Carmen Sandiego series

The Carmen Sandiego series (*Where in the World Is Carmen Sandiego? Where in the USA Is Carmen Sandiego? Where in Time Is Carmen Sandiego?* and others) puts the student in the role of detective. A crime has been committed, and the thief is dashing from city to city or country to country (this aspect varies with the version of the game). As the detective, the student must attempt to trail Carmen or her partners, using the clues that are revealed (kind of currency the villain is using, some characteristic of the city). Reference materials (*World Almanac Book of Facts* reference guide) supplied with the software help students interpret the clues. The newest CD-ROM version includes colorful graphics and allows the detective to question a witness, search the crime scene, compare notes with other detectives, log evidence in a database, and issue warrants. Students can play the game over and over again without encountering the same case. The game does acquaint students with several aspects of geography (location of cities and countries, factual information about specific places), requires the use of reference materials, and encourages note taking.

SimLife

Now consider something a bit more exotic. *SimLife* gives a player the tools to create a world complete with oceans, mountains, and deserts; to populate this world with plants and animals; to mix in a few natural and manmade disasters; and finally, to stand back and watch what happens. Which plants and animals will survive? Will the living organisms mutate, and what will the surviving species look like five hundred years after the artificial world was created? It is nearly impossible to describe the full scope of this activity. If the player desires, nearly any imaginable characteristic of the world or the flora and fauna living within the artificial world can be manipulated. Temperature, soil quality, characteristics of the seasons, rainfall, and many other features can be precisely determined. For each animal or plant, the player can adjust sliders, buttons, and menus to set numerous characteristics (see Species Genome for Yellow Jacket in Figure 3.8). A different set of controls allows characteristics such as intelligence, method of locomotion, and preferred habitat to be established.

The game comes with a large number of actual animals and plants, but players can also adjust characteristics of these species or create fanciful creations of their own. How would the world change if elephants could fly? A large number of data-gathering and charting features are included so that a player can chart the population statistics of each species across time, study patterns of mutation, list the organisms that have become extinct, and determine which species is eating which other species. If this sounds overwhelming, it is — it's supposed to be! It takes hours just to explore all of the features available, and building a world with a mix of plants and animals that will survive isn't easy. In a way, complexity is part of the challenge of any sophisticated game. It is probably the reason some people play bridge all of their lives, while most people quickly grow tired of Old Maid.

How *SimLife* can be entertaining may be obvious, but it may not be apparent how it can be enjoyed as a game. Like so many other features of this activity, the player or players create their own games. The complex data-acquisition features provide plenty of opportunities for scorekeeping or establishing standards of excellence. Perhaps the goal is to create a creature that can most quickly and extensively populate an unknown world. Perhaps the goal is to create the world that will sustain the most species of plants and animals for five years. As soon as players can agree on a challenge, the game is afoot.

FIGURE 3.8 Screen Display of Genome Tool and Sample World from *SimLife*

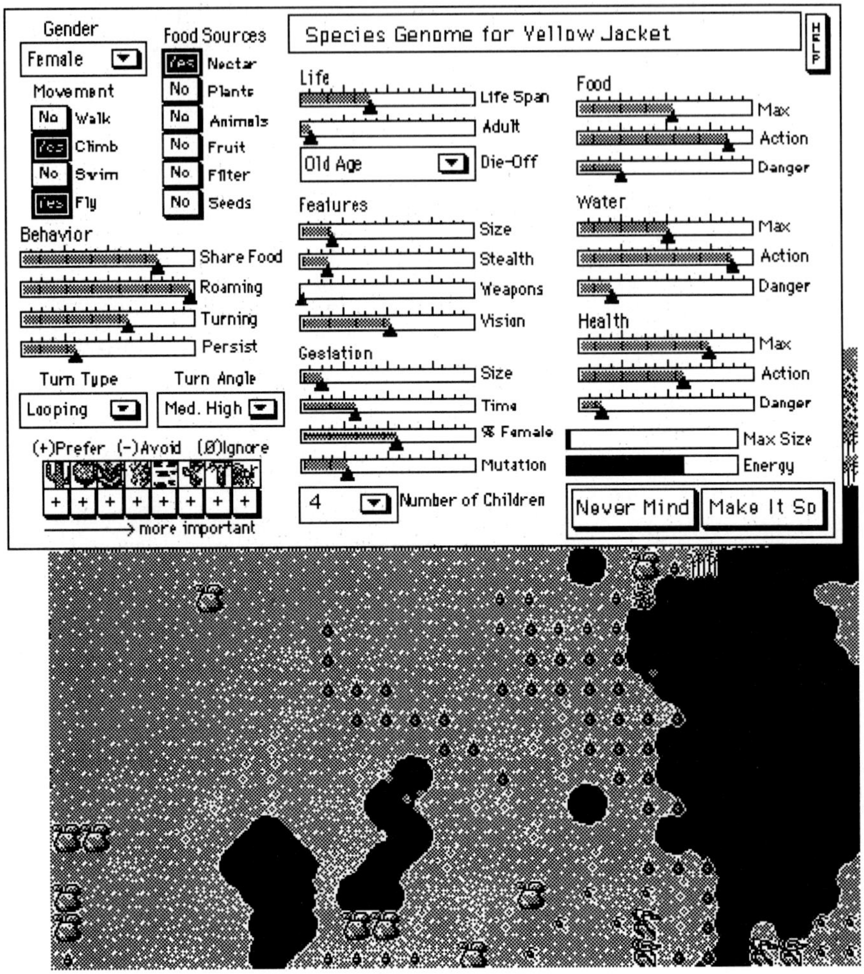

Classroom Uses of Games

Benefits of educational games

Teachers use educational games in several ways. Some, such as *The Oregon Trail* or *SimLife*, provide interesting ways to initiate related areas of study. Like simulations, carefully selected games may activate existing knowledge and pique student interest in the more traditional academic work that follows.

Although games are often equated with competition, games can also be used to enhance cooperation. In some games, the competition is with the computer and not with other students. The complexity of some games provides opportunities for teamwork. *SimLife*, for example, encourages extensive record keeping and planning. Students can share these tasks and benefit from opportunities to discuss strategy or evaluate game consequences. The Carmen Sandiego games make heavy use of travel guides and almanacs. Several students can work together to look up information.

Finally, teachers may also use educational games to reward hard work or achievement. There is nothing wrong with using technology in this way, but you should be aware of potential problems. Sometimes, students who always get their work done first are the only students who get to spend time with the computer games. Teachers need to take care that computer games do not become an exclusive opportunity for certain categories of students. Teachers must also be aware of the proportion of precious computer and classroom time devoted to games. Game use must be kept in check, and care must be taken that time on the computer does not become play time.

EXPLORATORY ENVIRONMENTS

Computer-based worlds to explore and manipulate

Exploratory environments provide manageable and responsive computer-based worlds for students to explore and manipulate (Hsu, Chapelle, and Thompson, 1993; Joyce, 1988). Such computer-based activities have also been described as intentional learning environments (Scardamalia et al., 1989) and interactive environments (Kozma, 1991).

An exploratory environment offers elements for students to work with and a setting in which the manipulation of these elements allows students to explore a cohesive body of information or a rule system (Hsu, Chapelle, and Thompson, 1993). The specific nature of the elements, information base, or rule system depends on the content area the environment was developed to represent. Exploratory environments present information, but they are not directive in the manner of tutorials. The material students spend time examining or manipulating is largely self-selected. One difference among the types of exploratory environments mentioned here is in whether or not they contain a task, goal, or problem to be solved. One difficulty with these nondirective environments is that a rich database of information is not always enough to engage many students in active learning. So, whether an assignment is embedded in the exploratory environment or suggested by a teacher, guided interaction with the environment appears to be most productive. This issue will be raised again after you have had an opportunity to become more familiar with exploratory environments.

Characteristics of Exploratory Environments

A high degree of learner control

It is difficult to list an exact set of requirements for an exploratory environment. One consistent characteristic, though, is a high degree of *learner control*. Clearly, exploratory environments encourage and may actually require that students exercise control over their experiences. The environment is

Active learning anchored in realistic situations, experiences, and goals

responsive to the student and tends to offer a great deal of flexibility in what might be done. *Flexibility* is a second characteristic of exploratory environments. Students can typically do many different things. They can even do the same thing in several different ways, revisiting the same concepts from different perspectives or using different approaches. Exploratory environments are designed to provide opportunities for active learning that are anchored in realistic situations, experiences, and goals.

Hypermedia and Interactive Videodisc Environments

Exploring settings that are rich in information

Environments developed using hypermedia or interactive videodisc technology resemble simulations in many ways and allow the student to explore settings rich in information. Some environments of this type allow the student to exercise control only through movement. The student moves from setting to setting, and each setting reveals certain information or makes certain experiences available. Settings may reflect different physical locations (different regions of a state) or points in time (important dates in history). Other environments allow the student to select an action from among a specific set of actions. The student selects this action in a particular setting and then experiences the consequences of that action. Programs of this type are useful in representing social situations. For example, a brief scenario might describe a social dilemma such as a classroom disciplinary situation. The software might then present alternative courses of action the teacher might take. When the student using the software selects one of these alternatives, the social interaction moves to some kind of conclusion based on the alternative selected.

One approach for presenting environments of this type involves interactive video. Videodiscs allow the storage of individual images, segments of video, and audio. There are many videodiscs available for instructional purposes. Although they are rich sources of information, most of them are designed to allow users to locate images or segments at will. This capability represents only the crudest level of exploration. Other videodiscs are designed specifically to represent more complete environments. More powerful forms of interaction built into the videodisc or a combination of videodisc and computer software allow students to explore and take action within these environments. The computer software controls which audio and video segments and images are presented.

If you are familiar with "choose your own adventure" books, you have some understanding of how one approach works. In a "choose your own adventure," the reader follows the text to a choice point and is presented several options. Each alternative is accompanied by a page number, and the reader moves to the page number of the desired choice to follow the story. The computer can control videodisc presentations in a similar way. Choices allow students control, and greater control allows the creation of more complex exploratory environments.

The Adventures of Jasper Woodbury. *The Adventures of Jasper Woodbury* is a series of learning activities based on a combination of video, text, and computer software. Originally developed by the Learning Technology Center of Vanderbilt University as a research program focused on "contextualized learning" (see Chapter 2, page 66), the videodisc adventures are now available commercially to schools.

A problem-solving approach

The Jasper adventures present students with believable stories, each ending with a challenge. The challenge is a complex problem that includes several subproblems. The typical classroom approach is to have the entire class view one of the adventures and then have small groups of students work to propose solutions to the challenge at the end of the adventure. To solve the challenges, which require a problem-solving approach and focus on mathematical concepts, students have to carefully examine the content of the videodisc for data relevant to the problems. The developers of the Jasper series argue that this "embedded data design" improves the transfer value of skills that students develop.

A CTIVE
C OOPERATION
T HEME-BASED
I NTEGRATED
V
E VALUATION

In *The Big Splash,* one of the Jasper adventures, a high school student decides to help the school fund the purchase of a video camera by setting up a "Dunk a Teacher" booth at the school carnival. Because the dunking booth itself will cost some money, the student approaches the principal for a loan. The principal agrees to provide the loan if the student can produce a business plan demonstrating the likelihood that the project will make a profit. To produce the business plan, the student must estimate the potential revenue and probable expenses. The potential revenue is determined by surveying students to determine whether they would spend money to dunk a teacher and how much they would be willing to pay for the chance. Consideration of how to conduct a survey provides an opportunity for the exploration of research methodology and statistics.

The student eventually locates a dunking machine and a pool. Since the pool must be rented by the day, the time the pool is in the possession of the school is an issue. The dimensions of the pool, but not the capacity, are known. The amount of time required to fill and drain the pool poses another problem to take into account. Several methods for filling the pool are available and vary in cost and risk. The school hose is available, but slow. A water truck is available, but it charges by the mile and has an added fee each time it is filled. The water truck also cannot carry enough water in one trip to fill the pool. The fire chief volunteers the local fire truck but warns that the truck will not be available if a fire should occur. While these are not all of the issues and variables that students must consider, this list should give you some idea of what would have to be considered in producing the business plan.

Analogous problems and other content areas

The Jasper adventures have also been developed to be extended to analogous problems and other content areas. The analogous problems modify the original story to create opportunities for students to transfer what they have learned. For example, students can consider whether a Jell-O slide would generate more income than the dunking pool. To extend the Jasper adventures into other content areas, teachers are given suggestions for further study following up on some issue raised in the adventure. For example, *The Big Splash* raises the issue of taking out a loan. Students might explore how someone applies for a loan at a bank, how the bank makes money on the loan, what collateral is, and other concepts related to the lending of money.

Another format for presenting exploratory environments

Hypermedia Exploratory Environments: *Grandparents' Attic.*   Hypermedia allows another format for presenting students with an exploratory environment. Hypermedia allows the integration of text, drawings, sounds, video, and animation in a common computer-accessible database, and the purposeful exploration of these information sources can provide effective learning experiences (Scardamalia et al., 1989). The example that follows is not a commercial project, but is an example of a project we have been working on with our university and middle school colleagues. (We will discuss hypermedia in greater depth in Chapter 7.)

An authentic context for understanding history

History is a discipline that students often fail to appreciate. They regard it as a bland list of facts, dates, places, generals, and battles, and seldom connect with the subject matter or understand the work of historians. The exploratory environment we describe here was developed to expose students to important elements of the history of their state during the period of the late 1800s and early 1900s. The project is called *Grandparents' Attic*. The metaphor of *Grandparents' Attic* is quite powerful: it provides an authentic context for understanding history, as a summary of the experiences of real people, and it provides an intuitive interface for the hypermedia environment students are allowed to explore.

If you ever had a chance to explore your grandparents' attic, you can probably anticipate how this exploratory environment works. The computer version of *Grandparents' Attic* was designed to replicate some of the same experiences you might remember. You might remember finding photographs of your grandparents when they were first married and laughing at how funny they looked. Maybe you wondered about what it would have been like to live in those times. Perhaps as you rummaged around the attic you ran across old newspapers or old school books. If you were lucky, you may have stumbled across a radio that contained tubes and required huge batteries or old phonograph records that had grooves only on one side. If you realized that modern radios have no tubes and that records of any type and certainly 78s are very rare, you were starting to develop a sense of the history of tremendous technological changes some of us have actually experienced. *Grandparents' Attic* and your history book both allow a look at history, but the subjective feeling is very different.

Students explore *Grandparents' Attic* by using the mouse to click on objects appearing on the computer screen. Many objects give some type of response. Some responses identify the object, and some responses are just humorous. In some cases, clicking on an object generates a more dramatic response. A prominent item in one attic is an old trunk. Clicking on the trunk makes the trunk open, revealing letters, a diary, a photo album, maps, official documents, and newspapers (see Figure 3.9).

FIGURE 3.9 Screen Display of Grandma and Grandpa's Trunk

Clicking on the diary opens it and allows the student to read about grandma's life (see Figure 3.10). Selecting the photo album allows the student to move through page after page of photographs. Clicking on a photograph flips it over to reveal an explanatory message on the back. The attic presents a hypermedia environment that organizes a huge amount of information for student examination. In addition to the items already described, the attic contains old books, a pump organ capable of playing a variety of popular melodies of the period, furniture, clothes, and a magical door allowing access to other resources (country museum, library). The description provided here

The hypermedia environment organizes information

FIGURE 3.10 Screen Display of Sample Diary Entry

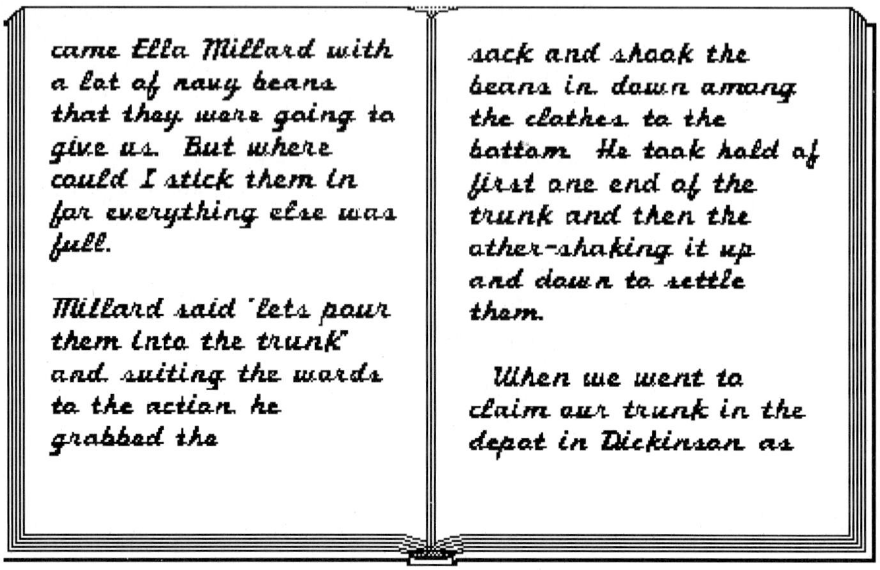

came Ella Millard with a lot of navy beans that they were going to give us. But where could I stick them in for everything else was full.

Millard said "lets pour them into the trunk" and suiting the words to the action he grabbed the

sack and shook the beans in down among the clothes to the bottom. He took hold of first one end of the trunk and then the other–shaking it up and down to settle them.

When we went to claim our trunk in the depot in Dickinson as

is actually a bit simplified. Parallel versions of the attic have been developed to reflect the immigrant experiences of several ethnic groups (Germans from Russia, Norwegians), as well as of the Native American people of the region.

Our work with the attic has included not only the development of the exploratory environment, but also the creation of tasks that we feel encourage students to carefully analyze the information they encounter as they explore. For example, students might be given writing assignments: Write a fictional diary account describing the experiences of a sixteen-year-old girl during the wheat harvest. Discuss the role of railroads to the homesteaders. We have also made the attic environment open ended, and students can add new material to the attic. The images in the photo album were taken from a recreated historical village some distance from our community. We purposely avoided the local historical museum so that students could visit this facility and collect their own images for the photo album (see procedure described in Chapter 9). Students can also create new documents based on their research at this museum or the library or based on interviews they have conducted with elderly people they know. The existing attic provides a shell into which new documents, images, drawings, and nearly any other kind of student-generated information can be incorporated. You will learn more about student-constructed hypermedia as a learning activity in Chapter 10.

Some commercial products would qualify as exploratory environments or would at least allow some exploratory experiences. *A House Divided: The Lincoln-Douglas Debates* was developed to supplement courses in American

Tasks that encourage students to analyze information

Lincoln-Douglas debates

history, government, or African American studies. The multimedia CD-ROM allows students to contemplate circumstances leading to the Civil War. However, the causes of the Civil War are not presented through direct instruction. Instead, students are provided the opportunity to read transcripts from the Lincoln-Douglas debates; view video reenactments of important events (e.g., the Dred Scott decision), photo essays (e.g., living conditions of slaves), and political cartoons; listen to diary excerpts of slaves and music of the period; and examine a time line of important events. These elements of information are encountered as students move about the rooms of an "interactive" mansion (see Figure 3.11). The rich assortment of primary sources and diversity of perspectives allow students to play an active role in developing personal explanations of the positions taken by the eventual combatants. Teachers can help students work with this material in a variety of ways, including introducing students to the basics of formal debate. However, the emphasis is always on helping students develop their own insights into the material.

Effectiveness of Exploratory Environments

Encouraging research

With the exception of evaluations conducted with LOGO (an exploratory environment allowing student programming) and the Jasper Woodbury interactive video materials developed by the Cognition and Technology Group at Vanderbilt University (Cognition and Technology Group, 1990, 1996; Goldman,

FIGURE 3.11   One Room from the Interactive Mansion

et al., 1996), exploratory environments have not been thoroughly evaluated. The benefits to students of exploring LOGO are discussed in Chapter 4 (Learning from Programming). The work with exploratory interactive video is much less extensive, but the research conducted with the Jasper Woodbury adventures is encouraging. It appears that the realistic and dynamic experiences provided by video encourage students to develop mental models to account for the phenomena they have observed. Learning is described as being anchored in the realistic problems and experiences provided through interactive video. Some of these ideas were discussed in greater detail in Chapter 2.

One element that experiences with LOGO and the Jasper Woodbury adventures have suggested is important is the presence of structuring tasks or problems. Experience has suggested that it should not be assumed that students will engage in the most desirable types of active exploration and generative thinking when exposed to exploratory environments (Grabe, 1992; Hsu, Chapelle, and Thompson, 1993).

The importance of structuring tasks or problems

HOW TO EVALUATE AND USE COMPUTER-ASSISTED INSTRUCTION

There has been a great deal of research evaluating the effectiveness of computer tutorials and other forms of CAI. Over the past twenty-five years, well over two hundred studies have been completed (Lepper and Gurtner, 1989). Because of this huge volume of information, it is common to rely on reviews in evaluating the effectiveness of CAI (Fletcher-Flinn & Gravatt, 1995; Liao, 1992; Niemiec et al., 1989; Niemiec and Walberg, 1987; Thomas and Hooper, 1991). Tutorials and drill activities have been studied most extensively. These studies have found that technology seems to offer a moderate advantage over traditional instruction, with tutorials somewhat more effective than drill activities, particularly for younger and less-able students (Lepper and Gurtner, 1989). The effect is labeled "moderate" because 66 percent of students taught using CAI performed better than the average for a group taught more traditionally. One of the more recent reviews compared more current CAI research with older studies and suggests that the advantage of CAI may be increasing. However, the general benefits are still described as moderate (Fletcher-Flinn & Gravatt, 1995). A review of the research evaluating simulations reached a similar conclusion (Thomas and Hooper, 1991). With the exception of LOGO (see Chapter 4) and the work done with the Jasper Woodbury interactive video materials (see earlier comments), research evaluating exploratory learning environments is much less extensive.

The moderate advantage for CAI instruction has been questioned, however. Critics point out that studies producing no advantage for CAI are less likely to be published, that many studies involving CAI do not control study

Arguments

time to make certain that students receiving CAI do not work longer, and that computers in many situations are so novel that students may respond to them more positively because of the uniqueness of learning with technology. Others accept the findings that CAI may offer an advantage but argue that CAI materials are often just more carefully developed and that there is no intrinsic advantage in the actual method of instruction (Clark, 1985; Fletcher-Flinn & Gravatt, 1995).

HELPING TEACHERS WITH CONTRADICTORY FINDINGS

What should classroom teachers make of these confusing findings? Teachers should not expect miracles from technology or from any other approach to instruction. However, when used thoughtfully and with common sense, many commercial products make learning opportunities available to students. Teachers need to use sound judgment in selecting quality software and need to pay careful attention to the conditions under which students use it. Technology does not eliminate the need for teaching, nor does it eliminate the need for teacher supervision. Students will have questions in response to a learning activity presented by the computer just as they may have questions during a science laboratory or about a social studies reading assignment.

Continued need for teaching and teacher supervision

We suggest that teachers keep the four phases of instruction in mind as they consider instructional software. Table 3.1 is our own attempt to summarize previous comments regarding how different types of software benefit students. In general, the ratings indicate instructional software provides positive — but incomplete — experiences. The summary also suggests that guiding the student, especially in ways necessary to develop complex mental skills, is frequently beyond the capabilities of present applications of technology. Recall from Chapter 2 that techniques such as cognitive apprenticeship attempt to model effective thinking and problem-solving behaviors and don't just help students identify problem areas. Teachers must continue to provide some of the guidance necessary for effective learning, which will often mean that teachers and students may want to interact together with the technology. For example, a teacher might use the Eco-Simulator (see the introductory example for this chapter) to demonstrate the desert biome food chain. By verbalizing thoughts as foxes and rabbits are added to the environment and the resulting population graphs are interpreted, the teacher would both familiarize students with the operation of the software and provide insights into decisions aimed at stabilizing plant and animal populations. Students might then move on to explore other biomes on their own.

Keep the phases of instruction in mind

There may be some situations that lend themselves especially well to CAI (Alessi and Trollip, 1991). Many of the following suggestions appear throughout this chapter but are summarized here for emphasis. Technology is often of

TABLE 3.1 Potential Software Effectiveness by Stage of Instruction

	COMPONENTS OF INSTRUCTION			
	Presentation	Guidance	Practice	Assesstment
Tutorial	* * *	*		
Simulation	* *	*	* *	* *
Drill/Practice			* * *	
Educ. Game	*	*	* *	*
Exploratory	* *	*	*	*

APPLICATIONS

We have ranked effectiveness on a scale of 0–3.

Summary of situations where CAI is of unique value

unique value when: (1) prolonged individual practice is necessary (math facts, typing); (2) traditional approaches fail to make the content exciting (history); (3) learning the skill presents a significant danger to the learner (flying an airplane); (4) concepts to be learned are difficult to visualize or conceptualize (calculus, physics); (5) students progress at significantly different rates and need to proceed at their own pace (any content area that builds heavily on prerequisite knowledge); and (6) practical limits of time, space, or money make certain experiences impractical (genetics experiments). Individual teachers might use this list as they think about the various experiences they want to provide their students.

EVALUATING SOFTWARE

Issues to consider

The final section of this chapter is intended to prepare you to make decisions about purchasing software. We alert you here to issues you might consider, rather than tell you what kinds of software you should buy. Our primary concerns are that you buy programs that will get used and that you will feel comfortable making available to your students.

Individual and group decisions

At some point, someone will have to decide which software products to purchase. Sometimes the decision is left up to individual classroom teachers. Each teacher might be given a budget to spend as desired. In other situations, a curriculum committee or a technology committee works as a group to decide what to buy. A number of situations might recommend group decision making. Perhaps the software to be purchased should be used for a variety of classes over a number of years, but there are different opinions concerning which product might best meet these needs. This situation occurs frequently with tool applications such as word processing or graphics programs.

Keeping Current

Locating Appropriate Software

A tremendous amount of commercial instructional software is available today. In purchasing software for your own classrooms or for your schools, you should develop an awareness of a reasonable sample of the products that are available and then proceed to gather more detailed information about the quality and curriculum appropriateness of specific products that seem most interesting. This process is probably more difficult than inexperienced individuals might anticipate. Unlike the tool applications discussed in other chapters, individual instructional software products target niche markets. Major tool applications such as word processing programs are used in homes, business settings, and schools. The marketing budgets for such products are huge, major computer magazines publish in-depth analyses and comparisons of the major products, local retailers are likely to have demonstration copies available, and it is probable that other computer users will be able to provide advice. Often, these same sources are less useful in helping you locate quality instructional software. The companies producing most instructional software are relatively obscure in comparison to companies producing general-purpose computer tools, local retailers cannot afford to maintain an extensive inventory of instructional materials, and other technology-oriented teachers with whom you work may teach in other disciplines and not pay attention to products that might interest you.

So, how do you become acquainted with the software you might purchase? Here are several suggestions:

◆ Attend conferences and conventions. State teacher's conventions frequently have sessions on instructional technology, and many vendors' booths are devoted to product demonstrations. It is also possible there will be a conference in your region devoted specifically to educational computing. Such conferences provide an excellent opportunity to meet other teachers interested in technology and to see what vendors have to offer.

◆ Take a class or workshop. If you are using this book as part of a college course, you are already in a setting in which you are likely to work with a variety of software products. This experience will be valuable in developing your awareness of useful software. But remember, if you are an undergraduate student, many new products will be available by the time you are working in a school and able to recommend software for purchase. Many colleges and universities sponsor brief workshops for practicing teachers. Sometimes teachers gather for a special Saturday session at a local college. Sometimes people from the college go out to the schools. School districts able to fund a position for a computer coordinator may provide their own staff development activities. In most locations, to be cost effective, workshops must cater to a cross section of teachers and will be unlikely to discuss a large number of individual instructional software products. Still, workshops are a great way to develop your background and refine your ideas about effective instructional software.

◆ Browse through magazines for educators. A number of magazines are written specifically for computer-using educators. Publications like *Learning and Leading with Technology, Electronic Learning, Journal of Computers in*

Math and Science Teaching, and *Computers in the Schools* carry software reviews. Educators' interest in technology has prompted other magazines to provide reviews as well (see the list of publications provided in Chapter 2). Teachers may subscribe to these publications themselves, schools may purchase the magazines and make them available through school libraries, or teachers may find them in a local college library. It is often informative to read reviews by many different authors, keeping in mind that they have biases just like anyone else. Reading several reviews will provide some balance in the information you gather.

Interact with other teachers using telecommunications. The Internet and commercial network services allow a teacher to interact with other teachers. The teachers involved have already self-selected themselves as computer users. It is common to see messages such as "We have $4,000 to spend on software for the science department. Do you have any recommendations?" (You will find information on telecommunications in Chapter 6.)

◆ Communicate directly with software companies. The software companies obviously have a vested interest in making sure educators are aware of their products. However, these companies cannot be expected to provide an unbiased evaluation of their own products and are unlikely to offer information on the programs of other companies. Contacting a company can be especially useful if it is willing to provide a review copy. If you are attempting to obtain an examination copy, it usually works best if the company is approached by an administrator or computer coordinator. Companies are quite concerned with the pirating of their products and seem more comfortable with an individual in an administrative capacity. Some companies provide sample programs that have been altered in some way from the originals. Often, only some of the content of the program is included, and certain functions such as saving or printing have been disabled. Finally, companies are beginning to offer previews of their products on World Wide Web sites. These previews consist of program descriptions and samples of what the student would see on the monitor. ✳

Allowing a number of independent purchases would probably mean that students would have to learn several different programs to do the same kind of work. Working with a variety of word processing or graphics programs would be desirable if the priority was to develop sophisticated computer users, but less desirable if the priority was to efficiently apply computer tools to content-area learning. Groups make some different types of decisions when selecting instructional software. A group of middle school math teachers might attempt to identify areas of their curriculum that need improvement and then try to find applications suited to these needs. Money might be tight, and priorities for purchases might have to be established. A group might compare several products to determine which one seems most effective. Sometimes it is necessary to decide *when* a particular program will be used, so that different teachers do not ask students to repeat the same activity. It isn't a bad idea to coordinate this kind of decision before spending the money that is available, lest some classrooms inadvertently be ignored. Group software selection also allows educators with more computer experience to offer advice to less-experienced educators. This can be helpful even when the teachers work in different content areas.

The process of selecting software must be regarded as subjective. If you have the opportunity to serve on a curriculum committee charged with selecting software, you will soon discover that committee members often have very different opinions. A subjective decision should not be confused with an arbitrary one. The curriculum committee participants are likely to have plenty to say in support of their recommendations. Teachers have different styles, philosophies, and insights into how students learn, and they may value certain learning outcomes over others. These differences account for some of the variability in the classroom behaviors of teachers; they also explain why reactions to a particular piece of software can be so different. One teacher might value the methodical and organized way in which a particular tutorial presents information, and another teacher might feel that the same tutorial leaves too little room for student independence. One teacher might feel that a genetics simulation is a great way to learn about dominant and recessive genes, genotypes, and phenotypes, and another teacher might feel that using a simulation is much less efficient than providing this same information through direct instruction. Teachers will use techniques and materials that are consistent with their values and beliefs (Hannafin & Freeman, 1995).

Different teaching styles and opinions

Teachers consider many factors when selecting software. However, the discussion of things to think about and the lists of things "experts" suggest ought to be valued should not obscure one essential question. As teachers examine software, the most important question is: Would I be able and willing to integrate this activity into my existing curriculum? Schools should purchase software that teachers are committed to using.

Formalized evaluation procedures

Formalized evaluation procedures do have a place. These methods are of value when several people must collaborate in making software selections. Formalized procedures provide a convenient framework for discussing strengths and weaknesses, as well as a way to retain for later consideration information gathered through the review process. Inexperienced teachers and inexperienced technology users may also benefit from a formalized evaluation process and a checklist of desired features. The expectations raised by a checklist may make less-experienced teachers think about issues they may not otherwise have considered. The benefits may be immediate, or the formal process may hasten the development of personal standards. Ring (1993) has demonstrated that a checklist increases the accuracy with which inexperienced teachers are able to predict how well they will like programs after extended use. If experience with a checklist would prevent inexperienced teachers from purchasing software they would not use, working with a checklist would be time well spent. For these reasons, we have included an evaluation form for teachers to use when selecting software.

EVALUATION FORMS

*Sources of software
evaluation forms*

Evaluation forms can be found in many sources (Bitter, Camuse, and Durbin, 1993; Ring, 1993). The form that follows is typical. The program title, publishing company, cost, and other general information are included for archival purposes. Often money will not be available immediately, and it may be necessary to put some potential purchases on hold. When money is available again, the more positive reviews can be assembled, and the teachers who generated them can be contacted to determine whether their interest is still high. Certain items are included to remind the reviewer to check system and hardware requirements. Some packages require additional memory or add-on hardware items such as a speech synthesizer, or function only with the most recent operating system. Unless the buyer is careful, it is very easy to purchase software that will not run on existing equipment.

The remainder of the form asks the reviewer to consider how students might use the software and to comment on certain characteristics of the software that could influence how productive and valued student experiences might be. You will notice that the review form is designed so that the form itself does not identify how important any given characteristic or issue should be in the final decision. The form asks the reviewer to make such value judgments.

*The reviewer makes
value judgments*

Two approaches are included. The reviewer either reacts to open-ended questions requesting descriptive and subjective comments or responds to a checklist of important program characteristics. The checklist requires the reviewer to indicate the perceived importance of each characteristic and the extent to which the program under review satisfies each characteristic. In this checklist, the weight for the perceived importance of each characteristic and the rating of the extent to which the program satisfies the characteristic fall on a six-point scale (0 to 5). The product of the weight and the rating results in a score for each characteristic. In theory, the sum of the scores for all characteristics should indicate the quality of the application as perceived by the reviewer. If you look at the characteristics listed and think about your own values, you should be able to see how this system works. For example, suppose you feel that the ability to integrate computer activities into your existing curriculum, the perceived instructional effectiveness of computer activities, the extent to which computer activities encourage active thought, and the extent to which software motivates students are particularly important (see evaluation checklist for a list of all characteristics). You probably would weigh these characteristics as 5. Other program characteristics, such as "Student can save work in progress" or "Quality of student supplemental materials," may be less important to you, and you might weigh these areas as 1 or 0. If you feel the program satisfies the criterion of "Program encourages active thought," you might award the program a rating of 5, resulting in a score for active thought of 25. The maximum rating for "Student can save work in progress" would result in a score of only 5 and would have a much smaller impact on the overall evaluation of the product.

We hope you will have an opportunity to apply this evaluation procedure to a number of software products and to discuss your conclusions with your classmates and instructor. This process should help you clarify what you will eventually look for when you find yourself in the position of purchasing software for your students' use.

Review Summary Sheet

General Information

Reviewer _____

Title _____

Publishing company _____

Publication date _____

List price _____

Availability of site license _____

Site license agreement _____

     Price _____

Hardware and Operating System Requirements

Host microcomputer _____

Operating system compatibility _____

Requires _____ K of memory

Is product network aware? _____

Storage _____ Hard drive _____ MB approximate capacity required

_____ CD-ROM player

Other hardware requirements _____

Program Format

_____ Drill/practice _____ Tutorial _____ Simulation _____

_____ Other (Describe:) _____

_____ Combination (Describe:) _____

Brief Description _____

_____

_____

Curriculum Compatibility

Subject area _____

Grade level _____

Specific topics _____

Reviewer Recommendation and Comments _____

_____

_____

Checklist

Rating: Extent to which the software successfully meets objective
Weight: Extent to which the objective is important to the rater
Total: Product of rating and weight
(Higher values are intended to indicate greater quality and importance.)

EVALUATION CATEGORY	RATING (0–5)	WEIGHT (0–5)	TOTAL (0–25)
CONTENT			
Easily integrated with existing content			
Content presented accurately			
Content presented efficiently			
Content presented effectively			
Presentation approach is motivating			
Program encourages active thought			
Content avoids offensive representations			
Quality of content justifies cost			
Comments:			

PROGRAM FUNCTIONS	RATING (0–5)	WEIGHT (0–5)	TOTAL (0–25)
Program is easy to operate			
Pace is appropriate			
Student can save work in progress			
Student can control rate of progress			
Student can change shift among activities			
Feedback is appropriate			
Saves data on student performance			
Comments:			

SUPPLEMENTS	RATING (0–5)	WEIGHT (0–5)	TOTAL (0–25)
Quality of student supplemental materials			
Quality of instruction manual			
Useful suggestions for program use			

Useful followup ideas   _____   _____   _____

Comments: _____

_____

_____

Total score   _____

SUMMARY

In contrast to other educational applications of technology, computer-based instruction (CBI) exerts greater control over the content to which students are exposed and how students are expected to interact with this content.

A complete instructional experience takes the student through four stages: (1) the presentation of information or learning experiences; (2) guidance as the student struggles to develop knowledge and master skills; (3) extended practice; and (4) assessment. Not all activities, computer or other, should be expected to provide all four stages of instruction. Often, lower-quality instruction occurs because it is assumed that an experience satisfies the expectations of all four stages, or because a task suited to one stage of instruction is used inappropriately to provide the experiences of a different stage.

Tutorials, simulations, drill and practice, games, and exploratory environments are categories of CAI. Commercial products seldom represent a pure example of any single category.

Tutorials are designed to present information and guide learning. Teachers must continue to participate actively when students are working with tutorials.

Simulations attempt to replicate the key elements of an actual experience. Although it is unlikely that any one product will provide for all four stages of instruction, simulations can provide for all of them. Fidelity, the exactness of the match between a simulation and reality, influences both learning and transfer. The relationships between fidelity, learning, and transfer are complex, and the best situation for rapid learning is not always the best situation for effective transfer. Simulations offer potential solutions to a number of instructional problems. Simulations can make learning experiences more concrete, more controllable, less expensive, and safer.

Drill-and-practice activities have a bad reputation. However, drill-and-practice applications are appropriate when information and skills need to be overlearned. Care must be taken not to emphasize memorization unless it is actually the intended objective of instruction.

Games put a premium on motivation, entertainment, and competition and can engage students with appropriate academic content. Educators might consider games as a way to introduce students to new topics or as ways to motivate. When a game is used to motivate work independent of the game itself, care must be taken for all students to have a realistic chance of receiving this reinforcement so that students do not perceive that technology is only for play.

Exploratory environments allow a student-centered approach to learning in a specified domain. For best productivity, teachers need to remain involved as students work with exploratory environments.

Research evaluating the effectiveness of CAI has been extensive. In general, comparisons seem to demonstrate a moderate level of success. Teachers should not expect miracles of technology and must realize that thoughtful implementation is the key to providing students with valuable experiences.

Software selection is an important, but subjective activity. In making purchasing decisions, teachers are encouraged to carefully consider their own instructional priorities and to determine how they would integrate the software into their curricula.

REFLECTING ON CHAPTER 3

Activities

◆ List simulations, computer or otherwise, that you have experienced. What principles or causal relationships was each simulation constructed to represent?
◆ Analyze several games, and list the specific characteristics you feel make each game enjoyable.
◆ Use the evaluation forms included at the end of the chapter to evaluate a commercial software product. Discuss your evaluation comments with your classmates.
◆ Locate one of the journals mentioned here as providing useful information for teachers. List the types of information you discovered in reviewing one issue. Share this information with your classmates.

Key Terms

automaticity (p. 98)
branching tutorials (p. 86)
computer-assisted instruction
   (CAI) (p. 82)
computer-based instruction (CBI)
   (p. 82)
constructionism (p. 83)
drill (p. 97)
edutainment (p. 100)

exploratory environments (p. 103)
fidelity (p. 91)
games (p. 99)
instructionism (p. 83)
linear tutorials (p. 86)
practice (p. 97)
simulations (p. 87)
tutorials (p. 85)

Resources to Expand Your Knowledge Base

Technology Journals
There are a number of journals written to inform K–12 teachers about issues related to classroom applications of technology. These journals can be helpful in several ways. Teachers can learn about new developments in hardware and software and can

also learn how other teachers are applying technology. As was mentioned earlier in this chapter, these periodicals frequently carry critical reviews and side-by-side comparisons of hardware and software products. Information about the strengths and weaknesses of products can be very helpful when planning purchases.

CD-ROM Today, 1350 Old Bayshore Highway, Suite 210, Burlingame, CA 94010

Computers in the School, 75 Griswold Street, Binghamton, NY 13904

Learning and Leading with Technology (formally *The Computing Teacher*), International Society for Technology in Education, 1787 Agate Street, Eugene, OR 97403

Electronic Learning, 902 Sylvan Ave., Englewood Cliffs, NJ 07632

Journal of Computers in Mathematics and Science Teaching, P.O. Box 2966, Charlottesville, VA 22902

NewMedia Magazine, 901 Mariner's Island Blvd. Suite 365, San Mateo, CA 94404

Technology and Learning, P.O. Box 49727, Dayton, OH 45449-0727

World Wide Web Sources

Interactive Frog Dissection
    Kinzie, M. (1994).
    http://teach.virginia.edu/go/frog
Virtual Frog Dissection Kit
    Lawrence Berkeley National Laboratory (1996).
    http://www-itg.lbl.gov/vfrog/dissect.html

Software

A House Divided: The Lincoln-Douglas Debates. A House Divided was developed by Grafica Multimedia and C-SPAN for Macintosh and Windows computers. The program requires a CD-ROM. Grafica Multimedia is located at 1777 Borel Place, Suite 500, San Mateo, CA 94402.

The Adventures of Jasper Woodbury. Jasper Woodbury was developed by the Learning Technology Center, Vanderbilt University. Six adventures were copyrighted in 1992 and are available through Optical Data Corporation, 30 Technology Drive, Warren, NJ 07059.

Eco-Simulator. The *Eco-Simulator* is one program within a package called *Ecology,* produced by Earthquest, Inc., 125 University Ave., Palo Alto, CA 94301.

Math Magic. Math Magic is a product of Mindplay Methods and Solutions, 3230 North Dodge Blvd., Tucson, AZ 85716. Versions are available for Apple II, MS-DOS, and Macintosh computers.

Operation: Frog. Operation: Frog is available in MS-DOS and Macintosh versions from Scholastic, Inc. Scholastic Software, P.O. Box 7502, 2391 E. McCarty St., Jefferson City, MO 65102.

The Oregon Trail. The Oregon Trail exists in several formats for several different computers. The latest version is available on CD-ROM. Minnesota Educational Computer Consortium (MECC), 6160 Summit Drive North, St. Paul, MN 55430.

SimLife. SimLife is a product of Maxis, 2 Theatre Square, Suite 230, Orinda, CA 94563. Maxis also has produced *SimEarth, SimAnt,* and *SimCity* for Macintosh, MS-DOS, and Windows.

Where in the World Is Carmen Sandiego? Where in the World Is Carmen Sandiego? (1992) and other games in the Carmen Sandiego series are products of Broderbund, P.O. Box 6125, Novato, CA 94948. Software is available for Apple, Macintosh, and MS-DOS machines. The latest versions of these products come in deluxe CD-ROM versions.

Chapter 4

Learning from Programming Experiences

ORIENTATION

In this chapter we address teaching students to program, establish some potential benefits of learning to program, and evaluate whether these potential benefits are realized. As you will see, programming is a great way to learn about computer technology and possibly about certain content areas as well. Programming gives students the opportunity to control powerful technology. Programming the computer to do useful things can be challenging, and in these challenges are some real opportunities to develop problem-solving skills. If at all possible, take the time to locate the appropriate software and work through the examples you encounter in this chapter. You should be able to understand the examples from your reading, but the experience of trying to solve the challenges yourself will help you appreciate the active process of problem solving that is involved. As you read, look for answers to the following questions:

FOCUS QUESTIONS

◆ Describe three ways students may benefit from the combination of high-quality programming experiences and thoughtful instruction.
◆ What are the major characteristics of the LOGO programming language?
◆ What is the rationale for introducing young students to programming through graphics applications?
◆ Explain the concept of a microworld. What does this idea have to do with LOGO, and how might it also apply to education in a more general way?
◆ What is the educational significance of the concept of transfer?

◆ What do studies evaluating transfer from programming experiences suggest about conditions necessary for transfer?

WHAT IS PROGRAMMING?

A definition of programming

Programming is the process of instructing the computer to perform some desired action. Think of it as teaching a student with perfect memory but very limited capacity to interpret what you say. Unless your instructions are very explicit, accurate, and detailed, the computer will be unable to understand what you would like it to do. To get this point across with younger children, we sometimes ask them to explain to a robot how to make a peanut butter and jelly sandwich. One child is the robot, with access to bread, a knife, peanut butter, and jelly. The robot is cautioned to execute only the exact commands given. For example, the robot cannot pick up a slice of bread until the bag containing the bread has been opened. Students will quickly point out that the command "Open the bag of bread" would also not be understood by the robot. Although it might seem that the process of making commands more and more specific could go on forever, this doesn't really happen. Programming languages contain commands that the computer — or, in this case, the robot — can understand. Once students understand these commands and the rules for combining them into valid expressions, programming becomes mostly a matter of careful planning and detailed explanation.

What is your image of a programmer?

If you are familiar with the classes computer science majors take, you might equate programming with some image you have of a programmer sitting at a computer terminal typing in code in BASIC, FORTRAN, Pascal, C, or some other recognizable high-level programming language. It is useful to take a somewhat broader perspective.

Early programming

Programming has not always involved these specialized languages. Actually, it used to be more difficult. Early programmers did not type in computer programs using keyboards but used a series of toggle switches to painstakingly enter commands in **binary** (1s and 0s). The world of technology has changed a great deal. The programming techniques of the future may also be very different from today's techniques. Already, some programming environments take a "visual approach" and allow the "programmer" to arrange **icons** (miniature pictures) representing different computer actions. So instead of programming with the words of a particular language, the programmer might select from a set of symbols. If you feel skeptical about this as the trend of the future, consider that the early pioneers entering 1s and 0s probably would also have smiled at the prediction that a computer would ever understand and respond to "If Card Field 'Input' is empty then Ask 'Where are your data?'" The part of programming that involves communicating with the computer is becoming easier, but planning exactly what you want the computer to do remains as challenging as ever.

WHY LEARN TO PROGRAM?

Functions of programming experiences in schools

Programming experiences in schools serve three functions. First, programming is a skill that some feel is important to learn because, for a few students, it may eventually become a profession. For most, however, it provides an understanding of the functioning of the computer and computer software and thus is one way to develop certain aspects of general computer literacy. Second, programming has been advocated as a powerful environment within which problem solving or some other general cognitive skills can be developed. As you will see later, this claim, though exciting, has been only marginally substantiated. A great deal of work is in progress to test this claim and to create classroom environments in which the overall benefits of learning general problem-solving skills through programming might best be realized. Finally, programming may allow students to learn the content of some other discipline, such as geometry. It appears possible that programming can provide an active way to explore and construct a personal understanding of content within certain disciplines.

Exploring and constructing personal understanding of content

As this chapter proceeds, we will explore these final two claims in some detail. We emphasize these issues because we see them as important to decisions educators must make about how students will spend school time. Will students have programming experiences or not? Before this discussion will make much sense, you will need to gain some insight into the programming experiences students might encounter.

WHY EMPHASIZE LOGO?

Strengths of LOGO

In this chapter we emphasize the LOGO programming language because it allows discussion of the whole range of potential programming benefits. It is a language for developing programming skill and possibly for developing content-area knowledge and general problem-solving ability. LOGO is somewhat unique because it is frequently taught at several grade levels, usually with students of a range of aptitudes. In comparison, other popular programming languages (BASIC and Pascal) seem frequently to be applied primarily as a way to develop programming skill. These languages are more likely to be taught in specialized courses for students with specialized interests.

Hypermedia development environments

Other computer experiences may also develop programming skills, problem-solving skills, and knowledge in a variety of content areas. You will find this book sprinkled with examples of HyperCard projects. HyperCard and similar products (LinkWay Live!, ToolBook) are best thought of as hypermedia development environments (see Chapter 8) rather than as languages. The language HyperTalk is one component of the HyperCard environment. The hypermedia development environments provide access to

HyperTalk

a variety of text and graphics tools and a wide assortment of functions that the user can manipulate directly or indirectly through HyperTalk programs. If HyperTalk is considered in isolation, it is a full-featured programming language with many of the same capabilities as more traditional programming languages (Henry and Southerly, 1994). In some educational situations, programming classes have even been based on HyperCard (Brown, 1989–1990). We emphasize traditional programming languages and experiences in this chapter and discuss hypermedia development environments in later chapters.

Focus

Seymour Papert and LOGO

At first glance, Seymour Papert might seem an unusual person to be advocating radically different approaches to elementary education. Proposing new ways children can use technology is not something you might expect from an individual who has earned two doctorates in mathematics and cofounded, with Marvin Minsky, the Artificial Intelligence Laboratory at MIT. However, there is a good deal more to Papert's story.

Before the AI Lab, Papert studied with Jean Piaget for five years. The view that children construct their own understanding of the world in response to personal experiences in their environment is strongly Piagetian. In 1968, Papert proposed the concept of Mathland. The basic idea was to develop a learning environment for mathematics that provided an experience equivalent to immersing a foreign language student in a foreign country. This general objective, together with the goal of developing a computer language suitable for children, produced the design guidelines for LOGO.

The LOGO programming language first used with junior high students in 1968 contained no graphics and no turtle. Students used the language to accomplish tasks such as translating English to pig Latin and designing strategy games. Papert added the turtle and graphics later to provide a more interesting environment for younger children.

The early work with LOGO was not focused entirely on screen-based experiences. An early version of the turtle was a robotlike device resembling an inverted salad bowl with wheels for legs and a pen for a tail. This device could be programmed to roll around on a sheet of paper and draw designs as it went. Papert believed in putting powerful resources in the hands of children. Early LOGO activities required computational power that did not exist in schools, and the salad-bowl turtle cost about $4,000 (without computer). Now the computational power of LOGO can be implemented with computers commonly available in schools, and LOGO is being used to control a variety of machines that students build themselves (see "LEGO-LOGO" beginning on page 145; Papert, 1980; Turkle, 1984). ✳

PROGRAMMING IN LOGO

BASIC and Pascal

A number of programming languages are used in elementary, junior high, and high school settings. BASIC probably has the longest history. Pascal has gained some prominence, particularly because it encourages a more disciplined style of programming (see comments on programming style on page 137). LOGO, a powerful, full-featured language, was developed with specific educational goals in mind (see "Focus: Seymour Papert and LOGO" on page 126). LOGO is intended to develop more than programming skill, and many educators use it because they believe their students will develop problem-solving and math skills.

The turtle

The customary method for introducing students or teachers to the LOGO language is through experiences with **turtlegraphics**. The most common version of turtlegraphics relies on a small-screen turtle (see Figure 4.1) that moves and draws on the computer monitor. The screen turtle's actions are controlled directly by commands issued from the keyboard or indirectly by programs constructed by a programmer. Examples of drawings created with turtlegraphics are scattered throughout this chapter.

Commands must follow an established syntax

The individual commands in LOGO are called **primitives** (see Table 4.1 for some LOGO primitives). As is true with commands in all programming languages, LOGO commands must follow an established syntax. The **syntax** for individual commands consists of rules for combining keywords,

FIGURE 4.1   The LogoWriter Screen, with Turtle

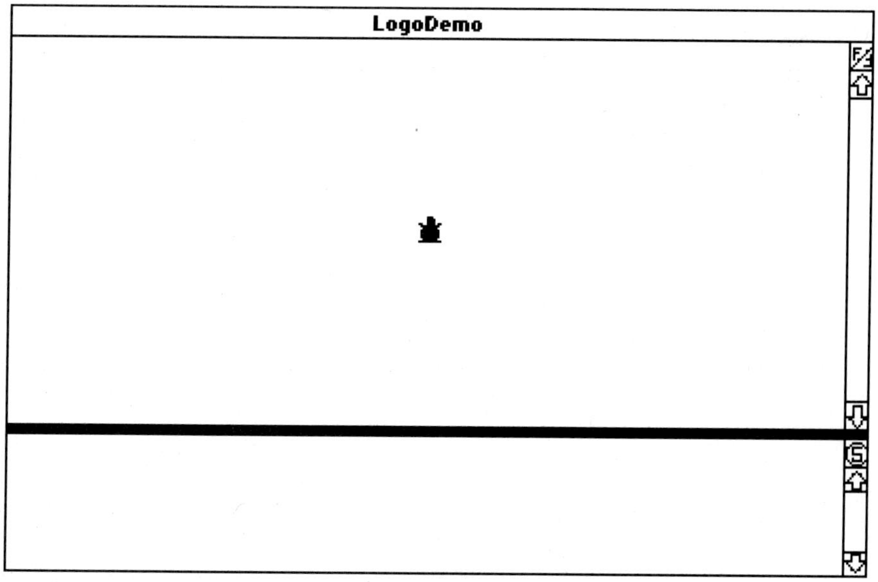

LOGO commands are entered below the solid line. The turtle constructs its drawings above the solid line.

LogoDemo

punctuation, and arguments. In LOGO, commands follow the format *keyword* [space] *argument* (Fay and Mayer, 1988). If you wanted the turtle to move ahead ten turtle steps, you would issue the command *forward 10* (abbreviated as FD 10). In this example, the keyword is *forward* (or FD), the punctuation is a space, and the argument is the number 10. Expressions such as 10FD, 10 FD, or FD10 are incorrect and will not work. If all of this seems unnecessarily complex for young children, just stop to think about the rules they follow in writing English. Whereas young students would probably be unable to apply appropriate terms to the components of a LOGO command, they are quite capable of learning and following the rules necessary for constructing commands the computer can interpret.

Hands-on experience

The best way to appreciate LOGO is to spend some time at a terminal exploring the features of the language. Once again, we strongly encourage you to take the time to experience programming. Also, contemplate your own thinking as you begin exploring. Insights you have about your own thinking might be helpful when you work later with other beginners. You might want to consider the following questions. What about your experiences do you find frustrating or exciting? What approach do you take when something does not work as expected? How do you feel when you finally solve a problem that has stumped you for some time? (One of us has been known to cheer and punch his fist in the air!)

TABLE 4.1 Some LOGO Primitives

PRIMITIVE	EXAMPLE	ACTION
cleargraphics	CG	Clear the screen
forward	FD 10	Move ahead 10 steps
back	BK 10	Move back 10 steps
right	RT 90	Turn right 90 degrees
left	LT 90	Turn left 90 degrees
penup	PU	Leave no trail
pendown	PD	Leave trail
home	Home	Return to center screen
hideturtle	HT	No turtle in graphic
showturtle	ST	Turtle visible in graphic

Different versions of LOGO may use slightly different commands. This list of primitives is from the LogoWriter version of LOGO. If you are using LogoWriter to try out some of these commands, you can obtain a complete list of primitives by entering .primitives.

In the following pages, we provide a brief overview of selected LOGO (LogoWriter) features. For more detail, you might consult a textbook or manual written to provide a more complete account of LOGO (Yoder, 1994).

PROGRAMMING IN DIRECT MODE

LOGO allows the keyboard input and execution of commands in direct mode. In **direct mode**, each time you press the return key, the command or commands that you have typed are executed. This is a good way to explore in the early stages of learning to program and is also a way to work out the details of sophisticated programs after you have become more proficient. Try some of the individual commands (primitives) from Table 4.1. If you type the following commands, you should see the turtle move as indicated in Figure 4.2

What is direct mode?

FIGURE 4.2   Result of Some LOGO Primitives

FD 30   RT 90   BK 30

By the way, if you don't want the effect of your commands to accumulate on the screen, you can enter CG *(cleargraphics)* at any point to clear the display.

Now, instead of individual commands, try entering the following sequence of commands before pressing the return key:
FD 30 RT 90 FD 30 RT 90 FD 30 RT 90 FD 30 RT 90
Figure 4.3 shows what you will see on your screen.

FIGURE 4.3   Square Resulting from LOGO Commands

A few limitations of direct mode

As you are probably beginning to discover, there are some limitations to working in direct mode. For example, if you have been working on a project of some complexity and decide to modify your approach (such as the size of the shapes), you essentially have to quit and start over. You also will be unable to save your commands for reuse. What if you want to return to the computer tomorrow and have LOGO repeat the process of constructing the same graphic design? Are you going to want to type the same set of commands again? For all practical purposes, your program in this mode (the direct mode) is also available only to you. If you want to pass this plan on to someone else, you need the capability of storing the plan you have developed.

PROGRAMMING IN INDIRECT MODE: WRITING PROCEDURES

What is indirect mode?

When working in **indirect mode**, the programmer constructs a set of instructions to be stored for execution at a later time. Because the programmer has to mentally anticipate the effect of each command, this approach to programming makes some new demands on the programmer. Often the programmer makes an error in thinking through what will happen when the entire sequence of commands is executed, and unexpected consequences occur (computer programmers refer to the errors in their programs as **bugs**; see "Focus: The Original Bug"). One very nice feature about a stored program is that, if the programmer can determine the cause of the flaw in the program, he or she can locate the bug in the stored program and change the offending command or commands. In a way, this is similar to using a word processing program to edit a written document. Editing requires the writer to correct only the offending statement — not redo the entire document.

In LOGO, a set of stored instructions is called a **procedure**. The general format for a procedure is:

TO *procedurename*
commands
END

LogoWriter provides a location for writing procedures in indirect mode. If you examine the upper right-hand corner of the LogoWriter screen in Figure 4.1, you will see an F and an inverted F. Clicking the mouse at this location will move the user between the display space allowed for the turtle and the page for writing procedures.

To generate a square as a procedure, you might write the following list of commands:

```
TO SQUARE
    FD 30
    RT 90
    FD 30
    RT 90
    FD 30
    RT 90
    FD 30
    RT 90
END
```

The advantage of a stored program

In direct mode, the entire sequence of commands can now be executed by simply entering SQUARE (then press return). The procedure SQUARE has been added to the LOGO vocabulary. In a way, the programmer increases the power of LOGO by contributing to what LOGO knows how to do. This is what we mean by describing programming as instructing the computer.

What if you made a mistake — say, you incorrectly entered 3 instead of 30 for one of the sides? The figure drawn by the procedure would not be what you anticipated (see Figure 4.4)!

FIGURE 4.4   Result of Flawed Square Procedure

However, the process of correcting the error is relatively easy. You simply return to indirect mode, examine the procedure to find the error, and make the necessary correction. You can now execute the procedure again, and if your modification fixes the actual bug, your program should execute as intended.

ADDITIONAL FEATURES OF LOGO

Familiar features

To help you gain some insight into the full potential of LOGO and the exploratory environment this language provides, we will describe some additional features of the language. If you have programmed in other languages but have not had experience with LOGO, you will find that LOGO allows most of the features you are accustomed to. For example, the procedure SQUARE is written in a manner that is not particularly elegant. The two

Focus

The Original Bug

The term *bug,* which is so familiar to computer programmers, has an interesting origin. The term is usually attributed to Grace Hooper, a famous computer pioneer who worked for the U.S. Navy. Computers used to contain many moving parts and, as a result, generated heat. Because air conditioning was not always available, the windows were some- times left open to contend with the unpleasant temperatures and also to keep the computer cool. On one occasion, the machine Grace Hooper was working on quit, and workers were painstakingly searching for the failed component. The problem turned out to be a moth that had probably come in through an open window. Hooper reported that she had to "debug" the machine, and this expression for fixing a computer problem has been used ever since. ✳

primitives FD and RT are repeated over and over again. What if the procedure involved some cyclical process that had to be repeated hundreds or thousands of times? It would be rather impractical to enter any set of commands that many times. The command REPEAT *number* [*commands*] tells LOGO to repeat the commands within brackets the designated number of times. You could rewrite the procedure SQUARE as follows:

TO SQUARE
    REPEAT 4 [FD 30 RT 90]
END

Powerful programming languages also make use of **variables**. The value of a procedure such as SQUARE would be limited if you had to rewrite the procedure every time you wanted the turtle to draw a square of a different size. In a way, variables allow you to establish the sequence of actions to be taken when the program is written and defer assigning specific arguments to these actions. To write a more flexible version of the square procedure, you might want to establish the length of a side when the procedure is actually executed. You could write this more flexible version of the square procedure this way:

TO SQUARE :SIDE
    REPEAT 4 [FD :SIDE RT 90]
END

Executing the procedure

Once you have created the square procedure, you execute the procedure by entering SQUARE followed by the length of the side you want (for example, SQUARE 40). If you forget and enter only the procedure name, LOGO will request that you provide the missing value.

The way LOGO designates and uses variables might be a bit confusing at first. SIDE is a variable name. When a variable name is preceded by a colon (as in :SIDE), this means the value of a variable. When the REPEAT command encounters FD :SIDE, it substitutes the value of SIDE. To establish the value of a variable, you can also use the primitive MAKE "*variablename value* (as in MAKE "SIDE 40). Instead of entering SQUARE 40 to draw a square 40 turtlesteps on a side, you could also enter the command MAKE "SIDE 40 and then the command SQUARE :SIDE to accomplish the same thing. To keep these different ideas straight, you might think of a variable name as a storage place, like a box somewhere in the computer's memory. The MAKE command attaches the variable name to a storage location and allows you to put

Overcoming confusion

information in this storage place. When the value of a variable is requested (as in :SIDE), LOGO will check the designated storage location to obtain the needed information. If LOGO finds an empty storage location, LOGO will generate an error message and ask for the needed information (in LogoWriter, SQUARE NEEDS MORE INPUTS).

From your own educational experiences, you probably know that variables play an important general role in math and science. The general concept

Variables in math and science

of a variable is not easy to understand at first, and experiences with variables in programming may be an effective way to help younger students gain an understanding of the concept. Again, we will consider the topic of what students learn from programming experiences later in this chapter.

BUILDING A PROGRAM WITH PROCEDURES

"Calling" a procedure

LOGO allows one procedure to "call" another procedure. That is, once a procedure has been written, the action generated by the procedure can be called by inserting the name of the procedure within a second procedure. Sometimes the main program or procedure is called a **superprocedure**, and the building block procedures are called **subprocedures**. Often, the superprocedure is very simple, consisting only of a series of procedure names (subprocedures). This method is efficient because it allows the programmer to isolate tasks and work on them as more manageable units. As we will point out later, the ability to identify problem subgoals is also an important general problem-solving skill. Experience with programs that utilize subprocedures may help students develop this technique for handling complex problems.

Students love to explore recursion

A procedure in LOGO can even call itself. This is accomplished by inserting the name of the procedure within the procedure. When the procedure is activated, the computer executes each command it encounters until it reaches the procedure name. When the computer encounters the name of any procedure, it begins to execute that procedure. In this case, this amounts to starting the sequence of actions generated by the procedure all over again. This special method is called **recursion**. Recursion is an idea that students find extremely intriguing and love to explore (Papert, 1980). Somehow, the idea of a self-perpetuating process is just fascinating. For example, consider the childhood riddle: If you have two wishes, what would your second wish be? The answer is: Two more wishes (or make one wish and then wish for two more wishes). If you could express the riddle as a procedure, it would look something like this:

```
TO WISH
    MAKE WISH1
    WISH
END
```

Extending and producing interesting effects

Recursion can also be demonstrated as a way to extend and produce some interesting effects with procedures that have already been written. The procedure that follows uses SQUARE. There are no repeats in this procedure, but many squares of decreasing size have been drawn. In fact, an IF statement was included to stop the program from going on and on. The results are shown in Figure 4.5.

```
TO BLACKHOLE :SIDE
```

```
SQUARE :SIDE
RT 12
Make "SIDE :SIDE*.985
IF :SIDE.5 [STOP]
BLACKHOLE :SIDE
END
```

FIGURE 4.5   Results of Blackhole Procedure

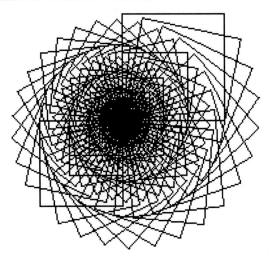

Now that you have had a brief exposure to the kinds of programming younger students might do, the question becomes what these experiences accomplish. The remainder of this chapter will address this question.

PROGRAMMING AND THE DEVELOPMENT OF PROBLEM-SOLVING SKILL

A nearly classic problem-solving activity

One major reason for involving students in programming is the assumption that programming experiences will help them learn to become more effective problem solvers. On the surface, the argument that students can learn general problem-solving skills from programming experiences seems logical. Programming is nearly a classic problem-solving activity. Your efforts to follow the programming examples here may have convinced you that programming tasks require a variety of mental skills. Descriptions of what experienced programmers do (Pea and Kurland, 1987) are almost identical to more general descriptions of the problem-solving process (Bransford and Stein, 1984; Hayes and Simon, 1974). As the programmer attempts to accomplish a programming task, he or she must:

A CTIVE
C OOPERATION
T HEME-BASED
I NTEGRATED
V ERSATILE
E VALUATION

An assortment of research studies

1. understand the task;
2. develop a plan for completing the task on the computer;
3. convert the plan into programming code; and
4. evaluate the extent to which the program functions as desired and modify the program when necessary.

Do students learn to become better problem solvers because they have spent time learning to program? Providing a direct answer to this question is difficult. Various reviews of the research attempting to summarize this issue have not reached a unanimous decision (Keller, 1990; Pea and Kurland, 1987; Salomon and Perkins, 1987). While frustrating to those looking to research for guidance, research in education can generates as many new questions as it provides answers.

An Overview of the Research

The collective body of research about the relationship between programming and the development of problem-solving skill is important in several ways:

Why consider the research?

1. If you decide to provide your students with programming experiences, you should really attempt to determine whether programming benefits them and which approaches to teaching programming seem most productive. Becoming familiar with the research will help you when you are trying to make effective decisions about how to integrate technology into your classroom.
2. The research literature provides an example of the evolution of theory and related ideas about classroom applications. Consideration of this body of work demonstrates that the results of research studies can cause recommendations for practice to change.
3. Because nearly all of the research on programming and problem solving was conducted in classroom settings, it provides insights into how teachers actually use LOGO. The impact of LOGO on student behavior is directly determined by the actual experiences of students and not by the potential experiences that are never realized.
4. The studies seem to lead to recommendations for practice that fit very nicely with many of the ideas developed in Chapter 2. These ideas include cognitive apprenticeship, authentic tasks, and learning for transfer or application.

Early expectations of LOGO may have been overly optimistic. When new and promising educational ideas do not deliver as advertised, the educational community often drops the ideas and looks for the next innovation. We agree with those who caution against this reaction and suggest that educators treat the educational application of LOGO itself as a LOGO program that does not work as anticipated. Even an inexperienced programmer realizes that a complex program often does not run on the first attempt, and the appropriate response should be to carefully evaluate the program and its assumptions rather than to abandon the work that has been completed.

Conditions for Low- and High-Road Transfer

A useful place to begin considering the existing research is with the influential analysis provided by Salomon and Perkins (1987). They noted the contradictory results of studies investigating whether or not programming would improve problem-solving performance and proposed a theory to reconcile the lack of consistency in the findings. The assumption that programming experience will lead to improved problem-solving performance in some other domain is an assumption about transfer. **Transfer** basically assumes that specific skills and knowledge learned in one situation will prove generally useful in a variety of new situations. When you think about it, transfer is what formal education is all about. Unless what we teach and learn in our classrooms has some general value in other classrooms and outside the school setting, why bother acquiring the knowledge in the first place?

Reconciling inconsistent findings

Transfer can occur in two ways sometimes referred to as low- and high-road transfer (Salomon and Perkins, 1987). In *low-road transfer,* behavior is practiced extensively and in a variety of situations. Behavior is learned to the point of **automatization**. Automatized behavior is behavior that a person has learned to the point at which he or she can complete a task without thinking about it. For example, if you drive or are a competent typist, you have practiced skills extensively and in a variety of situations and have likely automatized behaviors related to typing and driving. When you type the letter q, the fact that the little finger on your left hand moves straight up one row is probably not something you are aware of.

Low-road transfer

Automatized behavior

In *high-road transfer,* skills must be deliberately transferred from one context to another. Two requirements must be met. First, the individual must be capable of re-representing the original skill at a level that will include a greater range of cases than was covered by the context in which the original skill was first acquired. For example, if a student both observes from experiences with programming and is capable of explaining that it is often useful to take a complex problem and identify individual tasks to be accomplished, the student has re-represented programming knowledge in an abstract and verbal fashion that would apply to many tasks. Second, the student must be willing to make a conscious effort to use past experiences to attack current problems. Such an approach requires both motivation and metacognitive skill.

High-road transfer

Identifying whether studies met the requirement for either high- or low-road transfer turned out to be an accurate way to predict whether the studies were successful in demonstrating the transfer of problem-solving skills (Salomon and Perkins, 1987). To summarize, when students did not (a) spend enough time programming to develop a reasonable level of skill or accumulate enough diverse experiences, (b) consider and discuss how they solve problems when they program, and (c) consider how the problem-solving skills involved in programming might apply to other domains, the research studies were unlikely to demonstrate that students could transfer programming skills to other areas.

Issues in Implementing LOGO

The original philosophy of LOGO stressed the importance of personal discovery within a responsive exploratory environment. Many teachers appear to have interpreted the initial guidelines for working with LOGO as advocating little planning or intervention on their part (Keller, 1990). As a result, students typically had only brief introductions to commands or techniques and then were allowed to explore on their own. Observation of students' behaviors under these circumstances did indicate that they find the LOGO environment to be motivating. However, whatever the expectations, most younger students working in LOGO do not spontaneously engage in the general problem-solving skills thought to be prompted by programming environments. Without specific guidance, many students would find some set of commands that produced an interesting pattern and play with this pattern by entering slightly different values for the key variables (Littlefield et al., 1988; see "Focus: Computer Play"). Students might continue variations on the same theme for several class periods using a trial-and-error approach. It was noted that students seemed very motivated and intrigued with the interesting results their programs would produce, but that they were frequently unable to predict what a specific version of the program would do before they ran it or explain why particular results were produced. These observations suggest that many students engage in weak problem-solving practices when allowed complete freedom to explore. In terms of the principles we discussed in Chapter 2, it seems that the external activity of programming within a discovery environment often does not engage internal processes thought to be important components of problem solving (see pages 55 through 59).

LOGO is motivating

A teacher-guided approach

A Matter of Style

Even when students are task oriented, some educators believe they tend to work in a way that may be successful in the short run, but that does not lead to advanced problem-solving skills in the long run. Observation suggests that most young LOGO programmers use a style described as "product oriented," "brute force," and "linear" (Kurland et al., 1987). In this approach, the student has some desired screen effect in mind and generates a sequence of individual commands (linear approach) to achieve the desired effect (product oriented). The highly interactive nature of LOGO programming almost rewards this kind of behavior; the student can note bugs and insert or change individual commands very easily (by trial and error or brute force). A more disciplined approach would emphasize careful analysis of the problem to identify subproblems, the generation of procedures to solve the subproblems, and the

Interactive nature of LOGO programming

construction of superprocedures to integrate the procedures. Some teachers require students to sketch out a plan on paper before working at the computer. This approach is an attempt to encourage students to think the task through before they begin to enter code, like asking students to construct an outline before writing.

MORE EFFECTIVE PROGRAMMING INSTRUCTION

What do these observations of students' programming suggest for teachers and schools wanting to use LOGO or other languages to develop problem-solving skill?

First, the analysis suggests that educators take a more realistic look at what they expect LOGO to accomplish. At best, students in elementary and junior high school settings are likely to spend thirty to fifty hours in a year programming (Pea and Kurland, 1987). Schools have many instructional responsibilities, and it may not be practical to assume that they can improve this time commitment substantially. Perhaps it is necessary to accept the reality that students will not become very proficient as programmers in thirty to fifty hours — especially when they use much of the time in self-directed discovery. The solution may be to switch away from pure discovery experiences. This is the approach taken by educators who advocate more structured and mediated (but not lock-step) approaches to LOGO instruction.

Structured approaches to LOGO

Second, it appears that the development of problem-solving skills requires guidance. Increasing the amount of structure present in the learning environment seems to improve student knowledge of LOGO, but it does not appear to be sufficient to develop general problem-solving skills (Littlefield et al., 1988). It appears that more general skills can be developed when teachers employ *mediated instruction* (Keller, 1990; Littlefield et al., 1988). In a **mediated instruction** approach, the teacher works directly to develop the thinking skills or strategies associated with the academic task the student is performing. The teacher must take pains to establish that he or she is as concerned with the development of important thinking processes as with more visible products. When the content taught by mediated instruction is programming, key thinking processes might include planning, breaking complex problems into smaller problems, and using a systematic approach to identify and fix bugs. In contrast, the products are the program code and the result of the program (a graphic design when using turtlegraphics).

What to explain to students

Students need to be told that planning and other cognitive activities are important, taught how to perform these skills, and monitored to make certain they use the skills. Because of the broad educational expectations associated with programming, it might also be useful to ascertain that students understand that the targeted cognitive behaviors may be processes involved in general problem solving.

Focus

Computer Play — Action Without Cognitive Processing?

If you haven't spent time programming, the claim that students spend hours making trial-and-error modifications of a program to produce different visual effects may sound rather strange. Perhaps an example will provide some insights into how such classroom behaviors can develop. The students in this example are not K–12 students, but teachers we have met while providing in-service experiences in schools. Often, in-service classes consist of a two-day workshop in which teachers spend several hours working with a number of different applications of technology. In some cases, one of the applications has been LOGO. Although LOGO isn't something that can be mastered in a couple of hours, the basic objective of such a training session is to interest teachers in the potential of LOGO by introducing some of the basic concepts and providing some programming experiences. Near the end of the time set aside for independent programming activities, some teachers have often completed their assignments, and we sometimes give them the following program to experiment with:

```
TO SPIRAL :REPS :TURN :SIDE :INC
    REPEAT :REPS
        FD :SIDE
        RT :TURN
        MAKE "TURN :TURN+ :INC
    HT
END
```

As you may be able to tell from your introduction to LOGO, this program accepts four inputs. The inputs represent the number of it-erations of the repeat loop (REPS), the initial number of degrees the turtle is to turn (TURN), the number of turtle steps to advance after each turn (SIDE), and the number of degrees the turn variable is to be incremented each time through the loop (INC). Variations on this program appear in many books on LOGO. What this program generates is not obvious. In addition, changes in the variables produce very different results. The examples in Figure 4.6 give some feeling for the variations that occur.

FIGURE 4.6 Patterns Resulting from Spiral Procedure

SPIRAL 500 2 8 2   SPIRAL 800 2 8 2.5   SPIRAL 500 2 4 3.5

The teachers often became fascinated with this program. Those who showed up early for class on the second day would start plugging different numbers into the program to see what patterns would result. Often during the class, we would notice a student working with this program instead of the application we were actually presenting. In most cases, these teachers exhibited exactly the same reaction to this program that Littlefield et al. (1988) described in complaining about student behavior. Many teachers frequently did not know why the program worked the way it did, nor were they attempting to analyze what was happening. They could not predict what would happen before the different variations of the program executed. They were content to work in a trial-and-error fashion just to see what would happen. If you have access to a computer and LOGO software, try the program yourself. You will likely find it fascinating, too. The teachers we describe provide a great example of rote discovery (see Chapter 2, pages 50 through 55), demonstrating that activity without thinking does not produce much learning. How do you think this activity might be improved? Some (Karoly, 1996) claim that this type of activity can be useful and with proper preparation students will attempt to think through the program because they are intrigued by the seeming unpredictability of what is produced. ✷

Planning, breaking down complex problems, and debugging are useful processes in many arenas, but it appears the transfer of these skills to general applications is not automatic. Thus, mediated instruction might also concern the conscious transfer of skills learned in one domain to other settings and other problems. Teachers might ask students to think about how planning or debugging skills emphasized in programming might apply to writing or preparing a speech. Students must understand that they are learning skills they will be expected to apply in a variety of areas.

Mediated instruction

Mediated instruction involves a number of techniques. First, the teacher makes critical strategies explicit. Then he or she can mention specific skills and demonstrate them through think-aloud techniques. The teacher can demonstrate how to debug a faulty program and discuss how to bridge thinking skills learned in programming to other areas. For example, Littlefield et al. (1988) discuss applying processes involved in programming to planning a class party: What are the components of the problem, what has to be done to prepare for each component? Second, mediated instruction attempts to involve students in thinking about and analyzing their own thinking and behavior. This can be a very different process than telling students what to do or evaluating the product of what they have done. Teachers seem to communicate differently when teaching LOGO than when teaching other subject matter. Teachers provide fewer instructions and ask more questions (Emihovich and Miller, 1988). The questions often are not requests for information but are intended to get the students to think about their own behavior. A sequence of such questions might include: What did you tell the turtle to do? What did you want it to do? How are you going to fix it? (Au, Horton, and Ryba, 1987; Clements and Gullo, 1984). The use of questions is also opportunistic; teachers must generate the appropriate questions in the appropriate situations.

Focusing students on their thinking

Other forms of classroom interaction can also focus students on their own thinking. Teachers can ask students to explain to the teacher or to the class how they carried out important processes. How did you plan your program? How did you find and fix the problem you were having with your program? Several experts suggest that LOGO lessons end with a discussion or with student presentations (Au, Horton, and Ryba, 1987; Clements and

Merriman, 1988). Finally, teacher guidance and prompting of cognitive activity is gradually faded, and students must take responsibility for guiding and evaluating their own cognitive behaviors (metacognitive control). This combination of techniques may remind you of reciprocal teaching and cognitive apprenticeship (see Chapter 2, pages 67 through 69). Although the advocates of these techniques may not use the same terminology in describing how teachers interact with students, many of the techniques are very similar. Guidelines teachers might follow to more actively involve students appear in "Focus: A Process-oriented Checklist for LOGO."

Advances in the programming environment

Finally, as educators and researchers have gained experience in how students use LOGO and how to encourage students to focus on effective problem-solving approaches, attempts have been made to improve the programming software so it provides a better learning environment (Clements and Sarama, 1996). For example, one new version of the software has attempted to make it easier for students to see the connections between the program and the result. The version of LogoWriter described here allows students to view either the program or the drawing (see Figure 4.1). Why not make both views visible at the same time? A second way to improve the connection between representations is to allow the learner to manipulate the image and watch as the program changes. This is difficult to do in every case, but in simple cases it has been possible to do things such as allow the learner

Focus

A Process-Oriented Checklist for LOGO

1. Resist the impulse to solve problems for students. Keep your hands off the students' keyboards!
2. Make certain you give students the opportunity for individual discussions. Walk around the room when students are working.
3. Ask that students explain their solution strategies in their own words.
4. Require that students apply general problem-solving processes to non-LOGO situations. Have them analyze and develop plans for other tasks, such as preparing for a field trip. Discuss how general problem-solving techniques apply.
5. Ask students to describe the problem they are working on in concrete terms (What do you want the turtle to do?).
6. Encourage students to be flexible thinkers. Require that they write a different procedure to draw the same shape.
7. Ask followup questions when observing student work (Why do you think the turtle did that?).
8. Allow students to work on some problems in small groups. Have groups share their strategies for arriving at solutions. ✻

Source: Selected from a larger list provided by Au, Horton, and Ryba, 1987

to drag the corner of a square to make it larger and watch as the number representing the length of the side in the program adjusts. Finding why a program produces an unexpected result — a bug — can also be made easier. Sophisticated programming environments often make available a feature that allows the programmer to step through a program one command at a time. This helps the programmer identify exactly which command is being executed when something unexpected happens. When included in educational programming environments, this feature is a great way to find errors and provides learners a very interesting way to examine the programs they have created.

A
C OOPERATION
T
I
V
E

Small groups and peer-directed learning

PROGRAMMING AS A COOPERATIVE ACTIVITY

A review of many research studies providing a positive perspective on the potential of LOGO experiences reveals an important, but perhaps overlooked fact: teachers in these studies often worked with very small groups of students (Clements and Gullo, 1984; Emihovich and Miller, 1988; Littlefield et al., 1988). Instructional groups of two to six students are common in these studies because teachers can perform certain roles or functions with that number of students that would be very difficult in a large group setting. Many classroom teachers find it difficult to work with such small groups on a continual basis. Peer-directed learning may provide a practical way to supplement interaction with the teacher.

In theory, working within a group is beneficial for the following reasons:

1. Students should clarify concepts for themselves as they attempt to explain them to others.

2. A group provides a collective expertise that should enable the group to take on tasks beyond the capabilities of individuals. Students can correct and fill in the gaps for each other. Gradually, individuals should acquire the knowledge and develop the processing skills provided by others.

Resolving conflicts in groups

3. Groups naturally encourage some conflicts. In the process of resolving these conflicts, there are many opportunities for knowledge use, knowledge examination, and restructuring of personal beliefs (Webb and Lewis, 1988).

Here are some suggestions for establishing effective programming groups:

Effective programming groups

1. Don't assume that students know how to work as a group. Even basic skills, such as how to ask for assistance and how to provide assistance, may not be well developed. Skills can be modeled and practiced. Teachers should also continue to monitor group functioning and discuss group effectiveness with group members.

2. Teachers can encourage members of the group to help each other master essential skills by using a group reward structure. In a group reward structure, part of the grade for each individual depends on the performance of others in the group.
3. Teachers might require groups to plan and discuss a programming assignment before group members are allowed to start working at the computer. Some variations of this principle require the group to construct a diagram or written description to explain how the program will function.
4. Encourage group members to rely on each other for assistance in planning and debugging. The group should approach the teacher only when group resources have been exhausted (Webb and Lewis, 1988).

The teacher's role

A couple of other comments may be helpful. Having students work in groups does not mean that you, as the teacher, should be passive. You can be involved without directing or controlling. You also need to constantly monitor group effectiveness. There may be some situations in which you will need to intervene (one student dominates the terminal and writes the program for the group). Group work has much to offer, but like many other good ideas, it should not be used exclusively. Students also need the challenge of taking on programming tasks on their own.

PROGRAMMING TO LEARN IN OTHER CONTENT AREAS

A general relationship between programming and other content areas

The relationship between programming and other content areas may not be intuitively obvious. The programming examples in this chapter may have involved concepts you recognize from other content areas. For example, you may relate the concept of variables to an algebra course. Papert (1980) saw the relationship as potentially much more general. To understand his view, it is useful to appreciate his vision of a computer *microworld*. A computer **microworld** provides an environment representing some discipline. The student can explore and manipulate this environment and experience systematic consequences as a result of actions taken. These consequences allow the student to construct an understanding of the environment through processes of assimilation and accommodation (see discussion of constructivist theory in Chapter 2, pages 60 through 72).

Students' experiences when they test their ideas and skills

Papert adopted the ideas of assimilation and accommodation from Jean Piaget. In **assimilation**, external experiences are interpreted as fitting with existing mental structures. In **accommodation**, mental structures are changed to fit experiences. Most individuals probably think of such mental structures as general insights based on experience and probably would not label them in the way educators or psychologists would. When we experience unanticipated consequences, it is often because our mental structures are incorrect or at least not sufficiently specific. In this case, the mental structures need to be refined. In this view, mental structures (knowledge or personal representations of reality) begin to represent the microworld through a combination of action, consequences, and the processes of mental adaptation. This position is important for you as a teacher using technology in your classroom because it suggests that students learn a great deal when they discover that what they know or the way they try to do something does not bring the expected results. Students are most likely to have such experiences when they are involved in activities that allow them to test their ideas and skills.

Turtle Geometry

The turtle's style of doing geometry

The LOGO turtle provides access to the microworld of turtle geometry. Papert (1980) argued that geometry is understood through action and that turtle geometry is just another style of "doing geometry." Euclid's style was logical, Descartes' style was algebraic, and the turtle's style is computational. If you find this a bit abstract, think about your own understanding of the concept "circle." You may represent a circle as a definition: a closed plane figure with all points equidistant from a common point. As an algebraic expression, a circle can be represented as $x^2 + y^2 = r^2$ (assuming the Cartesian center is 0, 0), with r representing the radius of the circle. If you fix the radius as 1, the *unit circle* can be defined as $x^2 + y^2 = 1$. A circle can also be represented as the product of a LOGO program. Most students willing to experiment with LOGO eventually come across the simple program REPEAT 360 FD 1 RT 1. For a more sophisticated method for generating a circle, consider the following procedure (based on Yoder, 1992).

```
to CIRCLE :RADIUS
    REPEAT 360
        FD :RADIUS
        WAIT 10
        PD
        FD 1
        PU
        BK 1
        BK :RADIUS
        WAIT 10
        RT 1
    END
```

If you have an opportunity, enter these commands and run the program. The program draws a circle with the radius you specify. The turtle moves forward the distance you have specified as the radius, puts the pen down, and moves forward one step. This creates a point. The turtle then puts the pen up and moves back to the center of the circle. Finally, the turtle turns one degree to the right. This sequence is repeated 360 times. If you watch the turtle repeatedly run out, make a mark, and then run back as it generates the circle (the WAIT commands have been inserted so that program execution slows down), you may understand what a circle is in a different way than you would if you just thought about "a closed plane figure with all points equidistant from a common point."

Certainly, the computational method of defining shapes is the only method among those briefly presented here that defines geometry in terms of action (movements of the turtle). Young children intuitively understand spatial notions in terms of action and the LOGO approach (Battista and Clements, 1988). One experience cited in support of this claim is the very frequently observed tendency of children (or adults) to "become the turtle" to solve LOGO problems. You can watch children moving their bodies as they think about a problem. Teachers often suggest that students become the turtle when students want help. Try it. Can you walk in a circle? Translate what you are doing into LOGO commands. Would your program read "Move ahead a little, turn a little, ahead a little, turn a little, and so on"?

Becoming the turtle to solve LOGO problems

Although it is most frequently used with elementary or junior high school students, LOGO is not limited to understanding only the most basic features of geometry. Turtle geometry can be used to explore advanced topics in geometry as well (Abelson and diSessa, 1981; Yusuf, 1995).

LEGO-LOGO

Building simple machines

An interesting recent extension of LOGO is LEGO-LOGO (Rosen, 1993; Shimabukuro, 1989). LEGO-LOGO allows the student to build simple machines and then uses the computer to control the machines through an interface box. The LEGO kit includes blocks, motors, gears, touch and photo sensors, and a counting mechanism. These extensions allow some new and interesting programming problems. New LOGO primitives (such as ON, OFF, REVERSE DIRECTION) are provided. In addition, the LEGO-LOGO microworld allows the exploration of certain topics in physics, engineering, and mathematics. Because the machines move and lift, physical properties such as force, work, weight, friction, speed, time, and distance come into play. The sensors can be used to gather data for analysis. For example, the photo sensor can detect when an object breaks a beam of light. The object could be the car a student has built, and detecting when the car passes a certain point can be used to determine how long it took the car to move a certain distance — from the start line to the finish line, for example. You can imagine the potential for a LEGO-LOGO drag strip and a little friendly competition! However, the LEGO-LOGO microworld should also encourage the development of both programming skill and content-area knowledge. Could you write a program to determine the speed of the cars? What *is* speed, anyway?

Understanding physical properties

It is probably fair to suggest that while research and development efforts related to LOGO software and instructional techniques associated with learning from programming experiences continue, the prevalence of instructional use is declining. LOGO activities are quite consistent with the main themes of this book. Programming activities integrated into the instruction of certain

Emerging Technology

Using Computers and Calculators as Laboratory Tools

LOGO applications that gather data or control devices external to the computer are hardly unique. These functions are quite common in science and industry so LOGO applications of the type described here provide students some insights into authentic computer use. Using technology to gather data and control devices can do much more than familiarize students with technology applications. Math and science teachers have the opportunity to take advantage of this technology to engage students in authentic projects that connect the principles learned in the classroom with the everyday world.

Several companies offer educators the resources necessary to carry out these projects. These resources include curriculum guides, computer software, some form of *I/O* *(input/output)* interface (a hardware component allowing the computer to communicate with external devices), and the external devices. While some external devices allow simple robotic activities, most educational projects presently use probes that gather data. Probes are purchased to perform specific functions, whether to monitor heart rate or measure dissolved oxygen, acceleration, magnetic fields, pH, temperature, galvanic skin response, or humidity. Many types of probes are available. In contrast to LOGO applications, these activities emphasize data acquisition and

Students can use probes connected to a computer or a calculator to gather information for a variety of problem-solving activities. *(© Michael Zide)*

analysis and are conducted with the assistance of sophisticated programs that are provided.

It may surprise some to learn that these relatively sophisticated data acquisition techniques do not require a computer; they can be accomplished with hand-held calculators. Calculators have become much more powerful than those you may have used when younger and make available to high school students features such as graphic displays and complex stored mathematical and statistical functions. Calculators can be attached to the various probes we have already described. The calculator can be used to analyze and display data or it can be linked to a computer for data transfer. Calculators have some unique advantages. First, even the more powerful are inexpensive in comparison to computers. Another important feature is transportability. Students can easily carry their calculators home or from class to class. The connection of probes to a calculator also allows students to gather data in the field in ways that would not be practical with a computer. For example, students in a physics class might want to study acceleration during different phases of a roller coaster ride. It is not *that* difficult to imagine a student carrying a calculator along on carnival rides.

This discussion of ways in which technology can be connected to external devices is admittedly very brief. We provide it because of the emphasis such approaches place on authentic tasks and on integrating technology into content area instruction. If you are interested in high school math or science, you might locate some of the devices we describe in scientific supply catalogs. We have also provided a few mail and World Wide Web addresses for relevant companies at the end of this chapter. ✳

content areas can involve students in meaningful tasks that will be perceived as authentic (Lafer and Markert, 1994) and may offer a useful way to increase the involvement of women and minorities in math and science (the seriousness of this problem is discussed in Chapter 11) (Bernhard and Siegel, 1994; Hutchinson and Whalen, 1994–1995). However, learning from programming requires time and skilled guidance. We are confident there will continue to be pockets of interest in the types of programming activities we have described here. We also see a possible transition toward activities offering similar experiences.

Other Integrated Programming Opportunities

We have emphasized the LOGO programming language because it allows discussion of the range of potential programming benefits. It is a language for developing programming skill and possibly also for developing content-area knowledge and general problem-solving ability. LOGO is also somewhat unique because it is taught at several grade levels and usually with students with a wide range of aptitudes. In comparison, other popular programming languages (BASIC and Pascal) seem frequently to be applied primarily as a way to develop programming skill.

You may remember from earlier in this chapter our claim that HyperCard development activities may provide the same programming, problem-

Learning from multimedia authoring

solving, and content-area explorations available with more conventional programming languages. As we end this chapter, we want to offer a few more comments on this claim. One of the arguments for LOGO turtlegraphics is that it provides a computational way of "doing geometry." This statement implies that key concepts can be represented and explored through programming. Multimedia authoring environments (see discussion in Chapter 7) may serve a similar role in other content areas. Multimedia authoring environments (such as HyperStudio, HyperCard, Web page authoring progams) allow the manipulation of ideas expressed as numbers, text, graphics, and sounds. Constructing products with these programs allows students to create external representations of course content that require them to think carefully about what they are learning and make gaps in understanding readily apparent.

Manipulating ideas expressed as numbers, text, graphics, and sounds

Some hypermedia authoring environments allow traditional programming experiences; for example, HyperCard, HyperStudio, and ToolBook incorporate a programming language. Web page authoring can involve the use of simple commands that control the appearance of web pages and the transitions among them (see Chapter 6). The problem-solving skills involved in traditional programming tasks also apply in the design of complex multimedia projects (Brown, 1989–1990).

There are some potential benefits to this combination of multimedia design and simple programming that relate specifically to the educational goals of problem-solving and higher-level thinking (we will consider general content goals in later chapters). These benefits could be summarized under the general heading of *educational efficiency.* Explanations for the failed expectations of programming have included the lack of programming expertise actually developed and the lack of experience in using programming to solve a diversity of relevant problems. These difficulties do relate to the issue of efficiency. Students simply need to spend more time on a greater diversity of programming tasks. However, educators must make practical decisions about how students will spend their school time. Many laudable goals compete for valuable instructional and study time.

Educational efficiency

It can be argued that multimedia projects provide an efficient way to allow a relatively large amount of practice with diverse tasks. How can this claim be justified? First, multimedia experiences can be integrated into the time allocated to the instruction of many different content areas. Second, a variety of projects can be created across grade levels (see Chapter 10, pages 351 through 353). Basic skills can be developed in the early grades and expanded as the student progresses. Some programming experiences can be incorporated into these tasks.

SUMMARY

Programming is the process of instructing the computer to perform a desired action. Some (Taylor, 1980) describe this as placing the computer in the role of tutee. Programmers communicate with the computer through specialized languages, each of which has a unique vocabulary and requires the use of a formalized syntax.

LOGO was developed for the educational environment. An important characteristic of the LOGO language is the use of procedures — stored sets of instructions. Ideally, procedures are developed to perform one clearly defined task. Procedures can also be combined to performed more complex tasks.

Programming experiences in school are provided to develop programming skills, general problem-solving skills, and content-area skills. Although programming is a good example of problem solving, evaluations of the use of programming experiences as a way to teach problem solving are as yet inconclusive. Careful examination of programming experiences provided for this purpose reveal some potential problems:

1. Students do not become very proficient as programmers and thus may not spend much time actually engaged in problem solving.
2. Programming has often been interpreted as an activity for students to engage in with little instruction or guidance (pure discovery), and many students do not function effectively in this type of environment.
3. Students are not taught to apply skills learned as programmers to other settings.

Proposed solutions to these limitations include the development of more structured learning experiences and the use of mediational teaching methods. Mediational methods focus on the cognitive processes used in performing particular skills. In general, the teacher attempts to make these internal processes more understandable to the student and attempts to directly influence the development of these skills.

Programming can also provide an active way to learn a content area. The LOGO turtlegraphics environment was developed as a geometry microworld. When operating in this setting, the student can engage in a computational style of representing geometric principles and concepts. LEGO-LOGO may provide a similar type of environment for learning principles of physics. Programming may also be integrated with the exploration of other content areas. Multimedia projects are another way to bring programming experiences into many new content areas.

Activities

REFLECTING ON CHAPTER 4

◆ Consider how you would explain what programming is. Develop an explanation of programming that you might present to third grade students. Develop an explanation of programming that you might present to eighth grade students.

◆ High-road transfer requires that students be taught to transfer what they have learned. Provide an example of a nonprogramming learning task that might provide an opportunity to discuss transfer from programming experiences. How would you help students see the connections?

◆ Write the outline of a superprocedure for making a peanut butter and jelly sandwich. Write the steps involved in one subprocedure from this superprocedure.

Key Terms

accommodation *(p. 143)*	primitives *(p. 127)*
assimilation *(p. 143)*	procedure *(p. 130)*
automatization *(p. 136)*	programming *(p. 124)*
binary *(p. 124)*	recursion *(p. 133)*
bugs *(p. 130)*	subprocedure *(p. 133)*
direct mode *(p. 129)*	superprocedure *(p. 133)*
icons *(p. 124)*	syntax *(p. 127)*
indirect mode *(p. 130)*	transfer *(p. 136)*
mediated instruction *(p. 138)*	turtlegraphics *(p. 127)*
microworld *(p. 143)*	variables *(p. 132)*

Resources to Expand Your Knowledge Base

Books Exploring Programming as a General Learning Environment

Papert, S. *Mindstorms: Children, computers and powerful ideas.* New York: Basic Books, 1980.

Papert, S. *The children's machine: Rethinking school in the age of the computer.* New York: Basic Books, 1993.

Turkle, S. *The second self: Computers and the human spirit.* New York: Simon and Schuster, 1984.

Resources for Teachers Interested in Using LOGO

The International Society for Technology in Education (ISTE), 1787 Agate St., Eugene, OR 97403, has been helping teachers apply LOGO for years. ISTE is committed to demonstrating the cross-curricular versatility of LOGO. The following list summarizes some of its more recent products.

Flewelling, G. *Math activities using LogoWriter — High school math.* Eugene, Ore.: International Society for Technology in Education, 1994.

Flewelling, G. *Math activities using LogoWriter — Probability and statistics.* Eugene, Ore.: International Society for Technology in Education, 1994.

Logo Exchange. A periodical published four times a year by the LOGO Special Interest Group.

Yoder, S. *MicroWorlds — Hypermedia project development and Logo scripting.* Eugene, Ore.: International Society for Technology in Education, 1996.

Yoder, S., and D. Moursund. *Introduction to MicroWorlds — A Logo-based hypermedia environment.* Eugene, Ore.: International Society for Technology in Education, 1994.

Yoder, S. *Introduction to programming in Logo using LogoWriter.* 3d ed. Eugene, Ore.: International Society for Technology in Education, 1994.

Calculators

One calculator capable of the activities described here is manufactured by Texas Instruments. Contact Texas Instruments, P.O. Box 6118, Temple, TX 76501 or their World Wide Web page http://www.ti.com/calc/.

Probes

Several companies make probes educators can use in math and science instruction. Contact Vernier Software, 8565 SW Beaverton-Hillsdale Hwy., Portland, OR 97225 (WWW address http://www.teleport.com/~vernier/) or Acculab Products Group, 614 Scenic Drive, Suite 104, Modesto, CA 95350 (WWW address http://www.delta.com/star/asl/acculab.htm).

Chapter **5**

Using Tools: Word Processors, Databases, and Spreadsheets

ORIENTATION

In this chapter you will read about word processing, spreadsheet, and database applications. Tools for using the Internet have generated so much recent interest and offer so much promise we have decided to consider the use of these tools in a separate chapter. These are the most common computer tools in educational use and they play somewhat similar basic roles in influencing student behavior. Tools can increase students' productivity, help them become more active learners, and allow them to acquire knowledge and develop skills in unique ways. You will read about ways you can introduce these tools to your students and apply them in your classroom. As you read, look for answers to the following questions:

FOCUS QUESTIONS

◆ What are three different levels on which students benefit from applying tool applications in content-area tasks?
◆ Why are the capabilities of word processing applications especially well suited to teaching writing using the writing process approach?
◆ What are some classroom word processing, spreadsheet, and database activities that lead to more active processing of course content?
◆ What are the general characteristics of tool activities that increase the probability of meaningful learning?

Mark Grabe's Use of Computer Tools

You are in the office of a typical college professor. The computer on my office desk, for instance, is old and loaded with less sophisticated software than exists in most of the elementary school classrooms we describe in other parts of this book. A week for me is probably not that different from a week for many other teachers. Certain tasks, for example, are common:

◆ Preparing instructional materials for classroom presentations or for distribution to students.
◆ Preparing and scoring exams.
◆ Recording data on student performance and calculating grades.
◆ Communicating with students, colleagues, and a variety of other individuals, through several different mechanisms.
◆ Writing for many purposes.
◆ Gathering information to facilitate instruction and scholarly work.

I use my computer and one or more common tool applications in each of these activities. Surveys of teachers' use of technology reveal that teachers make the most frequent use of word processing in their own work. I'm no exception; I generate all of my written material, including overheads for classroom presentations, with a word processing program. If I do anything out of the ordinary with word processing, it would probably be including more graphics, particularly scanned images and images captured from videotape, in the documents I produce. (We'll discuss some of these techniques in later chapters.)

A second way many teachers use a computer is to record grades. There are computer programs developed specifically as gradebooks, but like many other teachers, I prefer to use a spreadsheet program to record student scores. Once mastered, a spreadsheet program is relatively easy to use, and I prefer to use one because I can adapt it to several atypical evaluation techniques I use in my classes. In the large lecture courses I teach, students are allowed to retake alternative versions of unit exams. This means that three different tests are available for each exam period, and students can decide to take one, two, or all three versions. The highest score is the score counted. The spreadsheet is useful because it offers the versatility I need to calculate final grades under these different circumstances. The description of spreadsheet applications provided later in this chapter should provide enough information for you to understand how to create your own gradebook for most straightforward grading procedures.

Databases: Generating and Improving Tests

Like most teachers, I devote a considerable amount of my time and energy to evaluating my students' performances. Because some of my classes are large, I give tests that include one essay question and many multiple-choice items. Multiple-choice items are frequently criticized for being shallow, but I feel that the often-negative emphasis on factual knowledge in such tests occurs because items of this type are the easiest to write *and* the easiest to defend when students disagree with the answer. In any case, my approach is to write a substantial proportion of questions that require students to apply knowledge gained from the textbook and classroom presentations. My development of questions is a process that takes place across semesters. When I find items that seem to work well, I keep them. When I can identify flaws in items I've used, I modify the items and try them again. The evaluation procedure I use in my courses requires me to generate a very large number of test items. A database plays a significant role in the way I generate my tests. The approach I take may or may not end up saving time, but I think it improves the quality of the testing process for my students.

Rather than generating test items immediately before each exam, I write and store items continuously. I usually spend part of the hour before each class going over the material that I'm going to present. This is usually also a good time to write a few items. I find that I can be more creative in preparing questions if I don't try to write all of the questions at once. Preparation time is also a good time to write questions because the content is fresh in my mind. Ready access to the computer makes this an efficient process. I just turn from my notes to the computer and work on a question.

I store the questions in a HyperCard database. Because database applications are designed to assist the user in storing, organizing, and retrieving large amounts of information, a collection of one thousand test items represents an almost perfect application for this tool. In creating a database, the user establishes *fields* for the different types of data to be stored. A database developed to store my test questions contains individual fields for the chapter number, the answer, and the question and several fields allowing storage of data on student performance and dates of use. After I write new items, I always sort the database on the chapter field. This process reorganizes the database so that items from each chapter appear consecutively. I use a special field to designate the individual items to be used for a particular exam. When I click on this field, the computer automatically enters a check mark. To prepare an exam, I search the database for questions related to particular chapters, select the items I want to include from each chapter by checking the selection field, and then click on the "dump test" button, shown in Figure 5.1. The database then creates one output file containing the test items I've selected and a second file containing the test key (that is, the correct answers and a unique number designating each question). The output file containing the test items is edited with a word processing program and then printed.

Once the examination has been scored, I return to the test item database, search by identification number for items administered, and enter the date I used the item and the student performance on the item. I enter the date so that I won't use the question too frequently. I may want to remember that I've already used the item in a particular semester and shouldn't use it again on the final. The proportion of students answering the question correctly gives me an indication of how difficult the question is and how well students understood the material covered by the item. Entering these data also provides an opportunity to consider the quality of the item and possibly to modify the question.

I consider a number of sources of information in modifying questions. During or after taking the tests, students may raise issues or ask questions that let me know that something about the question needs to be fixed. For example, recently I used the word *gist* in a question, and a

FIGURE 5.1 Screen Display from Test Generation Database

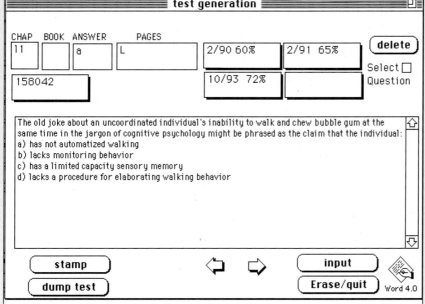

large number of students didn't know what this word meant. Students may argue that an alternate answer for a particular question should also be counted as correct because it is true in at least some cases. You've probably raised similar questions with your own instructors. Sometimes the students' logic makes me see a problem in the question that I hadn't considered before. The university test-scoring service also provides some statistical data that allow me to spot questions that seem particularly problematic. With these sources of information in mind, I can modify the database; that is, I can delete items. I can replace the word *gist* with the phrase "the main idea of the passage." And I can write new, less-ambiguous answers. Generating tests isn't an easy process under any circumstances. However, the use of a database allows a systematic and efficient approach to item collection, test production, and item improvement.

Internet Tools: Accessing People, Interactive Services, and Communicating with Students

Although Internet tools are presented in the next chapter, allow me to complete this discussion of personal tool use with a brief description of some of the ways I use the Internet. Including the Internet activities will allow a more complete description of tool applications from the perspective of a teacher.

The computer on my desk is connected directly to the campus local area network (LAN) and the Internet. From my desk, I can connect to people and services across campus and around the world. When we discuss telecommunications in the next chapter, we organize the discussion around communicating with people, interacting with remote services, and transferring resources. These three categories cover my own activities as well.

Because teaching is a highly social profession, teachers spend much of their time interacting with other people. Many of my own conversations don't take place in person. The people with whom I want to communicate may not live in my own community or may not be available when I want to tell them something. I make the same use of the telephone and traditional mail as others, but there are some serious time delays in communicating through the mail, long-distance telephone calls are expensive, and telephone calls are often frustrating because the person I want to reach may not be available when I am able to talk.

Electronic mail (e-mail) has been a valuable addition to the ways in which I can interact with others. I exchange electronic mail with my students, with administrators to whom I report, with local teachers, with colleagues around the country, with the editor of this textbook, and with my wife and coauthor. I am also on several mailing lists and receive thirty to forty messages a day from people with things to say or ask about HyperCard, ToolBook, computers in education, outdoor education, and the field of psychology. A mailing list is similar to the bulletin board in the teacher's lounge. You post a request or an idea and see if anyone responds. I respond to the mail sent directly to me, and I mostly read the mail generated by the mailing lists to keep up on topics that interest me. Electronic mail has become an integral part of the way I do my work.

I also use my office computer to access a number of remote computer services. Probably the most common application of this type involves doing literature searches. The college and university libraries in my state and the public library in my community allow a computerized search of library holdings. In other words, I can determine whether a book I want exists in a higher education library collection somewhere in the state or in my local public library. The library at my university also allows me to determine whether the book I want is on the shelf. When it is 20 degrees below zero, I only want to take the cold walk across campus if I know the book I want is there. Computerized library searches are available in many elementary and secondary schools. Students may also be able to conduct similar searches in local public libraries. Perhaps you've already made frequent use of the kind of search process described here.

Another kind of search procedure allows an even more exploratory approach to finding library resources. Most students in colleges of education have made use of the **E**ducational **R**esources **I**nformation **C**learinghouse (ERIC) services. ERIC provides a directory of published resources in the field of education. The resources include articles in education journals and other materials, such as the print version of conference presentations, which have been stored in many libraries on microfilm. You may have searched through a paper version of an ERIC directory in your own library to find references for a class assignment or, if you are a teacher, to find ideas to use in your classroom. Perhaps you are lucky, and your local library has the facilities to search the ERIC directory on CD-ROM. If you've worked with this type of technology, you've actually been working with a huge, computer-accessible database stored on compact disc. I sometimes find it most convenient to search the ERIC database by using the computer in my home or office to connect to an ERIC service on the Internet.

The Internet, which we discuss in the next chapter, is actually a network of worldwide computers. By navigating the network from my office, I can connect to an ERIC search facility located on another campus in another state. Because my library does provide ERIC on CD-ROM, I'm probably not the type of user they had in mind when ERIC services were made available through the Internet. The professionals most likely to benefit will be elementary and secondary school teachers and administrators with the necessary skills and the opportunity to use the Internet. Access to educational resources isn't always convenient for school personnel, and the opportunity to access ERIC or other sources of information from a computer in their schools seems a very useful service.

Gaining awareness and understanding about using tools

We hope these descriptions of how Mark Grabe uses computers in his teaching have begun to show you just how helpful computer tools can be. As you continue, you will learn more about the various computer tools we have just described. You will acquire a greater awareness of how you and your students might apply these tools and gain a basic understanding of how the tools are used. We cannot take total responsibility for teaching you how to use computer tools; there is just too much variability in the hardware and software you might encounter. Your instructor will be able to provide more specific information and may, we hope, provide you with some hands-on experiences. We hope we can get you excited about the potential of these applications and start you thinking about classroom uses.

Computer can function as many different tools

A *tool,* by definition, is an object that allows the user to perform tasks with greater efficiency or quality. For example, a calculator allows a student to add a series of numbers more quickly and accurately than the student could add them with pencil and paper. The computer, in combination with different kinds of application software, can function as many different tools. The tool functions performed by the computer can improve the efficiency and quality with which the user manipulates information — much as the calculator does. Nearly everyone has some occasion to manipulate information every day. Certainly, teachers and students are heavily involved with information and could benefit from tools that improve the efficiency or quality of their work. This chapter and the next will familiarize you with some of the basic computer tools that teachers and students might find useful. The specific computer tools we will consider in this chapter include word processing programs, spreadsheets, and databases. Other computer applications, such as graphics programs and computer tools used to explore and communicate using the Internet, also meet the general definition of a computer tool, but you will encounter these applications in later chapters. We want you to understand the type of tasks computer tools allow the user to perform and to gain some insights into what the user does as he or she works with each type of tool.

Ways computer tools may benefit students

As you learn about computer tools, consider that working with them may benefit students on several levels (Perkins, 1985). As you have already seen, tools can help the user work more efficiently and effectively. In part, students learn to use computer tools because tools can help them perform school work (such as writing papers) more effectively or perhaps provide them with valuable occupational skills. These skills are part of what constitutes computer literacy. There is the potential for more, though. Computer tools in content-area instruction may allow students to acquire knowledge and develop skills in unique and powerful ways. It appears that educational experiences with computer tools result in students' (1) learning to use the computer tools; (2) performing certain academic tasks more effectively and efficiently because of the tools; and (3) learning domain skills such as writing and problem solving or acquiring content-area knowledge through the application of computer tools to content-appropriate tasks. Others have noted and are attempting to help teachers make these same distinctions. Sometimes new descriptive terms can help bring new insights. For example, the functions we have just listed have also been described as *technology as tool* and *technology as intellectual partner* or **mindtool** (Jonassen, 1995). The notion that ordinary computer tools can be more than a means to boost efficiency is an intriguing possibility.

Results of educational experiences with computer tools

Technology as mindtool

In the material that follows, we will consider all of the levels on which tool use might be beneficial. However, we continually emphasize that student mastery of how the computer can be used to perform basic tasks is not enough. We need to find ways to allow students to apply the skills they acquire and, we hope, to apply these skills in a variety of meaningful circumstances. As you encounter each computer tool in the presentations that follow, think carefully about potential applications of the tool in your area of interest and about the several levels on which students might benefit from experience with that tool.

The broader role computers can play

WORD PROCESSING

Word processing, an application allowing the entry, manipulation, and storage of text, is the single most popular use of computer technology in schools, for several reasons (Becker, 1993). First, word processing is the most widely used computer application in the work and home environments, and educators are sensitive to the development of skills valued in these settings. Second, writing is one of the fundamental skills taught in schools. Features of word processing programs may help students write more effectively and develop writing skills more quickly. Third, writing is a skill that may contribute to the generation and integration of personal knowledge in nearly all content areas. Writing forces students to externalize what they know as they attempt to put ideas on paper (or in this case on the computer screen) and requires an active use of knowledge. Remember from your reading of Chapter 2 that the active processing of information increases the likelihood of meaningful learning.

The most widely used computer application

Data about word processing use

Surprisingly, although many students are exposed to word processing in school, the extent to which they *use* word processing is disappointing. Students are often introduced to computer applications, but then are not engaged in relevant tasks or provided the opportunities to use their skills (Becker, 1993). Sadly, word processing may be one of the best examples of learning *about* the computer and what it can do instead of actually learning *with* the computer. Once you get past English teachers, who run classes that fall into the frequent use category 45 percent of the time, use of word processing drops off quickly. Only 11 percent of science teachers and 4 percent of math teachers had their students use word processing programs on a frequent basis. This situation may exist because schools do not have enough computer equipment and students have difficulty gaining immediate access to the technology that is available (see Emerging Technology: Inexpensive "Keyboard" Computers). However, it is clear that access is not the only issue. Teachers can increase the use of writing as a learning activity and can expect that this writing be accomplished using word processing applications. Because opportunities for writing exist in all content areas and because the necessary hardware and software for word processing are now more likely to be available, educators have a real opportunity to expand computer use in this area.

A
C
T
I NTEGRATED
V ERSATILE
E

CHARACTERISTICS OF WORD PROCESSING PROGRAMS

Basic functions of word processing

Most word processing programs, even those designed for younger students, allow users to accomplish nearly the same set of basic functions. These functions can be described as text input, storage and retrieval, formatting, editing, and printing. Because many word processing programs also allow the integration of graphics, the storage and retrieval, formatting, editing, and printing functions potentially apply to the combination of text and graphics created by the user.

Text Input

Word wrap

Word processing programs have some special features that optimize a writer's ability to input text from the keyboard. One feature that most computer users take for granted is word wrap. When working on a typewriter, writers have to pay attention to how close they are coming to the end of a line and decide when to press return to move to the beginning of the next line. With **word wrap**, the computer automatically moves to the beginning of the next line when the word being entered would extend beyond the right margin. Similarly, the computer program also breaks to the next page when the specified number of lines has been entered. Word processing programs also allow writers to insert a forced page break at any time.

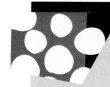

Activities and Projects for Your Classroom

Word Processing Activities for All Grade Levels

Word processing software can be used even with students in the *primary grades*. Young children can write stories with software that defaults to a large-size font and prints out on primary-style paper. This software still allows for the complete editing features of deleting, cutting, copying, and pasting. Young children can:

Write stories using predictable patterns ("The House That Jack Built").

Create alphabet books (the ABCs of space, winter ABCs).

Keep a daily journal.

Create lists of factual information from reference books and write reports with this information.

Create a class book, with one page of personal information for each child.

Create content-area class books, such as "Animals Where I Live" or "People in My Community."

In the *intermediate grades,* students can extend the word processing activities they started in the primary grades. They can:

Write and revise factual reports using cut and paste and spell checking.

Create journal entries using the "insert date" feature.

Use the thesaurus to expand vocabulary and eliminate redundancies.

Write collaborative stories.

Create cooperative reports, with each member of the group responsible for a different topic. Cut and paste to organize the report.

Write poetry and publish it using center alignment or acrostic poems using a larger-size font for the first letter of each line.

Write creative stories using different font styles to express emotions such as fear or shyness.

Publish historical newspapers.

Middle school and *high school* students can:

Write scientific reports that include tables and graphs.

Use outlining features to organize reports.

Create questionnaires using tab set fills to draw the lines for answers (tab fills draw a solid or dotted line to the next tab that has been set).

Create lists of information using the columnizing feature to align the list entries.

Publish newsletters with columns and clip art.
✳

Storage and Retrieval

Saving a copy to disk

Storage and retrieval involve the processes of saving a copy of the document to disk and loading a saved document from the disk back into the computer memory. These processes allow work done with a word processor to be extended over time. They have special significance for students learning to write with a word processor, because students can submit documents for evaluation and then rework them in response to the comments of peers or their teacher. Storage and retrieval of the original document allows the student to spend time addressing the specific areas of difficulty noted in the comments rather than wasting time regenerating parts of the document that didn't require additional attention.

Formatting

The physical appearance of a document

Formatting concerns the physical appearance of the document created with a word processor. Writers may apply formatting features at the level of the character, the paragraph, or the entire document.

The character level

At the character level, word processing programs usually allow the user to control font, style, and size. The **font** refers to the design of the character. All characters from the same font share certain design features. For example, this is Geneva, this is Palatino, this is New York, and this is Times. Font **style** alters a particular font in terms of slant or thickness. This is **bold** and this is *italic*. Underlining is also included as a style. Characters can also be displayed in a variety of sizes. A writer might want to control character formatting for several reasons. Think for a second about the material you read and how character style is used. The daily newspaper uses large bold type for headlines and story titles. Textbooks use bold print, italicized type, and underlining to bring readers' attention to particular words or phrases. Text written with some variability in character appearance is more interesting and thus allows the author additional mechanisms for communication.

The paragraph level

At the paragraph level, formatting typically allows setting tabs and margins, text justification, and line spacing. **Tabs**, **margins**, and text **justification** control the alignment of text on the screen and the printed page. A few formatting features apply to the entire document. For example, some word processors allow the user to designate how many columns of text will appear on a page. Teachers or students creating newsletters may find this feature useful.

Integrating Graphics

Pictures, diagrams, and charts

Some word processors allow the integration of text and graphics, such as pictures, diagrams, and charts. Positioning graphics within text presents a somewhat different set of issues than those applying specifically to text. Graphics give inexperienced computer users some challenges they may not anticipate. For example, once inserted, does the graphic remain at a fixed position on the page as new text is inserted above the graphic, or does the illustration slide down the page with the rest of the text? Does a particular word processing program allow text to flow around all sides of a graphic; can the graphic appear in the middle of a page, with text to the left and right? Some programs, particularly older ones, allow graphics to be included but do not allow text to flow around them. Newer programs differ drastically in the ease with which they can incorporate graphics.

Why the concern over such features as fonts, styles, printing multiple columns on a page, and manipulating the position of graphics within text? One initial reaction might be that such features are frills having little to do with the message of the text or the educational benefits of creating the text. But a very different perspective is possible.

The role of purpose and motivation

Consider the importance of purpose and motivation in effective writing and in learning to write. Writers need to be engaged in tasks in which they have authentic opportunities to communicate what they know, want, or feel. Appearance can influence perceptions of authentic authoring and perceptions of importance. The value to young writers of creating a book that really looks like a book or a newspaper that really looks like a newspaper should not be underestimated.

Editing

Editing involves modifying text at any time after it has been generated. Many mistakes are noticed and modified immediately; most writers composing at the computer will notice and correct typing errors as they appear on the computer screen or will immediately attempt to improve a sentence that does not sound quite right. Other changes occur much later in the writing process. Some methods of writing instruction require students to have their papers critiqued by the teacher or other students before they write a "final draft." In this case, the original material would likely be loaded from disk and reworked in response to the comments generated by the original draft.

Standard editing features

There are some standard editing features in nearly all word processing programs. These features include the character-level functions of **insert** and delete and the block operations of delete, cut, copy, and paste. A change in the existing format of a block of text (for example, making plain text bold) might also be considered editing. Once a body of text has been generated, it is possible to move the cursor within this existing text using the arrow keys on the keyboard or a mouse attached to the computer. The **cursor** is a highly visible indicator (it often blinks) that marks the point on the screen where any designated action will be implemented. If the writer enters new text from the keyboard, the position of the cursor marks the location at which the new input will be inserted. If the writer presses the backspace key, the letter or space to the left of the cursor will be erased. Since one character is added or removed with each key press, these changes represent editing at the character level.

Character-level editing

Block editing

Block editing involves making a change to a designated segment of text. The first step in block editing is to **select**, or mark, the segment of text to which the change will apply. Again, how the segment of text is selected will vary with the word processor program and the computer. If the computer allows it, one of the easiest approaches is to use a mouse to drag the cursor across the text to be modified. This process selects the text for further action and usually highlights the selected text. Once a block of text has been selected, the writer can execute such commands as delete, cut, paste, or copy. The

delete function erases the selected text. The **cut** function removes the selected text and stores it temporarily in the computer's memory for insertion at a different location. The process of moving the text from the computer's memory back to the screen at a point designated by the cursor is called **pasting**. The **copy** function temporarily stores the selected text in the computer's memory but differs from the cut command in not removing the text from its original location. Text copied to memory can also be pasted. Writers can use block editing to make major changes in a document; it is particularly useful to reorganize larger documents or to move segments of text from one document to another.

Special Tools

Tools to improve a writer's effectiveness

Word processing programs often come equipped with special tools to improve the writer's effectiveness. The most common tools include an outliner, a spell checker, and a thesaurus.

Most students are familiar with outlining. Incorporating an outlining tool in a word processing program allows the writer to plan the structure of his or her document. Often, the outline entries become headings within the actual document, and the writer can move back and forth between the outline view and the extended text as an aid to organizing a major project. This capability helps the writer to escape the detail level and regain a sense of the overall purpose and structure of the document.

Spell checkers

Spell checkers check text for spelling errors. Most spell checkers are menu driven and will attempt to offer suggestions for the word the writer may have intended. They have shortcomings, however. Unique terminology and proper names are initially reported as spelling errors. Spell checking a list of references is difficult because the spell checker will find an "error" in nearly every line (authors' names are reported as spelling errors). Words that a writer knows are correct can be added to the dictionary to make the spell checker more efficient over time. But spell checkers also cannot detect typing errors that result in a different valid word (*then* instead of *the,* for example), so writers must always proofread their work. Spell checkers have some instructional value in that they point out words that are consistently misspelled. The awareness that you often misspell a certain word — a form of metacognition — can help you learn to spell the word correctly or prompt you to look it up.

An electronic thesaurus

An electronic thesaurus allows a writer to generate a list of words with roughly equivalent meanings. This list allows the writer to find a word with just the right shade of meaning for a specific situation or to search for a different word when the writer feels he or she has been using a particular word too frequently. For example, we considered the word *nuance* for the previous sentence, but the word seemed just a bit too formal. The thesaurus recommended eight other words and phrases as potential equivalents, and *nuance* became *shade of meaning.*

WRITERS, WRITING, AND WORD PROCESSING

Writing has sometimes been regarded as a mysterious craft practiced by unusual characters with special talents. Some common educational expectations about word processing seem to leave these myths intact (Pea and Kurland, 1987). Many people assume that writing with a word processing program will lead to better products and that making frequent use of word processing while learning to write will produce better writers. Perhaps this powerful machine can somehow magically transform all of us into competent authors.

Will word processing make better writers?

In learning, as in other areas of life, you seldom get something for nothing. Still, a logical case has been proposed for how simply working with word processing for an extended period may improve writing skills and performance. Perkins (1985) calls this the "opportunities get taken" hypothesis. The proposal works like this. Writing by hand has a number of built-in limitations. Generating text this way is slow, and modifying what has been written comes at a substantial price. To produce a second or third draft with a pencil or typewriter requires the writer to spend a good deal of time reproducing text that was fine the first time, just to change a few things that might sound better if modified. Word processing, on the other hand, allows writers to revise at minimal cost. They can pursue an idea to see where it takes them and worry about fixing syntax and spelling later. Reworking documents from the level of fixing misspelled words to reordering the arguments in the entire presentation can be accomplished without crumpling up what has just been painstakingly written and starting over.

The "opportunities get taken" hypothesis

With word processing, writers can take risks and push their skills without worrying that they are wasting their time. The capacity to save and load text

---

Focus

Learning Word Processing Features

Many word processing features can be introduced as needed. The teacher can demonstrate each new feature within the context of a learning activity that will take advantage of that feature. Teachers can also:

Create "how-to" posters that can be posted by the computer or small "how to" cards that can be kept by the computer in an empty disk box.

Create text files purposely written to allow students to

◆ Edit paragraphs with punctuation and capitalization errors.
◆ Delete unnecessary information.
◆ Sequence the events of a story or a set of directions using cut and paste.
◆ Use the thesaurus to find alternatives for underlined words.
◆ Add charts and graphs.
◆ Move and resize clip art. ✳

Revising drafts easily

from disk makes it possible to revise earlier drafts with minimal effort. Writers can set aside what they have written to gain new perspective, show friends a draft and ask for advice, or discuss an idea with the teacher after class, and use these experiences to improve what they wrote yesterday or last week. What we have described here are opportunities — opportunities to produce a better paper for tomorrow's class and, over time, opportunities to learn to communicate more effectively.

Better products?

Do writers take the opportunities provided by word processing programs? Do writers produce better products when using word processing programs? The research evaluating the benefits of word processing (Bangert-Drowns, 1993; Cochran-Smith, 1991; Perkins, 1985) is not easy to interpret. Much seems to depend on the experience of the writer as a writer and computer user and on what is meant by "a better product." If the questions refer to younger students, it also seems to depend on the instructional strategies to which the students have been exposed. General summaries of the research literature (Bangert-Drowns, 1993) seem to indicate that students make more revisions, write longer documents, and produce documents containing fewer errors when word processing. However, the spelling, syntactical, and grammatical errors that students tend to address and the revision activities necessary to correct them are considered less important by many interested in effective writing than changes improving document content or document organization. Many writers bring their writing goals and old habits to the new medium. They revise in ways they already know to fix errors they are aware of. Beginning writers may thus not have the orientation or capabilities to utilize the full potential of word processing, and their classroom instruction may also emphasize the correction of more obvious surface errors. Thus, there are differences in the products generated when working with word processing tools, but the areas in which younger writers seem to improve are not regarded by many as involving some of the most important characteristics of effective communication: content, clarity, and organization.

Many of the potential educational advantages of word processing will appear only as students acquire considerable experience writing with the aid of technology. Perkins's (1985) argument that writing with word processing programs will improve writing skills because word processing allows students to experiment with their writing makes sense only in situations in which students have written a great deal and experimented with expressing themselves in different ways. The fact that most research evaluating the benefits of word processing has examined performance over a short period of time, with students having limited word processing experience, thus represents a poor test of the potential of word processing (Owston, Murphy, and Wideman, 1992).

The importance of how teachers and students apply technology

The role of word processing in developing writing skills depends on different factors: the goals of the teacher and individual students, the social context provided for writing, and the amount of writing students do with the assistance of word processing. Certain combinations of these factors appear to allow word processing to have a more profound impact on the development of writing skills (Cochran-Smith, 1991; Cochran-Smith, Paris, and Kahn, 1991; Owston, Murphy, and Wideman, 1992; Snyder, 1993).

THE WRITING PROCESS APPROACH

The stages of the writing process

Features of word processing are particularly well suited to what is often called the **writing process approach**, which includes the stages of planning, drafting, editing/revising, and publishing (Graves, 1983). Process models are constructivist in orientation (see Chapter 2, pages 60 through 66), and the components involved in the composing process emphasize that the writer's tasks are to create and communicate meaning. The development of composition skills within this orientation often involves collaboration, and writers frequently receive help and feedback from classmates and their teacher during all of the stages. The purpose of feedback is to improve performance. Feedback is given during the stages of composition to help writers improve their work rather than at the conclusion of a writing assignment as a summary evaluation. Students are expected to revise, and they learn to critique their own work and the work of others. The publication step implies that student compositions are authentic products prepared to entertain or inform a real audience. The process approach is often described as operating within a writing community in which students write, rewrite, read what others have written, and discuss the activities of writing (Montague, 1990).

Collaboration

A CTIVE
C OOPERATION
T HEME-BASED
I NTEGRATED
V ERSATILE
E VALUATION

Word processing and editing/revising

Word processing fits with the writing process approach in a number of ways. The most obvious application involves editing/revision. The recursive nature of process writing — that is, the expectation that ideas will be generated, written, considered, and rewritten several times — is ideally implemented within a system that allows written products to be saved, retrieved, and modified efficiently. Specific strategies for process writing encourage writers to do things like put what they have written aside for a day and then reread and revise it the next day; exchange papers with a writing partner and request ideas for improvement; or discuss what they have written and what they are trying to say with a teacher, to generate some new ideas for improving their papers. These activities are likely to be perceived more positively if the revisions they lead to can be implemented efficiently.

Word processing and other stages of the writing process

Word processing can also contribute to the other writing process stages. For example, a variety of word processing activities can contribute to the planning phase. Students can develop an initial structure using the outlining tool available in many word processing programs. Pon (1988) proposes a variety of brainstorming techniques that take advantage of technology. With a single classroom computer, the teacher can request story ideas from students and record them in a single file. This list of ideas can be printed and distributed to all students. The teacher can generate a list of key questions that might help a student come up with ideas for a project. For a paper on friendship, students might be asked to list five qualities of a good friend, briefly describe their good friends (without providing names) and why they like them, and describe how they try to be a friend to others. These tasks could be saved in a file for each student, and each student could be asked to respond individually to the questions. Responses could be discussed in class before students go on to write about friendship.

The publishing stage

The publishing stage is also important if classroom tasks are to be perceived as authentic. Younger children need to see their work displayed on the bulletin board or in the halls. They see their stories as more meaningful when they are compiled into a classroom book that students take home and read to parents. Older students can publish their work in school papers or occasionally send it to local newspapers. Students' informative writing or opinion papers can become required reading in subsequent classes covering similar topics.

Benefits of an authentic audience

The World Wide Web is also becoming a way for students to present their work (see Focus: Publication on the Internet). Having an authentic audience has some positive benefits. Material written to be communicated to peers through telecommunications has been found to be better organized, mechanically more correct, and more informative than papers on identical topics written to be graded by the teacher (Cohen & Riel, 1989). Having a peer

New products have emerged as alternatives to traditional computers. The eMate was designed to be a rugged and inexpensive product students can use in a wide variety of educational settings. *(courtesy of Apple Computer, Inc.)*

audience seems to be more motivating than the red marks, gold stars, or grade the teacher might attach to the paper.

KEYBOARDING

A long-term controversy

One of the long-term controversies over computer use at the elementary school level concerns whether or not precious computer time should be devoted to the development of keyboarding skills. Those who favor making keyboarding part of the curriculum make two points. First, students must achieve some level of typing proficiency before writing at the computer can really be very effective. Second, encouraging students to write at a computer without adequate training allows them to develop bad habits. These bad habits will be more difficult to overcome when students do attempt to develop typing skills. The opposition in this dispute is not really against the development of typing skills, but against holding off access to writing on the computer until students achieve keyboarding proficiency. With the number of computers and the time each student can spend working at the computer

Focus

Publication on the Internet

The World Wide Web (see Chapter 6 for an extended discussion) provides a number of opportunities for student publication. The more formal outlets operate much like print publications. Potential authors submit manuscripts for consideration; these submissions are reviewed by an editorial board. For example, *MidLink* publishes the work of 10- to 15-year-old students four times a year. Each edition has an announced theme and published material is kept on-line for one year. The decision to include a particular manuscript is made by a student review board with teacher supervision. *KidNews,* set up as a wire service, takes a different and unique approach. Students are invited to submit news articles and to use the articles submitted by other students in local publications. Any article used is expected to be accompanied by proper credits to author and source.

Be forewarned: sites of this type seem to frequently change host machines and may cease to exist as the individuals responsible no longer have the time to maintain them. Sites that change locations can usually be found by searching the World Wide Web for the site name (e.g., KidNews).

The addresses for several student publication sites are provided at the end of this chapter. Contacting one of these sites is also a good way to learn about other opportunities for student publication.

There are other opportunities for publication on the Web that are much more immediate and less formal. Many schools sponsor their own Web sites and provide individuals, classes, and student organizations opportunities for publication. ✳

each day so limited, some educators question whether allocating time to developing keyboarding proficiency makes sense. There may not be enough time to really develop skill, and time might be more productively spent on other activities.

How much training does a student need to become an adequate typist? The answer depends to some extent on what level of proficiency is considered adequate. Students in the upper elementary school grades write with a pencil at a rate of about ten words per minute (Wetzel, 1990). Without keyboard training, upper elementary school students will write at the keyboard at about

Emerging Technology

Inexpensive "Keyboard" Computers

Immediate and unlimited access to computers is a distant goal for most schools. There simply is not enough equipment to allow every student to use a computer any time a computer might be useful. Several companies have recognized this reality and have developed simple computers that can take over some of the demand for computer time. The products look very much like the keyboard of a traditional computer and are designed to perform limited word processing applications. Positioned above the keys is a simple liquid crystal display (LCD) panel capable of presenting eight lines of eighty characters of text each (some models present four lines of forty characters). Again, depending on the model, present versions of these machines can store up to eight text documents, a total of sixty-four pages. Simple editing is possible in all machines and some are capable of underlining and bolding. Some also include a built-in dictionary and thesaurus. All connect to a computer so stored text can be uploaded for storage, editing, and printing. The machines are much lighter than notebook computers, have a much longer battery life (up to 100 hours), and are quieter. And the most important feature: the least ex-

pensive of these machines, when purchased in bulk, costs approximately $200.

Naturally, the companies producing the machines recommend that schools purchase them in quantity. One company offers a package deal including a special security cabinet for storing and recharging forty machines. This storage area is positioned beneath the work space for a full-function computer and printer. This one piece of furniture can be rolled from classroom to classroom as needed and provides an instantaneous word processing lab.

The advantage of such equipment is that activities such as keyboarding or the early phases of writing can become much more familiar without monopolizing the computer lab or classroom computers. In addition, the size and cost of these machines makes them more transportable. Students can carry them to the library or to the laboratory to take notes, or even take them home because the risk of damage or loss doesn't carry the same financial burden as a regular computer. The companies claim these products are extremely easy to use and thus less threatening to technophobes.

Information on two of these products, AlphaSmart Pro and DreamWriter, is included at the end of this chapter. ✳

Spotlight on Assessment

Electronic Portfolios

A *portfolio* is a systematic and selective collection of student work that has been accumulated to demonstrate the student's motivation, academic growth, and level of achievement. Portfolio assessment is most commonly used in classes in which much of the work takes the form of written or artistic products, but depending on the content area, portfolios can also contain video or audio tapes, computer programs, science laboratory reports, and virtually any other product that can serve to demonstrate learning. To understand what a portfolio is, imagine a file folder for each student containing carefully selected work samples, the student's comments about these products, and various types of evaluation data contributed by the student, peers, and the teacher. What you have imagined is probably a collection consisting entirely of sheets of paper: written documents and reports, drawings, evaluation forms, and summary evaluation reports. This is a good starting place. Now extend this understanding to a broader set of materials: products generated with technology can also be incorporated in a portfolio.

Suggestions for Creating and Using Portfolios

◆ The development of a portfolio should be a joint activity between teacher and student. Teachers might suggest certain categories such as "the piece I am most proud of," "something I had to really struggle to learn," "my attempt to do something very different," and so on. Teachers should also require that certain standard items — for example, the major paper for the course, be included.

◆ Students should be encouraged to think carefully about the process and purpose of portfolio construction. For each item, students might be asked to write a brief explanation of why the item was selected, what was to be learned from the task, and the student's assessment of his or her success in meeting task objectives.

◆ Portfolios should allow the teacher and student to evaluate the whole learning process. For example, the portfolio should contain preparatory materials (notes), early drafts or works-in-progress, and the final product. The collection of similar examples over time also allows student progress to be assessed.

◆ With the students' permission, keep sample portfolios that other students can use for ideas for their own collections.

◆ Attach evaluation instruments, such as checklists and rating scales, to individual items in the portfolio. Periodically enter comments summarizing across portfolio contents to evaluate student progress.

(Paulson, Paulson, and Meyer, 1991; Porter & Cleland, 1995; Tierney, Carter, and Desai, 1991).

Portfolios and Technology

Certain applications of technology and portfolio assessment are ideally suited to each other. Products generated with technology, ranging from word processing documents to major student-created multimedia projects, can be components of a portfolio. As you think about the previous section on the writing process, consider how easy it would be to collect and compare multiple drafts a student has generated. Students might be asked to reexamine these drafts and comment on how they worked to create a better final product.

Technology supports the practice of

portfolio assessment in another way. Products are available to assist teachers and students in creating, organizing, and evaluating portfolios (Barrett, 1994). Some of these products are essentially electronic portfolios. Student work samples (text, scanned images of writing samples and artwork, audio generated from oral reading) are stored and then evaluated using one of several existing modifiable checklists.

Comments can also be attached to work samples by students, teachers, and even parents. At present, commercial products of this type have focused on the early grades. However, some of the same ideas can be applied to all grade levels using existing multimedia tools (see Chapter 8) and other forms of technology, such as videotape (Barrett, 1994). ✳

half the rate they can achieve with a pencil. To equal the proficiency elementary students are able to achieve with a pencil requires approximately twenty to thirty hours of keyboard training. After that, students must use their typing skills regularly, or they will regress to an unacceptable level of proficiency. Given what you know about the number of students in a typical classroom, the number of computers available, and the length of the elementary school day, you can see what a challenge this requirement represents. Teachers would have to devote a large proportion of the time actually spent on computers to keyboarding instruction in order to make students proficient typists. Exposure to keyboarding software without close monitoring by the teacher and without teacher understanding of proper technique also is not likely to produce competent typists (Balajthy, 1988). Cochran-Smith, Paris and Kahn (1991) give a more optimistic view. They contend that two to three twenty- to thirty-minute sessions will be sufficient to get elementary school students familiar with the keyboard and basic computer functions (insertion, deletion, block moves) and into writing. They do recommend a more intensive style of adult-student interaction, called coaching, during writing time.

Resolving this dispute with the present level of resources may not be possible. The development of keyboarding proficiency and the application of computers in content-area instruction represent different values, and student use of technology will require value-based decisions about how computers should be used.

SPREADSHEETS

Spreadsheets are a common computer application and an important reason for the microcomputer's rapid growth in popularity. **Spreadsheets** provide a convenient way to store and manipulate numerical data and have long been useful to businesspeople. A spreadsheet allows an accountant or a small business owner to organize numerical information, to perform calculations on

*Storing and
manipulating numerical
data*

*Numerical data in
context areas*

A
C
T
I NTEGRATED
V ERSATILE
E

*Numerical data and
grading*

these data, to display the results of these calculations in informative ways (charts or graphs), and even to ask hypothetical questions about the data, such as what would happen to total profits if three more cents were charged per unit.

The processing and interpretation of numerical data are more meaningful in some content areas than in others. Teachers and students recognize that manipulating numbers is part of mathematics. However, storing and interpreting numerical data and asking questions related to those data are also essential to political science, sociology, economics, geology, chemistry, physics, and biology. Consider the following diverse set of questions. What total electoral vote would have resulted if a particular presidential candidate had received 5 percent more votes in a specific block of southern states? How much would a 200-pound man weigh if he were transported to each of the other known planets? Is it colder in November in Fargo, North Dakota, or in Juneau, Alaska?

Teachers manipulate numerical data as part of their work, too. Consider, for example, the tasks of assigning grades and the amount of time that goes into the calculations associated with complex grading schemes. Teachers often come up with complicated methods for combining scores from several sources. For instance, a teacher might decide to base the course grade on a combination of homework assignments, two projects, three tests, and a final. Individual homework assignments might contribute different point totals determined by the amount of work required to complete the assignment. Students will be allowed to drop the lowest of their three unit test scores. Daily assignments, projects, unit tests, and the final examination might then be weighted equally in determining the final grade. A spreadsheet provides a convenient tool for performing these kinds of calculations.

Consider a very different situation of interest to teachers. Teachers and the school board are negotiating over next year's salaries. The board has suggested a $100 adjustment to the base salary and a 2.5 percent cost of living raise. The negotiating team for the teachers counters with a proposed 5 percent cost of living raise. What would each plan cost the district in total salary? This comparison would require the consideration of the existing salaries of all present employees. How would a new teacher and a teacher presently making $28,000 be affected by the two proposals?

A spreadsheet (Figure 5.2) is a grid of columns (designated by letters) and rows (designated by numbers). The intersection of a column and a row is a **cell** (designated by a letter and number, such as A2). The spreadsheet user can do two very different things with any cell. The first is to place a data item in the cell. Although titles and labels can be entered in cells to make it possible to interpret the spreadsheet, numbers are the most frequently entered data in cells. Each cell contains one number. A cell entry may also be the product of a formula. The attachment of a formula is the second action that can be applied to any cell. The formula defines what will be entered in a cell and how the data

FIGURE 5.2 Screen Showing Blank Spreadsheet

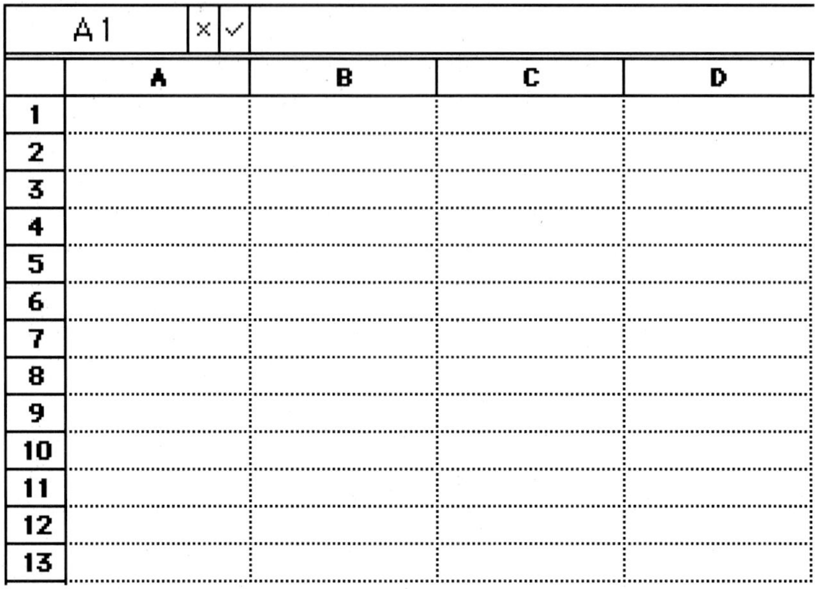

A1	✕ ✓			
	A	**B**	**C**	**D**
1				
2				
3				
4				
5				
6				
7				
8				
9				
10				
11				
12				
13				

to be entered will be generated. Here is an example. The simple formula =C2+C3 defines the cell to which the formula is attached as containing the sum of the values from two other cells (C2 and C3).

Conventions built into spreadsheets and stored functions allow some very complex operations to be expressed very simply. For instance, the expression =average(C2..C200) will generate the average of all the numbers contained in cells C2 through C200 (C2, C3, C4, . . . C200) and place the result in the cell to which the expression has been attached. This simple expression combines the convention for identifying all of the values within a range of consecutive values and the stored function for calculating an average.

Helpful conventions

The functions that can be pasted into a cell allow students to perform a wide variety of calculations or manipulations. Some functions perform statistical calculations, such as the average or standard deviation. Other functions provide mathematical information familiar to secondary school math students, such as the logarithm of a number to base 10 or the tangent of an angle. Some functions perform operations generating data that at first seem to have little practical value, but do seem to appeal to students' curiosity. One such function allows the calculation of the exact number of days between any two dates. The spreadsheet program assigns a unique number to each day. The difference between serial numbers, the number for today minus the number for the date on which you were born, would indicate the number of days you have lived. One of us — Mark — used this function to discover that he was exactly 17,598 days old. There are undoubtedly some very practical business applications for functions like this, but sometimes it's fun (and informative) just to play. (I wonder how many days old I'll be on the first day of the year 2000?)

COMPARING WINTER TEMPERATURES: A SPREADSHEET PROJECT

Let's work through a quick classroom example to see how a spreadsheet works. Assume that a seventh grade class has decided to compare the winter temperatures in various cities. The data here happen to be from cities in North Dakota and Alaska. For a class project, it is easy to examine data from many more cities — perhaps a city selected by each student in the class or a city from each state. (One method for obtaining these data is described in Chapter 6, page 216.)

Each day, at approximately the same time, students record the temperatures from the cities of interest. Entering these values in a spreadsheet is simple. A student selects the desired cell of the spreadsheet by clicking with the mouse or designating it with the arrow keys and enters the value. The same process is used to assign labels to the rows (the dates) and columns (city names). Students can attach a formula to a cell in a similar manner. In this example, the intent is to calculate the average temperature for each city. In the particular software program used for this example (ClarisWorks spreadsheet), the = sign designates a formula. A cell entry beginning with the = sign is automatically understood by the spreadsheet program to be a formula and not data. The easiest way to calculate the average temperature for Juneau is to attach the formula =average(C3..C11) to cell C12 (see Figure 5.3). As soon as the return or tab key is pressed to indicate that the formula has been entered, the result of the calculations appears in the designated cell.

FIGURE 5.3 Spreadsheet Example: Average Temperatures

E15	x ✓					
	A	**B**	**C**	**D**	**E**	**F**
1						
2			Juneau	Anchorage	Bismarck	Fargo
3		11/20	15	2	37	41
4		11/21	15	12	18	20
5		11/22	18	35	9	16
6		11/23	30	33	3	21
7		11/24	30	29	9	17
8		11/25	30	22	10	27
9		11/26	31	14	19	28
10		11/27	30	21	20	11
11		11/28	33	13	33	33
12			25.77777777	20.111111111	17.55555555	23.77777777
13						
14						

One very powerful feature of spreadsheets is that formulas are automatically adjusted when applied to different cells. For example, assume that it is decided to add the temperature for November 29 to this spreadsheet. The insert command allows a new row of data after row 11, and the average is now automatically calculated for rows 2 through 12, instead of 2 through 11. The formula developed to determine the average temperature for Juneau can also be copied and pasted to cell D12, and it now generates the average temperature for Anchorage. When copied to cell D12, the variables C2..C11 in the formula are automatically changed to the variables D2..D11 to produce the correct result. The capacity of a spreadsheet to make this kind of adjustment may not seem like a big deal in this example, but consider the benefits if the example contained fifty cities and students wanted to compare average temperatures as new data were added each day for a month. Instead of entering fifty formulas each day, one formula could be entered one time and quickly copied to the columns for the other forty-nine cities, and the formulas would adjust as the rows of data for each new day were added.

Most spreadsheet programs also allow numerical data to be represented in a variety of chart and graph formats (line graphs, pie charts, bar graphs), as in Figure 5.4. The opportunity to visualize numerical data may provide a useful perspective when students try to interpret the data. Students may also use the charts and graphs generated with a spreadsheet program in reports summarizing their research and analyses.

Working with charts and graphs provides opportunities for students to learn to interpret them. Since newspapers, magazines, and all types of educational materials communicate important data using charts and graphs, learning to interpret and critique them is an important educational objective.

CLASSROOM APPLICATIONS OF SPREADSHEET PROGRAMS

Spreadsheet applications could certainly be used more frequently in classrooms. Becker (1993) reports that only 1 percent of middle and high school computer-using math teachers had students use spreadsheets more than five times during the previous year. Because of the frequency with which spreadsheets are used and the roles they have played in the classroom, spreadsheet applications have received very little attention from researchers. Since evaluation data are not available, suggestions for how students might most productively use spreadsheets must be based on common sense and on general principles advocating that students play a more active role in their own learning. This situation does not mean that interested teachers will have difficulty locating ideas for how they might use spreadsheets themselves or with their students. Journals for teachers, such as *Learning and Leading with Technology*, carry articles providing exemplary projects teachers might adapt for their own classrooms. Books focused on popular tool software programs are often

FIGURE 5.4 Bar Graph Summarizing Average November Temperatures

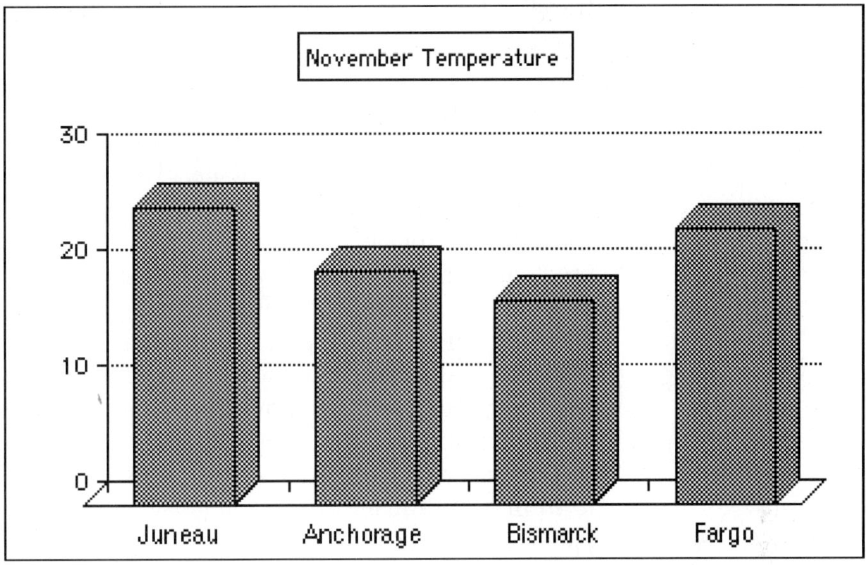

November Temperature

Juneau   Anchorage   Bismarck   Fargo

written for teachers and students to provide lesson plans and suggested activities (Rathje, 1996; Robinette, 1996). Often these books come with a disk of sample files. Such resources provide step-by-step instructions for such activities as creating a gradebook, studying the life of bubbles created with different solutions of corn syrup and water, and analyzing lunchroom litter.

DATABASES

What are databases used for?

Database programs are used to organize, store, and search for information. Although different software companies may describe their products a bit differently, all databases are organized into three hierarchical levels: *fields, records,* and *files.*

Individual elements of information are stored in fields. Each **field** holds a user-designated category of information: flower pictures, last names, phone numbers, dates of birth, favorite baseball players, bird songs, or virtually any other category of information the user can imagine. Fields themselves are containers. In creating a field, the user establishes a field name, such as zip code, last name, or flower picture, and indicates the type of information that will appear in the field (a zip code would contain a number, a last name would contain text, a flower picture would contain a graphic).

A **record** is a meaningful collection of fields and is really the defining feature of a database. Many computer applications allow the storage and retrieval of text, graphic, and numerical data, but the database requires the user to organize information so that the same set of fields is used consistently to describe the attributes of whatever happens to be the focus of the database.

Flexibility of databases

It is difficult to be much more specific about the purpose of a database, because a database can be prepared to organize categories of information on nearly any topic you might imagine. Commercial databases might be used to describe the attributes of the parts sold by an automotive supply store or the characteristics of potential customers a business might try to interest in its products. For the automotive parts database, fields might include part name, part number, a picture of the part, cost per item, number of items in a minimal order, and the name of the company manufacturing each part. The fields in a school's database might include student name, grade level, teacher, birthday, parents' or guardians' names, home phone number, work phone number, and emergency phone number. Students might use a database to investigate the characteristics of different countries (country name, population, size, form of government, primary language, capital city, GNP, present government leaders), or they might create a database for information they have gathered about the nutritional characteristics of different foods adolescents

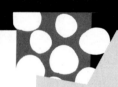

Activities and Projects for Your Classroom

Spreadsheet Activities

Here are some ideas for spreadsheet projects.

Take surveys on topics such as favorite foods, hobbies, sports, and pets. Graph the frequency with which the more popular alternatives were mentioned.

Keep track of money earned from classroom projects or schoolwide fund raisers.

Keep personal grade records.

Keep records of calorie intake.

Plan a budget.

Calculate actual expenditures for different rate mortgages.

Make conversion tables for weights and measures.

Calculate age and weight on different planets.

Plan a trip and calculate distances for different routes.

Collect litter for a week. Sort, weigh, and measure the litter. Use charts and graphs to motivate a campaign for recycling.

Grow bean plants under different conditions (temperature, light), use a spreadsheet to keep track of data and represent the data with charts and graphs. ✳

consume. The total stored information about one automotive part, one customer, one student, one country, or one food represents a record within the appropriate database. The total collection of records making up one of these databases is called a **file**. The file contains the entire collection of information about automotive parts, customers, students, countries, or foods.

DEVELOPING A DATABASE

The first and perhaps most important step in developing a database has nothing to do with the computer. The database developer needs to think carefully about the purpose of the database: who will use it, what kinds of backgrounds end users will have, and what questions they will want to ask of the database.

First steps in database development

Consider the relatively popular suggestion of having elementary students develop a database of library books they have read. What would be the purpose of this database? The primary purpose might be either to provide information the teacher can use to evaluate student understanding or to provide a resource other students can use to find an interesting book to read. This distinction would influence the categories of information included and what specific information students would provide in the database. If the purpose of the database is to interest other students in reading new books, it probably should not provide a complete summary of the books, because this would diminish the excitement of reading mysteries and many other types of fiction. Maybe the teacher would prefer that students writing for the database describe just enough to let the teacher know they have read the book and purposely try to entice others to read it. In other situations, whether to inform the teacher of what they have learned or perhaps to establish a factual summary of the content of the book for others, students writing for the database could be encouraged to be complete and accurate. What categories or fields of information would be important to include? There are many possibilities, including author, illustrator, publication date, topic, genre, storage location of book, other books by the author, perceived difficulty, and perceived interest value.

Creating a template or layout

Once the database developer has established its purpose and scope, the second step is to use the database software to create a **template** (sometimes called a *layout*). In this process, the developer specifies the fields and, in some applications, positions them as they should appear on the computer screen. Many database applications allow the developer to establish attributes of fields. Depending on the program, it may be necessary to specify how much space (that is, how many characters) to set aside for each field and what type of information (text, number, date, picture) to include in each field.

Specifying the type of information has a purpose you might not expect. In some programs, a field holding the information 06-09-93 could be identified to the program as containing text or a date (if this were to be recognized as a date, each program has a specific way in which the information would have to be entered, as in 06/09/93). One implication of establishing a field as containing a certain type of data relates to the types of searches that database users can conduct using that field. When databases grow very large, it is often most efficient to view only records having certain characteristics. How this is actually accomplished will be discussed in greater detail later. For now, imagine that the records in a database maintained by an automobile dealership contain information about all sales and that it becomes necessary to locate the owners of all cars sold between January 1991 and January 1992. If the field containing dates of sale contained information stored as a date, the appropriate records could be found. If the information had been stored as text, the program could locate only a specific match (say, 01/03/91), not all records falling in a range.

Important conventions

One final issue is important to consider. The usefulness of a database may depend on how closely the individuals entering and retrieving information follow conventions. In the next example, you will see a database used to organize information about wildflowers encountered on a biology field trip. One characteristic of the flowers noted in this database was color. Different students using this database might have entered information in different ways — "white," "it was white," "off-white." It is helpful to know that the entry in this field should be a single word and perhaps that it should be one of a predetermined number of alternatives.

INVESTIGATING WILDFLOWERS: A DATABASE PROJECT

The following wildflower database was the result of a summer biology field trip. The purpose of the database project was to give some structure to the field trip itself and to generate continuing activities that students could pursue once they had returned to the classroom. Before the trip, students decided on the layout, or template, for the database. The purpose of the information collected in the database was to help students investigate the relationship among location (open meadow, heavy woods, woods clearing), species of wildflowers identified, and physical characteristics (particularly height and color) of the flowers. The students also decided to record any other characteristics that students locating the flowers might find interesting. With these general goals in mind, the layout was to include fields allowing entry of common name, scientific name, location, habitat, observation date, flower color, and flower size. A general field was also included for extended comments, and a graphics field was included to hold an image of the flower. The layout for the wildflower project appears in Figure 5.5. The database application for this project was FileMaker Pro.

Students went into the field with a wildflower field guide, video camera,

FIGURE 5.5 Wildflower Database Template

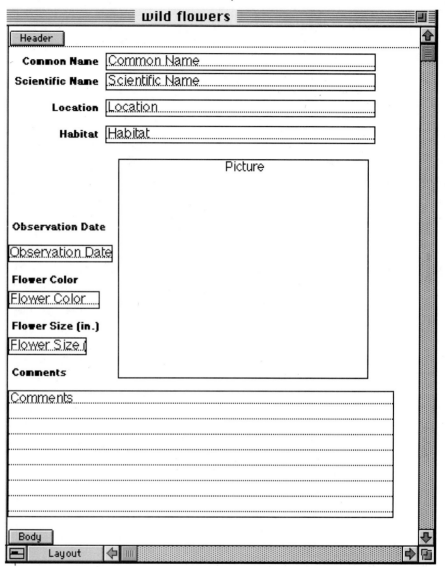

notebooks, and insect repellent. They worked in pairs to locate and identify as many wildflowers as possible and used the video camera to record an image of each flower that could later be digitized once they returned to school and inserted it in the database. See Figure 5.6 for a sample record from the completed database. You might wonder why we would use a video camera instead

FIGURE 5.6 Record from Wildflower Database

Common Name Dwarf Cornel Bunchberry

Scientific Name Cornus canadensis

Location Webb Lake, Wisconsin

Habitat Forest - Cross Country Ski Trail

Observation Date

06-09-93

Flower Color

White

Flower Size (in.)

6

Comments

This plant was found on a slope along the ski trail. The plant seems to grow in bunches. The white flower is not really a flower - the flower identification book says the white structures are bracts - the flowers are small green structures in the very middle. The book also says the flower grows in cold northern woods and has scarlet berries later in the season. Leaves occur in whorls of 6. The flower blooms May-June. The flower belongs to the dogwood family.

of simply collecting specimens. In part, this decision was made because of interest in using the technology. However, the unnecessary collection of living materials is also an issue students need to consider; in fact, some species of wildflowers, such as the lady's slipper, are protected by some state laws.

Once the records were complete, students applied sort and find functions to ask different questions of the database. Most database programs allow the output from a sort or find operation to be described in a new version of the original layout. Often it is useful to create a layout containing a subset of the fields contained in the database and perhaps to organize this layout differently. For example, it is possible to create a two-column display sorted by habitat in which the first column contains the habitat (forest or meadow) and the second column displays the common plant name. In this display format, data from several records are displayed on the screen or printed page at the same time. If the records were sorted alphabetically on the habitat field, the initial rows of this report would list the plants found in the forest and the later rows would list plants found in meadows. This would allow students to discover which plants were unique to the forest and which plants were found in both habitats.

Learning with and About Databases

On-line databases in libraries

One general point we have made about computer tools is that they seem to offer educational benefits on several levels; there is an advantage in learning how to use the tool, and using the tool can help students learn content-area knowledge and skills. As with other computer tools, skill in using a database can make certain educational tasks easier and more productive. One common application of database skills is library searches. Most college libraries, many public libraries, and many larger K–12 school libraries allow patrons to search library holdings using on-line databases. Online searches are much more thorough and certainly quicker than library patrons could conduct in any other manner. To use this type of database, the student needs to learn how the database operates and how to conduct effective searches. Learning how to search a library database is an appropriate use of class time, because the skills have long-term benefits.

Developing higher-level thinking skills

On a different level, it has been argued that creating databases and working with existing databases can develop higher-level thinking skills and provide insights into course content (Hartson, 1993; Jonassen, 1995; Lai, 1991). Not a great deal of research has tested these proposals directly, but database projects seem justified based on student enthusiasm and on analyses of the process skills necessary to complete projects. In Chapter 2 we discussed the advantages of experiences that involve students in manipulating and using content-area information. Creating and working with databases require students to be active learners. In creating the layout for a database, students need to carefully consider the purpose of the database and determine categories of information relevant to this purpose. Once the structure of the database has been established, students must conduct the research necessary to locate or generate data relevant to the database and then reformat these data to conform to the categories of information the database requests. In generating the records for the database, students must generate and organize knowledge. Once a database contains a substantial number of records, students can use the database to evaluate their hypotheses. Students learn to form hypotheses about relationships the database might reveal, propose ways to obtain the information necessary to test hypotheses, and evaluate the validity of the relationships they discover. In summary, databases encourage the active manipulation of information to generate knowledge, as well as the application of problem-solving skills to pose questions and evaluate conclusions.

CONCLUDING COMMENTS

Data from classrooms indicate that tools are used infrequently. When tools are used, much of the instructional time is focused on learning the tools rather than on applying the tools to learning activities. In some cases, this situation can be explained by lack of time and equipment. However, lack of teacher experience with tool applications and with the ways tools can be used in classroom activities is also an important limitation. This chapter describes the characteristics of each tool application and provides an example to demonstrate how each tool is used. In addition, we have attempted to identify learning processes that teachers might encourage as students use these tools in projects. This discussion will continue as we consider telecommunication activities in the next chapter. With the exception of the rather extensive work related to word processing, the educational potential of computer tools has not been carefully evaluated. The findings associated with word processing would likely generalize to the application of the other tools. The mere exposure of younger students to tool applications does not necessarily result in more meaningful learning. At least with the modest levels of experience students typically have, students will likely apply their traditional approaches to learning when using the tools. To be realized, the potential inherent in projects based on tool applications will require careful structuring, guidance, and modeling on the teacher's part.

SUMMARY

The most common computer tool applications are word processing, spreadsheets, databases, and telecommunications. In general, computer tools allow users to perform tasks with increased efficiency or quality. In addition, the most common computer tools can be applied in content areas in ways that give students a more active role in learning.

You might think of the difference in the purpose of word processing–based writing activities as the distinction between learning to write and writing to learn. Teachers are urged to consider word processing as one component of a writing environment. An effective environment for developing communication skills seems to emphasize coaching, authentic tasks, the writing community, and the writing process approach.

Database and spreadsheet applications are also described in terms of the power of these tools and the potential benefits of using these tools to explore content-area topics. Database programs are suited to the organization of factual information and the exploration of potential relationships within this information. Working with a completed database allows students to propose and test hypotheses about different relationships among the stored data. Spreadsheet programs allow many of the same opportunities in exploring quantitative data. Students can manipulate the data, evaluate hypotheses, and visually represent conclusions in the form of graphs and charts.

Activities

REFLECTING ON CHAPTER 5

◆ Create a paper layout for a database on an area of interest. What fields would be included? How would the fields be arranged? What questions should potential users be able to ask of the database?

◆ Evaluate the suitability of a particular word processing program for the type of general across-the-curriculum use described in this chapter. Consider such issues as ease of use, cost, formatting capabilities, and the ability to incorporate graphics. Describe or demonstrate for your classmates what you have learned.

◆ Create a simple paper spreadsheet gradebook capable of determining the final percentage for two tests and two quizzes, each worth a different number of points. In your sketch of a spreadsheet, indicate the cells in which student name, test and quiz scores, and final percentage should appear. Write the formula for calculating the final percentage for two students, and indicate the cells to which each version of this formula should be attached. You should be able to complete this task using the sum function =sum(b2,c2,d2) and division =b4/a4. *Hint:* Use one row of your spreadsheet to keep track of the points possible on each test or quiz.

Key Terms

cell *(p. 173)*	mindtool *(p. 159)*
copy *(p. 164)*	pasting *(p. 164)*
cursor *(p. 163)*	record *(p. 178)*
cut *(p. 164)*	select *(p. 163)*
database *(p. 177)*	spell checkers *(p. 164)*
delete *(p. 164)*	spreadsheets *(p. 172)*
field *(p. 177)*	style *(p. 162)*
file *(p. 179)*	tabs *(p. 162)*
font *(p. 162)*	template *(p. 179)*
formatting *(p. 162)*	word processing *(p. 159)*
insert *(p. 163)*	word wrap *(p. 160)*
justification *(p. 162)*	writing process approach
margins *(p. 162)*	*(p. 167)*

Resources to Expand Your Knowledge Base

Word Processing, Database, and Spreadsheet Applications

Some companies and some enterprising authors have written books explaining how general software tools can be used in the classroom. These books provide general instruction in the use of the tools, as well as content-area ideas for teachers. Following are a few examples:

Brownell, G. (1996). *A Mac for the teacher: ClarisWorks version.* St. Paul, MN: West Publishing Co.

Rathje, L. (1996). *ClarisWorks for students.* Eugene, OR: HRS Publishing.

Robinette, M. (1996). *The ClarisWorks reference for teachers.* Indianapolis, IN: IDG Books.

Computer magazines for teachers often provide content-area ideas making use of tool software. One example consistent with the writing process approach is Pon, K. (1988, March). Process writing in the one-computer classroom. *The Computing Teacher, 15* (6), 33–37.

Student Publication Sites on the World Wide Web

KidPub provides opportunities for both classes and individual students to present their work. The address for *KidPub* is http://escrime.en-garde.com/kidpub/

KidNews accepts news stories written by students with the understanding that the stories may then be taken from the Web site for use in local publications. *KidNews* also encourages discussion about news gathering, writing, and computer applications in education. The address for *KidNews* is http://www.vsa.cape.com/~powens/Kidnews.html

MidLink is an electronic magazine for 10- to 15-year old students. Theme issues are announced and student submissions are evaluated for possible publication. The address for this web site is http://longwood.cs.ucf.edu:80/~MidLink/

Global Show and Tell exhibits works in a variety of formats created by children up to age 17. When we visited the site, a drawing from a 2-year-old was included. *Global Show and Tell* can be reached at http://www.telenaut.com/gst/

Keyboard Computers

The *AlphaSmart Pro* is available from Intelligent Peripheral Devices, 20380 Town Center Lane, Suite 270, Cupertino, CA 95014. This machine stores fifty to sixty pages of text and has a four-line, forty-character display. Stored files can be transferred to either a Macintosh or a PC with Windows. The company manufacturing this product maintains a Web site at http://www.alphasmart.com.

The *DreamWriter* is available from NTS Computer Systems, Unit 10, 11720 Stewart Crescent, Maple Ridge, British Columbia, Canada, V2X 9E7. This machine has an eight-line, eighty-character display and comes with a built-in spell checker and thesaurus. Stored files can be transferred to either a Macintosh or a PC with

Windows. The company manufacturing this product maintains a Web site at http://www.dreamwriter.com.

Computers and Writing Instruction

The role computers play in teaching writing has generated so much interest that it now represents an area of research and practice complete with its own academic journals, professional organizations, annual conventions, college courses on how it should be done, Web sites, and listservs. There are some very practical issues to address, such as the level of keyboard competence necessary for effective writing, and some areas in which the field is pushing the boundaries of traditional writing, such as the rhetorical elements of Web authoring and idea processing software for authors.

Computers and Composition is a new journal from Ablex Publishing (355 Chestnut St., Norwood, NJ 07648) developed for those with special interests in this area. The journal hosts a related Web site at http://human.www.sunet.se/cc/index.html

The *Alliance for Computer and Writing (ACW)* is an organization offering support to K-12 and college faculty. The organization has affiliated regional and some state chapters. Its Web site is a great way to become familiar with the issues in the field, locate a variety of resources, and learn about other groups interested in related topics. The ACW Web site is located at http://english.ttu.edu/acw/

Chapter 6

Learning with Internet Tools

ORIENTATION

In this chapter you will read about various Internet tools that will allow you and your students to connect to other people, to interactive services, and to stored information in a variety of formats. We will demonstrate how you can connect to these resources and use them in productive ways.

FOCUS QUESTIONS

◆ What are the different types of Internet tools available to teachers and students?
◆ What are some e-mail activities that can be adapted for the content area you plan to teach?
◆ How can course-relevant World Wide Web resources be found?
◆ With so many resources available on the World Wide Web, how can teachers structure Web projects to engage students in meaningful inquiry?

Meaningful Use of the Internet

At present we have several computers, lots of software, and a teenage daughter in our home. This combination has provided some interesting opportunities to observe how young people use technology in unstructured and informal situations. Access to the Internet has long been an interest in our house. E-mail and online chats were entertaining for a while. Early on, a small group of students would assemble in our home office after school, connect to a commercial online service, go to a chat room, and spend time talking with others about whatever it is young people talk about. After a couple of large monthly bills, however, we decided to curb this activity.

When home access to the World Wide Web first became available, there were many new opportunities for exploration and fun. Our youngest daughter, Kim, is learning to play the guitar. She has found a place on the "Net" from which to download the words and chords to some of her favorite popular songs. Her instructor had been doing this for some time and he has encouraged her to continue; apparently it's more fun to practice songs you hear on the radio than those in some dull old lesson book. Kim and many of her friends are also heavily involved in sports (Michael Jordan rules!). Kim has located color pictures of Michael in action on the Net, printed them out to hang in her room, and installed them as the screen saver on her computer. Kim is also interested in whales and thinks she wants to be a marine biologist. North Dakota is about as far from an ocean as you can get, so her whale watching opportunities are rare. Web sites dedicated to the observation and preservation of whales keep her interest alive.

Web use for Kim extends beyond hobbies. She searches for material for school reports and seeks information about issues that concern her. Recently, she informed Cindy that she had found "three different places on the Net where it said you should go to the doctor when you start getting zits." This real problem in her life (we've all been teenagers) led her to search the Internet for information that might help her solve it: Mom thought that the pimple on her forehead probably did not yet require a visit to the doctor, but she did agree that a visit would be helpful if acne became a serious problem. When I was that age, I too used to believe I had all kinds of serious conditions. I remember reading a book of medical advice my parents had, looking for answers. Perhaps all that has really changed is the information source.

The point is that although our daughter and her friends are not particularly interested in learning about how computers work, they have become quite adept at using computers and the Internet to learn about the things that are important in their world. Not all of the time they spend using the Internet is productive. Sometimes it's just for fun, and once in a while it gets a bit out of hand. However, the Internet is a useful tool, and they usually apply it in naturally productive ways.

Similar goals should be established for classroom applications. Students should have the opportunity to use the Internet to challenge themselves to address authentic tasks. As we discuss Internet resources available to students and educators, we will also explore how these resources can be used as part of content area learning.

EDUCATIONAL ACCESS TO INTERNET RESOURCES

Internet serves many purposes

The Internet provides highly efficient access to a variety of helpful and stimulating resources. Visionaries see the Internet as offering new opportunities in many areas. Although our intent is to concentrate on present and future educational applications, we will not ignore other developments entirely. From the outset it is important to recognize that the Internet is a shared resource — it provides opportunities for commerce, entertainment, and education. No single entity is developing it and certainly no single entity is paying for it. Educators must understand that they are tapping into a resource not designed specifically for their benefit. But it is a resource of unparalleled potential nonetheless.

Commitment to connect all students

The Clinton administration has made an effort to establish a national commitment to connect schools to the Internet. In 1994, Vice President Al Gore proposed a vision for a "different kind of superhighway that can . . . give every American, young and old, the chance for the best education available to anyone, anywhere" (IITF/CAT, 1994). The goal is to have all classrooms and libraries connected to the Internet by the year 2000. The Telecommunications Act of 1996 was an attempt to make school connections more feasible by establishing the expectation that states, communities, and the Federal Communications Commission would work together to lower the cost of telecommunications services to schools. These are all important goals. At present, Internet access is an example of blatant technology-related academic inequity, students most in need of more resources have access to less.

THE INTERNET

The **Internet** is an international collection of computer networks, with an estimated 40 million users in nearly 100 countries. Think of it as a

A network of networks

meta-network — that is, a network of networks. There are huge networks providing high-speed regional network backbones and there are small networks within individual office buildings. One of these networks might be located at your university or local school district. By running the right software on one of the computers on any one of the networks, you become an active part of the entire system.

A unique characteristic of the Internet is that no one company or country really owns it. Members of the Internet community have made a commitment to share resources and to transfer information over the network in an agreed on manner. This method of transferring information from computer to computer is called *transmission control protocol/Internet protocol* (**TCP/IP**). Each computer on the Internet has a unique identity or address called an **IP number.** Often the same computer also has a **domain name.** The difference between the two is that the IP number is expressed as a series of numbers and the domain name as an easier to remember series of abbreviated words, such as sage.und.nodak.edu. The unique designation for each computer is important, ensuring that data sent over the Internet get to the right place. You don't have to understand how TCP/IP functions to appreciate what it allows users of the network to accomplish. Files can be quickly sent and received by different kinds of computers over great distances with great accuracy. Messages and files end up where they are supposed to — a specific computer with a specific IP number. Once you get past the equipment, the software, and the mysteries of how it all works, the ability to communicate so easily with so many people, to share what you know and what you feel, is motivating.

Unique designation for each computer

Let's begin by investigating how successful schools have been in gaining access to Internet resources. A government survey (National Center for Educational Statistics, 1996) determined that 50 percent of U.S. schools have access to the Internet. This figure rose 15 percent between 1994 and 1995 — in just one year! School districts obviously feel access to the Internet is important and are finding the money to connect. However, to the average classroom teacher, what has happened so far may not provide the kind of access that is needed. Only 9 percent of classrooms are actually connected so access, at best, might be more inconvenient than it may appear. Most schools provide access at a single location such as the school library. Access may also not be available in every building. Opportunities also vary with school size and the general income level of the student body. Larger districts are more likely to be connected, as are schools with smaller proportions of poor families (equity issues are discussed in detail in Chapter 11).

Over 50 percent of schools connected

Access varies greatly

Our discussion will focus on the resources that are available and how teachers and students might take advantage of them. Occasionally we will present some of the details of how a particular program used to access Internet resources works. However, we will not take the time to teach you everything you need to know to actually accomplish all of the activities

Focus

Levels of Internet Connection

There are several ways to connect to the Internet and the number of options continues to expand as innovations developed through research become commercial realities. Here is one way to think about the most common current options.

Full-Time Internet Access

If you have full-time access to the Internet, you don't have to think about making a connection, because your computer is part of the Internet whenever it is turned on. To use the Internet, you simply have to start the appropriate software program (e.g., a Web browser) and begin working. Computers connected in this fashion contain a network interface card that links them to a **local area network (LAN)** or a **wide area network (WAN),** which, in turn, is connected to the Internet through high-speed and high-capacity connections leased from a service provider. For example, a *T1* line carries information at 1,544,000 bits per second. When applied in a school setting, the computers in a school lab (a LAN), in combination with other computers in a school district (a WAN), are connected to the Internet through the high-capacity line leased by the district. This is obviously a convenient system for students and teachers and is probably the only really practical way to connect large numbers of users. Internet access is fast and immediate and users do not need to know or do much to be able to take advantage of Internet resources. Behind the scenes, the story is a little different. This type of access is relatively more expensive and requires special equipment, special cabling, and personnel with specific technical skills.

Computers may also be connected to the Internet full-time by special leased telephone lines (see *ISDN* in the discussion of part-time access), but this kind of connection is more commonly used for part-time access.

Part-Time Internet Access (Modem Connection to the Internet Provider)

Computers connected part-time to the Internet do so with a telephone line and a modem. To get to the Internet, a connection is established with another computer that is connected to the Internet full-time (through a commercial service such as CompuServe or America Online) or to a **terminal server** that is connected full-time to the Internet. As you might expect, **Internet Service Providers (ISPs)** intend to make a profit and sell access. The ISPs must have enough modems to handle the incoming traffic and a high enough capacity connection to the Internet to keep data moving at an acceptable rate. If users are frequently unable to connect or are plagued with slow connections, they will soon search for another provider. It becomes a balancing act involving the outlay for equipment and connection capacity, the number of users, and the amount users are charged for access.

There are several different ways to make the connection to the service provider. At present, the most common way is to use an **analog modem.** This kind of modem has been around for years and works by converting a digital signal from the computer into an analog signal that is sent over a standard phone line. The service provider has a pool of modems, one of which accepts the call and converts the analog signal back into a digital signal so it can be passed on to the Internet. Most analog modems sold today offer transfer rates of 28.8 Kbps (kilobytes per second). Running serial line Internet protocol (**SLIP**) or point-to-point protocol (**PPP**) software allows modem users to take advantage of the same Internet applications (e.g., World Wide Web) available to users with a direct full-time connection.

In some locations, users can now take advantage of faster integrated services digital network (**ISDN modems**). A digital phone connection is at least four times faster than a traditional analog modem connection. However, fewer service providers make this kind of access available and access is more expensive.

Basic Statistics on School Internet Access

About half the schools in the United States have Internet access. Of those schools, most (81 percent) still reach the Internet by modem (analog). However, 23 percent of Internet-accessing schools take advantage of SLIP or PPP connections, 17 percent obtain access through a fast dedicated line (T1 or somewhat slower 56 Kbps connections), and 3 percent use ISDN. (*Note*: These percentages add to more than 100 per-

cent because some schools have several kinds of connections.) Schools are acquiring Internet access at a rapid rate (an increase of 15 percent in one year) and are moving toward faster transmission connections, so these statistics will change quickly (National Center for Education Statistics, 1996).

A school's location can present very real problems in acquiring Internet access. Even connecting to an Internet provider using an analog modem, the most basic type of connectivity, is not always possible with a local phone call. Faster connections are not practical for an even larger number of schools. Providing the resources necessary for universal high-speed access is the goal of a federal initiative referred to as the National Information Infrastructure Act (IITF/CAT, 1994). In some ways, the Internet is like the interstate highway system: it is simply more cost effective to provide access in some locations than in others. A political initiative will be necessary to offset these differences and provide equal access for all. ✳

described here. If you are interested in step-by-step instructions, you might consider one of the sources listed at the end of this chapter.

INTERNET RESOURCES

Access people, files, and interactive hypermedia

One way to organize a discussion of the educational value of the Internet is to suggest that the Internet provides access to other people, to files or stores of information and programs that can be copied for personal use, and to the multicomputer interactive hypermedia resource referred to as the World Wide Web. We will describe each of these resource categories, provide basic information about the computer tools and techniques needed to access each type of resource, and discuss ways to use these resources in classroom settings.

ACCESS TO PEOPLE

One of the most powerful uses of technology is putting people in touch with other people. Students and teachers can convey ideas and information nearly instantaneously over great distances, or the students or teachers at the other end of the conversation can have the freedom to respond at a convenient time, when they feel prepared. These alternatives of immediate and delayed interaction can be quite useful. As any busy person who has attempted to call another busy person realizes, asynchronous communication has some very real advantages. It is often more convenient to leave your message for the other person to consider than to call repeatedly, hoping to make contact. Leaving a message that communicates what you want to say is also more considerate than requesting that the other person take responsibility for calling you. Often, participants sharing information, ideas, or feelings do not have to coordinate their individual lives to communicate efficiently. If this does not seem reasonable, consider that you or your students may want to communicate with teachers or students who live in a different part of the world and who may be sleeping when you are in school. Or imagine a situation in which you want to actively communicate with a large number of people, but that you would like to set aside a particular time each day for this interaction. Would you really expect all of the people you hope to interact with to set aside the identical time period just so you can work efficiently? In some educational settings situations like this arise more frequently than you might expect.

There are other advantages to messages communicated using technology. Messages are automatically stored, so information collected this way can be reviewed, integrated, and forwarded to other interested parties. If an interesting idea comes your way, it is relatively easy to forward a copy to others with whom you communicate. Obviously, communications should be stored and shared only when such activities are ethical.

Internet information exchanges among people fall into several categories. Real-time exchanges are possible. Sometimes this form of interaction is referred to as **chat mode**. "Keyboard conversations" might be a better description, since this kind of interaction is in the form of typed text. Commercial services such as America Online or CompuServe support a number of special interest groups, which often arrange specific times and topics for discussion. In some cases, the group will arrange for an expert to be available for a particular topic. All you need to do to participate in such a discussion is to log on to the service at the appropriate time and select the discussion you want from the various activities available. The comments in one of these discussions will appear on your screen as they are typed in by different people around the country. If you like, you may contribute your own thoughts when there is a pause. Commercial services often save transcripts of important discussions and make transcripts available as files. Chat opportunities are also available through Internet relay chat (**IRC**). An IRC works something like an

Value of asynchronous communication

Chat mode

Experts may participate

international CB radio (for those of you who remember CBs) complete with "handles" (nicknames) and channels. Once connected, anything you type is relayed to the screen of everyone connected to that channel. Your nickname will appear, followed by your comment. If you like, you can select a private channel for discussion with a smaller group.

Personal connections with e-mail

Probably the most common format for interpersonal telecommunication is electronic mail or **e-mail**. A teacher or student using e-mail composes a message and then sends it to the address of another individual. When this individual logs on to his or her account and searches for mail, the message is detected and brought to the computer screen to be read. Exchanging e-mail messages sounds simple, and it is. However, many creative projects based on the simple process of exchanging messages have demonstrated the educational potential of correspondence with other teachers, students, parents, scientists, the elderly, politicians, and potentially anyone in the world with access to a computer and a telephone. Among the more common e-mail projects are

Opportunity for creative projects

exchanges of correspondence with other students to learn about a different culture or to practice foreign language skills; projects that allow the collection and integration of data (for instance, on water quality) from many different locations; and projects that involve sharing student-generated literature or newsletters. Many students also seem to enjoy more informal opportunities to strike up friendships and correspond with a key pal. Newer e-mail systems allow a file to be attached to a message. Users with compatible systems can thus exchange whatever computer files they can create.

A CTIVE
C OOPERATION
T HEME-BASED
I NTEGRATED
V ERSATILE
E VALUATION

Telecomputing Activity Structures

Communicating through e-mail provides the opportunity for many kinds of activities and projects. Frequently, magazines written for computer-using educators (see Keeping Current in Chapter 3) provide descriptions of classroom projects. Harris (1995) suggests that instead of looking for projects they can duplicate in their own classrooms, teachers should understand the properties of different kinds of projects — Harris calls them "activity structures" — and then apply these structures to the content actually being studied. Harris contends this approach makes it more likely that classroom content will be emphasized. Here is a brief review of the activity structures Harris identified:

Emphasize classroom content

Interpersonal Exchanges. "Talk" among individuals, between an individual and a group, among groups.

Key pals unstructured exchange among individuals or groups; e.g., exchanges to develop cultural awareness or language skills

E-mail project categories

Global classrooms study a common topic and exchange accounts of what has been learned; e.g., themes in fairy tales

Electronic appearances e-mail or chat interaction with a guest, perhaps after some preparation; e.g., local engineer responds to questions from students in a physics class

Electronic mentoring ongoing interaction between expert and student on a specific topic; e.g., college education majors offer middle school students advice on class projects

Impersonations participants interact "in character"; e.g., correspondence with graduate student impersonating Benjamin Franklin

Information Collections.   Working together to collect and compile information provided by participants.

Information exchanges accumulation of information on some theme; e.g., favorite playground games, recycling practices

Electronic publishing publication of document based on submission by group members; e.g., publication of a district literary magazine of short stories submitted by elementary students

Tele-fieldtrips share observations made during local field trips; e.g., visits to local parks (a special case could be expeditions undertaken by experts; e.g., a bicycle trip through central America)

Pooled data analysis data collected from multiple sites are combined for analysis; e.g., cost comparison of gasoline

Problem-Solving Projects.   Focus of interaction involves solving problems.

Information searches solve a problem based on clues and reference sources; e.g., identify state landmarks or cities in response to a progression of clues

Electronic process writing post written works for critiques before revision; e.g., composition students comment on classmates' papers

Parallel problem-solving groups at different sites solve the same problem and then exchange and discuss methods and conclusions; e.g., compare ideas to improve school spirit

Sequential creations work on sequential components of an expressive piece; e.g., add a stanza to a poem about friendship

Social action projects groups take responsibility for solving an authentic problem and share reports of activities and consequences; e.g., cleaning up the environment, helping the homeless

Mailing lists for discussions

Not all e-mail messages need be addressed to a specific individual. In certain applications, users may send an open message to all interested readers. This process is accomplished in several ways. With one approach, the user sends the message to a designated address, where it is then relayed to a list of readers. Applications of this type are often called **mailing lists,** and the site from which the list originates is called the **list server.** There are many lists addressing both general and specific topics relevant to teachers. Members of active lists may receive several dozen messages a day. Some messages will request assistance with problems a reader knows nothing about or has no time to provide. For example, a school just connecting to the Internet might want to know what other schools have done to keep students from accessing inappropriate material. Of course, the reader also reads the responses of other

Focus

Joining a List Maintained by a Server

It is not difficult to join a list; the following is a description of the process. Electronic mailing lists usually have both a submission address and an administrative address. The submission address designates where to send messages you want included on the list. To subscribe to the list, you are usually asked to send a message to the administrative address. The message should have nothing in the portion of your message that asks for the subject of the message and should include the simple statement SUBSCRIBE LISTNAME FIRSTNAME LASTNAME as the main body of the message. Messages to be sent to members of the list are sent to the submission address.

When you first subscribe to a list, you may be sent a summary of the procedures that apply to that list. Often the procedures will explain what to do if you are going to be away from your computer for a while and would rather your "e-mail box" not be filled with mail from the list, how to receive the individual messages as a digest (a single file instead of many individual messages), and how to remove yourself from the list (our own description of this procedure follows). One of the major problems is that users frequently forget the administrative address. Although they constantly receive e-mail messages, the messages come from the submissions address, and the administrative address is not mentioned. However, the administrative address is needed to implement any of the procedures just described. *Save the list of instructions you receive when you first subscribe.* Print it out and pin it to the bulletin board next to your computer and save it as a file on that disk of very important documents. If you choose to ignore this advice, then you must be patient. The list administrator will usually send the list procedures out as a message every month or so.

It is sometimes difficult to tell if the list you subscribe to will be useful until you have tried it for a while. The purpose of the list may turn out to be something other than what you anticipated. You may also find, after subscribing to several lists, that the volume of mail is just too much. You can remove your name from a mailing list by sending a message to the administrative address (not the submission address). The message should read UNSUBSCRIBE LISTNAME (SIGN-OFF LISTNAME is also used in some cases). Sending an UNSUBSCRIBE message to the submission address rather than the administrative address is a common mistake; list readers often see messages from other members attempting to remove themselves from the list.

One more hint about using mailing lists: Often, telecommunications services have an automatic reply feature, which allows you to send a message in response to one you have just received. When reading a message on a mailing list, remember that the immediate source of the message is the list server, and not the person who actually wrote the message. Using the reply feature will send what you may intend to be a private message to all members on the list. More than one person has been embarrassed by such an error. The message author's address will appear somewhere in the message; this is the address that should be used when private correspondence is desired. ✶

members of the list to these requests. Many schools are interested in the issue of inappropriate material on the Internet, and of course you don't always have to be the person asking the question to learn something new. Some of the questions and messages sent through a list will be of little interest to you. These you can quickly scan and discard. A lot of information will come your way and relevant messages may provide some useful piece of information or identify an individual the user would like to contact for further discussion.

Follow a discussion thread

Often discussions will focus on a specific topic until the topic is exhausted and then move on to something new. This sequence of messages, called a **thread**, can be informative and the discussion sometimes gets quite heated. A thread is created when a user "replies" to a previous message. A reply is an option allowed within most e-mail systems that keeps the **header** (a descriptive phrase) from the previous message. Archived files of list discussions allow you to a follow a thread and ignore unrelated messages.

A different approach to the exchange of messages within a group does not

Keeping Current

Finding Useful Lists

Of all the Keeping Current sources we have provided in this book, list servers probably offer the most immediate access to new ideas and information. Current books on the Internet are constantly appearing in local bookstores and those providing broad coverage of Internet services will include thousands of lists.

Many lists come and go so quickly that it is not productive to attempt an exhaustive survey. We offer here a few relevant examples of mailing lists and the suggestion that you use the World Wide Web to locate others. To reach these Web sites, use a Web browser to connect to one of these locations: http://www.tile.net/listserv/alphabetical.html or http://www.liszt.com. We will discuss the World Wide Web later in this chapter. ✳

List Name	List Topic	Administrative Address
BGEDU-L	Forum on Educational Reform	listserv@lsv.uky.edu
EDTECH	Topics in Educational Technology	listserv@msu.edu
IECC	International Classroom Connect	iecc-request@stolaf.edu
KIDPROJ	Special Youth Projects	listserv@listserv.nodak.edu
KIDSPHERE	General List for K-12 Educators	kidsphere-request@vms.cis.pitt.edu
KIDS	Kidsphere Spinoff for Kids	joinkids@vms.cis.pitt.edu
MIDDLE-L	Middle School Topics	listserv@vmd.cso.uiuc.edu
WWWEDU	Educational Web Discussion	listproc@educom.unc.edu

result in a large number of messages being sent directly to you. Instead, the messages are "posted" to a network location, where users go to electronically review the material. To understand how this works, think of departmental bulletin boards in high schools that inform students of activities and news. Information on the upcoming orchestra concert, notice of band instruments for sale, and a notice of jazz band auditions would be found on the bulletin board near the music department. Other bulletin boards serving similar functions would be located throughout the school. High school students interested in different topics would peruse different bulletin boards. The electronic equivalent of the bulletin board, called a **conference**, **forum**, or **newsgroup**, can hold hundreds of messages and can be read by people from all over the world. Often, many conferences are available through the same electronic source. People who participate in conferences are encouraged to start relevant new discussions with a question or comment, respond to a posted comment, or just read the existing comments to glean whatever useful information might be available. Obviously, the more participants, the more material will be available.

Newsgroups like bulletin boards

ACCESS TO FILES

Various commercial, public, and government institutions maintain archives of files that users can copy, or **download**, to their personal computers. These files can be text documents, graphic images, sounds, or programs. If the archive has been developed specifically for educators or students, the files might be lesson plans for hands-on science activities, information about the latest shuttle mission, the text of *Moby Dick,* pictures from the Smithsonian, pictures of U.S. presidents, or a virus protection program for your computer.

Must eventually purchase shareware

You may initially feel that access to all of this material is just too good to be true. It is important to understand and appreciate the various commitments individuals have made to providing these resources. The resources to which you have access through the Internet are provided with different expectations. One term with which you should be familiar is *shareware.* A **shareware** product is distributed for evaluation, but the author has copyrighted the material and expects to receive payment if use extends beyond the initial evaluation. Some users of commercial services assume that the fees they pay for the service somehow cover the cost of the shareware products they download. This is not the case; software and other resources designated as shareware come with the expectation that the author will eventually receive some compensation. You will learn more about shareware and other copyright issues in Chapter 11.

Share your own resources

It is also important that teachers understand that file transfers are not a one-way process. Some resources, such as collections of lesson plans, would be greatly enhanced if more teachers took the time to contribute some of

Emerging Technology

Video Conferencing with CU-SeeMe

Videoconferencing is synchronous video and audio communication. Participants send and receive video and audio simultaneously. CU-SeeMe, free software developed by Cornell University (source provided at the end of chapter), allows anyone with an Internet connection, a computer equipped with video and audio digitizing hardware (see Chapter 9), a camera, and a microphone to participate in videoconferencing. Special black-and-white video cameras, specifically designed for the single purpose of feeding a video signal into computers, can be obtained for less than $100, or a camcorder can be used. Color cameras and a commercial color version of CU-SeeMe are also available. The high-speed connection to the Internet is likely to be the most common barrier. A 14.4 Kbps modem will allow experimentation in receive-only mode, but a 28.8 Kbps or better connection is required for minimal quality full participation. Faster connections (see Focus: Levels of Internet Connection, page 192) increase the number of video frames sent per second and make it less likely the audio will break up.

There are two ways to use CU-SeeMe. First, two appropriately equipped computers running the CU-SeeMe software can achieve a direct connection. One user simply enters the IP number or address of the second user to request a connection. The second user is informed of the request, and consents, and a connection is established. The second method is employed when multiple users want to connect to a single source. For example, NASA provides a live feed during space shuttle missions and many users may want to watch and listen. In this case, the NASA feed comes into what is called a **reflector site** to which multiple users connect.

Finding ways to use CU-SeeMe in the classroom requires teachers and students to have a sense of adventure. Classroom videoconferencing is unlike either tuning into a television news program or the interactive television you may have experienced in your college classroom. Sometimes the sound is garbled beyond recognition. The visual image can also be lost or change so slowly that parts of two images appear simultaneously. We watched some scenes come back from the shuttle this way and didn't mind a bit. Sometimes it was even possible to understand what the astronauts were saying. The experience was very different from watching mission coverage on television. Somehow, joining in on whatever was happening *at that moment* made us feel personally involved in the mission.

If this type of adventure appeals to you, there are many opportunities available now. You can locate the reflector sites (sources provided at the end of the chapter) and explore to find out what's available — look first for opportunities in science (e.g., active volcanoes, zoo and aquarium exhibits, shuttle missions) and foreign languages (a variety of experimental formats including simple news programs). Connecting two computers with CU-SeeMe is pretty easy — just launch the application program, turn on the video camera, and open a connection. If you are working in a school computer lab and want another user to connect to you, the most difficult part will likely be determining the IP number for your computer to be shared with the other user (ask a lab technician for help). Effective use of CU-SeeMe technology includes any situation in which a visual or audio signal would add to the authenticity of an online project. For example, questioning an expert is likely to be more spontaneous in real time. Many of the telecomputing activity structures recom- mended by Harris (1995) can be implemented using this technology. Ideas for how to make classroom use of student videoconferencing are available through periodicals (e.g., Andres, 1996) and are often shared on the Internet. ✳

FIGURE 6.1   CU-SeeMe Screen Images for Host and Remote

their better ideas. There are also circumstances in which students' work is a welcome addition to archives. Contributing a student project to an archive may be a valuable way to authenticate the original scholarship demonstrated by the project (see Chapter 10).

The process of transferring files over the Internet is relatively simple once a user has gained access and knows a bit about establishing an active network connection. The transfer of a file to or from the remote computer is accomplished using **FTP** (*file transfer protocol*). The following demonstration illustrates how a picture from a collection generated by the Smithsonian Institute is transferred from the archives maintained by Apple Computer (address: ftp.apple.com).

UNIX most common operating system

Most of the machines making files available on a large-scale basis are large computers running on the UNIX operating system. To transfer a file from the UNIX machine to your desktop machine used to require that you knew the UNIX commands to control the remote computer. You certainly

Painless UNIX

would be capable of learning how to do this, and we took the time to explain these procedures in the first edition of this textbook. Now software has been developed to execute these procedures automatically, and you need to work in UNIX only if you find it interesting. Our example in Figure 6.2 uses a program called *Fetch* (files can also be transferred to your computer using a Web browser, as you will see later in this chapter). We will be sending UNIX commands such as *cd* (change directory) and *ls* (list the files in the directory) without even knowing it.

FIGURE 6.2   Connecting to a Remote Host with Fetch

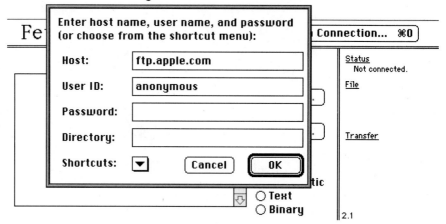

Connecting to the remote computer requires entering the address for the remote computer (in this case, ftp.apple.com). Like many sites allowing all interested users to have access to file archives, this site allows the user to log on using the name ANONYMOUS. Some sites will then expect a password (ftp.apple.com does not). This may seem a bit strange, considering the files are available to everyone. The desired password for anonymous logons is typically the user's Internet address. This is a courtesy that allows the host site to gather data on how many different users take advantage of the services that have been provided.

Searching for interesting files

Now what? The next step is to see what files are available. The server stores files within a hierarchical system of directories. A directory is represented within Fetch as a folder — in other words, there are folders stored within folders, as in Figure 6.3. Individual files (what we are looking for) are not accompanied by the folder icon (the small picture of a folder) and often have endings such as .txt (a text file) or .bin (a binary file such as a program or picture).

Learning about resources

How do we know this is where we are going? Often, a teacher might read in a magazine or an e-mail about a file that sounds interesting. In this case, an e-mail source has indicated that a collection of Smithsonian photographs has

FIGURE 6.3 Moving Through Server Directories with Fetch

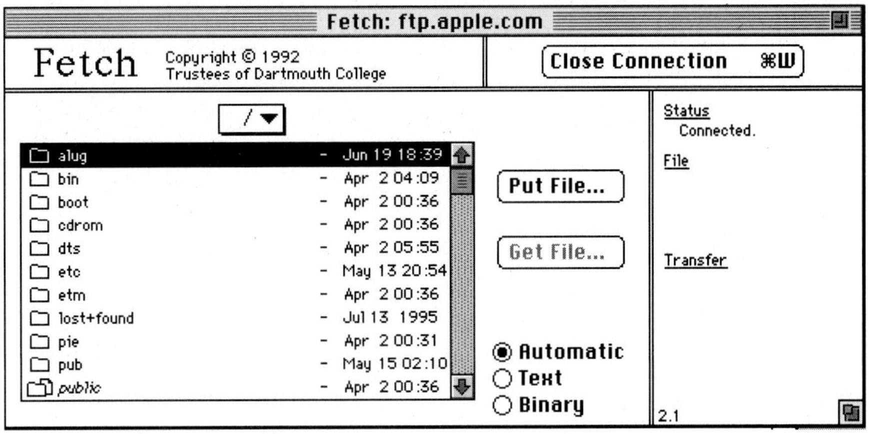

```
================ Fetch: ftp.apple.com ================
 Fetch    Copyright © 1992              │  Close Connection    ⌘W
          Trustees of Dartmouth College │
─────────────────────────────────────────────────────────────
                  ┌─────────┐            │ Status
                  │  /  ▼   │            │   Connected.
  ▢ alug              -  Jun 19 18:39 ▲  │ File
  ▢ bin               -  Apr  2 04:09    │
  ▢ boot              -  Apr  2 00:36    │   Put File...
  ▢ cdrom             -  Apr  2 00:36    │
  ▢ dts               -  Apr  2 05:55    │
  ▢ etc               -  May 13 20:54    │   Get File...
  ▢ etm               -  Apr  2 00:36    │
  ▢ lost+found        -  Jul 13  1995    │
  ▢ pie               -  Apr  2 00:31    │ ● Automatic   Transfer
  ▢ pub               -  May 15 02:10    │ ○ Text
  ▢ public            -  Apr  2 00:36 ▼  │ ○ Binary     2.1
```

been stored in alug/Smith/jpeg. This information indicates that it will be necessary to open the alug subdirectory, then the Smith (an abbreviation for Smithsonian) subdirectory, and finally the jpeg subdirectory to find the photographs. Opening each directory requires just a double click on the appropriate folder.

File types

Files are stored in different formats. The format might be determined by the type of computer that generated the file or by the type of information stored in the file. Again, teachers or students with limited computer experience should probably seek a local resource person's assistance. The Internet transfers files in **ASCII** or **binary** modes. If the transfer mode is not consistent with the format in which the file has been stored, the file will be sent in an unusable form. The file format is one of those small details that is easy to forget and that can easily create consequences that confuse novice users. The format in which the photographs are stored is easy to determine because of the suffix attached to the file name. Fetch, the software we are using, automatically recognizes file types and makes the necessary preparations for a file transfer.

To transfer the picture of a gorilla, the filename gorila.jpeg.bin is selected and the "Get" button is clicked. The results can be quite satisfying. Figure 6.4 shows an incredible image a student might use in a classroom report.

THE WORLD WIDE WEB

The resources available on the Internet are disorganized because they have resulted from the efforts of many institutions and individuals operating independently and contributing whatever they think might be useful. Because the Internet lacks a central directory, it can be challenging for inexperienced users

FIGURE 6.4   Download of gorila.jpeg.bin

© 1992 Smithsonian Institution

and time consuming for anyone to pull together resources related to a specific topic.

The **World Wide Web (WWW)** represents a significant improvement because it allows a variety of information sources to be interconnected through a special type of hypertext or hypermedia link (see discussions of hypertext and hypermedia in Chapter 7). The information sources might be text documents, graphics, sounds, or even other Web sites. The major advantage to educators and students of individual Web sites is that someone else has already done the work of locating and organizing meaningful collections of Internet resources.

World Wide Web is hypermedia

A Web site might be thought of as a special type of publication. In some cases, the entire contents of an individual Web site are contributed by the Web author. In other instances, a Web site consists of some material developed by the Web author and connections to other resources found on computers throughout the Internet. A Web user does not have to keep track of who authored what. The user simply follows links embedded within the content of Web pages from one topic of interest to another.

Follow the links

Focus

Web Excitement

People associated with the computer industry use the term "killer apps" (killer applications) to refer to a new application that is so powerful it will eliminate earlier applications and so impressive it will attract new users to the technology. People in the business of creating and selling new software and hardware are always looking for killer apps because such advances mean more business. The idea is to create something so attractive and useful that individuals or institutions (businesses and schools) will buy products they had not considered before, and current customers will feel what they have is inadequate and must be replaced. Applications that are attractive also interest developers, who see the potential in a new area, and a productive upward spiral occurs. "If you build it, they will come" does not always work, but there are certainly some technological innovations to which this maxim would apply.

Both the World Wide Web and the new software that allows users to explore it are great examples of killer apps. The Web has encouraged schools to connect to the Internet like nothing that existed before. To a lesser degree, the presence of the Web has probably even encouraged schools to purchase more

computers. Information consumers and information providers are linked symbiotically. You may have noted that it is nearly impossible to watch a television sporting event, news program, or educational program without being given a Web address related to that program. (*Note*: The address usually looks like this — http://www.tvprogram.com. This address is called a uniform resource locator (**URL**) and it provides the information needed for your computer to connect to the desired remote site.) The number of Web servers (computers offering information to the web) increased sixfold during one year alone (WebCrawler, 1996); the number of servers was estimated at 230,000 (Gary, 1996). While the quality and relevance of many sites is at issue, the total pool of information is staggering and users of many different types are rushing to connect. It appears the upward spiral is in full motion.

Will new killer apps come along? Absolutely, and rest assured that changes will come quickly. The trend toward increasingly powerful tools that have become more intuitive and easier to use should be both exciting and reassuring. It is becoming easier to ignore the technology and to concentrate on the applications. The key is to jump in and make a start. ✳

Browser software

Special software, called a **browser,** is required to connect to and interpret the protocol used by Web servers. A browser provides a graphic interface and interactive involvement with the full range of hypermedia — text, pictures, sounds, and movies. You can follow links from resource to resource in a variety of ways, including using the mouse to click on specially marked pictures or words that serve as links to other resources.

The example that follows shows part of the home page from the

VolcanoWorld Web site (http://volcano.und.nodak.edu) operated at the University of North Dakota by Dr. Charles Wood. As you can probably guess, VolcanoWorld was developed to provide information about volcanoes. We can show only a very small portion of this resource here, but it should be sufficient to give you an idea of what a hypermedia web site looks like and how such a site works. The **home page** is what you encounter when you first connect to a specific Web address. On this page are links that can be clicked with the mouse. The links can be words or pictures and are usually differentiated in some way. Picture links are identified by a color border. Text links are underlined and appear in a color different from the other text on the page. The color is not apparent here because of the need to reproduce these images in grayscale.

First encounter is home page

FIGURE 6.5 VolcanoWorld Home Page

Supported by NASA's Program:

Public Use of Earth and Space Science Data Over the Internet

Awards

VolcanoWorld Remote! An alternative interface to VolcanoWorld...

🏆 **What is VolcanoWorld?** May 17

🏆 **Volcanoes of the World** Dec 9

🏆 **Volcanic Parks and Monuments** Dec 6

🏆 **Learning about Volcanoes** Dec 10

🏆 **Test your Knowledge of Volcanoes Contest** Dec 3

🏆 **Kids Door** Dec 2

Clicking on the text "What is VolcanoWorld?" displays another page, part of which is shown in Figure 6.6.

FIGURE 6.6   Sample Page from VolcanoWorld Web Site

What is VolcanoWorld ?

Volcanoes are one of the most dramatic phenomena in nature, attracting millions of visitors each year to US national parks, and fascinating millions more children in school science courses. We will greatly enrich the learning experiences of these targeted groups by delivering high quality remote sensing images, other data, and interactive experiments that add depth, variety and currency to existing volcano information sources.

VolcanoWorld brings modern and near real time volcano information to specific target audiences and other users of the Internet. VolcanoWorld draws extensively on remote sensing images (AVHRR, Landsat TM, Magellan, Gloria, etc.) and other data collections. We add value to these data by relating each image to geologic processes, and by encouraging users to analyse images with provided algorithms. VolcanoWorld has a very easy to use, Hypercard-like interface which will ultimately have these options:

1. Update on volcanic activity
2. Volcanic regions
3. How volcanoes work
4. Historical eruptions
5. Submarine volcanoes
6. Planetary volcanoes
7. How to become a volcanologist
8. Ask a volcanologist
9. Volcano contests
10. Further explorations
11. About this volcano

Currently, some information is available for items 1, 2, 7, 8, and 10. Check us out frequently, because we add new information - and answer your questions - every day!

Can save images   Web browsers provide the first practical applications for viewing images as they are sent across the Internet. The images appear on the computer screen rather than being saved as a file for later viewing. (Browsers can also be

FIGURE 6.7   Sample Graphic from VolcanoWorld Web Site

Mount St. Helens, WA on 10/16/94 from STS-64 (STS064-51-025)

When Mount St. Helens erupted on 18 May 80, the top 1300 ft. disappeared within minutes. The blast area covered an area of more than 150 sq. miles and sent thousands of tons of ash into the upper atmosphere.

used to save the information that is received.) Figure 6.7 is an example of a graphic from VolcanoWorld: a satellite view of Mount St. Helens.

The World Wide Web is rapidly incorporating many earlier uses of the Internet, and the newer browsers allowing users to navigate the Web are incorporating many functions of programs needed to use the Internet. A Web browser can be used to send and receive mail, download files, and visit gopher and newsnet sites. The Internet continues to exist apart from the Web and software applications for using the Internet still exist, but there is no real need for most users to learn the intricacies of other ways to locate and interact with Internet resources.

Web Browsers

Web browser assembles pieces of information

The exciting multimedia displays you encounter when exploring the Web are sent to you in pieces and then assembled by your Web browser. The one essential piece among the assortment of file types is a simple file containing plain text. This file has no large headline-sized fonts, no centered headings, and even no mandatory paragraph breaks. There certainly are no integrated pictures of the sort you encountered when you read about word processing (see Chapter 5). This simple text document has one unique characteristic. Embedded within the text are the special tags making up the **hypertext markup language** (**HTML**). The tag <BR> tells the browser to break and start a new line of text. The tag set <I></I> surrounding text would cause that text to appear italicized. The IMG tag causes an image to be transferred and displayed (e.g., <IMG SRC="mark.gif">). (*Note*: You will learn more about HTML and how to actually construct Web pages in Chapter 10.) A Web

Browser interprets markup language

browser interprets — or, more accurately, tries to interpret — the HTML tags and builds the Web page before your eyes. Because different browsers may do this work in different ways, the appearance of a given Web page will depend on the browser you use. HTML is also constantly evolving and there are differences of opinion over which functions should be included. If your browser is out of date or is not designed to implement one of these new functions, some feature the Web page author included will just not be displayed.

Expanding variety of formats

The variety of formats available over the Web is constantly expanding. We have already mentioned text, pictures, movies, and sounds. New additions include 3-D virtual experiences (based on **VRML — virtual reality modeling language**), "live" video and audio, and small programs (**applets**) that are transferred to your computer and run within your browser (e.g., Java applets). This variety of formats is available because of special applications software that works as a companion to the browser. Usually, developers first

Helper applications and plug-ins

create what are called **helper applications,** which function like a second program. The browser downloads a file (e.g., a quicktime movie) and the helper application presents it, in this case, the movie. Newer browsers that have been developed allow **plug-ins**. A plug-in is a special type of software developed to function within another software application. Many helper applications have been converted to plug-ins. Plug-ins perform their roles *within* the browser — for example, by presenting a movie within the browser window rather than in a separate window. As newer versions of browsers are developed, the more popular functions once provided by helper applications and plug-ins are sometimes incorporated into the browser.

Plug-ins and helper applications must be obtained independently of the browser. This usually means they must be downloaded from a different Internet source, which can often be accomplished using the browser. Sometimes when a Web author uses an uncommon multimedia element (e.g., a VRML scene), the author will also point you to a Web site where the player for that element can be obtained.

Get a free browser

For educators, one of the great things about browsers is that they are free. You simply connect to the host site of the company that developed the browser and download it. How do you get started if you don't have an old browser with which to download a new one? One suggestion would be to purchase a book about the World Wide Web for educators. Many books come with software. Another suggestion would be to get a copy from an educator who already uses the Web. Addresses for obtaining copies of four popular browsers (Netscape Communications Navigator, Microsoft Internet Explorer, NCSA Mosaic, and Cyberdog) are provided at the end of the chapter.

Keeping track of valuable sites

All browsers have the capability to store the location and perhaps even a brief description of Web pages you have visited and may want to find again. This is definitely one feature of browsers that you will want to learn to use. Depending on the browser, this list of important URLs may be referred to as "bookmarks," "favorites," or a "notebook." We will use bookmarks, to keep our description more concise. Adding a bookmark to the stored list is as simple as selecting the "Add Bookmark" option from one of the browser menus. Collecting valued sites in this fashion works well until you begin to accumulate a huge list. At that point, you are going to want to learn how to organize your list of favorite Web sites. Browsers all have some system for categorizing the list of stored URLs. A common system is to allow the user to create and name file folders and then to move individual URLs into the appropriate folders. An organized system becomes helpful when you have located hundreds of sites you want to remember. One final option may be helpful to teachers. It is possible to *export* a list of bookmarks as an HTML document (authoring HTML documents will be discussed in Chapter 10). A student can open this document with a browser, click on one of the options from your list, and visit that Web site.

SEARCHING THE WEB

Search engines locate resources

Search engines have sprung up as an answer to the extensiveness, disarray, and transitory nature of the Web. There is a tremendous amount of information available, but finding exactly what you want can be a challenge. Search engines are fed by robots that continually roam the Internet looking for new servers and new pages; indexing software that identifies key words contained in the Web pages that are found; and Web librarians, who examine Web documents and classify material they feel might be useful. Search engines access the rich databases of information these methods develop. More and more, making effective use of the Web requires developing some familiarity with several search engines.

Types of Search Engines

There are many search engines bidding for your attention. As soon as you connect to a commercial search engine, it will be immediately apparent that these resources are supported by advertising dollars. You have to maneuver among the colorful product displays to get your work done. However, it is hardly fair to complain about services that are free and that work so hard to get you to use them. The individuals responsible for developing and maintaining search engines have taken different approaches. It is worthwhile to be aware of the different strategies that are used and familiar with search engines implementing each strategy. Different strategies and different search engines produce different results.

Meta-index searches

Meta-Index Searches. Some search engines actually activate and cross-reference the results from several others. These searches take quite a bit longer than other searches because the results from several primary search engines must first be received and integrated, and the duplicates eliminated. Examples include MetaCrawlers and SavvySearch.

Concept searches

Concept Searches. A concept search is based on a cataloging system very much like that maintained by conventional libraries. Human editors examine Web material as it becomes available and organize useful material into some type of classification system. You can search by dealing directly with the hierarchical system of catalog topics or by searching the cataloged material for key terms. This type of search strategy will not provide access to everything on the Web, but the collective results of such a search will be of a little higher quality. Examples include Yahoo!, Lycos, and Excite.

Index searches

Index Searches. Index search sites rely on a computer-generated index of the contents of Web sites. The techniques are more sophisticated than a simple list of all the Web pages containing a specific word. Rule-based artificial intelligence systems built into search engines might use variables, such as the number of times key words are mentioned in an article or how close to the top of a document a key word appears, in determining the most relevant Web pages for you to examine. Index search strategies are becoming more sophisticated but still can't do things like recognize synonyms for requested search terms. Examples include AltaVista and Infoseek Ultra.

Personal Indexes. Companies are just now releasing software that allows individuals to create personal index search engines. The technique works like that described for index searches, but is based on personal priorities.

Opinions differ on best search method

Every extensive user of the Web seems to have an opinion about which search engine is most useful. From time to time, articles appear in computer magazines in which an author attempts a more systematic approach and compares the different search engines on a standard set of search tasks (Seiter, 1996). Despite authors' recommendations based on these analyses, examination of the actual search data shows that search engine effectiveness differs between assignments. If anything, reading such articles has caused us to try different search engines than we might normally employ. If you feel information probably exists on a topic and the results from your favorite search engine are disappointing, it is worth trying both a different engine and a different combination of search terms.

Sophisticated searches

Web search engines usually present users with a very simple and easy-to-use interface. An unfortunate consequence of this normally desirable circumstance is that many users never really learn to take advantage of the powerful search features that are available. It is so easy to just type something into the little text field, click the "Submit" button, and see what you get. Usually you will get something, but it would be unfortunate if you assumed that the links at the top of the list were the best resources the Internet had to offer. Search engines are usually capable of conducting a variety of Boolean searches (see Chapter 7, page 244), and learning at least some of the rules a particular search engine uses to conduct such searches is important to anyone using the Internet for serious research.

Results of different search methods

Let's use the search requested in Figure 6.8 as an example. The request as submitted actually generates more than 50,000 hits. If the request were submitted as "civil war battles" (with the phrase enclosed in quotations), the search generates slightly more than 200 hits. The search engine interprets these two requests in very different ways. In the first situation, the search process locates all web pages containing civil, war, or battles. In the second situation, the search engine finds pages containing the phrase "civil war battles." Actually, the links available at the top of the list are similar because this particular search engine places documents containing several of the targeted terms before documents containing fewer targeted terms. As you might expect based on this explanation, the links at the end of the two lists are very different.

Boolean search strategies

Let's see what you remember. You probably learned the basics of Boolean logic in a high school math class. Boolean operators (e.g. AND, NOT, OR) define ways in which sets can be combined. What is accomplished by the

FIGURE 6.8 AltaVista Search Page

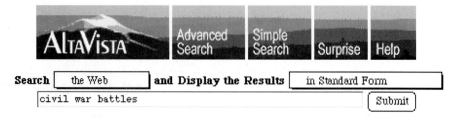

following search request: bat NOT baseball NOT computer? The answer is the generation of a list of Web resources about bats — the furry flying kind. You can probably guess the purpose of NOT baseball. This excludes the large number of Web pages containing information about different baseball players that often contain information about whether they *bat* left- or right-handed, pages devoted to collecting baseball *bats*, and other pages focused on the game of baseball. The request to exclude pages about computers may stump you. Some computers include *bat files,* which list special instructions the computer is to follow. Many hardcore computer users find it useful to discuss such things. At any rate, excluding Web pages about baseball and computers generates a list of resources containing a much higher proportion of hits on the topic we really want to review.

In some situations, knowing how to search efficiently is nearly essential to achieving satisfactory results. A search such as the one we have proposed using the word *bat* can generate thousands of hits. Some search engines limit the size of the list of Web sites returned to the user. In such cases, many good resources might never be found. Even if a list containing several thousand potentially valuable pages were given it would take hours to go through the list to identify the sites that provide relevant information. As the resources of the Web have grown, learning to search those resources effectively has become an essential skill.

Search techniques to master

How search procedures are implemented will vary with the search engine. Here are some things you might want to find out about the search engine you decide to use.

◆ How to search for a phrase — e.g., *civil war battle*
◆ How will upper- versus lower-case letters be interpreted in a search request — a lower-case request probably finds both lower- and upper-case matches and an upper-case search only upper-case matches; a search for maRK would find nothing
◆ Whether there is an option for wild card searches — e.g., battl* would find battle, battles, battleship, battlefield, and so forth, with some search engines
◆ How to request AND, OR, NOT combinations of search terms — e.g., some engines use + and - and some AND and NOT (all in caps).

USING THE WEB FOR ACTIVE LEARNING

The Internet — particularly the large body of information available through the World Wide Web — is a tremendous educational resource. The intuitive nature of browsers and the power of search engines allow students to easily find information on almost any topic imaginable. The quantity and breadth of what can be explored is impressive and educators should be excited by the potential. Students can visit the museums of the world; access the same satellite images and meteorological data available to local weather forecasters; and tag along as adventurers climb mountain peaks, explore the depths of the oceans, or bicycle through parts of the world most of us will never see — all without leaving the classroom. The Internet presents educators and learners with tremendous opportunities, but the resources alone are not enough.

In a way, the Internet is the world's largest and strangest library. It holds all the wonderful and exciting resources we have described and many more. Because there are so few restrictions on who can publish in this forum, it also contains information that is clearly biased, potentially offensive, in poor taste, or inaccurate. We are turning students loose to wander around in this environment and we must recognize certain potential problems. We don't want students to become focused on the offensive or inappropriate (see Chapter 11 for more on this issue). But other challenges are not as obvious. A popular and fairly accurate description of what many Internet users do is "surf the Net." The user drifts from resource to resource as first one link and then another attracts a click of the mouse. As we have emphasized repeatedly, exposure to information is not the same as meaningful learning. Exposure does not necessarily result in the depth of thought necessary to discount biased or

Mere exposure allows passive learning

The World Wide Web provides access to a tremendous number of different information resources. Here students use the World Wide Web as part of a collaborative project. (© Michael Zide)

inaccurate information. It also does not guarantee the mental activity necessary to construct personal meaning.

To get students to use the Web productively, teachers are going to have to play an active role. They might require that students "study" specific Web resources (for example, visit specific URLs) or they might require students to use the Web to gather resources to generate a product (for example, a paper on a specific topic). These approaches may provide an **incremental advantage** over existing practices in that students have access to many more resources and can access these resources more efficiently than is presently the case, but they do not offer a **transformational advantage**. Student experiences would still emphasize similar classroom activities and the same cognitive skills, even without the Internet. The transformational advantage of Internet activities would be realized if students were engaged in different learning activities emphasizing cognitive skills that have some unique value. These skills might be unique in emphasizing new areas, such as information literacy, or in finding ways to effectively target skills that have always been valued, but that are difficult to develop in some content areas, such as critical thinking and problem solving.

Here is a somewhat different way to think about how you might want to use Web resources. Consider how Web access might contribute to an ACTIVE learning environment. The Web can provide factual answers to simple objective questions, but it can also provide information that students can use in trying to resolve complex problems and questions with no definitive answers. Using Web resources in the investigation of complex problems is a good way to integrate the use of technology into nearly any content area and a way to take on challenges that students can attack collaboratively. Giving students the opportunity to use knowledge and skills in ways that are authentic to the discipline provide valuable opportunities for assessment.

Incremental versus transformational advantage

A CTIVE
C OOPERATION
T HEME-BASED
I NTEGRATED
V ERSATILE
E VALUATION

Creating an ACTIVE learning environment

OBTAINING CURRENT WEATHER DATA: AN INTERNET PROJECT

Here is an example of a project that uses the Web as a source of authentic scientific data. Working with data allows students the opportunity to use knowledge and skills in ways that are appropriate to a particular subject matter domain (see the discussion of authentic activities in Chapter 2, pages 65 to 66). The teacher's role in this example is critical. He or she must help students propose questions that are interesting and appropriate to their backgrounds and abilities. The teacher's involvement as the project unfolds is also essential in challenging students to think deeply about what they are doing and what they are discovering.

The Weather Underground has provided current weather data on the

Internet for several years. The present system makes use of the World Wide Web and is easy to learn.

Consider a project based on the question "Are winter temperatures in Alaska colder than winter temperatures in North Dakota?" This question might seem relatively simple, but determining a valid way to find the answer requires some careful thought. Are there places in Alaska that are colder than places in North Dakota? Are there places in North Dakota that are colder than places in Alaska? Is Alaska the coldest state? What would be a reasonable way to summarize winter temperature as a single variable? Why might people hold stereotypes about what particular places they have not actually experienced are like?

Simple data can address complex issues

One way to begin is to explore to determine what information is available. The Weather Underground provides current weather conditions for designated cities. After examining the city list for each state, as in Figure 6.9, students know that they can obtain weather information for ten Alaska cities and four North Dakota cities. It might occur to them that to provide a complete answer to the question, they may need to gather information related to more than one location in each state. How many cities and which to include are important questions. Perhaps it would be enough to simply select every other one on each list. Perhaps it might be useful to examine a map and select cities from different parts of each state, or cities reflecting different geographic characteristics. To continue this example, assume that students have selected Fargo and Bismarck in North Dakota and Anchorage and Juneau in Alaska.

The data gathered from a day in mid-December indicate that the current

FIGURE 6.9 Weather Underground Information for Alaska

City	Temp. (F)	Humidity	Pressure (in)	Conditions
Anchorage	26°	44%	30.36	blowing snow
Barrow	-15°	77%	30.64	Clear
Fairbanks	-9°	77%	N/A	light snow
Juneau	30°	100%	N/A	Clear
Ketchikan	35°	89%	29.66	Clear
Kodiak	32°	45%	N/A	Clear
McGrath	-22°	74%	30.85	Mostly Cloudy
Nome	19°	87%	30.54	light snow
Valdez	38°	28%	30.16	Mostly Cloudy
Yakutat	26°	100%	29.91	Mostly Cloudy

Use Web with other computer tools

temperatures were Bismarck, 21; Fargo, 17; Anchorage, 26; and Juneau, 30. At this point, students might want to determine whether they can now answer the original question. There are always abnormally warm and cold days during the winter. Perhaps the data are not representative of typical winter temperatures. Perhaps Juneau is having an unusually warm spell. A more scientific approach might be to gather data over several weeks and then to calculate an average to determine the typical temperature. Having easy access to data and thoughtful guidance from a teacher can help students learn some of the skills of thoughtful inquiry. Students could use a spreadsheet to record the data from several cities over several days and calculate an average temperature for each city (see the spreadsheet and graph from study in Chapter 5, pages 175 and 176). Some parts of Alaska are warmer and others are colder than the typical winter temperatures in North Dakota. The teacher and students might want to know why this is the case. Of course, finding out why will require that students go to the library or the Internet and do more research.

SCAFFOLDING WEB EXPLORATION

Scaffold Web experiences

How do we help students use the Web effectively, particularly when we want to encourage them to use Web resources in ways that are likely to be unfamiliar? One approach is based on cognitive apprenticeship, scaffolding, and some of the other concepts you first encountered in Chapter 2. The basic idea is to gradually ease students into what are likely to be challenging tasks by creating a supportive structure to guide their work. In other words, as the teacher you would initially do some of the work for students.

Why students need help

Here is how the process would work and how the teacher might create a scaffold to support novice students. Assume that you would like your students to write a position paper on a controversial topic. If the student were working independently, he or she would have to find resources related to the topic, examine a number of the resources in an attempt to determine both the opposing positions and the basic arguments for and against each position, select a position to defend, find particularly good sources related to that position, carefully review the sources to obtain key data and develop sound arguments, and then write the paper. Consider just a couple of areas that might cause difficulty. Students may lack the experience to use a Web browser in a sophisticated way, such as to conduct a sophisticated search or bookmark potentially relevant resources. Students might be unable or unmotivated to find truly good sources among the many that are available or they might lack the reading or inquiry skills necessary to identify different positions or the arguments for and against these positions.

Guidance from the teacher

Now consider how the teacher might participate to assist the student. The teacher might conduct an initial Web search, generate a list of potential sites, and then designate three helpful sites students must review. For each of these sites, the teacher might offer guiding comments, such as, this resource presents a good description of the general problem and outlines positions A and B or this site provides some very persuasive arguments for position B. The teacher might also deal with some computer skill issues by authoring a simple Web page presenting this background material to the students and directly linking students to the more productive sites (Chapter 10 will discuss Web authoring). If the students have even the most basic competence in using a browser, this Web page would allow them to connect directly to the suggested resources. The cognitive apprenticeship model assumes that students will gradually take on more and more of these skills. Perhaps the process might begin by having students search for their own resources to augment those provided by the teacher or by having students review key resources without suggesting specific things they should try to learn from each resource.

The WebQuest

Bernie Dodge (1995) has proposed that educators provide scaffolding through what he describes as WebQuests. A WebQuest is a document (usually prepared as a WWW page) consisting of (a) a brief introduction to a topic, (b) the description of an inquiry task related to the topic, (c) a set of primary WWW resources students can use in performing the task, and (d) a description of specific processes students should employ in performing the assigned task.

A CTIVE
C OOPERATION
T HEME-BASED
I NTEGRATED
V ERSATILE
E VALUATION

Other active techniques

Others have proposed similar mechanisms for engaging students in "active" involvement with Internet resources. Some of the first demonstrations of Apple Computer's Cyberdog browser and Cyberdog DocBuilder were structured Internet inquiry activities. (*Note*: DocBuilder uses a unique approach in which "parts" are embedded in a "container" document. Parts and container documents are special features of a method of software development called opendoc architecture. With this approach, small chunks of code performing specific desired functions can be used to assemble useful programs.) Pictures and text fields (areas for displaying or entering text) could be combined with "parts" that are links to Web sites or even an active Web site embedded within the document. The earliest demonstrations of these free products showed how educators could easily create structured Internet experiences for their students. The basic idea was to create a document that provided background and proposed an inquiry activity using text and graphics and then directed students to relevant Internet resources using embedded links (see Figure 6.10).

Teachers don't have to master any particular authoring software to present Internet inquiry activities to their students. The Cyberdog Docbuilder approach is interesting because it allows the creation of an informative "document" that has integrated within it the tools necessary to access the Internet. A similar approach could be taken by teachers who have learned some of the advanced techniques available within HyperStudio (see Chapter 8, pages 285 to 293). A conventional paper document listing the actual URLs could be prepared for distribution to students and would work nearly as well.

FIGURE 6.10   Web Inquiry Task Prepared with DocBuilder

Paying Farmers Not to Farm: Everyone Benefits!

Background: Some farmland areas would make great habitat for ducks and deer. The same land could be used to hold rainwater and snow melt so that it does not run into rivers too quickly. However, farmers cannot raise crops on land that is used in these ways. In most cases, this land is not great for crops, but it is still better than nothing. The government uses tax money to pay farmers not to grow crops on such areas. Whether this is necessary and how much money should be provided are always controversial.

Activities: (pick one)

• Write an editorial for your local paper urging your congresspersons to support Conservation Reserve Program legislation.

• Write a newspaper article explaining to farmers the long-term benefits of accepting modest subsidies to set aside low-yield land for conservation purposes.

Primary Internet Resources

▢ Lists ways the public benefits from land taken out of production.

▢ How original wetlands were formed, the functions wetlands serve in nature, and how they can be restored.

▢ Description of Conservation Reserve Program

Other Resources

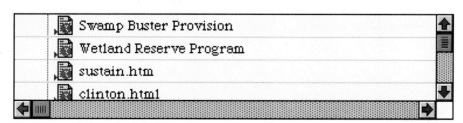

- Swamp Buster Provision
- Wetland Reserve Program
- sustain.htm
- clinton.html

Focus

Citing Internet Sources

Research is one of the most common reasons secondary and elementary students use the Internet. Students need to learn to provide citations for Internet resources just as they cite the sources of other information. Some feel citing Internet sources is especially important because the nature of the Internet makes it so easy to copy and paste material. Providing accurate citations makes students aware of their responsibilities and provides teachers a way to follow up on the resources students have used (Li, 1996).

Here is the basic citation format:

Author/editor. (Year). Title (edition), [Type of medium]. Producer (optional). Available: Protocol (e.g., FTP, HTTP): Site/Path/File [Access date].

Sample WWW Resource

Li, X. (1996). Electronic Sources: APA Style of Citation, [On-line]. Available: http://www.uvm.edu/~xli/reference/apa.html [1996, June 22].

Sample FTP Resource

Smithsonian Institution. (1992). gorila.jpg.bin, [On-line]. Available: ftp://ftp.apple.com/alug/Smith/jpg/gorila.jpg.bin [1996, June 22].

One of the frustrating things about Internet resources is that they have a tendency to disappear as host sites come and go. The access date indicates when that resource was found. This date may be helpful to someone following up on a large list of citations. Chances are, more recent access dates would still be available, and perhaps the later citations would be the place to start. ✳

SUMMARY

The Internet, the vast web of interconnected computers that spans the globe, has been growing at a phenomenal rate. Educational interest in the resources of the Internet has heightened, too. Approximately 50 percent of schools have some form of access to the Internet, but few students can connect from their classrooms or transfer information at a rapid rate.

The Internet provides access to other people, to files that can be downloaded for personal use, and to the interactive hypermedia environment called the World Wide Web. Teachers and students can communicate directly with other individuals through e-mail or take part in discussions by sending comments to a list server that will relay those comments to all members who subscribe to the list.

Under the older system for transferring stored information across the Internet, the user connected to a remote computer and transferred a file to the local computer. The user could then choose the appropriate software to examine the information (for example, a text file with a word processor) or, if the transferred file was a program, use the program. An alternative approach now provides this capability and some exciting new features. This system, called the World Wide Web, transfers information from a remote computer to the host computer in somewhat the same manner as the older system, but allows a more interactive approach because information is presented by the same software used to access the remote computer. In addition, those preparing resources for access by World Wide Web browsers are able to present multimedia content and include links users can follow to other resources found on other servers.

Whether students communicate with other people or explore information resources, access alone is not sufficient for meaningful learning. Teachers need to give serious thought to how they will help students use the vast resources of the Internet to learn and solve authentic problems more effectively. This chapter suggested a number of introductory activities that require students to work with the information the Internet makes available.

REFLECTING ON CHAPTER 6

Activities

◆ Subscribe to one of the listservs described in this chapter or in another resource for educators (make sure you take note of the procedure for unsubscribing). After one week, summarize the topics discussed on the list and evaluate how helpful you feel the list would be to educators.

◆ Compare the productivity of several Web search engines. Select a search engine from each of the categories described on pages 211 and 212 and submit an identical search request (e.g., webquest) to each. What do you note about the results you generate? Does the search topic seem to make a difference?

◆ Design the "paper equivalent" of a WebQuest for a topic that interests you. Describe a problem, propose inquiry questions, and identify key Web resources as described on pages 218 through 220.

Key Terms

analog modem *(p. 192)*
applets *(p. 209)*
ASCII *(p. 203)*
binary *(p. 203)*
browser *(p. 205)*
chat mode *(p. 194)*
conference *(p. 199)*
domain name *(p. 191)*
download *(p. 199)*
electronic mail (e-mail) *(p. 195)*
forum *(p. 199)*

FTP *(p. 201)*
header *(p. 198)*
helper application *(p. 209)*
home page *(p. 206)*
hypertext markup language (HTML)
    (p. 209)
incremental advantage *(p. 215)*
Internet *(p. 190)*
Internet service provider (ISP)
    (p. 192)
IP number *(p. 191)*

IRC   *(p. 194)*
ISDN modems   *(p. 193)*
list server   *(p. 196)*
local area network (LAN)   *(p. 192)*
mailing lists   *(p. 196)*
newsgroup   *(p. 199)*
plug-ins   *(p. 209)*
PPP (point-to-point protocol)
   (p. 193)
reflector site   *(p. 200)*
shareware   *(p. 199)*
SLIP   *(p. 193)*

TCP/IP   *(p. 191)*
terminal server   *(p. 192)*
thread   *(p. 198)*
transformational advantage
   (p. 215)
URL   *(p. 205)*
VRML — virtual reality modeling
   language   *(p. 209)*
wide area network (WAN)
   (p. 192)
World Wide Web (WWW)   *(p. 204)*

Resources for Teachers Using the Internet

Resources to Expand Your Knowledge Base

Any good bookstore is likely to carry a number of publications describing the Internet and providing detailed explanations for using different World Wide Web browsers. We have found the following more specialized publications for teachers to be useful.

Classroom Connect Staff. (1996). *Educator's Internet companion.* Lancaster, PA: Wentworth.

Classroom Connect Staff. (1996). *Educator's World Wide Web tourguide.* Lancaster, PA: Wentworth.

Frazier, D. (1995). *Internet for kids.* Alameda, CA: Sybex.

Technology journals for teachers carry features and regular columns dealing with Internet activities. In 1992, *The Computing Teacher* (now *Learning and Leading with Technology*) initiated a column called "Mining the Internet." ISTE, 1787 Agate St., Eugene, OR 97403.

Classroom Connect, Wentworth Worldwide Media, Inc., P.O. Box 10488, Lancaster, PA 17605-0488. This is a monthly publication providing information on using the Internet and commercial telecommunications services.

Locating the Software and Services Mentioned in Chapter 6

CU-SeeMe can be downloaded for your use. Try using FTP to connect to gated.cornell.edu or ftp.classroom.net.

Following are the URLs for the various search engines described in Chapter 6:

AltaVista http://www.altavista.digital.com/

Excite http://www.excite.com

Infoseek Ultra http://ultra.infoseek.com

Lycos http://www.lycos.com

MetaCrawler http://metacrawler.cs.washington.edu:8080/index.html

SavvySearch http://guaraldi.cs.colostate.edu:2000/./

Yahoo! http://www.yahoo.com

The Web browsers described in this chapter can all be downloaded for educational use:

Cyberdog http://cyberdog.apple.com

Microsoft Internet Explorer http://www.microsoft.com/ie/iedl.htm

NCSA Mosaic http://www.ncsa.uiuc.edu/SDG/Software/Mosaic/

Netscape Communications Navigator
www.netscape.com/comprod/mirror/client_download.html

The weather project used the University of Michigan's *Weather Underground.* This Web site provides current weather data, maps, satellite images, and curriculum guides for teachers at http://www.wundergound.com.

Unique Web Experiences

With thousands of educationally relevant Web sites, it isn't feasible to provide a list of sites you must see. Here is a list of unique sites that demonstrate the breadth of what students can experience on the Web.

Trip Quest provides travel route and distance information based on origin and destination provided by the user (http://www.mapquest.com/)

Fast Food Calories recommends menu items when user enters desired grams of fat and fast food establishment (http://www.olen.com/food/index.html)

The Why Files? discusses scientific findings associated with news stories (http://whyfiles.news.wisc.edu/index.html)

Foreign Languages for Travelers provides audio pronunciation of useful travel phrases for selected languages (http://www.travlang.com/languages/)

Real Audio is real-time programs from radio stations around the world (http://www.prognet.com/)

White House tours the White House and offers a message from the president (http://www.whitehouse.gov/)

Robotics allows students to move a robotic arm and plant a seed (http://www.usc.edu/dept/garden/)

Chapter **7**

Introducing Multimedia Applications for Classroom Learning

 ORIENTATION

The goal of this chapter is to identify ways students can use multimedia tools to explore, think about, and involve themselves with course content in personally meaningful ways. First, we look at ways multimedia can be used as a delivery system for the computer-assisted instruction (CAI) you read about in Chapter 3. Then we look at other types of multimedia software, such as talking books, that are not CAI materials. Finally, we examine the educational advantages of multimedia and hypermedia as applications that present information in a variety of ways. As you read, look for answers to the following questions:

FOCUS QUESTIONS

- ◆ What changes might multimedia tools bring about in the functioning of schools?
- ◆ In what ways can multimedia and hypermedia support verbal instruction?
- ◆ What kinds of content can multimedia present to students in particularly powerful ways?
- ◆ What are some of the unique advantages offered by multimedia environments?
- ◆ What are some concerns related to multimedia applications that classroom teachers need to recognize?
- ◆ How do multimedia applications support students' meaningful learning?

WHAT ARE MULTIMEDIA, HYPERMEDIA, AND HYPERTEXT?

The terms describe different combinations of media and communication methods.

Official definitions of *multimedia, hypermedia,* and *hypertext* don't really exist. There are no "industry standards," and different people use the terms differently. Educators sometimes use the terms interchangeably, even though they are intended to describe different combinations of media and communication methods. We have developed the definitions offered here based on product characteristics, and our system seems in agreement with the distinctions others have drawn in efforts to differentiate the terms (e.g., Tolhurst, 1995). A product is whatever the developer gives to the consumer to communicate information, experience, and emotion. This book is a product that you and we are using to share information, experiences, and some feelings.

If a product uses more than one modality (say, visual and auditory); at least two symbol systems within a modality (words and pictures); or at least two genres within a symbol system (prose and poetry, a still image and video), the product includes multiple media — that is, multimedia. *Multimedia* thus translates as "many formats." By this definition, a child's story illustrated with drawings or a series of slides with musical accompaniment is multimedia.

How multimedia has changed over the years

The term *multimedia* has been around since the early 1970s. Instructional media courses used to refer to slide-and-sound or filmstrip-and-sound presentations as multimedia. You may remember filmstrip and tape combinations in which a beep from the tape recorder told someone to advance the filmstrip.

This book concentrates on forms of multimedia in which a computer is involved, one way or another. The computer either presents information directly or controls the presentation of information from some other source, such as CD-ROM or videodisc. Some would prefer that the term *multimedia* (and *hypermedia*) refer to the entire system, including hardware, software, and document, used to communicate with the system user (Marchionini, 1988). The term *document* here refers to the actual data file or files storing the text, graphics, and sounds. The combination of hardware, application software, and document is probably what most educators now understand multimedia to be. This definition would exclude a textbook with pictures, for example. **Multimedia** is a communication format that integrates several media — text, audio, video, and animation — most commonly implemented with a computer.

The definition of multimedia

The definition of hypermedia

Hypermedia allows multimedia to be experienced in a nonlinear fashion. In this format, units of information, such as individual words, segments of text, segments of audio, pictures, animations, and video clips, are connected to each other in multiple ways. The individual working within a hypermedia environment exerts a high degree of control over the order in which he or she experiences these individual items. Hypermedia environments are often described as *interactive* because the hypermedia user must direct the software and hardware environment to present the next unit of information to be experienced. Because control is vested in the user, different individuals potentially have very different experiences as they work in hypermedia environments. If the same student works with a hypermedia environment on several occasions, it is also likely that the student will explore the environment in different ways.

The definition of hypertext

When the information in hypermedia consists entirely of text, the term **hypertext** is sometimes used. Hypertext was actually the first form of hypermedia (see Focus: A Brief History of Hypermedia, on page 228), but now this format rarely exists in educational settings.

What is linear organization?

The idea of an organized yet nonlinear system might be a bit confusing. Here's a comparison that might help explain how hypermedia works. Traditional books are organized in a linear fashion. As you read them, you encounter a series of ideas. An author orders the ideas in this series based on his or her opinion of the structure that will make the information most interesting, most persuasive, or easiest to understand. If you were to read a section of a chapter a second time, you would obviously encounter the same series of ideas in the same order. In fact, every student reading that section would move through the same set of ideas in the same order.

How is a hypermedia format different?

Now, consider how the same textbook, perhaps in a science, might be presented in a hypermedia format. From a particular segment of text describing scientific discoveries, the reader might be able to access the definition of any term appearing in bold print, view a picture of the famous scientist responsible for each discovery, read a short biographical sketch of the scientist, and review the scientific principles on which scientific breakthroughs were based. Some scientists and some scientific principles might be associated with several different discoveries. Different students might explore this environment in different ways. Some might just review the scientific discoveries. Some might read all the biographies of the scientists. Some might take each discovery in turn and learn about the discovery, the scientist, and the principles associated with that discovery. Some might review everything available about a famous scientist's work. In contrast to the predictable pattern of readers' working with a textbook, the exploration of a hypermedia environment offers much more variety.

Although multimedia and hypermedia are distinct, a separate discussion of each would be unnecessarily complicated. In this book, we use the term *multimedia* to discuss issues that apply to both multimedia and hypermedia. We use the term *hypermedia* only when an issue relates exclusively to hypermedia.

WHAT ARE CD-ROM AND VIDEODISC?

Discussions of multimedia and hypermedia always seem to include some reference to videodiscs and CD-ROMs. There is a practical reason for this association: both CD-ROMs and videodiscs are large-capacity storage media. Multimedia and hypermedia require access to tremendous amounts of information. The connection between the applications and the storage media is thus a very logical and necessary one. Some basic information about videodiscs and CD-ROMs should help you understand how they work and when they can be of particular value in classrooms.

Unlike the blank diskettes you might buy to store data from a word processing program or other computer tool, CD-ROMs and videodiscs are nearly always purchased already loaded with data. **CD-ROM** stands for *compact disc read only memory*. In other words, information stored on a CD-ROM can be read from the disc[1] into the memory of the computer but cannot be erased or modified. Until recently, this also meant that compact discs were used only for distributing commercial products and that consumers could not take advantage of compact discs' large capacity to store their own information. Because of our experience with music CDs, this is probably a limitation we take for granted. However, recordable CD technology is available to consumers. As you will read in the material that follows, recordable CDs will likely become very common because of the great storage capacity of blank CDs at very low cost.

What does CD-ROM mean?

Recordable CD technology

VIDEODISC TECHNOLOGY

The **videodisc** is the older of the two formats as a popular commercial product. A videodisc is about the size of a 33-rpm record and silver in color. It requires a special videodisc player, which spins the videodisc at a very high speed while a laser beam is bounced off the disc's surface. Microscopic pits in the surface of the disc cause variations in the way the laser beam is reflected back to a pickup device and allow the pickup device to read information from the disc. Since nothing really touches the surface of the disc, there is no wear, and discs should last indefinitely. Videodiscs are sometimes called **laserdiscs** because of this method of reading information from the disc. A videodisc is capable of storing both video and stereo audio. Instead of stereo, the two auditory channels are sometimes used to store two auditory sources, perhaps descriptive information in two different languages or a computer program.

Videodiscs are sometimes called laserdiscs.

---

[1] You may have wondered about the peculiar spelling of *disc*. This is a convention. Optical discs are spelled with a *c* and magnetic disks are spelled with a *k*.

A Brief History of Hypermedia

A scientist first imagined hypermedia as a tool to mimic and extend what he felt was the way people actually thought. In 1945, Vannevar Bush, President Franklin D. Roosevelt's director of scientific research and development, was given the task of coordinating the work of 6,000 scientists contributing to the war effort. Bush noted two things. First, there was the daunting task of keeping up with an ever-expanding body of knowledge. Second, the method of storing the existing knowledge base was inconsistent with the way Bush perceived the human mind to work. Bush observed that people seem to think by association. One idea tends to make you think of others. In contrast, information in files or books is stored serially and is referenced alphabetically or numerically. Bush's proposal was to create a form of technology capable of organizing and retrieving information in a manner more compatible with his perception of the way humans organized information in their memories. He wanted to develop physical tools that would be coordinated with and amplify human mental processes. In introducing the article in which Vannevar Bush (1945) first presented his ideas, the editor of the *Atlantic Monthly* magazine commented,

> For years inventions have extended man's physical powers rather than the powers of the mind. Trip hammers that multiply the fists, microscopes that sharpen the eye. . . . Now, says Mr. Bush, instruments are at hand which, if properly developed, will give man access to and command over the inherited knowledge of the ages. (p. 101)

The proposed machine, called a "memex," was never actually built. The memex was based on the mass storage medium of the time: microfilm. Bush imagined a special adaptation of the existing form of microfilm in which a code could be added to a particular image on microfilm. He envisioned a system in which a memex user might locate two related items of information and project both simultaneously. Using a special photographic feature, the user could mark each segment with a special code. In the future, the code attached to one microfilm segment would allow the memex to go directly to the associated microfilm segment. Users could also use the photographic coding capabilities of the memex to add their own notes and attach them to existing segments of microfilm. Using present terminology, the connection between segments would be called *links* and the segments would be called *nodes*.

Douglas Engelbart is regarded as the next hypervisionary. Engelbart, a radar operator during the war, had read Bush's classic *Atlantic* paper and was captivated by his ideas. When he heard about computers, he combined what he saw as the processing potential of this new technology with ideas about knowledge tools and his experience with visual displays from his background as a radar operator. In 1962, he wrote a paper describing his intentions to develop systems that would augment how individuals thought and how they worked together to solve complex problems. He proposed functional hypermedia systems for collaborative problem solving and the enhancement of writing. As the ideas were being developed, Engelbart's Augmentation Research Laboratory also contributed to the development of the mouse, windows, electronic mail, and computer conferencing. These computer tools and applications have become integral parts of they way we use technology today.

The third hypervisionary in this brief history is Theodor Nelson. The coining of the term *hypertext* is attributed to Ted Nelson. He described hypertext as "nonsequential writing" — a series of text chunks connected by links allowing a reader to select different pathways at will. In attempting to communicate his vision, Nelson offered the rather metaphorical suggestion that documents be modeled after the onion and not the potato. If desired, a reader should be able to peel back the layers to explore what an author has to say at a deeper level.

Nelson strongly supported personal freedoms, and his beliefs are evident in his proposals and projects. He believed in a national and international hypertext of information that everyone could explore. He even proposed convenient establishments, called "Silverstands," which citizens could visit to explore the "universal hypertext." If you glance back at Chapter 6, on computer tools, you will note a discussion of the Internet, a present-day, fully operational system with at least some of the features in Nelson's proposal. The World Wide Web seems very similar indeed to what Nelson proposed.

Bush, Engelbart, and Nelson did not create highly successful commercial hypermedia products or systems. Their contributions lay in concepts or in demonstrating how ideas could actually work. The first commercially successful hypermedia product for the microcomputer was called Guide. A few years later, in 1987, Apple Computer released HyperCard to run on the Macintosh computer. (*Note:* HyperCard and similar products will be discussed in detail in Chapter 8.) Since 1987, commercial products allowing microcomputer users to develop their own hypermedia have become commonplace. New hypermedia authoring environments show a tremendous range of power, sophistication, and cost. Some are designed as tools for elementary school children. Others allow professionals to create commercial products of great sophistication. Early forms of hypermedia resided on a single computer. Now, the World Wide Web links thousands of individual computers and millions of documents, pictures, sounds, and movies. These computers are located in every corner of the world. One sits on the corner of my desk. All have their roots in Bush's imagination and in his proposal of a tool that would work "as we may think." ✳

The storage capacity of videodiscs

Videodiscs store visual information as a series of frames or pictures. This is also true of videotape. The videodisc or videotape player sends these images to the screen at the rate of 30 frames per second, giving the illusion of motion. There is an important difference in the way a videodisc and a videotape store these individual images. A videotape stores the images in a series. A videodisc stores the images as concentric circles on the disc. With at least one type of videodisc, the same circle of information can be read over and over to provide a stationary image of very high quality. Because there are 54,000 frames on each side of this type of videodisc[2] and individual frames can be accessed very

---

[2] Most come with information stored on only one side.

quickly, a tremendous number of high-quality images are nearly instantly available with videodisc technology. To appreciate this storage capacity, translate this as the equivalent of 54,000 photographic slides that can be accessed at will, and you will begin to imagine how much information can be stored on one of these platters. In contrast, videotape is unable to provide practical access to individual images in a reasonable amount of time.

Videodisc Formats

The videodiscs themselves come in two formats: **CLV** (**c**onstant **l**inear **v**elocity) and **CAV** (**c**onstant **a**ngular **v**elocity). A CLV videodisc can hold about one hour of video but is really useful only for showing continuous video. A CAV videodisc holds only thirty minutes of continuous video but offers several very useful advantages. CAV discs allow the display of individual frames. CAV discs also allow the user to step through a sequence of video one frame at a time and to play video segments at different speeds, both forward and reverse. The instructional advantage of examining individual frames and precisely controlling the display of specific segments is well worth the difference in storage capacity.

Accessing videodisc images

Most educational videodiscs contain images to be displayed as individual frames, short video segments, and audio. The images can be accessed manually from the control panel on the front of the player, from a remote device similar in appearance to the device you use to change channels on your television or to control your videotape player, from a bar code reader, or by using a computer connected to the videodisc player. When the videodisc player is controlled by a computer, the images from the videodisc are often displayed on a separate monitor. In this case, the student could watch both the computer monitor and the monitor attached to the videodisc player. Images can also be viewed through the computer monitor. Depending on the type of computer, watching video through the computer monitor may require that special hardware be added to the computer (Barron et al., 1994).

Video and sound are stored on a videodisc in **analog format**. This format provides high quality and efficient storage, but does not allow the computer to manipulate the information without first capturing and digitizing the information. The information is not stored on the videodisc in the **digital format** used directly by your computer. One way to understand the difference between analog and digital is to think of the difference between a traditional and a digital clock. The time is expressed discretely by the digital clock. With a traditional clock, the expression of time is continuous and always changing. Computers need information represented in a discrete fashion.

Types of Videodiscs

There are several types of videodiscs, labeled level 0, level I, level II, and level III. Level 0 videodiscs are intended for movielike presentations and are viewed from beginning to end. Some years ago, movies were released on videodisc, but this format never really caught on. Level 1 videodiscs are controlled with a hand-held controller or a bar code reader. The hand-held controller allows the user to display a segment of video or advance to a specific frame.

Using the bar code reader

The bar code reader uses the technology you know from grocery store checkout lines. The bar codes indicate commands (forward, reverse), frame numbers, or the beginning and ending frames of a video segment, and are often printed in teacher's resource materials. Along with the videodisc, the teacher might receive a looseleaf notebook containing sample lesson plans and bar codes. As the teacher moves through the lesson with the class, the bar code reader is simply swiped across the bar code at the appropriate time to present an image or video segment on the monitor.

Software is also available (BarCode Maker, Videodiscovery MediaMAX) to create your own bar codes, like those shown in Figure 7.1. These bar codes can be printed by themselves or inserted in computer-generated text documents or graphics. A teacher or students can do some very interesting things with this kind of program. A teacher can create and print a list of bar codes representing the images the teacher might want to display during a presentation. During the presentation, simply running the bar code reader over the appropriate bar code displays the desired image on a monitor attached to the videodisc player. Students might prepare presentations of their own or create bar codes and stick them on maps, a globe, diagrams, or even a skeleton. Running the bar code reader over the bar code would present whatever image the student wanted the viewer to see (Barron et al., 1994).

FIGURE 7.1   Sample Bar Codes Produced with MediaMAX

18516 (President Kennedy)

18516

19522 (Berlin Wall)

19522

Level 2 videodiscs contain a program on the soundtrack that can be interpreted by a microprocessor in specially adapted videodisc players. Few of these specially equipped machines exist in educational settings.

When operating in level 3 format, the videodisc player is controlled by a computer. In some cases, the program running on the computer simply makes the selection of frames or segments easier for the viewer. A menu might appear on the computer screen, and the viewer can then just select the segment to be displayed on the monitor. A teacher might use this menu to present images as part of a classroom presentation in much the same way he or she might have used the hand controller or the bar code reader in the level 1 format. In some cases, the specific selections to accompany a presentation can be sequenced and stored in the computer ahead of time. The teacher can then move smoothly from one frame or video segment to another as the class proceeds. In the other main application of level 3 technology, the video frames or segments displayed are a component of the instructional program with which a student is interacting. Here, the student is involved in computer-assisted instruction of one form or another, and the videodisc is used to supply video and auditory information. The computer presents text, accepts student responses from the keyboard or some other input device, and makes decisions or offers choices in order to control how the instruction should proceed.

Repurposing to prepare presentations

Level 1 videodiscs can be used as level 3 videodiscs if software is developed to control them. Software of the type just described or software such as HyperCard or HyperStudio (we discuss these programs in Chapter 8) can also be used to control the display of images and video segments. Adapting a level 1 or level 3 videodisc originally developed for one use to a different kind of application or a different method of controlling the presentation is called **repurposing**. It is feasible for teachers and students to repurpose discs to prepare the presentations they wish to offer.

CD-ROM TECHNOLOGY

A CD-ROM holds about 600 **megabytes** (1 million bytes) of information on a disc that costs about $2 to produce. You are probably familiar with the appearance of CD-ROMs because CD-ROMs have nearly replaced records as the format of choice for music. With computer programs becoming larger and larger, CD-ROMs have become the most common format in which commercial software is made available. New computers usually come with a CD-ROM player already installed.

The advantage of digital format

CD-ROMs store information in digital form. This means that CD-ROMs can store not only music and pictures as data files, but also computer programs. The advantage of the digital format is that the computer user can

What Can You Do with 600 Megabytes of Storage?

It is difficult to appreciate what can be stored on a single CD-ROM. Here is the list of contents from Microsoft's Encarta, an electronic multimedia encyclopedia (Gates, 1995). ✳

◆ 9 million words of text on 26,000 topics
◆ 8 hours of sound
◆ 7,000 images
◆ 800 maps
◆ 250 interactive charts
◆ 100 animations and video clips

bring data of this type into the memory of the computer and work directly with the information. A picture from a CD-ROM can be modified using a graphics program or can be inserted in a word processing document.

The disadvantages of CD-ROM

The disadvantages of the CD-ROM approach include both capacity and speed. High-quality images may easily require 10 megabytes of space, and it takes a significant amount of time to load this much information into the computer. CD-ROM drives also tend to be slower than hard drives. Two variables — access speed and transfer speed — must be considered. *Access speed* is measured in milliseconds and reflects the average time it takes the CD player to locate a random piece of information. This variable is important when tasks involve a lot of searching. This might be the case with an encyclopedia CD. *Transfer speed* is the time it takes to transfer information to the

Transfer speed

computer. This is important when transferring large files, as might occur when retrieving large images, and critical when displaying video. Slower transfer speeds do not allow digitized video to compete with the quality allowed by videodiscs. When run from a slow player, digital video, such as **QuickTime** movies, runs at fewer frames per second than traditional video and thus appears of poorer quality. The original CD drives transferred data at 150 kilobytes per second. When you read advertisements for computers that come equipped with a CD drive, you will note that the drive is described as a 2X, 4X, 6X, or 10X drive. This designation expresses the speed of the drive in comparison to the speed of the original CD drives; for example, a 2X drive operates at 300 kilobytes per second.

The time is rapidly approaching when schools will be able to purchase, for a reasonable price, the equipment to generate their own CDs. The equipment exists now, but it may still be a bit beyond the price range of most schools. The technology works a little differently from the approach used to produce commercial CDs. The commercial process generates a master expensively and stamps individual CDs cheaply. The alternative approach is to burn information into a special CD blank. This process is much less expensive for producing individual CDs, but very expensive if you want to create many. An individual blank for this process is presently under $20. Even now, spending $20 to save 600 megabytes of information is incredibly inexpensive. Just imagine how many high-density floppies it would take to save that much information (approximately 500).

CD players in schools

CD players are more prevalent than videodisc players in schools. Roughly 63 percent of secondary schools and 47 percent of elementary schools own CD players. About 41 percent of secondary schools and 30 percent of elementary schools own videodisc players. Recent investment in both forms of technology has been heavy. Between 1992 and 1996, the number of CD-ROM players in secondary schools grew by 48 percent and the number of videodiscs by 27 percent. The same four-year period saw a 43 percent increase in CD players and a 48 percent increase in videodisc players in elementary schools (Quality Education Data, 1996). Because most new computers now come equipped with a built-in CD drive, it will eventually become more appropriate to discuss what percentage of computers have a CD drive rather than what percentage of schools.

Emerging Technology

Digital Video Discs

Because multimedia requires a tremendous amount of storage capacity, advances in multimedia educational experiences are linked to advances in storage technology. *Digital video disc (DVD)* technology promises some changes. A DVD looks very much like a standard CD, but the DVD player uses a more sophisticated laser system that allows the disc to contain more tracks and more densely packed pits, and to spin faster. In addition, a DVD potentially allows two layers of information on both sides of the disc (a CD has one layer of information on one side). How much capacity do these changes make available? The lowest-capacity DVD (one-side, one information layer) will hold 4.7 gigabytes and the high-end DVD will hold 17 gigabytes. The most obvious benefit of this amount of storage will be in the delivery of high-quality video for entertainment or educational purposes. A standard movie of the quality you are used to seeing on your television will fit comfortably on the lowest-capacity DVD and the high-end disc will hold 8 hours of video. The opportunity to integrate extended high-quality video segments into educational multimedia will provide experiences that are not now possible with standard CD technology. ✳

EDUCATIONAL APPLICATIONS USING MULTIMEDIA AND HYPERMEDIA

Multimedia and computer-assisted instruction

Multimedia can be used as a delivery system for the CAI activities described in Chapter 3. Often a multimedia environment will combine a number of different CAI activities. For example, *Animal Pathfinders* combines access to videodisc frames and video segments with various computer-based CAI activities to present a number of lessons about animal behavior. One lesson, "Bee Dances," explains how bees communicate the location of a food source. The capabilities of the videodisc and computer simulations are important in helping students grasp animal behaviors and many other phenomena that would be difficult to describe with other techniques. The observation of an actual event in any content area is nearly always a highly desirable option, and students should not have to rely on simple diagrams or written accounts.

Establishing a richer context for student understanding

When dealing with animal behaviors, the use of video segments can also give students a richer context for understanding (you might want to review the discussion of situated cognition in Chapter 2, pages 43–48).

Students learn about biological phenomena in order to better understand the natural world. The key is whether students will form these associations when confronted with information separated from the actual phenomena the information seeks to explain. Some students will, and some will not. For some, the concepts will be learned but will remain inert, instead of useful outside the classroom situation in which the information was encountered. Video segments depicting the inside of a beehive or bees searching for flowers may allow the student to connect with experiences not found in the classroom.

Among other examples, the *Animal Pathfinders* videodisc shows how a scout bee uses the "waggle dance" to communicate the location of a food source to other bees in the hive. The dance consists of a pair of looping movements separated by a running motion. The direction of the run explains the direction of the food relative to the position of the sun. The duration of buzzing during the run indicates the distance to the food source. Probably the most difficult part of this phenomenon to understand is the way both the direction of the bee's run and the position of the sun must be used to determine the direction of flowers. It may also be difficult to imagine what a bee's dance might look like. Perhaps our definition of two loops surrounding a running motion has not been sufficient for you to visualize a bee performing this dance. Does the bee lead with his (it would be a male) left foot or his right? Viewing a short video clip quickly solves the problem of recognizing the dance, but viewing the video clip cannot by itself do much to solve the more complex problem of understanding the relationship between the dance, the position of the sun, and the location of the flowers. The developers of "Bee

Combining a tutorial, a simulation, and a game

Dances" combine a tutorial, a simulation, and a game to present information, to assist students in achieving understanding, to provide extended practice, and to evaluate understanding (the four stages of instruction from Chapter 3). The tutorial uses text, a few simple diagrams, and images from the videodisc to explain the communication techniques of the honeybee. One simulation provides an opportunity to learn the geometric relationship between dance, sun, and flowers. One simulation lets the student become a bee and attempt to find flowers.

Dances with Bees

Teacher: What does *communicate* mean?

Student: It means to talk — kind of. It means to tell someone what you are thinking.

Teacher: Are animals able to communicate?

Student: Sure, my dog tells me when he wants to go outside.

[*Laughter*]

Teacher: How does your dog tell you he wants to go outside?

Student: He gives a few yips and moves toward the door.

Teacher: Okay. Do you think insects communicate?

[*Silence*]

Teacher: How about honeybees? Do you think they communicate? How would they communicate, and what would they have to say?

Student: They would buzz, I suppose.

Teacher: What would they want to tell each other?

[*Silence*]

Teacher: [*Starts the "Bee Dances" tutorial. Plays initial video segment.*] So tell me what you observed.

Student: The bees were flying to the flowers. They took nectar from the purple flowers and flew back to their hive. They put the nectar in the honeycomb. Eggs are laid in those holes in the honeycomb, too.

Teacher: Did you see the eggs?

Student: No, I just know they do that.

Teacher: Did you see any dances? Watch this again. [*Points to dancing bee.*]

Student: Oh, that one wiggling its butt is dancing. [*Imitates; everyone laughs.*]

Teacher: I guess we'll have to call this lesson "Dances with Bees." Why don't you work on this program on your own? Click on the arrow keys when you're ready to go to the next page. Watch for buttons telling you there's some special demonstration to look at. Sometimes you will watch more video on the monitor, and sometimes you will see something special on the computer screen. [*Steps back to watch.*]

[*One student controls the keyboard, and the other watches. Initial part of tutorial explains that dances are used to direct other bees to sources of food that have been discovered. When the flowers are close to the hive, the bee performs a round dance to inform other bees that the flowers are close. Bees then use their olfactory sense to find flowers.*]

Student: What does *olfactory* mean?

Teacher: It means the bees can find the flowers by smell.

[*The student continues with the tutorial and now learns about the "waggle dance." The waggle dance consists of two loops connected by a running movement. The orientation of the run explains the position of the flowers relative to the position of the sun. The combs are positioned vertically in the hive. If the run is toward the top of the comb, the dance means the flowers are toward the sun. Straight down means they are away from the sun. Movements that depart from the vertical indicate that the flowers are located at an angle away from the sun. The duration of the waggle indicates the distance from the hive. The students move from the tutorial to a simulation that allows either the flowers or the sun to be moved. Clicking on the hive indicates the direction of the dance that would indicate this relationship between sun and flowers (see Figure 7.2). Students spend some time working with the simulation.*]

Teacher: Do you understand that [*refers to simulation*]?

Student: It is like the direction of the run in the hive shows how far you have to turn away from the sun to find the flowers. [*Students are having some difficulty orienting the bee dance to the picture of the hive, flowers, and sun.*] It would be easier to see if you could move this part [*points to part of simulation showing the orientation of the dance*]. You should be able to point the top of the hive at the sun.

FIGURE 7.2 "Bee Dances" Simulation Allowing Student to Experiment with Position of Food and Sun

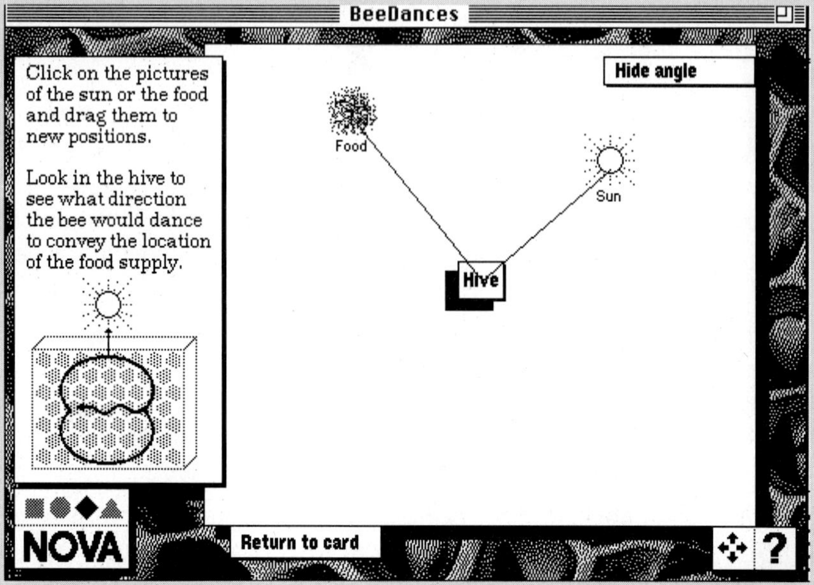

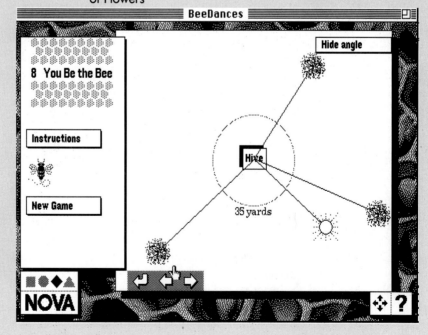

FIGURE 7.3 Screen from "Bee Dances" Allowing Student to Select Position of Flowers

Teacher: I don't think the bees are allowed to do that.

[*Student works a while longer and then moves to final activity — a game called "You Be the Bee" (see Figure 7.3). In this activity, the student clicks on the hive and views a dancing bee. The run of the dancing bee (see Figure 7.4 — the dancing bee appears near the middle of the picture) is oriented at an angle of about 100 degrees relative to the top of the picture. (The student attempts to interpret the dance and clicks on a potential food source; refer to Figure 7.3). The program then displays the flight of the bee from the bee's perspective. As the bee flies through the meadow, the student experiences moving through the meadow. If directed properly, the bee finds the flowers. If misdirected, the bee ends up at a bush.*]

Student: I knew it was this one. It's the only one turned to the right from the sun this much [*points to computer screen and the angle displayed*]. Click on "New" and let's do another one.

FIGURE 7.4   Image of Dancing Bee from "Bee Dances"

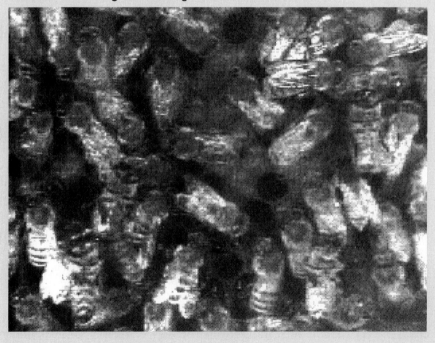

OTHER FORMS OF MULTIMEDIA FOUND IN CLASSROOMS

There are some unique types of multimedia software that are not really CAI materials. The following section presents some of these applications and the classroom situations in which you might choose to use them. These applications include talking books, collections, references, cooperative problem-solving activities, and report makers. We hope the discussion helps you better understand existing applications of multimedia and leads you to consider how multimedia applications might involve students in meaningful learning. You should recognize that commercial multimedia products very often integrate a number of components. If you have the opportunity to work with products of the type described here, you may find that some include several forms of CAI and several of the applications listed in this section. We isolate these applications here primarily to make it easier to describe and discuss each type of software.

Involving students in meaningful learning

Talking Books

The storage capacity of CD-ROMs has made possible the creation of talking books. These products are most commonly based on popular and award-winning children's literature and are characterized by colorful artwork, optional access to narrators reading the story "in character," access to pronunciation and definitions by clicking on words, and objects within the artwork that perform simple actions when clicked. The CD-ROM is important because it provides the capacity necessary for the high-quality sound, graphics, and simple animations hidden in the artwork. As you can see in Figure 7.5, these products purposely mimic the appearance of books.

When encountering these products, teachers can often appreciate how young students might be intrigued by the uniqueness of this use of technology, by the high-quality narration, and by the fun of looking for the hidden treasures in the artwork. The questions teachers often ask are, "Is it worth spending this much money when you could buy the actual book for much less?" and "Will students be less interested in reading if the computer will read books to them?" The value in talking books is in helping children develop a relationship with books and in building excitement about reading (Chomsky, 1990). Literacy develops when children read because they want to. Reading educators have long appreciated the value of reading to children — even to children very capable of reading to themselves — as a way to involve them with books and as a way to share an interest in reading. Experience with talking books can be an effective way to introduce quality books to a child, to practice "reading while listening," to develop fluency, and to review a book a student has already read and enjoyed. Talking books may also provide some unique benefits for children whose second language is English.

The value of talking books

Content-area reading materials for young readers have also been developed

FIGURE 7.5   Screen Display from *Scary Poems for Rotten Kids*

using the talking book approach *(National Geographic Wonders of Learning CD-ROM Library)*. Instead of presenting children's literature, this software explores topics such as "The World of Plants" and other topics from science, nature, and geography. Like the previous example of children's literature, the content-area reading materials appear as a colorful book on the computer screen. *Scary Poems for Rotten Kids* and the *National Geographic Wonders of Learning* collection were both developed by Discis Knowledge Research, Inc. This particular collection allows the user to select from a number of features in addition to basic narration. Individual words can be pronounced and explained in context, in either English or Spanish. The Spanish language option is intended to assist students learning English as a second language.

The talking book concept has also been developed into a system for language arts instruction. *WiggleWorks* is based on a series of lavishly illustrated stories and nonfiction works published by Scholastic for young children. The students have the option of reading the "books" to themselves or having the computer read the books to them. Each student's oral reading can be recorded, played back, and contrasted with the narrated version. The WiggleWorks materials take an approach that emphasizes the connections between reading and writing. In one option available for each selection, students are presented a "coloring book" version of the original book. This coloring book version can be modified in a variety of ways with several different types of

ACTIVE

ACTIVE

EVALUATION

tools. The text from a particular page can be retained and paint tools and image stamps appropriate to the theme of the story can be used to create a new illustration. Or the image can be retained and "colored" and new text suited to the image can be added (see Figure 7.6). The student could write new sentences from scratch or descriptive sentences including key words taken from a list appropriate to the theme of the book. Some writing tasks make available story prompts that provide ideas students might develop in their stories. Whatever the student ends up writing can be read by the computer. These varied opportunities to construct meaning through the interpretation (reading) and manipulation (writing) of words and images allow young learners active and scaffolded learning experiences (see the emphasis on these characteristics in Chapter 2).

The WiggleWorks materials contain sophisticated management/assessment tools. The computer keeps track of what students do with each text selection (listen, read, write) and saves any products created by the student (written samples, recordings of oral readings). The teacher can review this information, add notes for archival purposes, and export any of this information for inclusion in a student portfolio.

Collections

CD-ROMs and videodiscs are now being distributed to provide collections of information about a particular topic or issue. Examples of issues for such col-

FIGURE 7.6 Sample Screen from WiggleWorks "Coloring Book" Activity

lections include mammals, plants, AIDS, Hurricane Hugo, butterflies, and many topics of historical interest. Collections can be differentiated as visual databases and multimedia libraries (Barron et al., 1994).

A **visual database** can be likened to a large collection of photographic slides. Whereas visual databases would not technically be considered multimedia because they provide only one form of information, material from visual databases commonly ends up being used in combination with other sources of information. A teacher might use such images as part of classroom presentations, as part of instructional materials prepared for students, or as artwork for noninstructional uses, such as different types of school publications. Students given access to visual databases could use the images for nearly identical purposes. Students might put together presentations for classmates, use images to embellish their reports, or include images in materials for extracurricular activities. Some visual databases are advertised as "royalty free." This means that users have more freedom in how they can legally use the images in the collection (we discuss legal issues in Chapter 11).

A **multimedia library** offers a collection of still images, video clips, sounds, text, and simple graphics focused on a theme. These sources of information have not been fashioned into lessons or some other organized form suitable for direct instruction. Rather, multimedia libraries offer teachers and students a collection of resources they can browse, organize, and use in many of the same ways visual databases are used. These resources, sometimes assembled from the archives of national news agencies or organizations such as the National Geographic Society, provide materials that would often be impractical for teachers or students to obtain on their own.

Just how extensive are these collections? Corel distributes a large number of CDs, making 100 royalty-free, photograph-quality images available on a large number of topics (see resources on page 262). Collections exist for butterflies, trees, Africa, monkeys, deserts, and similar topics. *The American History Videodisc* includes 2,500 still images and 70 video clips. A printed guide accompanying the videodisc contains a descriptive paragraph, frame number, and bar code for each image. If you are an elementary school teacher who wants to do a unit on deserts or a secondary school history teacher looking for ways to present the realities of World War I, you would find *Deserts* or *The American History Videodisc* tremendous resources. Similar opportunities exist for many other content areas.

Multimedia References

School libraries and some classrooms commonly have certain references that students can consult. Reference materials such as encyclopedias, almanacs, globes, and atlases have general value in many content areas. Students usually use these sources for questions of an immediate nature and consult other library resources when pursuing projects requiring more extensive research. Alternatives to each item on this list of references are available on CD-ROM.

Using collections for students' presentations or reports

HEME-BASED

Sources of information focused on a theme

Advantages of CD-based multimedia references

CD-based multimedia references offer several advantages. In some cases, the CD-ROM version is less expensive. This is true with encyclopedias. Although current CD-ROM encyclopedias are not the equivalent of some of the more extensive paper alternatives, the price does make the CD version an attractive resource. Multimedia resources offer a second advantage in making information available in multiple formats. Some information sources cannot be presented in text format, and some information sources that could be presented as text are more motivating when presented in other ways. For example, reading about the cry of a loon is not the same as hearing it. Reading the words of President John F. Kennedy's inaugural address is less moving than hearing the speech in his own voice.

Search and exploration options

Multimedia encyclopedias allow powerful search features. CD-based encyclopedias have hypertext links among articles that allow powerful searches using individual terms or various combinations of terms. Searches using multiple terms are often called **Boolean searches**. Boolean searches refer to the logic involved in defining when certain conditions have been met. Searches are usually classified as AND or OR searches. In an AND search, a successful search would result when *all* of the search conditions have been met. For example, a student might search the encyclopedia using the terms *fish* AND *ocean*. This search would locate articles containing both the word *fish* and the word *ocean* and would be unlikely to include an article on the smallmouth bass, a freshwater fish. In an OR search, a successful search results when *any* of the conditions of the search is satisfied. Searches of this type are used when broad coverage is desired or when related information might be described using different terms.

Finally, references often allow a **copy and paste** capability. These two procedures allow material to be copied from the reference and then pasted into another application. This is sometimes described as cut and paste in manuals accompanying reference software, but this description is inaccurate because nothing is actually removed, or "cut," from the original source. The availability of copy and paste allows students to use pictures, maps, and tables from other sources in their own documents. You may be concerned that this option encourages students to literally copy when they are usually asked to summarize and organize the material they take from references. However, because copying is, in this case, so obvious, it actually gives teachers a convenient opportunity to explain students' responsibilities in using information from other sources.

Cooperative Problem Solving

Whole-class learning activities

Commercial multimedia specifically designed to encourage group work is not common, but is a powerful and practical use of technology in classrooms. The most unique characteristics of this category of learning tasks are that they are designed for use with intact classes and require that students work on the tasks as members of a group.

Learning activities involving entire classes have practical advantages. The equipment necessary for using multimedia may not be available in abundance, and group-based approaches can use available equipment more efficiently. Teachers are also often responsible for twenty-five to thirty students at a time, and activities allowing them to work with the entire group make supervision a bit easier. With the exception of methods for group-based information presentation, applications of technology are seldom designed with the group context in mind.

 COOPERATION

Cooperative problem solving involves groups of students with information in a nontraditional manner: students work in groups to solve problems posed through text and video. In the tasks developed by Tom Snyder Productions *(Great Ocean Rescue, Great Solar System Rescue),* several subproblems are set within a single scenario, and students work through these subproblems to resolve the central problem. In the following example, "Grief on the Reef," the central problem is to find an explanation for the widespread death of marine life on an ocean reef. To solve this problem, students have to first locate the reef and then decide which biological tests might provide useful information. Using the information from the tests, students then attempt to identify the reason for the reef's decline. The students go through a sequence of three subproblems to reach a final decision.

Types of group interdependencies

The cooperative nature of these activities is based on several types of group interdependencies (Johnson, Johnson, and Holubec, 1991). Students working with these problem-solving activities experience **reward interdependence**, because the point system allowing teams to compete against each other is based on the money whole groups must pay each time they make a choice regarding location, request that a test be administered, or suggest a reason for the problem (see description that follows). Because the group must make such requests as a group and must spend as little money as possible in competing against other groups, the team and not the individual wins or loses.

These activities also involve *resource interdependence.* Each member of a team is given a specific role and provided unique access to information related to that role. **Resource interdependence** exists when each group member has a portion of the resources necessary for a task to be completed and must combine these resources with those of others to complete the task. In this case, the resources are the information each student must master. This type of cooperative learning is sometimes described as **jigsaw cooperation** because each member of the group has a piece of the puzzle the group must assemble for success.

Emerging Technology

The Evolution of Multimedia Encyclopedias

Multimedia encyclopedias are becoming much more than just encyclopedias on a disc. The companies creating computer-based reference tools have always had vast stores of information to draw on, but competition and consumer interest have led to products that are both more powerful and augmented by activities and tools intended to involve students with information in a more active manner. The "old style" encyclopedia on a disc made limited use of powerful search features or true hypermedia. Now encyclopedias offer more sophisticated searches (i.e., Boolean searches) and embed links to related articles, images, interactive activities, and even games within articles. Companies may also develop thematic approaches that present a topic at a more general level or a historical approach based on a time line and then provide links to a number of individual encyclopedia articles.

No matter how sophisticated disc-based reference materials become they have one inherent weakness true of all reference materials: once published they are immediately at least partially out of date. New discoveries that may negate long-held beliefs and important events occur on a daily basis. Some companies have taken to the Internet in an effort to provide those purchasing their disc-based encyclopedia products with the most recent information possible and to provide other "value-added" features that will make their products more attractive to educators. For example, Grolier linked articles from its *1997 Multimedia Encyclopedia* with carefully selected World Wide Web sites through a special interface called the Internet Index. A staff will continue to add hundreds of new sites a month in an effort to expand the basic reference tool and provide the most current examples possible.

Microsoft has taken this approach even further in establishing the Web-based Encarta Schoolhouse. The Encarta Schoolhouse provides Internet links based on a series of "themes." Each theme, covering a topic such as the Civil War, life in the ocean, or earthquakes, is supported by suggested activities and links to some of the best related Internet content. Encarta has also developed what it calls the "Yearbook Builder," which makes use of the Internet to download a monthly review of that month's most important events and new articles that are linked to existing Encarta content. What is especially impressive about the approach that has been developed is that not only is it possible to examine the new material and then find related articles on the original CD, but it is also possible to click the "Update" icon while working with the CD to search for any updated material that has been downloaded.

How do companies receive payment for these services? At the time of this writing, it is fair to say that such details are still being worked out. Companies are making World Wide Web sites available at no cost to consumers as a way to develop interest in the products they sell and to offer some services that make the products more valuable to customers. In the case of Encarta, information updates are presently being provided on a free trial basis, but at some point it appears this practice will be discontinued.

The resources described here should provide teachers with some powerful opportunities to engage students in meaningful learning. The theme-based activities would provide great opportunities to develop WebQuests, as described in Chapter 6 (page 218). Teachers would need only to review some of the Internet resources and establish scaffolding activities. The links established between current events and more standard encyclopedia content offer a different kind of opportunity. In that case, students could use experiences that are more immediate and specific to understand issues and content that are likely to be more remote and abstract.

The Internet addresses for the two products described here are provided at the end of the chapter. ✳

Video resources available on videodisc or videotape can play a valuable role in many classroom activities. *(© Michael Zide)*

Grief on the Reef: A Group-Based Interactive Videodisc

Cully Gause is a life science and earth science teacher at South Junior High School in Grand Forks, North Dakota. We asked him to describe his experiences working with group-based interactive videodiscs.

Cully: Interactive video can work great with a group if you remember to do one important thing. You need to find a way to get everyone involved, make everyone accountable for something. I have used several of the Tom Snyder videodiscs. They were designed for group work and have good ideas for giving all students something to do. The tasks and worksheets are all set up and ready to go. I find most of the suggestions and activities work pretty well, so I haven't had to prepare new activities.

Here's what it's like to use *The Great Ocean Rescue.* This videodisc contains four "missions." A mission is really a problem the group is supposed to solve. I remember one of the missions was "Grief on the Reef," and the group had to determine why the sea life on a coral reef was dying. A student group is supposed to be made up of four people, in which each student is assigned a role. There is an environmental scientist, a geologist, an oceanographer, and a marine biologist. When students take a role, they take responsibility for learning certain information and for being able to answer certain kinds of questions. The materials support these responsibilities, because students in different roles are given different materials to study. All students view some common video sequences and read some common material from booklets. Each student also reads some material no other student in the group sees.

Assigning students to roles can be difficult. What if no one wants to be the geologist? Here's what I tried last. I made it the boys against the girls. There were twelve students in one group and sixteen in the other. Then I let the students in each group decide what they wanted to be. So each group ended up with several marine biologists and several students in each of the other categories. Each student gets a booklet for the role they have chosen. This seemed to work as long as someone would try each of the roles. I had the students stick with one role through all four missions so we didn't have to spend the time dividing them up and assigning roles for each mission.

Here's the way I used the activity. All students read from a booklet. They read some general information and some information specific to their own roles. Actually, each expert's manual is about thirty pages long. Each individual is responsible for a lot of information. The same information is used for all four ocean missions. By reading this information, the experts acquire ideas that might be helpful in solving the problems they will be asked to solve, and they learn something about what people in their role do. They need to have some idea of what kind of things they should look for.

When the video begins, students see a scene of a beautiful reef with lots of fish and living things. Then they see a reef that is dead. Information that is potentially useful for making future decisions is provided, so most students take notes. They can use the worksheet to write down any information they think might be important. They generally seem to want to contribute so that they won't let the group down.

The first task each group is given is to locate the reef. The screen displays four different locations, and students have to use the information they've gathered to make a selection. Each student tries to determine how the information at his or her disposal would argue for or against each location. The group talks it over, considers what each person knows, and comes to some conclusion.

After the reef has been located, the next step is to select a test that will determine what is responsible for the problem at the reef. Again, four tests are available. Taking a water sample provides information about the presence of any unusual chemicals. An inspection of the coral indicates whether certain diseases are present. Inspecting the fish tells you what fish are present, if there have been any changes in the fish population, and if the fish are healthy. Checking the coast tells you if anything happening on land might be causing damage to the reef. The way this activity works is that any choice costs money. The idea is to come up with the right answer quickly and spend the least amount of money.

Making choices about the location costs money; so do choices of tests and the selection of a solution to the problem. I can never decide exactly what to do about making choices. Obviously, when a group makes a choice, other groups usually get to see the outcome. How do you make this fair? I've tried a couple of different things. The group asked to make the first choice can alternate across each of the three questions. When it was the boys against the girls, I gave each group one choice, and both groups were allowed to see what happened when each choice was selected. Another thing I've tried is to have the students who aren't selecting a choice leave the room. If a group finds that a choice didn't provide the information or outcome they wanted, they may pay to try something else. Students seem to get into the competition and are very sensitive to what is a fair way to do things. Whatever you decide to do, it seems important to explain ahead of time how the competitive part of the activity will be conducted and make sure the groups understand and agree.

After the tests are completed, each group needs to give a reason for the problem and offer a recommendation. Each group writes out the recommended action on the worksheet. Again, picking a reason costs money. Once the choices are in, I allow the videodisc to evaluate each answer. If neither group is correct, I let them pick again.

I've used this activity three times. You do learn some things that work well, but each group is also different, so what worked last time may not work so well this time.

Interviewer: *Do you have students who are reluctant to participate?*

Cully: Some of my students do very little in class anyway. They just don't seem to care. These group activities have been helpful in getting junior high students to respond. The group activity may exert the kind of pressure or create the kind of interest to which some of these students will respond. I sometimes put a student in a key role, so they will have to do something. Maybe the student is the person to make and announce a particular choice for the group. It's kind of a gut feeling how each student will react to this.

Interviewer: *How did you evaluate these activities?*

Cully: The students came up with their own grading system. Since the activity is a competition focused on points, the team spending the least money gets 100 percent, and the groups spending more money get 90 percent. Everyone does well if he or she participates. I collect the worksheets to make sure students have filled in the information: notes, choices, reasons. Students must complete the worksheet to get full credit for the points their team has earned.

Report Makers

What report makers allow students and teachers to do

One application available on many CD-ROMs and accompanying many educational videodiscs is a report maker. The **report maker** allows a teacher or students to prepare and deliver presentations using the resources of the CD-ROM, videodisc, or user-created sources. Report makers are also available from independent commercial sources. Products that do not come as part of a package are often more powerful and flexible than those that do.

It might be useful to compare preparing a presentation to filling the slide carousel used with traditional slide projectors. Filling a slide tray amounts to sorting through your collections of photographs and finding the particular slides that will be most interesting or informative, and then ordering these slides in the tray so the presentation will make sense. With the more sophisticated report makers used with multimedia, the slides are obviously not the same kind of slides, and often they are not traditional still images. The multimedia presenter also does not have to worry about presenting an image that is upside down or backward.

Exploring content-area topics

MediaMAX, one multimedia presentation manager, can be used to create presentations using still images, video clips, text, or sounds. MediaMAX will load these different types of information from a videodisc, a CD-ROM, or the computer's hard drive, depending on which storage device is appropriate for each form of information.

Figure 7.7 shows the remote control from MediaMAX. When used on a computer attached to a CAV videodisc player, this program replaces the hand-held remote and serves other important functions. A teacher or student can use the computer version of the remote to explore the contents of the videodisc. The number appearing in the "Frame" field is that of the frame presently being displayed. When a video clip or frame of interest is located, the user can store data about it for future use. The procedure is fairly simple.

FIGURE 7.7 The Remote Control Used in MediaMAX

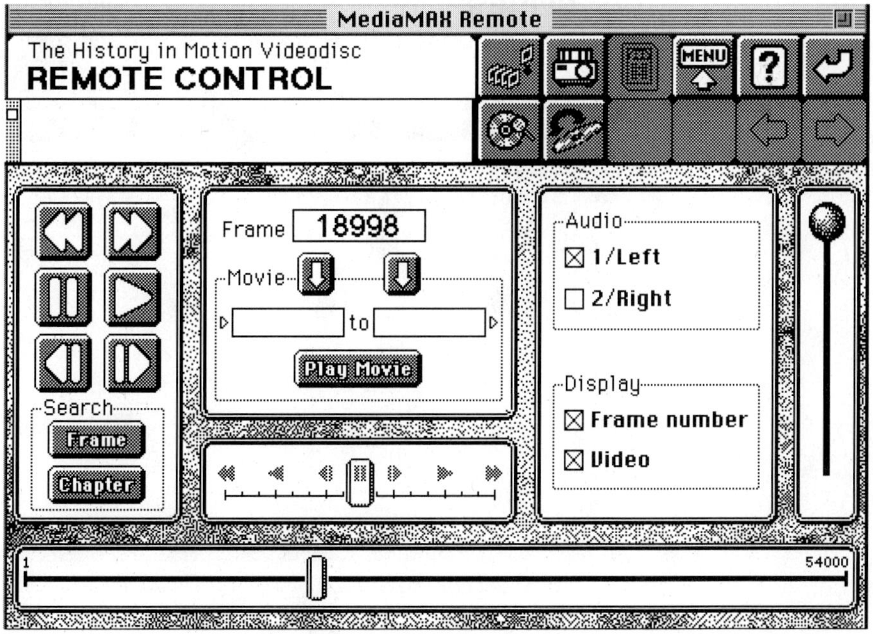

For a video clip, the user identifies the beginning and ending frames of the desired segment, enters these values in the two fields defining the beginning and end of the movie, and clicks the "Add Slide" button (the button sharing an icon of a sequence of slides). When the "Add Slide" button is clicked with no values entered for a movie segment, the frame identified by the frame number is defined as a slide. When a slide is defined, the user has the opportunity to enter a name for it.

As slides are created, they are added to the clipbook that is presently active (see Figure 7.8). As you may have guessed from the previous discussion, other types of slides (sounds, text, other types of graphics) can be developed with the tools available in MediaMAX. These slides are also available from the clipbook. Slides from the clipbook can be moved to the slide list (right-hand side of Figure 7.8) to create a presentation. The "Slide Notes" panel allows the user to write notes to accompany a series of slides. The notes can be printed out as a guide for the presenter or as notes for a viewer. The notes can also be used to create "hotlinks" that can be used to activate the slides. A slide name can be entered within the notes in angle brackets (for example <Berlin Wall>). If a user views the notes from within MediaMAX and clicks on a hotlink, that slide will be displayed.

FIGURE 7.8 Screen Display of MediaMAX Clipbook and Slide Preparation Tools

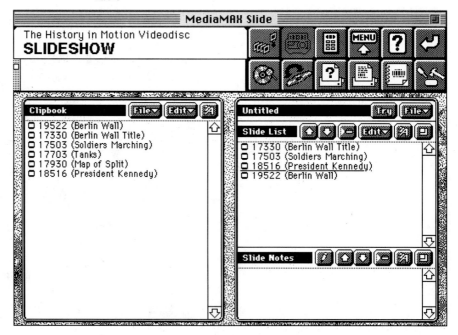

This discussion is not intended to teach you the ins and outs of any particular product, but to give you a few insights into the kinds of applications for which you can use report makers. We have a particular interest in convincing future and practicing teachers that elementary and secondary school students can use computer tools to explore content-area topics and create their own knowledge (see original discussion in Chapter 2). We also want to demonstrate to teachers that there are easy-to-use tools for working with information and to help teachers imagine what it would be like to have their students work with these tools. Usually this means that teachers must feel comfortable working with these tools themselves. Young students are quite capable of using the MediaMax remote control to view a videodisc. They can find pictures that interest them and that they want to learn more about. It is a reasonable task even for young children to write down the frame numbers of their favorite images so they can find them again to show their classmates or teacher. With some guidance by an experienced student or teacher, students working alone or in small groups can also create slides and slide shows. Some of the resources discussed here are intended to be both very general and extensive in coverage. It seems probable that many more resources of this type will become available as commercial organizations such as news services begin to make their vast archives available.

EVALUATING MULTIMEDIA AND HYPERMEDIA

New and readily available innovations such as multimedia and hypermedia often capture educators' imaginations. There is a certain excitement in promising new ideas and powerful innovations that allow students and teachers opportunities that were not previously available. However, there is also reason for caution. There is some degree of vulnerability present in the excitement connected with new opportunities. Merchandisers can play on this excitement to market products urging well-intentioned educators and school boards to take advantage of the newest resources for the benefit of their students. Although such situations may occasionally result from opportunism, there is also the real possibility that the potential of new products and new approaches has yet to be fully understood. Kozma (1991, p. 199) makes the point this way: "Little research has been done on learning with multimedia environments, in part because most efforts in the field are focused on development and in part because the field is still evolving."

Be an aware decision maker

As you make decisions, the best advice is to combine awareness of the general strengths and concerns expressed by experienced users and developers, the conclusions generated by the available research, and the qualities of a particular product with your particular instructional goals. Do these sources of information and values converge to recommend that a particular product and learning activity be made available to your students? The following paragraphs outline some of the available research on strengths and weaknesses of multimedia and hypermedia. Determining the characteristics of specific products and site-specific instructional goals will be up to you.

Multimedia's impact on student achievement

A number of reviews have summarized studies comparing traditional instruction with various types of videodisc-based instruction or interactive multimedia (Bosco, 1986; Fletcher, 1990; McNeil and Nelson, 1990; Nelson, Watson, and Busch, 1989). Although the research is much less extensive than the work on computer-based instruction summarized in Chapter 3 (pages 82 through 83) and although some of the techniques and strategies have yet to be thoroughly evaluated in the classroom, the existing research suggests that the use of multimedia has a moderately positive impact on student achievement. One must remember that there are many studies that do not find an advantage for technology and that studies comparing one method with another are prone to biases. Studies are often of short duration, frequently use dependent measures sensitive to new treatments, and are unlikely to be published unless they find significant differences between treatments.

Personally meaningful learning

As we mentioned in the orientation at the beginning of this chapter, a goal of the chapter is to identify ways students can use multimedia tools to explore, think, and involve themselves with course content in ways that are personally meaningful. These ideas might be used on occasion or as part of a much more pervasive attempt to change the way classrooms function. When applications of technology are intended to alter the way schools function, traditional outcome measures are less appropriate (Means et al., 1993).

Student-centered learning

It is important to understand that efforts at restructuring classroom learning are multidimensional. The differences between traditional instruction and inquiry-based or student-centered learning extend far beyond whether students make heavy use of technology. Such themes as creating a "community of learners" within the classroom, thematic or project-based learning, cooperative learning, and constructivism create an entirely different classroom culture. Although gains on traditional measures of achievement have resulted from the implementation of these themes (Brown, 1992), it may be more important to understand the role of technology in facilitating new approaches to learning than to demonstrate an advantage according to traditional measures of achievement. We explore some of the possible ways in which student's work with multimedia tools can facilitate learning in the following discussion of strengths and weaknesses. Chapter 10 provides a more extensive discussion of some of the ideas and techniques introduced here.

STRENGTHS OF MULTIMEDIA AND HYPERMEDIA

ADVANTAGES OF MULTIPLE FORMATS AND ALTERNATIVE PERSPECTIVES

Presenting information to students more effectively

Multimedia and hypermedia expand the number of ways in which a **courseware** (instructional software) designer can present information, and these alternative formats offer possible advantages. The availability of text, sound, animation, video, and still images for presenting information and the easy transitions among these formats can increase the clarity of explanations. Different methods of representation are potentially suited to explaining or demonstrating different concepts or skills, and multimedia and hypermedia make it easy to give students these different experiences. For example, it would be more effective to give a basic explanation of mitosis and then step through a time-lapse video of cell division than to struggle through a verbal analysis of how the chromosomes align themselves along the equatorial plate or how the spindle fibers pull the chromatids toward the centrioles. A teacher can easily point out these phenomena in the images displayed on a monitor. The teacher might first talk the students through the stages of mitosis by advancing the videodisc a few frames at a time, describing changes and pointing to interesting developments as they appear on the monitor. Then the teacher might run the entire sequence so students will have an opportunity to appreciate how the process unfolds.

Multimedia can support verbal instruction in other ways. Consider the challenge of helping students understand the form of musical composition called a fugue. It is easy to give a verbal definition, but will terms like *theme, imitation,* and *counterpoint* mean much to students? Of even greater importance, would students be able to identify a fugue if they heard one? Again, the teacher's definition or the definition in a tutorial could be supported by listening to a musical selection, such as an appropriate passage from Beethoven's Ninth Symphony. The teacher might play a few seconds of music, pause to ask if the students are able to hear different voices imitating each other at different pitches, maybe hum a few bars to identify the imitation, and then play the brief selection again. The appropriate CD and related software (such as *Analysis of Beethoven Symphony #9*) make this type of demonstration easy to implement.

Content multimedia presents in powerful ways

There are other kinds of content that multimedia can present in particularly powerful ways. Kozma (1991) argues that multimedia, particularly combinations involving video, is very useful when the content has to do with social situations, interpersonal problem solving, foreign language training, or moral decision making. Multimedia can encourage students to think about complex issues. Kozma uses the example of *A right to die? The case of Dax*

Cowart (Covey, 1990). This social documentary examines the actual experience of a young person who had been burned over 60 percent of his body and lost his sight. The patient would always be disabled but could survive if willing to submit to a long and painful treatment. The patient found the treatments unbearable and wanted to have them stopped. The video provides actual comments from the patient, mother, doctor, nurse, and lawyer. As the student works with this material, he or she is asked to make decisions. The student's decision making and the presentation of opposing perspectives, in the words and images of real people, provide a depth of experience that would not be possible without interactive multimedia.

Dual-coding Theory

The capability of efficiently offering related experiences in different forms may have other advantages. Paivio's (1986) dual-coding theory is often cited as support for exposing students to both pictures and verbal information. **Dual-coding theory** argues that imagery and verbal information are stored in different ways. You might recall that we distinguished different types of memory codes in Chapter 2 and that imagery represented a distinct memory code. Experiencing something verbally and through imagery offers advantages because the experiences may result in two memory codes instead of one. Students exposed to pictures or video *and* verbal input may store and retrieve information more effectively than students who do not have these multiple inputs because multiple representations allow them more direct retrieval options and more indirect retrieval options because of connections with other memory units.

Helping students retain information

It is possible to be even more explicit about the conditions under which multiple formats are advantageous (Mayer and Anderson, 1991). When explaining relatively complex phenomena, dual codes are most beneficial when students are able to interrelate the codes. For example, in explaining how a bicycle pump works, a computer animation with narration was found to lead to better understanding than allowing students first to hear the narration and then to watch the animation. Access to both sources of information also resulted in an advantage over access to only one source of information. In this example, hearing the narration while watching the animation resulted in greater integration of the two inputs. Students were less able to use two codes to support each other when the two codes were presented sequentially.

You should note that multimedia and hypermedia frequently allow sequential rather than integrated experiences with multiple media. Often, a student working with multimedia or hypermedia is allowed to voluntarily access a video segment or an animation when he or she feels that an additional form of input would be helpful. In many such situations, text and sometimes simple diagrams are used initially to present information. The information sources might be separated because of cost factors or because it was considered desirable to offer the student a choice of one or both sources of information. When multiple forms for conveying the same idea are presented sequentially, the student must work more actively to integrate the information sources.

Multimedia environments may provide other unique advantages (Bransford et al., 1990). The video format provides experiences that are both more complex and more like situations outside the classroom, exposing students to realistic experiences they may not have encountered directly. Video provides more information to sort through and think about, and video material can often be examined from multiple points of view. Working to process such a rich information source is one way to engage students in more active learning. Learning experiences that combine extended video segments and other resources and activities allow students to anchor what they learn in realistic goals, activities, and situations. The ideas of active learning, anchored instruction, and situated cognition were presented in Chapter 2. An example of anchored instruction relying heavily in videodisc-based video, *The Adventures of Jasper Woodbury,* was presented in Chapter 3 (pages 105 through 106).

Engaging students in more active learning

In summary, multimedia and hypermedia offer several advantages because students are provided efficient access to information presented in different ways. It can be argued that (1) certain ideas or procedures are easier for students to understand when experienced in other than a text-based format; (2) information experienced in multiple formats will be encoded in multiple ways, increasing the retrievability of the information; and (3) integrating extended video segments in learning activities allows students to anchor what they learn in more complex and realistic experiences.

Meeting Individual Needs

Both interactive multimedia and hypermedia offer students some degree of control over the information they experience. Students can get help when they need it. When they have difficulties, they can get supplementary information or experience information in a different format.

Allowing students to control information they experience

Other needs are also important. Sometimes a student understands the information but wants to know more. Imagine a learning environment in which a student can quickly ask for more depth, greater detail, or additional examples when he or she encounters something of great personal interest. The element of control allows students working in responsive environments to meet their own needs.

The flexibility allowed by present applications is limited, but these applications do suggest the potential for greater adaptability as software becomes more sophisticated. Some of the examples already provided demonstrate the adaptive value of multimedia.

You may recall from the earlier discussion of talking books (pages 240 through 242) that these CD-based products allow the reader to click on

Responding to diversity needs in classrooms

unfamiliar words to have words pronounced and defined. Students struggling with English can even listen in Spanish. The frequency with which these options are used and the individual words with which students need assistance vary greatly. Multimedia and certainly hypermedia programs often leave the decision to display a video segment, diagram, or supplemental text to the student. In theory, students needing access to a different type of explanation, or who are likely to find a visual representation helpful, have opportunities to customize their learning environment.

Opportunities to customize the learning environment

The point to note in both these examples is that multimedia offers more variety than traditional materials. Individual students can take advantage of this variety to find ways to solve individual difficulties. As multimedia and hypermedia environments become more sophisticated, options for students will become even more varied.

Multimedia and Hypermedia Are Motivating

Finally, the variety of formats offered by multimedia and hypermedia is motivating. For many students, seeing a human take the first steps on the moon or hearing Dr. Martin Luther King's "I Have a Dream" speech result in very different affective reactions than simply reading about the lunar landing or reading Dr. King's speech. Emotion is part of school learning and part of what makes learning exciting.

CONCERNS ABOUT MULTIMEDIA IN CLASSROOMS

Making informed decisions about multimedia in your classroom

Experts have raised a number of concerns related to the multimedia and hypermedia programs that are currently available and to some of the assumed benefits of multimedia and hypermedia. We want you to have a realistic sense of how multimedia applications are used in classrooms and to recognize that there are potential problems. Such awareness will help you recognize classroom situations in which problems might develop and help you make more informed decisions about how to use multimedia with your students.

Multimedia applications are often an unnecessary duplication of existing instructional materials

◆ Talking children's books and CD-based atlases, encyclopedias, and almanacs are clearly similar to the books already common in classrooms. Images of artwork, plants, whales, and other collections of photographs on a CD or a videodisc are similar to slide collections. Is this redundancy necessary?

Some computer-based resources are cost effective

◆ What exactly is wrong with duplication? One response may be "Nothing." There is nothing wrong with taking a good idea and making it available in a different form. Computer-based resources are sometimes less expensive than printed ones, have greater durability, and may be perceived as more interesting by students. Counterarguments can be offered. Computer-based resources are not always less expensive. A CD may be a cost-effective replacement for an encyclopedia, but is it a cost-effective replacement for a children's book?

◆ There is also the issue of how educators should use a valuable limited resource. If a limited number of computers or videodisc and CD players are available, why not make certain these resources are used for unique purposes? Perhaps the emphasis should be on using technology in ways that offer students experiences they do not have now.

◆ How multimedia is used will likely evolve in the next few years. If it is any consolation to those impatient for change, the tendency to first use new technological innovations to implement old strategies seems to be a familiar historical pattern (McLuhan, 1964). Many early radio programs were broadcasts of vaudeville acts, and early television was similar to radio except that viewers could see the source of the sound. It takes time for the potential of new technologies to be developed and accepted.

Students may not have the skills to learn from multimedia and hypermedia

Developing new learning skills

◆ Learning from any information source requires that students have skills suitable to both the format and the particular method in which information is made available. Young children are capable of learning by observing and listening before they are able to learn by reading. They have the necessary skills. They acquire strategies for learning from textbooks and from teacher presentations as they move through school and experience these types of learning experiences. Sometimes the strategies are taught formally. Somewhere during late elementary or junior high school, a teacher may take the time to talk with students about taking notes. Often, however, they develop their own study and learning strategies through trial and error.

◆ Multimedia and hypermedia are new learning environments. It makes sense that if they offer an alternative to learning from traditional sources, these new formats will also require the development of new learning skills. For example, it has been demonstrated that approaches combining text with extensive video can sometimes result in poorer learning. In one informative study, junior high earth science students worked with multimedia containing interesting video from the Great Quake of 1989 (Levin, 1991). When presented with text only, students seemed to be in a familiar element. When presented with text *and* the opportunity to watch interesting video, the students appeared to become distracted by the video and retained less essential information. By the way, this is not really a new phenomenon. It has been known for some time that pictures in books can interfere with the performance of young readers (Schallert, 1980). This early work with traditional reading material offers some additional insights. Pictures in any medium must serve a purpose. Pictures interfere when they do not convey useful information. As readers gain experience, they seem to learn to ignore pointless graphics. As students become experienced users of multimedia, they may adopt similar strategies. We can only hope that multimedia designers will use graphics and video effectively, and that students will have a reason for giving these sources of information careful consideration.

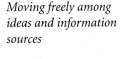

◆ Hypermedia can present students with a rather radical departure from traditional learning materials. As you learned earlier, hypermedia allows students to move freely among ideas and information sources. They can often jump from one text document to another or from a text document to a picture or video clip. There may be several ways such freedom could be problematic. It has been argued (Locatis, Letourneau, and Banvard, 1990) that hypermedia systems make the most sense to people already familiar with a particular domain. The links among ideas, documents, pictures, and other sources built by an expert author are most likely to make sense to someone else already familiar with the general topic. Students with little background may just wander about aimlessly, never really appreciating the ideas they are encountering. Students with less experience may prefer to be guided through a more structured experience.

Moving freely among ideas and information sources

◆ Hypermedia allows a great deal of student control. It is not yet well established that students can make effective decisions in service of their own learning needs. Given what is known about general metacognitive competence and student control (see Chapter 2), inconsistency in taking advantage of potentially helpful learning opportunities is not surprising. As multimedia materials become more common, the skills needed to benefit from flexible learning environments will likely receive more attention.

SUMMARY

Definitions of *multimedia* and *hypermedia* can be confusing because the terms are used inconsistently. In this book, *multimedia* describes a communication format implemented with a computer and involving the integration of several media, such as text, audio, video, still images, sound, and animations. *Hypermedia* is an interactive nonlinear form of multimedia in which the units of information are connected to each other in multiple ways. The hypermedia user has considerable freedom to choose which possible links to pursue and in what order.

Because information in the form of sound, high-quality pictures, or video requires large amounts of storage space, multimedia and hypermedia often make use of the large storage capacity of videodiscs or CD-ROMs.

Multimedia can be incorporated into traditional computer-based instructional activities such as tutorials, drills, and simulations. Other educational applications of multimedia and hypermedia include talking books, collections of pictures and other information sources, references, cooperative problem-solving activities, and report makers.

Although research provides some evidence that learning from multimedia is slightly more productive than learning from traditional materials, more impressive claims that multimedia and hypermedia may herald the restructuring of traditional education and result in experiences of greater personal relevance are still largely without strong empirical support.

Intuitively, however, multimedia and hypermedia offer several advantages. Multiple presentation formats allow students more diverse experiences. Some ideas may be easier to understand when portrayed in a realistic video, when heard, or when carefully outlined in text. Dual-coding theory holds that the redundancy present in multiple formats can allow more effective storage in and retrieval from memory. Multimedia also allows experiences that are more like the rich and motivating contexts found outside the classroom. To the extent that students have some flexibility in controlling what they encounter or the form in which information is presented, students may also be able to adapt learning experiences to their individual needs.

Concerns about multimedia and hypermedia do exist. Critics often lament the lack of imagination in many commercial products and observe that many products do not really offer alternatives to existing traditional instructional materials. Finally, students may not have the academic skills necessary to be responsible for their own learning.

REFLECTING ON CHAPTER 7

Activities

◆ Locate a review (try *Electronic Learning, Learning and Leading with Technology, New Media,* or one of the other technology sources listed at the end of Chapter 3) of a multimedia product relevant to your content-area specialty. Write a summary of the review.

◆ Compare a paper and a CD-based encyclopedia (preferably from the same publisher, such as Grolier). Look up the same topics in each source and write a summary of what you observe.

◆ Review the description of WiggleWorks presented on pages 241 to 242. What examples of scaffolding (structured support for learning) do you detect?

◆ Learn to use a videodisc player. You should be capable of connecting the player to a computer and monitor. You should also be able to locate and play designated video segments using a hand-held controller, a bar code reader, and appropriate computer software. Demonstrate these capabilities for classmates using a videodisc appropriate to your content-area speciality.

◆ Use traditional and CD-ROM encyclopedias to investigate a common topic. Contrast the experiences.

Resources to Expand Your Knowledge Base

For a more complete discussion of videodisc and CD-ROM applications and resources try the following sources:

Semrau, P., and B. Boyer. *Using interactive video in education.* Boston: Allyn & Bacon, 1994.

The videodisc compendium for education and training, 1994-1995. Available from Emerging Technology Consultants, Distribution Center, P.O. Box 102444, St. Paul, MN 55112.

Perhaps the best way to keep up with new developments is to review some of the technology magazines for educators. A list of these publications appears in Chapter 3.

Key Terms

analog format *(p. 230)*	laserdiscs *(p. 227)*
Boolean searches *(p. 244)*	megabytes *(p. 232)*
CAV *(p. 230)*	multimedia *(p. 225)*
CD-ROM *(p. 227)*	multimedia library *(p. 243)*
CLV *(p. 230)*	QuickTime *(p. 233)*
copy and paste *(p. 244)*	report maker *(p. 250)*
courseware *(p. 255)*	repurposing *(p. 232)*
digital format *(p. 230)*	resource interdependence *(p. 245)*
dual-coding theory *(p. 256)*	reward interdependence *(p. 245)*
hypermedia *(p. 225)*	videodisc *(p. 227)*
hypertext *(p. 226)*	visual database *(p. 243)*
jigsaw cooperation *(p. 245)*	

Other Software Resources Include

Software Examples

Analysis of Beethoven Symphony #9 (R. Winter, 1991) is one in a series of companion products offered by the Voyager Company. Each product consists of a CD containing a major musical work and related software. The software controls the CD and allows specific segments of music to be played.

Animal Pathfinders. Videodisc and software from Apple Computer and WGBH Education Foundation. Distributed by Scholastic Software, 730 Broadway, New York, NY 10003.

Guide. This product is available for MS-DOS and Macintosh computers from OWL International, 14218 NE 21st St., Bellevue, Washington 98007.

BarCode Maker. Creative Laser Concepts, 4449 Vista Nacion Dr., Chula Vista, CA 91910.

Talking Books

Scary Poems for Rotten Kids (1990). Original book written by Sean O'Huigin. Discis Knowledge Research, Inc., NYCCPO Box #45099, 5150 Yonge Street, North York, Ontario, CANADA M2N 6N2. Available for Macintosh.

A World of Plants (1993). One CD-ROM from the National Geographic Wonders of Learning CD-ROM Library developed by the National Geographic Society and Discis Knowledge Research, Inc. National Geographic Society, P.O. Box 96108, Dept. WOL CD LIB, Washington, DC 20077. Available for Macintosh.

WiggleWorks: The Scholastic Beginning Literacy System is a K-2 language arts system available on CD-ROM for Windows and Macintosh from Scholastic New Media, 2931 East McCarty St., Jefferson City, MO 65101.

Collections: Visual Databases

Butterflies. CD for Macintosh and IBM Windows. Available from Corel Corporation, PO Box 3595, Salinas, CA 93912.

Collections: Multimedia Libraries

AIDS. Videodisc available from Optical Data Corporation, 30 Technology Drive, Warren, NJ 07059. Software supporting this videodisc is available for Macintosh and MS-DOS computers.

The American History Videodisc. Available for Macintosh and IBM Windows from Instructional Resources Corporation. 1819 Bay Ridge Ave., Annapolis, MD 21403.

Multimedia References

Encarta Encyclopedia for Macintosh and Windows is available from Microsoft Corporation, Redmond, WA.

The WWW address for the Encarta Schoolhouse is http://www.msn.com/encarta/sch/default.htm.

Grolier Multimedia Encyclopedia for Macintosh, MS-DOS and Windows computers is available from Grolier Interactive, 90 Sherman Turnpike, Danbury, CT 06816.

The WWW address for the Grolier Multimedia Encyclopedia home page is http://205.185.3.2/interact/products/gme/docs/gmehome.html.

Cooperative Problem Solving

The Great Solar System Rescue and *The Great Ocean Rescue* are group problem-solving activities available on videodisc from Tom Snyder Productions, 80 Coolidge Hill Rd., Watertown, MA 02172.

Report Makers

MediaMAX. Videodiscovery, 1700 Westlake Ave. N., Suite 600, Seattle, WA 98109.

Chapter 8

Learning to Use Multimedia Tools to Create Multimedia Projects

ORIENTATION

This chapter has two broad goals. The first is to develop a simple system for classifying student multimedia projects. The second is to describe some of the software authoring tools students can use to produce multimedia projects. You have read about multimedia tools in other chapters, but here we present these tools more systematically and describe their capabilities more completely. After reading this chapter, you will know about and be able to recommend several specific software tools that students can use to generate each category of multimedia project. In addition to reviewing multimedia tools, this chapter introduces the concept of multimedia authoring environments. As you read, look for answers to the following questions:

FOCUS QUESTIONS

◆ What is an embellished document, and what are some examples that students could create for a content-area course?

◆ What is a linear presentation or slide show? What are some examples of assignments that could result in a student-created slide show?

◆ What is interactive hypermedia?

◆ What options and issues do you need to consider when you choose authoring software?

◆ How do students' multimedia projects encourage meaningful learning?

Multimedia in a Ninth Grade Classroom

As you know, we believe that student projects often encourage meaningful learning. Students engage in active learning and thinking as they work to complete projects appropriate to the content they are studying. Let's start this chapter by looking at an actual multimedia project. Monte Hahn teaches a ninth grade word processing course at Schroeder Junior High School in Grand Forks, North Dakota. If you have preconceived notions of what goes on in a word processing course, put your assumptions on hold for a bit. Teacher creativity presents surprising and wide-ranging options for working with the content of any course. We asked Monte about hers.

Grabes: *So how did you get starting doing multimedia projects in your class?*

Monte: We were working on a service learning activity at a home for the elderly around Christmastime. Our original plan was to play board games like Trivial Pursuit with the people at the home, in order to get better acquainted. Following this session, each student paired up with an elderly person and took dictation of a Christmas letter for that person to send. The students videotaped each resident so that an image could be captured as part of the letter. It was the first time we had worked with capturing images from videotape and using the images in computer applications.

The students really enjoyed this project, and we started talking about other things we might try. Somehow, the idea of a tour of the school came up. The school counselor had been talking about doing some kind of program that would inform parents and new students about our school. This sounded like a useful project.

Grabes: *Had your students worked in cooperative groups before?*

Monte: At the beginning of the year, we had a leadership training week and learned about roles within cooperative groups. As a class, we developed lists of ways to be a good leader and things to avoid. We did the winter survival exercise from the Johnson book [Johnson, Johnson, and Holubec, 1991, is referenced and discussed in Chapter 7]. This is a simulation that puts a group in the northern woods in the dead of winter and has the group make decisions about what they need to do to survive. I'm convinced that this type of training is important. Group projects have gone better when we've taken the time to *train* group skills than when we've just started in on the projects.

Grabes: *How were group skills applied in the multimedia project?*

Monte: Each group had a designated leader, an encourager, and a recorder. The groups began by talking about what new students needed to know. They brainstormed by trying to remember what had confused or scared them when they were new. I wanted the students to develop a formal plan, so they were required to use an outlining program to structure their presentation. The major headings were the major topics they wanted to cover, such as school activities, class schedules and options, administration, faculty, student council, library, and special events. Sometimes I suggested topics that the students had overlooked but that I knew should be covered—building entrances and access times, lunchroom rules. Then the students tried to think of images we could use for each category and added these suggestions under the appropriate headings.

One of the headings in our outline was "Student Council." The student council has sponsored several special events, and we wanted to show some of these activities. The student council had just completed a contest in which classes had decorated their classroom doors with class names. They came up with names like "The Weasel Easels" for the art teacher. My room was "Hahn's Hall of Famers." The students tried to decide which door decorations would be most interesting. They did the same kind of thing for the other categories. When we were finished, we had an organized list of the images we wanted to include in our project.

We used the completed outline as a way to keep the members of the group accountable. Students were assigned to provide each image. We were working with one video camera and one multimedia station for processing the images from videotape. Students signed up for the video camera, and we crossed images off the list as they were stored on the computer. In the beginning, all the students wanted to make sure they had their turn working with the video camera. After a while, the novelty wore off. Sometimes the pictures weren't that good, and the process had to be repeated. Then students started helping each other out; someone who had a free period might be sent back to get a better picture.

Grabes: *So you started with a project outline and then generated a series of pictures based on the outline. What did you do next?*

Monte: We created a series of screens using the slide show option in ClarisWorks. [We discuss this procedure in the section on slide show tools on pages 279 through 284.] Sometimes several images were combined in making one slide. We added text to some slides, but this was kept to a minimum because we didn't think it would be that easy to read information from the screen (see Figure 8.1). Each slide show ended up with about thirty-five different slides.

We made a decision to display each slide for ten seconds, which seemed a reasonable amount of time. Students then began to write the narration. Background music was selected, and the students tried to use some of the lyrics in the narration. Because we'd decided to display the slides at a fixed rate, developing the matching script was a challenge for the students. The script had to conform to the time a certain category of pictures was being shown, which took a good deal of trial and error and rewriting. One student was designated to do the final narration. This student practiced several times, trying to keep pace with the slide show program. Finally, the student recorded the narration on audio tape.

FIGURE 8.1 Captured Image Used in Schroeder Slide Show

The district had just purchased some AV Macintoshes, and we used one of these computers to produce the videotape. The AV computers can output a signal directly to a video recorder. You just connect the computer and tape recorder to the video recorder. You start the slide show on the computer and play the audio tape, and both sources are recorded. It may take a few tries to coordinate the two sources. If you don't like the recording, you can just rewind the videotape and try it again.

Grabes: *Any final comments on doing this kind of project?*

Monte: Well, as a teacher you have to be flexible and able to tolerate a little bit of chaos. Because of our equipment limitations, some students had down time. Students may need to have other things to work on. Students will need to mill around, look at each other's work, and talk with each other. We were also learning a lot of things as we went along. Neither the students nor I had much experience when we started, but that made it kind of fun. When you try something new, there has to be a time when you don't know exactly how everything works.

There were some unique benefits. Some students just aren't book-and-paper-type people, yet some of these students emerged as leaders. It was interesting to see some of these students spending time after school and working harder at the project than many of the others. Even parents talked about how interested their children were. I couldn't have gotten the same reaction by having the students type nine letters. This project seemed to give them a real sense of ownership.

Other word processing teachers may not understand this project. I think I see the purpose of this class a little differently. Computer applications will soon be much more than writing letters and constructing tables. The students now have a feel for how the computer can be used to communicate, and they're excited about what they've learned. I think you have to involve your students in things that challenge them to try something new. One of my college professors told me something I've always remembered. He said, "Don't be a textbook wired for sound."

A SYSTEM FOR CLASSIFYING STUDENT MULTIMEDIA PROJECTS

Three types of multimedia projects

The three types of multimedia projects that we will emphasize and differentiate in this chapter are embellished documents, linear multimedia presentations (often called slide shows), and hypermedia. Knowing about the different categories of multimedia projects should help you think about multimedia projects to use in your teaching. Figure 8.2 contains visual representations of these different project types. Look at them and read the brief

FIGURE 8.2   Categories of Student-Authored Multimedia

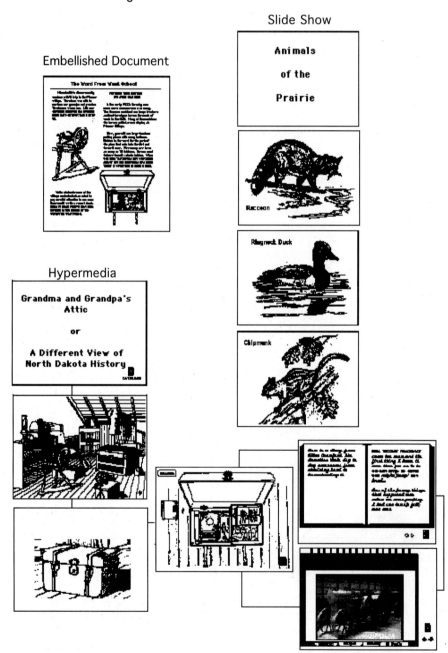

description of each category before moving on to the more detailed descriptions and examples that follow.

EMBELLISHED DOCUMENTS

Kinds of embellishments

An **embellished document** is a text document that has been enhanced with line art, high-quality pictures, access to video segments, or sound. (*Note:* Line art is not artwork made up only of lines. It is artwork that is purely black and white. You will learn more about such computer graphics in Chapter 9.) Student authors might add pictures, sounds, or video segments to text because information in these alternative formats seems more informative or more interesting than text alone. Students can prepare some form of embellished document with nearly every word processing program. Different word processing programs allow different formats to be incorporated.

Informative alternative formats

Examples of embellished documents

If an embellished document is to include sound or video, the audience will have to view the document using a computer. The author does not have to be present or use his or her own computer to show this kind of document to a reader. It is as easy to send someone a word processing file on disk as it is to send a letter and embellished documents can usually be sent as an attachment to an e-mail message. Students in other classrooms or schools can easily

Some programs students may use to create embellished documents allow them to incorporate video and sound. (© Michael Zide)

view the document containing sound and video that you or your students have created. If the document contains text and still graphics, students can print and distribute it. Common examples of embellished documents include student-authored newsletters, reports, and instructional manuals.

LINEAR MULTIMEDIA PRESENTATIONS OR SLIDE SHOWS

Viewing slide shows

A **slide show** is a **linear multimedia presentation** that might be used as a self-contained presentation or may accompany a speech or lecture. The defining attribute of this format is the linear nature of the presentation. Slide shows can be viewed from the computer screen or by using a projection system, recorded on videotape for presentation, or printed to produce a series of overhead transparencies. Like all the other projects discussed in this chapter, a slide show can incorporate text, several types of graphics, and sound. See "Activities and Projects for Your Classroom: Slide Show Activities" for more suggestions for student-authored slide shows.

HYPERMEDIA

Hypermedia users make many choices.

Meaningful units of information

Hypermedia as exploration

A **hypermedia** project differs from embellished documents and linear multimedia in the complexity of the pathways that are available through the information and in the degree of control that users can exercise in navigating those pathways. As you discovered in Chapter 7, anyone using hypermedia is in the position of making choices. These choices often make it possible for a user to pursue some topics in depth and to avoid or perhaps fail to encounter some other sources of information. Authors segment information into meaningful units and create pathways among the units. In creating the units of information and establishing the links, authors attempt to anticipate the types of information different users might find helpful and provide convenient ways for these users to explore. Users decide which of the options provided by the author they want or need to experience.

How do users experience hypermedia as exploration? The brief segment of hypermedia depicted in Figure 8.2 provides an example of how user-guided exploration might proceed. In this example, the user explores an attic. You may recognize this example as *Grandparents' Attic,* the exploratory history environment first described in some detail in Chapter 3. The student exploring the attic can move from scene to scene. Some objects in each scene react when the student acts on them. In some cases, a label appears so the user will know what the object is. The trunk in the attic opens to reveal a diary, a photo album, letters, and a stack of short stories. If the user decides to open the photo album, many color pictures are available. Each photograph displays an artifact or scene from the historical period. Clicking on a photograph

Activities and Projects for Your Classroom

Slide Show Activities

Many classroom activities traditionally done with paper, pencils, and crayons can easily be converted to slide shows incorporating text, color graphics, and sound. Slide shows can be either a whole-class activity, in which each student is responsible for one or two slides, or an individual or small group activity, in which the individual or group is responsible for the entire presentation. The following examples should get you thinking about the many opportunities for using slide shows in your classroom.

Examples of whole-class slide shows

Getting to Know You

◆ A parents' night introduction of class members

Theme-Based Alphabet Books

◆ Such as *The ABC Book of Space* or *The ABC Book of Birds*

Recycling Posters

◆ Student-created slides to encourage recycling

Parade of States

◆ Student-created slides depicting important facts about states

Seasonal Poetry

Our Favorite Books

◆ Student-created slides depicting favorite books could be kept in the library and viewed by other students.

Memories of Junior High

◆ Created by present students as an orientation for future students

Examples of individual or small-group slide shows:

◆ Book reports
◆ Creative stories
◆ Modern fairy tales
◆ Autobiographies
◆ Historical portraits
◆ Geographic travelogues
◆ Cartoons
◆ Animal reports
◆ Stages of meiosis or mitosis
◆ Stages in the development of a thunderstorm
◆ Chronology of world events, such as the breakup of the Soviet Union
◆ Differing viewpoints on controversial issues such as welfare ✳

turns it over to reveal a segment of text describing the photograph. The student can decide to abandon exploring a particular type of information at any time. The student can investigate or ignore each of these types of information depending on his or her interest and purpose.

THINKING BEYOND WHAT YOUR PROJECTS WILL LOOK LIKE

How might we sum all of this information up? Clearly, the three formats we have described differ in complexity. Embellished documents or slide shows can be used in any situation in which reports are used to develop communication skills and encourage students to think about course content. Nearly all classes require students to write reports or research papers or to give oral presentations of some type. Incorporating a few graphics or a short video segment takes a little additional time and new skills (see discussion of techniques in Chapter 9), but developing embellished documents or using a slide show to *Teacher commitment* improve an oral presentation would not call for a serious deviation from existing activities. On the other hand, creating an interactive hypermedia project does involve committing a significant amount of time to developing some new skills in using technology and to developing the project itself. In deciding to embark on involving students in developing hypermedia, you need to be committed to something that is presently quite out of the ordinary.

One of the greatest challenges in introducing student-authored multimedia projects is to get teachers thinking beyond what finished projects will look like. We want teachers to think about the skills that will be involved in completing the projects. Think about these questions, too:

◆ Why would you have students spend their time developing these projects?
◆ How will students gather and transform information as they prepare to create their multimedia project?
◆ How will you encourage active student involvement with the central course ideas that you want to emphasize in a particular project?
◆ How will you assess student projects?

ACTIVE
COOPERATION
THEME-BASED
INTEGRATED
VERSATILE
EVALUATION

Projects stimulate valued mental activities.

We hope that we can help you interconnect all these issues. Unfortunately, the linear format of a textbook does not allow us to interweave these ideas very effectively. It would be nice if we could insert buttons that would let you instantly return to Chapter 2 to review how external activities, such as projects, can stimulate valued mental behaviors or just as instantly glance ahead to later chapters, where we make the point that many important behaviors in project development have nothing to do with the computer. But since a textbook is not hypermedia, the best alternative seems to be to constantly remind you of (1) why projects are valuable activities that encourage your students to think, and (2) how to integrate projects within the social setting and curriculum of your present or future classrooms.

SOFTWARE TOOLS FOR CREATING MULTIMEDIA PROJECTS

A basic set of software tools can be used to construct the entire range of project types, and the project types can be applied to a variety of content areas, at many levels of sophistication, by students at all grade levels.

Why students should learn to use technological tools

The time students spend learning how to use the software tools and how to design each category of multimedia will be spent efficiently if they continue to use similar software tools to design similar projects. Consider this point as an extension of our general argument for why students should learn to use any technological tool. Students are not taught to use a word processing program to complete one term paper. Students learn to use word processing programs because this knowledge will help them complete a variety of school and nonschool tasks. Likewise, efficiency in learning to use multimedia tools occurs when students use the tools repeatedly. Whether students will eventually communicate with multimedia the way many adults now communicate with text remains to be seen, but it is reasonable to predict that multimedia—very possibly, student-authored multimedia—will play an increasingly important role in academic settings.

GETTING STARTED AUTHORING MULTIMEDIA

Students can create multimedia projects in a number of ways. In many cases, no specialized software is required, because many of the most widely used software tools already have built-in multimedia capabilities. You have already read about some of these tools in earlier chapters, but we will revisit them to discuss their specific multimedia applications. Keep in mind that multimedia capabilities are not found only in sophisticated application programs. General-purpose tools, such as word processing and paint programs targeting the K–12 market, emphasized integrating graphics and sound just as soon as the necessary hardware was available. Creating the categories of multimedia outlined here usually does not require that schools purchase a great deal of expensive new software.

Creating multimedia is financially realistic.

We will also consider specialized multimedia tools. Specialization implies that a software tool was developed to accomplish a well-defined set of tasks. A word processing program is a general tool. A tool designed specifically to link a number of pictures together into a slide show is a specialized tool. Specialized multimedia tools often offer more powerful options and may make similar functions easier to implement than general tools. Teachers will have to balance this additional power and ease of use against the added cost and training time needed for their students to create projects with more specialized tools.

Helping students develop their projects

The purpose of discussing multimedia tools in some detail is to help you link specific software tools with each type of multimedia project. It is important for you to feel confident that you would know where to begin in helping students develop their own projects. After you complete this section, you should be able to suggest several specific programs that could be used to author each category of multimedia project. You should also be able to describe in general terms what the author does in working with each type of software. Ideally, you will have the opportunity to work with similar software tools in a laboratory setting and create sample projects of your own. Your course instructor may emphasize a different program than we describe or feel it is important that you be exposed to several different programs. Our goal is to give you a comprehensive perspective on some exemplary programs. The general characteristics we describe should apply to whatever specific programs you actually experience. Working with these tools in a hands-on setting is probably the best way to develop your own knowledge and confidence.

CREATING EMBELLISHED DOCUMENTS WITH WORD PROCESSING PROGRAMS

Most word processing programs are now capable of producing multimedia. Some word processing programs not only allow a combination of text and graphics but also allow users to integrate video segments and digitized sound. These more flexible programs are used mainly to produce printed documents, but they have the added potential of creating a file containing information stored in the other formats. This file can be shared with others who own the same program.

A small embellished document appears in Figure 8.3. This simple file consists of three elements: a title (text), a QuickTime movie (video segment), and digitized sound. Figure 8.3 provides a glimpse of the movie. This video was digitized from a videotape made at a local zoo (we will describe the specific technique in Chapter 9). The video segment depicts a baby elk's antics as it struggles to eat grass. With gangly legs that are too long, the elk first kneels and finally collapses to the ground to eat more comfortably. To the right of the image is a small speaker icon. Clicking on this icon plays a recorded sound—in this case, a brief poem about the baby elk.

Publishing features in word processing programs

Computer applications capable of integrating text and graphics, using different text styles, and arranging text in columns are often described as desktop publishing programs. Historically, word processing programs and **desktop publishing** programs were distinct, but now they are much less clearly differentiated. Basic publishing features are included in many word processing programs. These features can do a great deal to increase student pride in authorship.

Some word processing programs developed for education have been

FIGURE 8.3 Word Processor Document Incorporating Video and Sound

Why is the grass so far away when you are small?

designed to make desktop publishing features easier to implement. Student Writing Center is a good example of such a program. As a student begins the process of creating a new document, he or she first determines if the pages of the document will be divided into columns and then if the first page will have a heading. Creating a heading and columns this easily can encourage even young students and their teachers to take on projects such as classroom newsletters.

Integrating and positioning text and graphics

Some of the most fundamental desktop publishing capabilities are the integration and positioning of text and graphics. Desktop publishing programs allow the author to lay out pages exactly as they are to appear to the intended audience. The author should be able to view on the computer screen what the printed page will look like and experiment until the desired appearance is achieved. The full range of text editing features described in Chapter 5 should also be available (see pages 160 through 164). In addition, the author should be able to treat segments of text and graphic images as objects and edit these objects. If you find the idea of a **text object** difficult to understand, think of it as a rectangular frame containing text. The sides of the frame are usually not visible. Any time you work with a word processing program, you are actually entering text into a frame of a sort. The frame is established by the left and right margins, and the text frame changes if you decide to change the margins. In desktop publishing, one text object does not cover the entire page, and there are likely to be several text objects used on each page. The author is able to position text and graphic objects on the page and to move these objects around to determine which arrangement is most effective. Programs differ a great deal in the capacity to edit at this level.

If a teacher wants to emphasize multimedia applications, it may not be enough for him or her simply to know that a particular program is capable of desktop publishing applications. Often, a decision will have to be made about tradeoffs among ease of use, the desktop publishing functions available, and price. There are a number of very useful products available, but teachers should have their own objectives and budgets in mind when making a decision.

Student Writing Center is a convenient example demonstrating the kinds of issues teachers should consider. On one hand, it is reasonably priced, and users can create headings and columns easily. On the other hand, video segments and sound cannot be integrated into documents prepared with this program, so it is not as versatile as some more expensive programs. What Student Writing Center does offer is a very easy method for inserting and positioning graphics. Once an image is inserted into a document, it can be resized and easily moved to a new position on the page. The author simply clicks on the image and then drags the image to the desired location. **Dragging** is accomplished by moving the mouse while holding the mouse button down. As the image is moved, text simply flows around it (see Figure 8.4). The process of inserting and moving images within text could not be accomplished more easily. These features may be just what some teachers want for their students.

Dragging images with a mouse

FIGURE 8.4   Text and Image Integration in the Student Writing Center

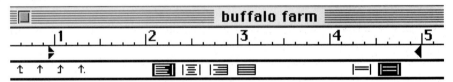

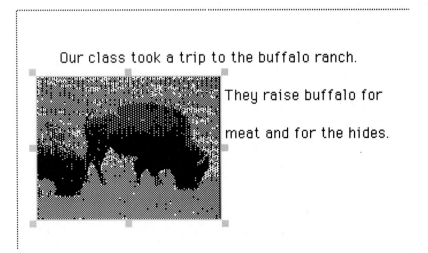

Student Writing Center is a registered trademark of the Learning Company, 1-800-852-2255.

CREATING MULTIMEDIA SLIDE SHOWS

Multimedia slide shows can be created using either general multimedia authoring tools or tools designed specifically for linear multimedia presentations. We will present good examples of tools that teachers and students have used to do some interesting things, but we are not claiming that they are the best. Your instructor and your own investigations may lead you to other applications that you end up liking better. However, these examples should get you started thinking about this category of multimedia tools and should give you a better understanding of how students actually use a slide show tool to create a project based on a class topic. As you read, try to develop your own examples of slide show projects for your content areas.

Developing your own project examples

ClarisWorks

Monte Hahn's students created their slide show project using ClarisWorks, a single product that integrates a number of the most commonly used computer tools. The applications described in Chapter 5 (word processing, spreadsheet, database, communications), as well as tools for creating and manipulating graphics (see Chapter 9), are all available within this integrated package. Schools often consider integrated packages as a way to make tools available to students because so many basic functions can be made available with one purchase. If ClarisWorks 4.0 or a later version happens to be available, students also have access to a very convenient tool for creating slide shows.

The slide show option is available when using several of the ClarisWorks tools (word processing, drawing, painting), but the draw tool is probably the best option. A slide show is developed by creating a multipage document. Think of a multipage document as a number of sheets of paper joined to each other at the top and bottom edges. Each page within the multipage document will eventually become a separate slide in the slide show. The draw tool allows the author to combine and precisely position different types of information on each page. You can enter text from the keyboard or import text from a stored file, load a color picture created with some other application, draw using the tools available within ClarisWorks, import charts from the spreadsheet, or add sound or a QuickTime movie. Once they are available on the page, you can move these elements around to create a more effective display.

Multipage draw documents as slide shows

The presentation of a multipage draw document as a slide show is accomplished by selecting the slide show option from the View menu. Selecting the slide show option produces the **dialog box**, or selection of options, shown in Figure 8.5. From this dialog box, you can present the slide show or add some final touches and refinements. If you like, you can change the order of the pages.

Selecting whether a page is presented as opaque, transparent, or hidden controls how the images will appear when you display them. When pages are presented as opaque, one page is experienced as replacing the previous page. When pages are presented as transparent, the image on one page is added to whatever appeared on the previous page. Transparent images are used when you want to build an image stage by stage. You have probably seen presentations in which the speaker wanted the audience to view a building list of points, with each new idea added at the time it was presented. To create this effect, the author of a multimedia slide show develops a series of slides with text positioned at the appropriate location on the pages and then presents the series of pages in transparent mode. The same thing can be done with pictures. Single images can be accumulated until the desired composite is achieved. This procedure is useful when an author wants to demonstrate stages, such as those in the metamorphosis of a butterfly, or to call attention to individual parts of a whole, such as the parts of a frontier fort. Once the series of cumulative images is complete, a page presented in opaque mode gives the viewer the impression of moving on to a different slide. Designating an image as hidden allows an image to remain part of the multipage document and not be displayed. This option might be used when the author wants to create and save a set of images, but perhaps use only some of them for a particular presentation.

Ways of running slide shows

A slide show can be set to run automatically or to operate under manual control. The distinction is established by selecting or deselecting the box next to the "Advance every" option. (The term **deselecting** means that selecting, or clicking on, an option that has already been selected will cause the option not

FIGURE 8.5   ClarisWorks Slide Show Options

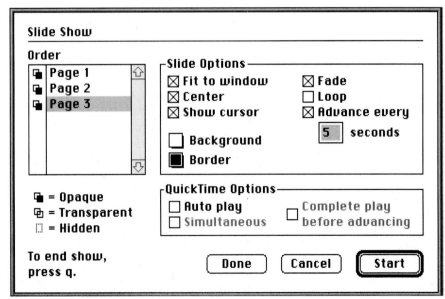

to be applied. If an author uses the mouse to click on a selection box containing an X, the X will disappear, and the option will no longer be applied.) When functioning automatically, the slide show will run from beginning to end on its own. If the "Loop" option is also selected, the slide show will run continuously. When functioning manually, the next slide is displayed when the user clicks the mouse. If a slide show is developed to accompany a presentation, it makes sense to allow the speaker or presenter to control the slides manually. If the slides are complex, it also makes sense to allow individual viewers to advance to the next slide when they are ready. If users are likely to be inexperienced, authors should include a message on the slide such as "Click anywhere to continue," as a prompt.

Kid Pix Slideshow

Kid Pix Slideshow was designed specifically to generate slide shows. As its name implies, it is a feature of Kid Pix 2, a popular inexpensive paint program designed for younger children (we will discuss Kid Pix further in Chapter 9) and is also included as part of Kid Pix Studio. Kid Pix allows a multimedia author to create color pictures, include text with the picture, and record sound. Each screen image is saved as a separate file. Kid Pix Slideshow allows several Kid Pix sound and picture files or graphics files created with other software tools to be organized into a slide show. (*Note:* The type of graphics files with which Kid Pix Slideshow can work is not really a function of the software tool producing the file, but of the file type. Many graphics programs can save files in several file formats. The Macintosh version of Kid Pix Slideshow works with PICT files [see Chapter 9, pages 305 through 306, for a discussion of file types].)

COOPERATION

This system of creating and then integrating separate files works well for school projects. In a fairly common application, individual students or student teams are given the assignment of creating one slide in a series. Each student or student group might provide information about one butterfly, one fish, one classmate, or one low-fat food to become part of an integrated series dealing with biological organisms, the class, or nutrition. As the project develops, students may work simultaneously on several different computers to develop their contributions to the final product. When the individual files have been completed, Kid Pix Slideshow allows the teacher or the students to integrate and organize the individual files.

Kid Pix Slideshow is a very easy product for students to work with. If you look carefully at Figure 8.6, you will notice three buttons below each miniature picture. When the first, or picture, button is clicked, a dialog box appears listing the graphics files available. The author selects the desired file, and a miniature of the picture appears. If you keep looking carefully at Figure 8.6, you will notice that a graphic has yet to be selected for slide 12. When the middle, or sound, button is clicked, the author is given the opportunity to record a segment of sound that will be played when the picture is displayed. Sounds previously recorded with Kid Pix will be attached automatically. The final, or transition, button allows the author to specify the visual transition that will be used between the present slide and the next slide to be displayed. Transitions show how one image appears to replace another on the computer screen. One image may appear to slide over the image on the screen, emerge and expand out of the middle of the existing image, or replace it in a number of other possible ways. Authors may use transitions to convey the relationship between the two images such as whether the information on the new slide continues the presentation on the same level or provides greater depth about what was presented on the previous slide. Transitions are also useful simply to keep the presentation a little more interesting. Inexperienced authors often take the potential for creating a more interesting presentation too far and use so many different transitions that the variety of changes becomes distracting. Young students often employ transitions haphazardly, and teachers have to decide whether or not to encourage a more systematic approach.

Transitions convey information

The miniature pictures in Figure 8.6 show spring wildflowers. This slide show was prepared to chronicle observations during a hike down a forest trail. Narration accompanying the images describes the surroundings and identifies the flowers. Kid Pix Slideshow is perfectly suited to this kind of

Slide shows to chronicle observations

A
C
T
I NTEGRATED
V
E

FIGURE 8.6 Kid Pix Slideshow Assembly Area

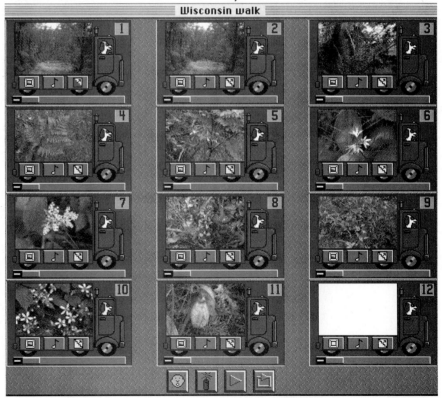

Presentation Tools

Presentation tools are specialized for the purpose of communicating information to others in a way that is structured, forceful, and transitory. The tools produce and present the computer-based equivalent of overhead transparencies or 35 mm slides. Although presentation tools can be used to create actual slides and transparencies, the more popular method of delivery is probably with an **LCD projection panel,** a **video projector,** or a large monitor. Presentation tools are designed to help users perform three tasks: organize the ideas for a presentation, generate the visual materials, and deliver the presentation. Often presentations are initially created with an outlining tool. An outliner allows the user to get ideas down quickly and to cluster and reorganize ideas efficiently. Projected presentations place a premium on the expression of ideas in a succinct fashion. An outliner provides a good way to prepare and organize precise statements.

The visual components of presentation images—think of them as projected slides—nearly always consist of text, graphics, and a background. A presentation tool allows these components to be combined into the composite images the audience will eventually view. Text must be displayed in a large font so it can be read easily. The carefully crafted text statements are often presented as **bullet charts** for easy reading. Often, the presenter uses a technique called a **build** and reveals bulleted items one at a time against a fixed background so the significance of each idea can be stressed as it is revealed. Projected visuals are often displayed against a white screen. To make the presenta-

tion easier to view, the text and graphics of the presentation are typically placed on some type of colored background. It is easier to read white lettering against a colored background than vice versa. A single background color and perhaps simple graphic elements (e.g., a company logo) may remain across the entire presentation. Most presentation programs allow the preparation of a **master slide** that contains all elements common to all slides, a technique that greatly increases preparation efficiency. Only the text and some graphics change from slide to slide. Many presentation tools provide templates to make the creation of the master slide even easier.

Finally, presentation tools are used to actually deliver presentations. While this primarily means controlling the projection of each slide, it is usually also possible to print out miniature images of the slides. Copies can be distributed to the audience so that they can follow along, read the slides if they don't happen to have a good view of the screen, and take some notes.

Presentations can be created with a variety of tools. HyperStudio, ClarisWorks, and many other multimedia products discussed in this book can be used to create effective presentations. In contrast, the tools described in this section are more sophisticated and designed for those who give important presentations as part of their work. As with many tools, we come to what might be described as the cost/time/benefit question. Is the cost to purchase and time to master a unique tool worth the benefit? It is certainly worth becoming acquainted enough with high-end presentation tools to answer this question for yourself (we list several of the more popular products at the end of the chapter). Our emphasis on student projects causes us to emphasize general-purpose tools, but some teachers may find it worthwhile to become skilled in the use of presentation tools for their own use and to have students use them as well. ✳

project. Once the images have been isolated and stored as individual files (see techniques described in Chapter 9), it takes just a few minutes to bring the individual images into Kid Pix Slideshow. High school students can very quickly learn all they need to know to work with the program and can spend their class or homework time developing the comments to accompany the images.

MULTIMEDIA AUTHORING ENVIRONMENTS FOR HYPERMEDIA

A multimedia authoring environment often achieves the following:

◆ Integrates a variety of tools frequently used to produce multimedia products.
◆ Allows basic multimedia functions to be included in products without requiring the author to engage in detailed programming.
◆ Allows the author to produce more specialized products either through programming or through inclusion of small specialized programs produced by others.

Support and power for student and teacher multimedia authors

The combination of these characteristics gives teacher or student multimedia authors a great deal of support and power.

Let's look at what each of the characteristics of a multimedia authoring environment contributes. Remember that at a basic level, multimedia is a combination of text, graphics, and sound. A multimedia authoring environment provides tools for manipulating and perhaps creating all these types of information. It should be possible to enter and edit text, to import or create graphics and video segments, and to import or record sound. Once the basic resources are available, the authoring environment should allow you to easily integrate and rearrange the different types of information. For example, the multimedia authoring environment should allow you to combine text and graphics and position these elements of information exactly as you would like to have them appear on the computer screen. Finally, the component that most clearly distinguishes multimedia authoring environments from the other applications we have discussed is the ability to create the means by which the user will interact with the multimedia content. The author may create presentation methods that range from giving the user no control over what or when anything is experienced to allowing the user always to select what is to be experienced next.

Multimedia authoring environments can generate embellished documents, linear presentations, and interactive multimedia, but it is the production of interactive hypermedia projects that most clearly demonstrates the full capabilities of authoring environments.

Multimedia authoring environments appropriate for teachers and students

There are a number of multimedia authoring environments appropriate for teachers and students; even more products of this type are likely to appear in the near future. We will review several of these products so that you will have some idea of what authoring environments are like and what can be done with them. *Do not worry at this point if you feel that you are not learning enough to actually develop multimedia materials on your own. You will learn more in the chapters that follow.* There are also many "how-to" manuals available to help teachers learn both the basics and advanced techniques (we list several appropriate references at the end of this chapter in "Resources to Expand Your Knowledge Base"). However, you will also see that you do not need a lot of know-how before you will be ready to start experimenting with simple projects. Keep in mind from the beginning that if your intent is to use development of a multimedia project to involve students in meaningful content-area learning, they should not have to spend a long time developing computer skills. The creative application of a reasonable number of simple skills should give them powerful experiences. Such experiences are available through HyperStudio, one of the most popular multimedia environments in school settings.

HYPERSTUDIO

Like other multimedia authoring environments, HyperStudio might be described as a multimedia construction set. It contains elements that might be seen as multimedia building blocks, and others that provide the tools to work with these building blocks.

Most HyperStudio tools are available directly from the menu bar. When you click on a heading in the menu bar, a menu "drops down." For this reason, you might hear this type of user interface called a drop-down menu bar. Several of the drop-down menus in HyperStudio are actually **tear-off palettes**, which can be detached from the menu bar and will then remain available wherever you place them on the screen (normally, a menu disappears when the mouse button is released). The top part of Figure 8.7 shows the drop-down "Objects" menu, the tools palette, and the patterns and colors palette for the paint tools. The individual tools from the tools palette are also labeled in the lower portion of Figure 8.7.

Using just the tools displayed in Figure 8.7, the author can (1) create some HyperStudio elements (button, field, graphic, sound, text); (2) access these

A variety of powerful tools for authors

elements to move and modify them (button, field, graphic, sound, and text tools); and (3) create and modify the appearance of what appears on the screen using the painting tools. As we proceed, we will provide additional information on how these tools (and others that are not displayed in Figure 8.7) perform their functions. The important point here is that HyperStudio and

FIGURE 8.7 Tools and Actions Available from HyperStudio Menu Bar

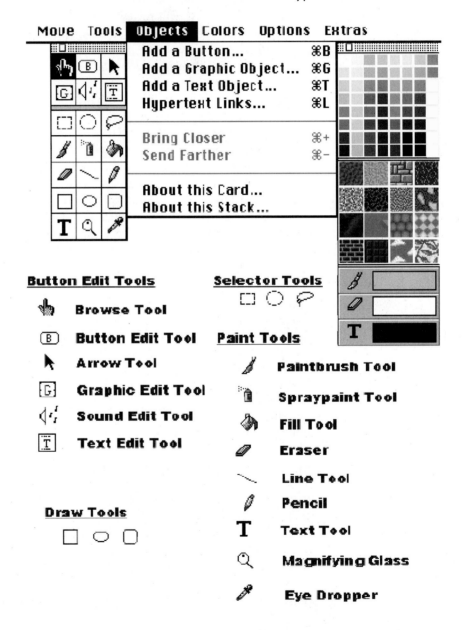

Button Edit Tools

🖐 **Browse Tool**

Ⓑ **Button Edit Tool**

▶ **Arrow Tool**

Ⓖ **Graphic Edit Tool**

◁ **Sound Edit Tool**

Ⓣ **Text Edit Tool**

Draw Tools

▢ ⬭ ▢

Selector Tools

▢ ⬭ ◠

Paint Tools

🖌 **Paintbrush Tool**

Spraypaint Tool

🖐 **Fill Tool**

◿ **Eraser**

╲ **Line Tool**

✏ **Pencil**

T **Text Tool**

🔍 **Magnifying Glass**

🖊 **Eye Dropper**

other multimedia authoring environments provide the author with convenient access to a variety of powerful tools for manipulating and integrating both the building blocks of multimedia and the actual information sources from which multimedia products are assembled.

Elements of the HyperStudio System

It is important for authors and users to have some understanding of the elements with which HyperStudio products are assembled. These elements include:

- Stack
- Card
- Background
- Button
- Field
- Script/NBA
- Other Objects

Cards

The **card** is the fundamental unit of the HyperStudio system. You can usually think of a card as equivalent to what you can see on the computer screen at any one time. What users see when examining a card are sources of information such as text, graphics, video, and some of the other elements of the HyperStudio system.

If you look at Figure 8.8, you will see a card containing a graphic, text contained within two fields (fields will be discussed shortly), and buttons providing access to other cards and to a sound.

With HyperStudio, it is useful to differentiate between the surface of the

FIGURE 8.8 HyperStudio Card

card, called the **background,** and objects placed on the card. The background may be painted with color or a pattern, with an image, or with text. If the hyperauthor wants several cards to share the background, a new card can be created with the background of an existing card. Objects are layered on top of the card. HyperStudio offers a variety of object types including graphics, text fields, and buttons. You will learn about objects later.

Stack

Imagine a stack as a pile of notecards.

A HyperStudio file is called a **stack** and consists of a series of cards. You might find it helpful to imagine a stack as a pile of notecards like those you would use to prepare a speech or study for a test. You can easily shuffle through the cards in a stack in sequential order using keyboard commands. Moving from card to card brings into view the information that each card contains.

Do not assume from this example that all stacks consist of cards containing exactly the same categories of information. This is the case only when using hypermedia strictly as a database. Again, HyperStudio is a multimedia authoring environment, and it can take on whatever form the author desires. If the author wants each card in a stack to have a unique appearance and to contain a unique combination of information types, then the stack can just as easily be put together in this format.

Fields

Why enter in a field?

A multimedia author can enter text directly on the card background or within a text field. The advantage of entering text in a **field** is that it allows you or a later user of a stack to take advantage of word processing capabilities built into the multimedia authoring environment.

When you enter text directly on the card, you sacrifice many capabilities. For example, if you decide to return and edit work that you've already completed, perhaps to enter text in a different font size or to insert or remove words, you'll have a lot of work to do. Text entered directly on a card is "painted" on the card, and you must remove it before you can add new text. Attempting to insert text does not work because existing text does not move aside to provide space for the new words. Similarly, when text is deleted, the remaining words do not slide back together. In most cases you must erase the work that you have completed and start again.

Sometimes it is useful to enter text directly on a card.

When you enter text in a text field, most of the editing features of a typical word processor are available (see characteristics of word processing programs in Chapter 5). You can very easily make font changes, as well as deletions and insertions. You can also cut, copy, and paste between fields or between applications. Keep in mind, however, that there *are* a few situations in which you might find it useful to enter text directly on the card. Painting text on a card can be useful when creating special effects, with text arranged in an unusual configuration—perhaps you don't want your text in a straight line, or you want to use a font that may not be available on user machines.

Adding a text field to a card is easy. The command "Add a Text Object" appears under the "Objects" menu. When you select this command, a field appears in the middle of the card. You may drag this field to the position you want it to occupy on the card and then drag the field by the edges to make it the size you want.

Set field characteristics

Other characteristics of the field can be modified using a dialog box, as shown in Figure 8.9. The dialog box appears when the area outside the field is clicked. You can also return to edit a field by selecting the Text Tool (Tools Menu).

Several characteristics of the text field can be determined using the dialog box. It is possible to set both the color of the text and of the field background. "Draw Frame" will determine whether the text will be enclosed within a visible frame. For some purposes, it may be preferable to have the text appear without a frame. Using unframed text is often preferable to entering text directly on the card (because editing capabilities are available), and the result will appear the same to the user.

The scrolling option is useful when the amount of text to be placed in a field exceeds the card space available. A field can contain approximately 32,000 characters. Obviously, this amounts to many pages of text. Using scrolling fields containing a great deal of information is a controversial technique. Many experts believe that presenting such large units of information defeats the whole purpose of hypermedia authoring. This is another one of the design guidelines that individual teachers may or may not endorse.

Finally, authors may want to consider setting the "**Read only**" property of

FIGURE 8.9 HyperStudio Text Appearance Dialog Box

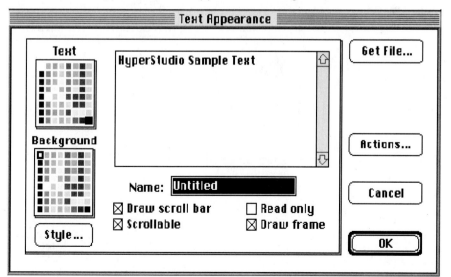

The "Read only" option

a field (right side of Figure 8.9). Setting a field to "Read only" prevents users from altering what the author has entered in it. There are times when the user is expected to contribute to a field and times when the author just wants the user to read what is written. If a stack has been authored to be used by many users, the authors may not want the first users of the stack to alter the stack before later users have had a chance to work with it. Although unlocking a "Read only" field is relatively easy for an experienced user, the danger is minimized because such a user will realize that the author did not intend for the text entered in a locked field to be altered.

Buttons

Optional actions with buttons

Buttons allow the HyperStudio author to prepare optional actions for the eventual user of the stack. The actions might allow the user to move to other cards, to reveal and hide color pictures and QuickTime movies, to play sounds, to manipulate a videodisc player, to reveal a hidden text message, or to perform many other actions.

Adding a button to a stack

Adding a button to a stack is similar to adding a field. The "Add a button" option from the "Objects" menu opens the dialog box shown in Figure 8.10. There are several options to note in the button dialog box. First, you can attach a name to each button. It is particularly useful for the button's name to describe its purpose. A button labeled "Song" near a bird picture, for example, suggests to most users that the button will provide that bird's song. The button name may be visible or invisible depending on whether the "Show name" option is selected.

FIGURE 8.10 Button Appearance Dialog Box

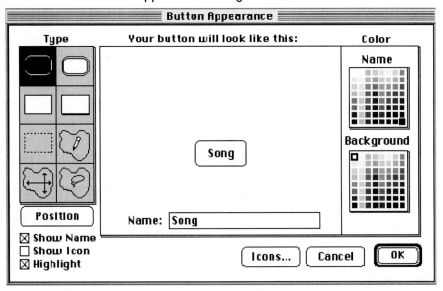

Setting the button style

Button style allows the shape and general appearance of the button to be set. A very important style option is transparent. The capability of creating a button that the user cannot see may at first confuse you a bit. The advantage in using invisible buttons—usually several different buttons—is to cover different objects or parts of an object. Sometimes an invisible button is used to cover the entire card. Clicking anywhere on the card will initiate any action attached to the button. Often the object to be covered is a graphic of some type. By carefully positioning invisible buttons over critical features of the graphic, a software author might allow users to reveal text describing each selected feature or to move to another card with a larger, more detailed image of the selected part of the original image. Or, instead of using buttons to present information, invisible buttons can be used as part of a method for evaluating understanding. Buttons can be used to program "test-like" events ("Click on the carburetor" or "Click on the part of the weather map showing the cold front") and to provide feedback.

Advantages of invisible buttons

From the dialog box, the author can choose the "Icons . . ." button to move to a collection of button shapes that can be incorporated into any new project (see Figure 8.11). **Icons** are pictures that are intended to represent functions. The icon's appearance should suggest the action that clicking the button will produce. Icons can save authors a lot of work, and using standard icons consistently can make stacks easier to use. Often authors combine the icon with a meaningful button name to make certain that users understand the button's function; for example, naming a forward arrow "Next Card."

Icons represent functions.

The purpose of buttons is to allow the user to take some action designated by the author. HyperStudio offers several ways to assign actions to

FIGURE 8.11 Button Icons

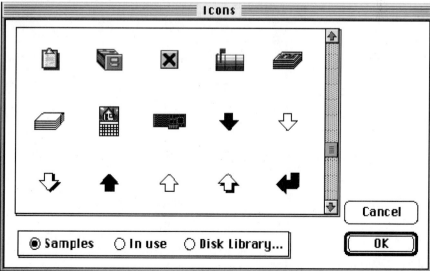

buttons. Some actions are simply assigned by selecting the desired action from the options provided on the button dialog box (see Figure 8.12). Additional button actions can be obtained by selecting the New Button Actions (NBA) option from the dialog box. (Focus: New Button Actions describes several interesting NBAs and an example of how each might be used.) Finally, you can program buttons to initiate actions of your choice using HyperLogo (the programming language available in HyperStudio). Perhaps because HyperStudio comes with many "preprogrammed" actions, we have seen few examples of students programming button actions. You will learn a little more about programming later in this chapter when we discuss HyperCard. You might also review some of the comments on programming in Chapter 4.

NBAs assign actions

Student authors will find that one of the most useful functions they can make available with buttons is the transition from one card to another. Think of this as moving from one source of information to another. The purpose of adding a button to provide this function may be as simple as giving users the opportunity to control when they proceed to new material. At the most basic level, having this ability to move from one source of information to another is like turning the pages in a book.

When an option is intended to move to another card, a special dialog box appears on the screen (see Figure 8.13).

Using the "Move To . . ." dialog box is a simple matter. Once this dialog box appears on the screen, you use the arrows to move to the desired destination for the link. The special dialog box will remain on the screen during these transitions. When the destination card has been reached, click the OK button in the special dialog box. The link will automatically be established, and the

Using the "Move To . . ." function

FIGURE 8.12 HyperStudio Button Actions

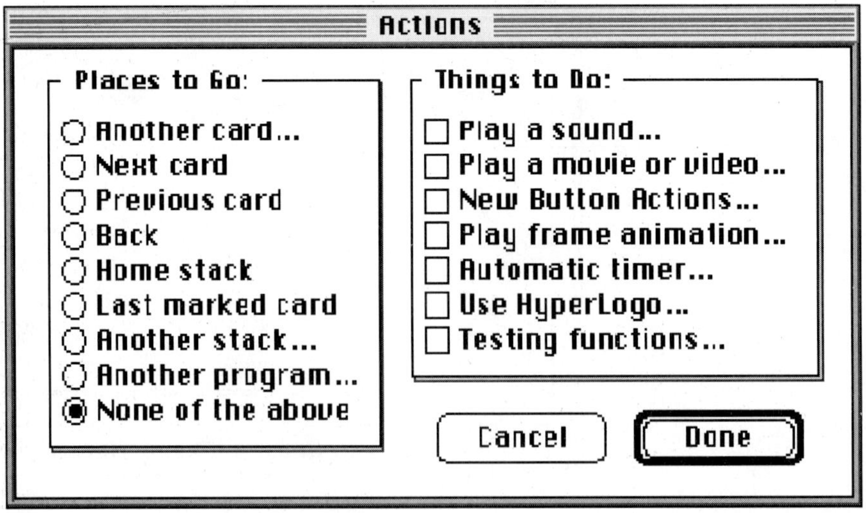

FIGURE 8.13   HyperStudio "Move To . . ." Dialog Box

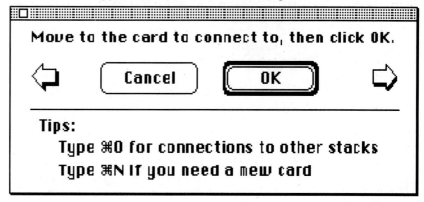

author will be returned to the location of the button. Now when the button is clicked, the user will move from the location of the button to the destination that was selected.

Assigning visual effects to buttons

HyperStudio also allows users to assign visual effects to buttons. Visual effects can be used to give the user the feeling of a certain type of movement when moving from card to card. Perhaps it is desirable that the user have the impression of turning the pages in a book. The visual effect involved in turning pages is sometimes called *binding*. Most textbooks have left binding. Some notebooks have top binding. The effects *left to right* and *right to left* are used to simulate left binding. The effects *top to bottom* and *bottom to top* are used to simulate top binding. *Iris open* is used to indicate movement to a deeper level of detail, and *iris close* is used to return to a higher detail level. In all, twenty-seven different visual effects can be assigned.

Multiple buttons provide multiple options.

Multiple buttons can also provide users with multiple options. For example, individual buttons covering each state in a U.S. map might allow the user to move to a larger map of a given state. Such buttons can give users the opportunity to choose the information they will encounter next. A key application of buttons is to give users a way to move to different places, such as different rooms in a house, parts of the body, buildings in a city, classrooms in a school, or exhibits in a museum. Buttons allow users to initiate the desired transitions. Learning to use buttons greatly expands the diversity of projects student authors can develop.

HYPERCARD

HyperCard is similar in many ways to HyperStudio, and authors familiar with one authoring environment will be able to function in the other almost immediately. Many of the projects you have seen or will see in this book could have been authored using either environment.

Focus

New Button Actions (NBAs)

An important factor contributing to the success of HyperStudio in school settings has been the relatively powerful techniques available to novice users. Although these techniques may be available in more expensive hypermedia authoring environments or in less expensive environments through author-generated programming, HyperStudio is not expensive and allows many options without programming. HyperStudio allows hyperauthors to assign New Button Actions (NBAs) to stacks, cards, and any object. NBAs are essentially small programs that have already been written. The user never actually sees the language of the program, but may be allowed to set certain parameters controlling how the program will work. The following are examples of NBAs and how they might be used:

Animator   Moves a user-designated graphic along a path estab-lished by the author. Example: A dog appears to move around the card.

Blabbermouth   Computer speaks text desig-nated by the author. Example: A message entered by the user is read back to the user.

HideShow   Button hides or shows a screen object. Example: Show a hidden text field to explain image on a card.

Netpage   Opens Netscape (a World Wide Web browser—see Chapter 6) and goes to a Web site selected by author. Example: Connects user to a Web site providing informa-tion to supplement Hyper-Studio presentation.

SlideShow   Shows all cards in a stack at speed and with transitions designated by author. ✳

HyperCard has been around since 1987 and has gone through several upgrades. HyperCard and the other products that are discussed in this final section were not developed specifically for schools or students, but all have loyal advocates in educational settings. These hypermedia tools were developed to be versatile, flexibility that comes, in part, from their programmability.

Programming in the HyperCard Environment

Programming called scripting

Programming in HyperCard is usually called *scripting*. Even when you write scripts with it, HyperCard is different from other programming environments. HyperTalk (its programming language) is direct and descriptive. Most commands tend to be terms that make sense even to beginning programmers. The statements "Go to the next card" or "Put the date into card field 'Date'" do just what you might expect. It would be deceptive to imply that mastery of HyperTalk comes easily or quickly, though. There are numerous commands, and advanced techniques require *algorithms* (techniques for accomplishing tasks that are encountered repeatedly) similar to those used by programmers of traditional languages. However, unlike some other languages, it is possible to jump in and do something productive with HyperCard quickly. Beginners can start by learning a restricted set of commands and techniques and can quickly add to the creativity of their products using this basic knowledge.

Scripts

Scripts are programs written in HyperTalk and are attached to buttons, fields, the background, or stacks—very much like the NBAs in HyperStudio. Hyper-Card even writes scripts for you when you use predefined options. HyperCard has a "LinkTo . . ." option that works very much like the "Move To . . ." option in HyperStudio. If an author working in HyperCard has created links and effects using the options available within the button dialog box, that author has actually asked HyperCard to attach a script written in HyperTalk to the button. The script can be observed and modified by clicking on the "Script . . ." button in the button dialog box. The script automatically created using the "LinkTo" and "Effect" options is shown in Figure 8.14.

Programming and problem solving

Although authors can certainly get by without programming, there are many good reasons for learning to program. Like LOGO, BASIC, Pascal, and other programming languages, HyperTalk can provide student multimedia authors with valuable problem-solving experience. The HyperTalk language is sufficiently powerful to give students the educational benefits of extended work with a programming language (see Chapter 4). Because HyperTalk is part of a multimedia authoring environment and because students working in this environment are likely to be creating projects of one form or another, the programming tasks are embedded in what most students will regard as an authentic task. In other words, programming accomplishes a necessary task within the project the student is designing. Multimedia authors may also learn to program because they find that the built-in options provided by HyperCard are too limiting. HyperCard is an impressively powerful multime-

FIGURE 8.14 Automatically Scripted Button Script

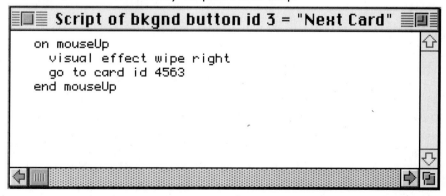

dia system, and many of its most sophisticated features are not available without programming. A classroom teacher can sometimes show students the program necessary to perform a specific function. For example, the teacher might show students a script that will display a color picture or a QuickTime movie. We have included the entire set of scripts associated with one project in Chapter 10. An examination of these scripts should provide some insight into what it is like to program in HyperCard.

Comparing HyperCard and HyperStudio

HyperCard and HyperStudio may be compared in the following ways. HyperStudio has more built-in features that users can employ by selecting preestablished options from menus or dialog boxes. Many of these features were developed specifically for educational presentations and educational authoring. Accomplishing these same things with HyperCard would require programming skill or the addition of other products that can be purchased and incorporated into HyperCard.

On one hand, HyperCard is more versatile because of the power of its programming language. Writing a HyperTalk script allows the author to develop an idea of how a multimedia product might function and then attempt to implement this idea, rather than attempting to see what can be done with existing functions. On the other hand, HyperTalk makes available powerful built-in functions. For example, it includes commands for listing the time and date; for performing mathematical, scientific, and business calculations (tangent, annuity, average, maximum); and for conditional decision making, in which actions depend on the existence of previous conditions (for example, if the user responded in less than 5 seconds, add 5 points to the player's score; otherwise add 2 points). Both HyperCard and HyperStudio make very basic features, such as creating text fields, adding simple graphics, creating simple drawings, and using buttons to control movement from card to card, easy for users. If more is desired, HyperStudio offers a number of built-in capabilities that students will find useful in creating projects. These same capabilities can usually be implemented in HyperCard, but with a little more effort or skill. If even more sophistication is desired, HyperCard has an advantage in the power of HyperTalk. This is another one of those situations in which individual teachers will have different opinions and may end up selecting different products.

OTHER MULTIMEDIA AUTHORING ENVIRONMENTS

Multimedia authoring systems for other operating systems

We have concentrated our attention on HyperStudio because it is a product available for both Windows and Macintosh platforms and on HyperCard because of its long-standing role as an educational authoring tool. Several other quality authoring environments appropriate for student projects have been developed and more appear to be on the way. We cannot devote space to a description of other products, but we do list several notable examples at the end of this chapter. With each item on the list, you will find a Web address where you can learn more about the product. Most of these Web sites also give curriculum-related ideas and examples of student projects. Even if you do not intend to purchase a particular product, it is worth examining the Web site for suggestions you might adapt to your content-area interests and choice of hypermedia authoring tools. Remember, Web sites come and go and you can always use the Web to search for information by name.

SUMMARY

Student multimedia projects can be classified as embellished documents, linear multimedia presentations or slide shows, or interactive hypermedia. An embellished document is a text document that has been enhanced with images, video, or sound. A classroom newsletter printed and sent home to parents or shared with other students is a common example of an embellished document.

A slide show is a linear multimedia presentation. Using elements of text, sound, still images and video, the author prepares a series of multimedia slides to inform and entertain an audience.

Interactive hypermedia is the most complex of the multimedia formats. This type of project differs from the others primarily in offering users choices instead of binding them to a single type of experience. The user has greater control over which sources of information to consider and perhaps the formats in which information will be encountered. Developing hypermedia is more complex because the author or authors have to prepare a much more extensive body of information to explore.

Teachers have many options available when selecting software tools that students might use to create multimedia projects. Students can create projects with general and common software tools such as word processing programs, or with more specialized multimedia tools designed to create slide shows, or with powerful hypermedia authoring environments, or a combination of the above.

The authoring environments offer project developers a variety of tools for creating and linking information resources and, in the case of programs such as HyperCard, a built-in programming language allowing nearly unlimited flexibility. Working with the programming language is optional and projects can be developed with only the tools existing within the authoring environment. When teachers consider the various ways in which multimedia projects can be created, they might think about a number of issues. How is the project intended to encourage thorough consideration of information? Does the project include additional objectives, such as the development of interpersonal skills, problem-solving skills, or communication skills? Finally, teachers might want to consider whether students are likely to use the same software to create other projects in the future.

Activities

REFLECTING ON CHAPTER 8

◆ Consider the unique advantages and disadvantages of slide show and hypermedia applications. Describe a classroom project most appropriately presented as a slide show. Describe a classroom project most appropriately presented as interactive hypermedia.
◆ Familiarize yourself with a word processing program capable of integrating text and graphics. Demonstrate the capabilities of this program to your classmates.
◆ Familiarize yourself with a slide show application. Demonstrate the capabilities of this program to your classmates.

Key Terms

background *(p. 288)*	icons *(p. 291)*
build *(p. 283)*	LCD projection panel *(p. 283)*
bullet charts *(p. 283)*	linear multimedia presentation
buttons *(p. 290)*	*(p. 272)*
card *(p. 287)*	master slide *(p. 283)*
deselecting *(p. 280)*	"Read only" *(p. 289)*
desktop publishing *(p. 276)*	scripts *(p. 295)*
dialog box *(p. 279)*	slide show *(p. 272)*
dragging *(p. 278)*	stack *(p. 288)*
embellished document *(p. 271)*	tear-off palettes *(p. 285)*
field *(p. 288)*	text object *(p. 277)*
hypermedia *(p. 272)*	video projector *(p. 283)*

Resources to Expand Your Knowledge Base

Software Resources

ClarisWorks is available for Macintosh and Windows computers. Claris Corporation, 5201 Patrick Henry Drive, Box 58168, Santa Clara, CA 95052.

Kid Pix products are available for Macintosh and Windows computers. Broderbund Software, 500 Redwood Blvd., P.O. Box 6121, Novato, CA 94948.

Student Writing Center is available for Macintosh and Windows. The Learning Company, 6493 Kaiser Drive, Fremont, CA 94555.

Hypermedia Authoring Environments

HyperMedia Authoring Environments for Both Macintosh and Windows

HyperStudio: Roger Wagner Publishing, 1050 Pioneer Way, Suite P, El Cajon, CA 92020. http://www.hyperstudio.com

HyperMedia Authoring Environments for the Macintosh

HyperCard: Apple Computers, Inc., 20525 Mariani Ave., Cupertino, CA 95014.

Digital Chisel: Pierian Spring Software, 5200 S.W. Macadam Ave., Suite 570, Portland, OR 97201. http://www.pierian.com

HyperMedia Authoring Environments for Windows

Superlink for Windows and *Multimedia ScrapBook:* Washington Computer Services, 2601 North Shore Road, Bellingham, WA 98226. http://alchmediainc.com

Presentation Tools

The following are some of the more popular presentation tools. All are available for both Macintosh and Windows.

Adobe Persuasion: Adobe Systems Incorporated, 411 First Avenue South, Seattle, WA 98104-2871.

Powerpoint: Microsoft Corp., One Microsoft Way, Redmond, WA 98052-6399.

Astound: Astound, Inc., P.O. Box 59, Santa Clara, CA 95052.

Newsletters

The ClarisWorks Users Group publishes *ClarisWorks Journal.* The publication is available from ClarisWorks Users Group, Box 701010, Plymouth, MI 48170.

The HyperStudio Network publishes a newsletter and an annual *Best of HyperStudio* disk and distributes commercial, shareware, and public domain HyperStudio stacks. There is a membership fee. HyperStudio Network, Box 103, Blawenberg, NJ 08504.

Chapter 9

Learning to Work with Images and Sound

ORIENTATION

This chapter explains some of the tools and basic techniques that allow students to produce the kinds of images and sounds described in multimedia applications throughout this book. After reading this chapter, you should understand how sounds and images are represented digitally and the function of sample software and hardware used to create these representations. As always, actually working with the applications is likely to provide a much more complete understanding. We encourage you to supplement your reading with hands-on experiences. As you read, look for answers to the following questions:

FOCUS QUESTIONS

♦ What distinguishes paint programs from draw programs, and what are some educational applications of each?
♦ Why must teachers pay attention to the file format used to store graphic images and sounds?
♦ How can teachers and students capture images for use in their own projects?
♦ Where might teachers find already-prepared images to use with computers?
♦ How do students benefit from the collection and manipulation of sounds and graphics?

Looking in on a Teacher's Workshop

The educational process continually presents students information in the form of sounds and graphic images, but students seldom have opportunities to manipulate information in these formats. Sound and graphics tools allow students some very concrete ways to act on information in this form. Take a look at some students learning how to work with images and sounds in one of our summer teacher-training workshops on multimedia applications for elementary school teachers.

Mark Grabe: Okay, here's what I want you to think about. Let's work on some ideas you might use at the beginning of the year. Let's develop a project in which we pair off students and have one student in each pair interview the other. Each student will then use this information to write a very brief segment introducing his or her partner. The introduction will be combined in some way with a picture of the student, and we'll put together all of the individual introductions in a slide show introducing the entire class. We'll try to simulate the parts of the project that involve technology so you will feel confident doing something like this in your own classrooms. We'll start by capturing your pictures using this video camera. [*A camcorder on a tripod is already connected by cable to a videocapture card in the computer.*] I want each of you to come and sit in this chair while someone else operates the video camera. Try to get a nice close-up of the face. I'll show someone else how to capture the picture from the computer screen. Who has some experience operating a video camera? All you have to do is point the camera and use the zoom adjustment to get a nice close-up.

[*A student volunteers.*]

Wait a minute. This isn't going to work. The image we're getting shows the date, the condition of the battery, and how far we're zoomed out on top of the person's picture. I guess we're going to have to record the pictures to tape and then play the tape back to capture what we need. Just press the red button to record.

[*Student records a few seconds of tape.*]

Now rewind the tape and press "play." Watch here. The video will be played in this small window on the computer screen. All I have to do is use the mouse to quickly drag a picture I want from the window showing the video to some other part of the computer screen [*demonstrates*].

Student: Wow, that's so easy! [*a typical first reaction*]

Mark Grabe: Okay, now someone else run the camera, and we'll record the rest of your pictures. Then you can each take a turn capturing your own picture when we play the tape back.

[*Students sit in chair for a few seconds to have their picture recorded.*]

Student: Mark, you should have to do this, too.

Mark: Fair enough [*sits down*]. Go ahead. [*when finished*] Now rewind the tape and start the playback. Each of you take control of the mouse and capture your own picture. We can stop the camera and rewind the tape if you don't have time to get your picture.

[*When finished, sets of pictures are transferred to disks, and students are sent off to work at their individual computers.*]

Here's your assignment. We'll start with Kid Pix Companion. Create a sequence introducing three of your classmates. We aren't going to take the time to interview each other. Record a message along with each picture just to show me you know how to use the record feature. If you don't know some factual information about your classmates, make something up. When we all finish, we'll go on to do a similar thing with HyperCard. With HyperCard, we'll write out the student descriptions rather than use voice recordings. Go ahead and begin. Call me over if you need help.

[*Students work for some time.*]

Student: Help! Look what happened.

Mark: You're already working on the HyperCard project.

Student: Yeah, the other one was easy and I wanted to move on. I tried to bring a picture into HyperCard, and look what happened.

Mark: You got a little ahead of me. I was going to explain that you can't really bring complex graphics into HyperCard. You can paste PICT files onto a card, but HyperCard immediately converts the picture into a simplified form. Everything becomes pure black or white. There is a way to show color pictures, but I haven't had a chance to show you how to do it yet.

Student: I guess I jumped the gun — you didn't say we couldn't start. I still don't understand what happened to your picture.

Mark: My picture is made up of many small dots of color. Many different shades are allowed. When HyperCard tries to convert the picture, only two colors are allowed. The program has to decide if each dot will become black or white. The lightest areas become white, and the darker areas become black.

Student: I can kind of see your glasses. What are those triangles in the middle of your head?

Mark: [*laughs*] Well, I am losing a bit of my hair. I suppose when light bounces off my head it creates a bright light area that HyperCard decided to call white. My hair must be dark enough that HyperCard decided to color it black. What you see is my bald spot. This is not a good thing to bring to your professor's attention. In a minute, I'll show you how to display color pictures, and then I won't look so bad.

FIGURE 9.1   Gray-Scale and Line Art Versions of the Same Image

TOOLS FOR CREATING, CAPTURING, AND MANIPULATING IMAGES

Differentiating created and captured images

Images can be brought into the computer environment in a variety of ways. To differentiate those applications in which images are *created* using technology from those in which images are *captured* using technology, think of the more familiar examples of an artist using paints and canvas to create a painting and a photographer using a camera to capture a photograph. Both processes require creativity and technique. The same is true in the application of technology. In the discussion that follows, we describe paint and draw programs as tools for creating and manipulating images, and scanners and video digitizers as tools to capture images.

PAINT AND DRAW PROGRAMS

Student access to a graphics program is essential to the multimedia project approach frequently mentioned in this book. Graphics programs are traditionally differentiated as paint or draw programs; this distinction will be explained later in this chapter. Paint programs are generally more useful for multimedia projects. In order to function successfully in this role, a paint program should allow students to

What a paint program should do

◆ Create graphics from scratch.
◆ Modify graphics from other sources.
◆ Save images in the format required for other application programs.

Creating Original Images

All paint programs allow users to produce original artwork. The quality of what they create depends on the users' talent and the tools the paint program makes available. The question of whether or not technology can enhance existing artistic talent is complicated. For people accustomed to creating art *Can technology enhance* with a pencil or paintbrush, initial attempts to draw or paint using a computer program and a peripheral device such as a mouse may prove frustrating and unsatisfactory. It helps to keep in mind that, with experience, artists do learn to work with the tools of technology to produce some remarkable products.

Can technology enhance talent?

Although technology will not allow all students to create impressive illustrations or pictures, a useful paint program at the very least makes tools available to allow students with limited artistic skill and experience to generate informative displays.

Modifying Existing Images

Sources of high-quality images

Much of this chapter deals with ways technology can be used to capture images from sources external to the computer environment (see the sections on scanners and video digitizers). We also provide some suggestions for locating graphic resources already converted into a format suitable for computer use. Both of these sources supply images that are likely to be of much higher quality than those students could create themselves and are most likely the equivalent of a photograph rather than a drawing or crude painting.

Reworking images

The opportunity to capture or acquire images without having to draw or paint them does not eliminate the need for access to graphics tool software, however. Existing images may not be suited to the exact purpose or presentation style students or teachers have in mind for their projects. They will frequently want the means to make modifications. Providing opportunities to rework images is important for another reason. Working with images allows students to work with the ideas and processes those images represent. Appropriate tools can more actively involve students.

A
C
T
I NTEGRATED
V
E

Here are some of the most frequently used tool capabilities. First, the

Loading graphics files

graphics program must be able to load, or open, existing graphics files. Although this may seem obvious, not all graphics programs were developed for the purpose of modifying graphics files created by other programs or methods. Files can be stored in many formats (see discussion of file formats on pages 315 through 317), and programs will differ in how many different file types they can access.

Second, programs should allow the user to copy and paste parts of images. Frequently, a student will want to take part of an existing picture and use this piece to create a new display. Students may want to take parts of several individual images and combine them into a new, composite image to demonstrate stages in some process or to make various comparisons. Perhaps they want to show the stages in a butterfly's development: egg, caterpillar, chrysalis, butterfly. Or they may want to contrast the painted lady butterfly with the monarch.

Copying and pasting

Finally, students should be able to enhance an existing image using a variety of tools. A student may want to use the text tool to label parts of an image. Students may also want to create a composite image of several small color pictures and a line drawing they have created themselves.

Composite images

Saving Images That Can Be Used by Application Programs

When developing projects, students use a paint or draw program at an intermediary stage. In most cases, the graphics program will not be the final host program for the images that have been created. The images might eventually appear in a multimedia presentation, be included on a Web page, be used as part of a record in a database, or be printed as part of a word processing document. The programs representing the final destination for the images are likely to have much less powerful tools for modifying images, so it is desirable that the graphics program be able to generate the exact images desired.

Compatibility issues

Compatibility issues can be important. The paint or draw program should be able to save images of the type required by the intended authoring or presentation program. Some graphics programs and some multimedia authoring environments are versatile in the file formats (such as PICT or BMP, discussed in detail later in this chapter) they allow, and some are not. Web pages, for example, use graphics saved in GIF or JPEG formats because these formats can be read by Web browsers running on different types of computers. Teachers may want to consider the issue of compatibility before beginning to work on projects. However, they should also be assured that there is usually some way to make the necessary adjustments if compatibility problems arise. Programs are available to convert graphics files from one format to another. (We discuss screen capture and file conversion — techniques that can be very helpful when compatibility problems arise — at other points in this chapter.) Often, the exact image desired can be temporarily copied to the memory of the computer and then pasted into a file opened by a different application program. In this way, the second application program does not have to actually open a file saved by the first program. Finally, you can also use a more powerful graphics program to make necessary adjustments when your students' program cannot generate exactly the final product they need.

A Comparison of Paint and Draw Programs

Graphics programs used in school environments tend to fall into two general categories: *paint programs,* producing bit-mapped images, and *draw programs,* producing object-oriented images. Each category has unique advantages and disadvantages.

Paint programs are used to create and manipulate bit-mapped images.

Focus

Screen Capture

Screen capture is the process of saving the screen image or part of the screen image as a graphics file. This is true even if the screen contains text; the process is very much like taking a picture of the screen. Screen capture capabilities are built into newer versions of the Macintosh and Windows operating systems. In Windows, the keyboard command is Alt–Print Screen. A copy of the screen is saved to the **clipboard**, a computer memory buffer from which it can be loaded into a paint program such as Windows' own Paintbrush. The Macintosh equivalent is Command-Shift-3. Executing this command should result in the reassuring sound of a camera shutter click that lets the user know the computer has taken the requested action. Screen capture for the Macintosh saves the screen as a PICT file on the computer's hard drive. Again, a paint program can then be used to load and work with the captured image.

Both Windows and the Macintosh require a multiple key command to capture a screen image. This sometimes confuses novices when they first encounter a description of this type. An effective way to think about multiple key commands is to compare them with the method for producing a capital letter with a word processor or typewriter: depress the shift key and then depress the letter to be capitalized. For screen capture on the Macintosh, depress the command key and the shift key and then press the 3.

It is also possible to purchase (often as shareware) small programs (sometimes called utilities) that extend the basic screen capture techniques. For example, such utilities usually allow the user to select and then capture any part of the image that appears on the entire screen and then to print or save the designated segment.

Screen captures can be used for many different purposes. One important use is capturing screens from application programs to use in material that explains to others how to use those programs. Many images in this textbook were captured from the screen for this purpose. Teachers may have opportunities to use this technique to prepare instructional materials for their students. If you wanted to prepare handouts explaining to students how to use a new program, this would be a useful way to display what the computer screen would look like at certain critical points. ✳

Bit-mapped images

With such bit-mapped programs, an image is created on a "page" that contains a set number of visual elements. You might think of visual elements as the individual points or dots that make up the image and background. A **bit-mapped** image is "painted" on the background by changing the color of these individual dots. In many early applications, the individual points making up the screen display, or the **pixels**, would be either black or white. Images made up of only black or white pixels are called **line art**. With the proper equipment and software, individual pixels can also be defined in terms of many colors or shades of gray. Working at the level of individual pixels offers the greatest flexibility in creating an image, but paint programs also have some disadvantages when modifying, storing, and printing images. There are problems in effectively adjusting the size of images, and the images tend to take more disk space.

Programs used to create and manipulate object-oriented images are commonly called **draw programs**. Object-oriented programs define the elements (points, lines, circles) making up these images in terms of mathematical equations. When an **object-oriented image** is saved to disk, it is this

Object-oriented images

mathematical information and not a record of the color of individual pixels that is saved. This does not mean that a young student working with a draw program needs to know the equation for defining a circle and locating the circle at a particular spot on the computer screen. The program takes care of the mathematics.

Creating an image from individually defined objects can be useful when great precision is required. Special versions of draw programs using **computer-assisted design (CAD)** are commonly used to create engineering or architectural drawings and may be used in specialized secondary school classes. Because object-oriented programs are composed of individual objects and these objects can be isolated and modified, certain editing functions are much easier with draw programs.

Draw programs store images efficiently.

Draw programs also tend to store images much more efficiently and display images with higher quality than paint programs. The display quality of an image in a draw program is limited only by the quality of the computer screen or printer used to produce the display. At issue is how much information — that is, **dots per inch (dpi)** — the screen or printer is capable of presenting. The mathematical formula defining draw objects can be used to produce basically the amount of information the display device is capable of representing. The quality of bit-mapped images is defined when the images are created and thus may be lower than the quality of image the display device can present.

It might seem from this comparison that object-oriented images would have replaced bit-mapped images by now. This is not the case. We will emphasize bit-mapped images and the programs and hardware used to create them because the images students use in content-area applications will often be captured from other sources rather than developed as original student artwork. It turns out that the various methods used to capture such images work by capturing bit-mapped information. You have already read about techniques for capturing images from the computer screen. Later, you will encounter procedures for capturing images from live sources, from student-recorded videotape, and from paper sources. It is these capture techniques and the information resources that these techniques make available to students that make so many student projects practical to implement. Many of the images students will have access to using these techniques will be complex, and any student editing will be minimal. Students may want to cut the picture of, say, a wildflower, a deer, or a classmate from some source and display it in another application. The emphasis here is on capturing and displaying realistic images rather than on reconstruction or drastic alteration. Actions of this type are easier in the bit-mapped paint format than in the object-oriented draw format.

Students will often capture images for projects.

ClarisWorks. One effective way to demonstrate some of the differences between draw and paint programs is to consider an application such as Claris-Works that makes both types of tools available. The left side of Figure 9.2 allows you to compare the ClarisWorks paint and draw palettes. You will notice that the paintbrush, pencil, paint can, airbrush, and eraser are available as paint tools, but not as draw tools. Paint tools allow the manipulation of individual pixels with great flexibility. The pencil tool provides a good example of this flexibility. A pencil can be used to sketch or to scribble. The complexity of either of these images would be difficult to represent efficiently in a mathematical equation. All of the other tools that are unique to the paint format can be applied with the same degree of flexibility.

Paint tools

You will note from Figure 9.2 that both paint and draw palettes offer tools for creating basic shapes, such as rectangles, lines, and polygons. Even when draw and paint tools are used to create identical images, the properties of the images are still very different. Compare the two rectangles on the right side of Figure 9.2. The rectangle created with the draw tool is really a single unit. If the user decides to remove it from the computer screen, it will be deleted as a unit. The small dark squares appearing at the corners of the rectangle are *handles* the user can drag (click with the mouse and move with the mouse held) to change the shape of the rectangle. If desired, these handles can be used to modify the rectangle to create a square. The handles disappear as soon as the user selects another tool or begins work on another part of the computer screen. The rectangle created with the paint tool is not a single unit; it is actually made up of pixels that can be manipulated independently. To demonstrate the difference between rectangles created with draw and paint tools, the eraser tool has been used to eliminate a corner of the painted rectangle in Figure 9.2. A set of pixels has been removed, and the rest of the rectangle remains. The eraser is not available when working on draw objects because draw objects must be treated as whole units. Similarly, because

Comparing draw and paint images

FIGURE 9.2   Paint and Draw Palettes from ClarisWorks

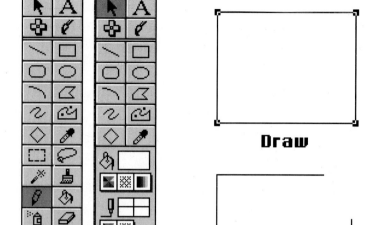

the painted rectangle is not one unit, it cannot easily be reshaped into a square.

Distortion with enlarged paint images

One other unique problem that users of paint programs encounter is the distortion that occurs when the size of an image is changed. The individual pixels that make up an image are like tiny blocks. When an image is enlarged, these blocks are simply magnified. In some cases, particularly with diagonal lines, this magnification results in a distortion often called **jaggies** (see Figure 9.3).

Do schools need both draw and paint applications? There are some very useful applications for object-oriented images in the fields of design and engineering, and educational experiences related to these areas offer opportunities for draw applications. However, these applications are relatively infrequent in comparison to the opportunities to use paint programs. The flexibility of bit-mapped graphics is extremely important for the general computer tool approach advocated here.

Kid Pix Studio — A Paint Program.   Kid Pix is one of the best examples of a paint program developed specifically for younger users. This inexpensive

FIGURE 9.3 Bit-Mapped Line Magnified Four Times

Paint programs especially for younger students

program combines a set of very functional graphics tools, an interface intended to make the program more intuitive for young users, and some special quirky tools and features just for fun.

The Kid Pix interface was designed to make the program's options apparent even to the inexperienced user. The idea is to use icons that visibly suggest what can be done with each tool so that the user does not have to learn or remember complicated procedures. Although most users have to experiment a bit to become familiar with what some of the options actually do, this **graphic user interface (GUI)** makes it easy to learn and remember how to use the program.

Icons represent tools.

If you have had little previous experience with computer paint programs, the structure of the Kid Pix interface might serve as a convenient model for understanding more complicated programs. As you examine a monitor displaying Kid Pix (see Figure 9.4), you will see a column of icons down the left side of the screen and a row of icons across the bottom of the screen. These icons represent *paint tools, color options,* and *tool options.* Although not all paint programs make these choices visible simultaneously to the user, other paint programs work in approximately the same way. The user selects a paint tool to work with; when applicable, the color the paint tool is to apply; and an option for the specific effect the tool will have. The tool options are presented in a particularly useful way with Kid Pix. When a tool is selected, the tool options available for that tool appear automatically. The young user does not have to remember the options that are available or how to implement them. In some cases, all of the available options cannot fit in a single row. When this is the case, a numbered arrow at the end of the row informs the user that more options are available. The user can view the additional options by clicking on the up or down arrow.

Most paint programs work in similar ways.

MY PET: USING GRAPHICS TOOLS IN A WRITING ASSIGNMENT

How are the various graphics tools used to construct a picture? The following description takes you step by step through the process of creating a simple

FIGURE 9.4 Kid Pix Monitor Display

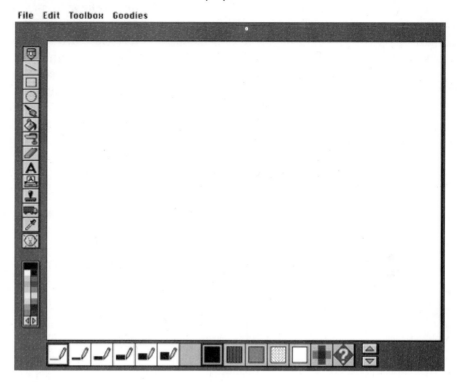

image, which was the cover for a writing assignment — "My Pet" — by our daughter Kim. The finished image is provided in Figure 9.6 on page 313. This image combines the picture of a dog, captured using a video digitizing technique, with simple line art and text created in Kid Pix.

The process begins with the original picture of the dog. In the original image, the dog is sitting under a kitchen table. To get just the part of the image that is needed, the area around the dog is carefully erased. One useful approach when doing very detailed work is to magnify an image several times. Working on an enlarged image calls for much less delicate control of a tool such as the eraser. It would be very easy to slip and erase a paw if it were necessary to work on a same-size image. Kid Pix does not allow image size to be easily manipulated, so the detailed work needed to isolate the picture of the dog must be done in a more sophisticated program.

Once the file containing the picture of the dog is opened in Kid Pix, the moving van tool is used to move the picture to the bottom of the screen, where it will be out of the way. One of the options available with this tool allows an area of the screen to be selected using the mouse and then relocated by dragging. When the mouse button is released, the selected material

For detailed work, magnify images.

Using the mouse to move images

remains in the new location. Having the picture of the dog present on the screen gave Kim a better feel for how large to make the doghouse.

The first step in constructing the doghouse is to generate a large rectangle using the rectangle tool. After it is selected, the tool is positioned in what is intended to be one of the corners of the finished shape. The mouse button is then depressed and the rectangle tool is moved toward the opposite corner of the intended shape. If the user starts in the upper-left corner, the mouse can be moved on a downward diagonal or over and then down (see Figure 9.5). As long as the mouse button remains depressed, the rectangle tool will draw a rectangle between the initial point and the point to which the tool is moved. When the mouse is released, the size of the rectangle is fixed. If the image does not meet the user's expectations, it can be removed with the undo tool and redrawn.

FIGURE 9.5 Technique for Using Paint Rectangle Tool

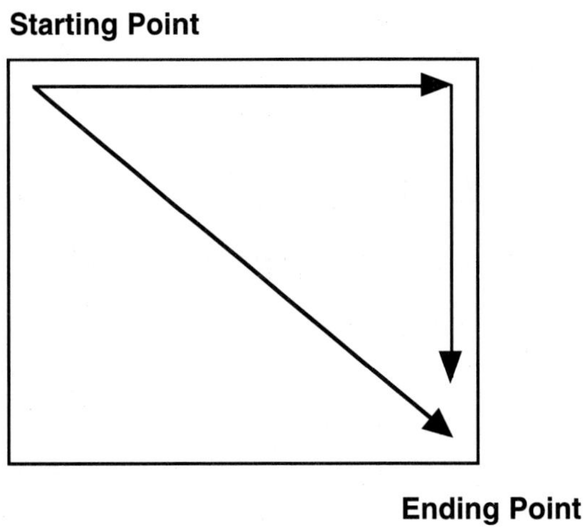

Starting Point

Ending Point

When you examine Figure 9.6, the fact that you no longer see a complete rectangle may at first confuse you. The oval tool was used to generate a large oval on top of the rectangle. Because the opaque tool was selected from the fill options appearing across the bottom of the screen (see Figure 9.4), the oval obscures part of the line making up the original rectangle. The technique for creating an oval is exactly the same as for creating a rectangle. Start at a point on one boundary and move the tool toward the corresponding point on the opposite side of the figure. With a little practice, users learn to create ovals of different shapes. Of course, you also do not see a complete oval in Figure 9.6. The bottom part of the oval was erased using the erase tool, beginning at the points where the oval intersected the rectangle. The result is the entrance to the doghouse.

Kim created the roof by using the line tool to draw three lines and the paint bucket to fill the enclosed area with a pattern selected from the available options. Remember from Chapter 1's description of Pam Carlson's ocean

Using the opaque option

project that it is important when using a fill procedure to make certain there are no gaps in the boundary of the area to be filled. If an opening is present, the fill color or pattern will leak out across any open area of the picture. If this should happen (and it happens to everyone, because breaks in lines are not always easy to see) the key is not to panic. Simply use the undo tool to delete the last action taken. It is also good practice to save your work every few minutes, so that you will never be in the position of losing work that has taken a long time to create.

Undo deletes the last action.

To finish the picture, text is added using the text tool, and the student's signature is added using the pencil tool. The image of the dog is then moved, using the moving van, to the side of the doghouse. Because Kid Pix moves only rectangular areas, some of the lines on the doghouse were covered up with the "white" space that surrounded the picture of the dog. These lines had to be redrawn. Obviously, some of the mechanical techniques used in computer graphics are a little different from those used with pencil, crayons, and paper. Learning these techniques is just a matter of awareness and practice.

FIGURE 9.6 Sample Kid Pix Picture

It is difficult to describe the process of creating a picture with a paint program. Some processes are best learned by experience, and if you have the opportunity, you should certainly take the time to acquaint yourself with at least one paint program. Paint programs can be used to good effect by individuals with some artistic talent. Kid Pix was one of the first purchases made for the elementary school computers in our community, and some interesting products surfaced very quickly. Teachers were allowed to take a classroom computer home for the summer to become acquainted with it and the software tools that had been purchased. Soon after taking a computer home, one of the teachers returned with the picture shown in Figure 9.7. It was created by her son, Joel Quamme, a high school sophomore. This is the kind of product one might expect from a more expensive draw or CAD program in the hands of an experienced user. Would you be able to create an image of this quality? If you have little artistic talent or experience, probably not. This student has an obvious appreciation of scale, shading, and depth perspective over and above his computer skills.

In some ways, it might be argued that creating art on the computer is more difficult than creating art with paper and pencil. As an input device, the mouse is probably more difficult to manipulate than a pencil. In some ways, though, creating art on the computer is easier than using paper and pencil. Lines and shapes can be drawn with great precision, and areas can easily be filled with colors or patterns. There are a number of sources for computer graphics projects (Bennett and Bennett, 1993; Chan, 1993). Make sure you take a look at the resources section at the end of this chapter.

It also should not be assumed that schools will need only a graphics program like Kid Pix. Because of the cost and intended users, Kid Pix does not have some of the tools or tool options that are available in full-featured graphics programs and does not meet all the needs of educational settings. There are a number of limitations that are important to recognize. Kid Pix opens only PICT files. Schools may want to work with graphic images stored in other formats and may need a program to open and save graphic files in other formats. In addition, all Kid Pix images appear on the same size canvas. Not all portions of larger images can be viewed, and small images will be surrounded with a great deal of white space. This lack of versatility makes for a number of limitations. For example, if the paint program is being used to prepare graphics files to be opened by other programs, it is often desirable to save images of different sizes. Kid Pix also lacks the capability to modify image size; that is, to shrink or enlarge an image, to transform images from color to gray scale, or to modify such image characteristics as brightness or contrast.

Benefits of a workstation with additional tools and features

Factors like these can come into play when schools work heavily with graphic images for multimedia applications. It is not necessary to invest in many copies of a higher-end program with these capabilities, but at least one workstation with additional tools and features should be available so that students and teachers can perform more sophisticated functions when necessary.

FIGURE 9.7 Joel Quamme's Mondo Castle

UNDERSTANDING GRAPHICS FILE FORMATS

When a graphics program stores a graphic image, the resulting file has a characteristic format. Users may encounter a bewildering variety of graphics file formats. This situation exists for several reasons. First, certain file types are associated with different hardware platforms. For example, BMP is a common format on computers running the Windows operating system, and PICT is a common Macintosh format. Second, certain file types were designed to accomplish certain tasks. The TIFF format was developed for scanned images, and the GIF format, for exchanging graphics through the Internet. Finally, many graphics programs have a "native format." This means that programs of this type save graphics files in a format that is intended to be loaded only by the same program. In most cases, however, programs offering a native format also allow files to be saved in other formats.

Why is there a variety of graphics file formats?

Why should teachers using computers in their classrooms bother to become aware of the various graphics file formats? Here are some situations you might encounter:

Teachers may encounter any of these situations.

◆ An elementary school teacher wants to scan some line art from a coloring book and then have his students paint the images using Kid Pix. The school's older scanner saves the scanned images as TIFF files. (*Note:* Scanners will be discussed at a later point.) Kid Pix loads and saves graphics only as PICT files. What should the teacher do?

◆ A high school science teacher finds some great photographs from a recent space mission on the Internet. The photographs are in GIF format.

Spotlight on Assessment

Using Peer Comments

Educational accomplishments take time and effort. Our understanding or the projects through which we demonstrate our understanding are seldom perfect immediately; they evolve as we work. Feedback can be very important in improving the efficiency of learning and constructive processes. Although we must learn to evaluate our own efforts (review our discussion of metacognition in Chapter 2), it is often very helpful to have input from others. We often think of teachers as providing this type of information. However, other students may also represent a very valuable resource. Here are two things to consider. (1) Providing enough individual attention for an entire class may be too much to expect of one person. Student reactions to the work of their peers can increase the amount of feedback available. (2) Students may also benefit from evaluating the work of others. Examining work that is less familiar allows students to practice their evaluation skills.

As students work to complete a classroom project, it can be useful to set up a system in which they receive feedback from peers before presenting the project to the teacher for more formal evaluation (Tierney, Carter, and Desai, 1991). Student work in progress can be distributed to peers along with a request for spe-

cific feedback. Students can contemplate these comments as they make final revisions. Consider questions that we might ask fifth grade students to guide their comments about a cover page they have all been asked to generate.

◆ Does the cover page make me want to read this report? What might be changed to make the cover more interesting?

◆ Does the cover page help me understand what the report is about? What might be changed so that the cover is more closely related to the report?

◆ Does the title provide a good summary of the report?

◆ Is the picture on the cover a good choice? Is it clear and of appropriate size? What might be improved?

◆ Are the picture and the drawing put together attractively? What might be improved?

Because students could be asked to consider many different things about the report and the cover page, the comments you request students to provide should be related to the characteristics you will evaluate in the more finished product. The issues you raise will determine the informativeness of peer comments and will also help students think about their own work. ✳

The school has Macintosh equipment. Should the teacher download the files?

◆ You have a great collection of free clip art stored in a HyperCard stack. A teacher friend of yours has ideas for using some of the images in a classroom newsletter, but the teacher uses an IBM PC. Is there some way to make the images available to her?

There are several ways to deal with the various file formats you might encounter. If you are lucky, you will be able to ignore them. Many programs have built-in **translators,** small utilities that allow the program to accept a variety of file formats. Programs of this type can also be used as an intermediary. For example, Kid Pix accepts only PICT files. Photoshop is a much more powerful and flexible program that allows files to be opened and saved in a variety of formats. If it were necessary to get a TIFF image into Kid Pix, Photoshop could be used to open the image in TIFF format and save the image in PICT format. Kid Pix could then work with the image. This is one of the reasons we recommend that schools invest in a more powerful graphics program even if students would only rarely use such a program. There are also utility programs that are designed primarily to convert files from one format to another.

Here is a limited glossary of graphics file formats you may encounter:

BMP

A glossary of graphics file formats

Common bit-map formats for the Windows platform.

EPS (encapsulated PostScript)

A format commonly used for storing object-oriented graphics files.

GIF (graphics interchange format)

Format created by CompuServe for efficient transfer of bit-mapped images to and from commercial telecommunications services. The GIF format continues to be popular for this purpose. Several Macintosh and DOS/Windows application programs support this format.

JPEG (Joint Photographic Experts Group)

A "lossy" compression format that produces high-quality images while drastically reducing file size. **Lossy** implies a form of compression in which data and thus some quality are lost during the compression process.

PICT and PICT2 (not acronyms)

A generic file format for the Macintosh, allowing a mixture of bit-mapped and object-oriented graphics. PICT and PICT2 files are often not differentiated, but PICT2 technically allows more color options.

TIFF (tag image file format)

The most flexible format for bit-mapped (not object-oriented) graphics; often the standard output file for scanning. Can be used to cross Macintosh and DOS/Windows hardware platforms.

CAPTURING IMAGES

Students can use scanners and video digitizers.

Students can use reasonably priced technology to transfer existing images from paper into a form computers can use and manipulate, or to capture images from their surroundings, much as they would capture images with a camera. **Scanners** are used for capturing images from paper sources or from photographic slides and transforming these images into a bit-mapped digital format the computer can store. **Video digitizers** are used to create graphics files from video sources such as camcorders, VCRs, video cameras, and laserdisc players.

Scanners and video digitizers working in combination with a computer were developed to convert an external image into a digitized graphics file. This means that existing images, such as a crayon line drawing created by a young student, a secondary school student's original pencil illustration, the view through a microscope, or virtually any image that might now be captured with a photocopier, camera, or camcorder, can be converted into the kind of digital information that a computer can use. Information in the form of a graphics file can be saved to disk, loaded back into the computer at a later time, displayed on the computer monitor, or printed. Once an image is present in a form the computer can manipulate, tool software can be used to cut sections from a larger image to form smaller images; to integrate images from several sources to form a new composite image; to add text to label parts of an image; to add color to black-and-white drawings; and to modify, combine, and manipulate the stored images in many other ways. Once brought into the computer with a scanner or video digitizer, and perhaps further enhanced with graphics software tools, images captured from an external source can become part of the multimedia products discussed in several other chapters of this book. You have already read how you and your students can use paint programs to modify and enhance computer graphics. In the following sections, we will describe the methods for bringing external images into a computer.

Scanners

Flatbed Scanners. If you have ever copied documents with a photocopy machine, you are well on your way to being able to operate a flatbed scanner. You begin by lifting the lid of the scanner and placing the sheet of paper with the image you want to scan face down on the glass. When the scanning process begins, you will notice the familiar light source moving along the length of the image beneath the glass plate. In a scanner, a lens or mirror system beneath the glass plate focuses the light reflected from the original image into the **charge-coupled device**, or **CCD**. The output from this device is translated within the scanner into the digital form acceptable as input to a computer.

Flatbed scanners operate in a way similar to photocopiers.

The camcorder lets students capture images in the field and allows them to continue learning from unique experiences even when they return to the classrooms. (© Michael Zide)

Hand-held Scanners. A hand-held scanner captures an image using the same basic process as a flatbed scanner but differs in the method used to sweep the scanning mechanism across the surface of the original image. With a flatbed scanner, the computer controls the movement of the light source and the device for directing the reflected light as they move across the original image. This mechanism is the source of the moving band of light you see below the glass plate of a flatbed scanner. With a hand-held scanner, the entire scanner is manually rolled over the image. The light source and light-sensing mechanism are contained in the apparatus you hold in your hand. When you consider the precise mechanism by which reflected light is captured and transformed into hundreds of digitally recorded dots per inch, it seems amazing that something as unsteady as the movement of the human hand could produce anything of quality. Hand-held scanners do not seem to have difficulty with variations in the rate of forward movement. A much more common problem concerns the alignment of the path of the scanner with objects in the image to be copied. For example, if there are vertical lines in the material to be scanned, it is difficult to move the scanner parallel with these lines. If the scanner is moved across the lines at a slight angle, the lines will appear jagged (see discussion of jaggies in earlier section describing limitations of bit-mapped files).

Hand-held scanners are considerably less expensive than flatbed scanners

Hand-held scanners are convenient but have limitations.

and provide a functional alternative when the major application is capturing small images. Hand-held scanners are 5 to 6 inches wide, which does limit the kinds of images you can capture. It would be difficult to recommend that individual schools rely on hand-held scanners. Teachers and students would quickly become frustrated with the limitations and might underestimate the ease with which quality images can be captured.

Video Digitizers

Scanners can be used to capture images from only a narrow range of sources. With the exception of specialized scanners designed to capture images from photographic slides, these would be the same sources suitable for photocopying. You cannot directly capture the images of a classmate or a zoo animal with a scanner. Video digitizers make other sources of images available. Among the additional possibilities, you or your students might use this type of equipment to bring into the computer environment the images from sources you might pursue with a camera. Two methods are available for digitizing video input: video digitizing boards and digital cameras. We will discuss digital cameras in the next section, "Recording Video Segments."

Video digitizing boards convert the analog video signal generated by a videocassette player, a camcorder, a television tuner, or a videodisc player into a digital signal. Without going into great detail, an **analog signal** is continuous, and a digital signal is discrete. The cable between the "video out" connection of your videocassette player and the "video in" connection of your television carries an analog signal, a signal capable of being represented by continuous values. This same cable can be connected directly to a video digitizing board to convert the analog signal to a digital signal and save still frames or video segments as graphics files.

Ask questions when your school makes a purchase.

As used here, the description of a "board," sometimes called a "card," is purposefully vague. Some computers, perhaps described as multimedia or audiovisual computers, may have this capability built in. If this is the kind of computer you want, you should ask specific questions when making a purchase to be certain the desired capabilities are present. The ability to create or display multimedia should not be confused with the capability to capture graphic images from an analog source. Many school computers can also be used to digitize video input but require additional hardware to make this capability available. There are several different commercial hardware products that can add the capability to digitize an analog signal. Whether the capability comes built in or must be added, the transformation from analog to digital signal is accomplished by a hardware device integrated with the other hardware components of the computer.

Video capture is accomplished by first activating a software program that accesses input from the video digitizing card. The active image from a camcorder, video camera, videocassette player, or some other input device appears in a window on the screen. This window can serve as a rather expensive

Emerging Technology

Personal Digital Video Cameras

A digital video camera is quite different from a camcorder. The camcorder captures visual images and stores them as analog information on tape. The digital video camera captures and digitizes images and sends this digital information directly to a computer (the video camera must remain connected to the computer). The computer can then be used to store individual images or video segments as files. We made reference to this kind of personal video camera when we described CU-SeeMe in Chapter 6 (pages 200 through 201). One of the major advantages of the special video cameras

built to provide input to personal computers is the price. Although high-end versions are available, these cameras are generally small and simple. Money does not need to be wasted on fancy lenses or on the mechanism that records to tape. The CCD is built into the camera unit, eliminating the need for special hardware. Black-and-white cameras cost approximately $100 and color cameras approximately $250 (one source is listed at the end of the chapter). These cameras are versatile and useful for generating digitized images for any classroom project in which the objects of interest can walk or be carried to the location of the computer. ✳

and very small television. The exact method for capturing images varies with the hardware and software that are used. The example in Figure 9.8 shows the video digitizing feature built into HyperStudio. You watch the video in a small window. When you find an image you would like to capture, you click the freeze button. At this stage, the image has not been saved. If the still image that results is what you want, you simply click the OK button and new tools are made available for selecting the exact part of the image you want to use and for placing the image on a card. If your reactions are a little slow and you miss what you wanted to capture, simply click at the location of the freeze button, and you are back watching live video. You might have to rewind the videotape and try several times to get the exact image you want.

Image size

Digitizing boards differ in the size of the image they generate when capturing images from a recorded source. This is one situation in which the cost of the product will come into play. Larger digital images require more memory and more time to generate. Less expensive boards digitize an image from several successive frames sent from the videocassette player. Video is commonly recorded at 30 frames per second, and the speed at which some boards convert the signal to a digital form requires that several frames be combined to produce the image. This can reduce the quality of the image.

Digital Cameras

Digital cameras have been around for several years. These devices appear similar to traditional cameras, but instead of capturing images on film, digital

FIGURE 9.8 HyperStudio Image Dialog Box

cameras use a charge-coupled device like that used in a camcorder. The older versions kept images on a special video floppy disk, and the method of storage was similar to that of videotape. These images were not digitized. The images stored on this type of disk still had to be converted to a digital format with a video digitizing card before they could be used in multimedia applications (Murie, 1993). Recently, newer products that store digital images have been introduced. For example, the Kodak DC40 can store 48 large (756 x 504 pixels or about 7 x 10 inches), fairly high-quality color images (24-bit color) or more images of smaller size and lower quality. The camera does not use a disk and must be attached to a computer with a cable to transfer the images. Products of this type will continue to evolve and prove useful in capturing images for a variety of school applications.

Products that store digital images

Recording Video Segments

As you have seen in earlier chapters, many class projects can incorporate video segments. Students and teachers can create their own video segments

Activities and Projects for Your Classroom

Images to Capture

Once you get the idea, generating a list of the types of images students might capture is almost too easy. The opportunities to provide examples, to demonstrate something, or just to liven up your writing are limitless. Here are a few ideas to get you started. Videocapture techniques could be used to generate images that:

◆ Contrast proper and improper weightlifting techniques.
◆ Reveal geometric shapes in your environment.

◆ Personalize a language board (a device used to communicate by pointing at pictures) for a seriously language-impaired student.
◆ Recall experiences from field trips to a farm, factory, museum, lake shore, or local business.
◆ Show the birds that have visited your birdfeeder.
◆ Expose instances of local pollution.
◆ Exemplify merchandise displays you feel are interesting and effective.
◆ Show the many ways computer technology is used in the workplace.
◆ Illustrate some of the things that make you happy. ✳

Incorporating video segments in class projects

using the hardware and software described here. It is important to realize from the beginning, however, that a video segment recorded on school equipment will probably have nowhere near the quality of the original motion sequences captured with a camcorder. Some of the reasons for the limitations are informative and worth considering.

First, there is the matter of speed. Most of us are used to video displayed at the rate of 30 frames per second. At this display rate, we are unable to distinguish individual images from continuous motion. To create a digitized video segment, a computer has to be capable of both digitizing and displaying many frames at a very rapid rate. Because of the large amount of data that must be manipulated and moved, these are not trivial matters. Display speed can also be limited by how quickly image files can be read from the disk. As you can probably guess from the previous discussion of capturing individual images, most computers cannot achieve the rate of capture and display needed to achieve the rate we have grown to expect from our experience with television, movies, and home videos.

Images can take up 1 megabyte of memory.

The other difficulty is capacity — both storage capacity and computer memory capacity. Quality full-screen images can require 1 megabyte of memory each to store. Imagine the problem of trying to store 30 such images for each second of video. This is one of the reasons why the digitized video you see is likely to use rather small images and why commercial applications of digitized video make the storage capacity of a CD nearly mandatory. This is also one of the reasons why digitized video is likely to be recorded and

What are compression techniques?

presented at a much lower rate of frames per second: 12 frames per second is an achievable speed. Finally, capacity problems have led to the development of compression techniques. Compression techniques such as JPEG (page 317) sacrifice only a small amount of image quality in order to save a large amount of disk space. Compression rates of 10 to 1 are possible with reasonable quality.

The QuickTime format is often used for storing video segments and presenting them as part of WWW pages. **QuickTime** is a software capability that can be purchased and added to a computer. It provides the compression methods and timing mechanisms necessary to keep video presentations synchronized. For example, different machines will not be able to display the same number of frames per second. With slower machines, some of the frames will automatically be dropped so that the sequence will run at the proper speed and remain coordinated with any accompanying sound (Murie, 1993).

LOCATING ALTERNATIVE IMAGE SOURCES

Searching for multimedia resources will take you into new territory. It has led us to carry our camcorder down tick-infested wooded trails and into county historical museums. We have become acquainted with student artists at all educational levels. We have scoured bargain bookstores and museum and zoo gift shops in search of unusual coloring books, as well as the backs of computer magazines for the ads of small companies offering collections of sounds, video clips, and pictures. Things have started to change and resources are becoming easier to find. The market for multimedia resources has just started to go big time and inexpensive collections are now available in every educational supplies catalog. We urge teachers not to rely completely on such material and to make project-by-project decisions about how best to gather resources. The convenience of providing students access to commercial multimedia collections should be balanced against the fun and educational value of searching for your own resources.

Huge range of multimedia resources

Because scanners are used to capture images that already appear on paper and because teachers tend to be familiar with many sources of this type, it may be most productive to comment on a few resources teachers may overlook.

Coloring Books

Coloring books provide images that are nearly ideal for scanning. Because coloring book images are drawn simply, emphasizing only the essential details, the quality of the captured images tends to be very high even when scanned with inexpensive equipment. Because coloring book images are already drawn in "line mode," images captured from coloring books can be

Coloring books offer an active role for students

Focus

Camcorder Tips

Students of all ages can use a camcorder effectively, but that does not mean that teachers should take camcorder skills for granted. Some opportunities, such as a major field trip, might come only once a year, and lack of experience can mean that students return from such a trip with little in the way of a permanent record. If we were to offer only one suggestion it would be to allow the students to practice using the camcorder before they attempt to record an important event. Give students some fun and simple recording assignments, such as a favorite cook in action, the school's messiest locker, plants on the school grounds, or close-ups of the contents of a pocket, and then take the time to critique their work.

There are many books that explain basic camera techniques to hobbyists and you will find it worthwhile to thumb through one. If you intend to use the video primarily to capture individual images for computer projects, here are some additional suggestions to consider:

◆ Students seem to capture video images that are too distant and too general. Show them how to identify what is informative or interesting and get a tight shot of it. There is nothing wrong with capturing images from a variety of distances, but generally the close views will be most useful.

◆ Do not pan a scene and assume you will be able to capture later what is useful. Capturing still images from video works best when you have a still image to work with. Pause for 10 to 15 seconds when recording individual scenes you expect to be useful.

◆ Most camcorders are capable of taking great close-ups — images an inch or so from the lens. Students intuitively take the wrong approach to capturing close-ups. They tend to stand at a comfortable distance from the object and then zoom in with the telephoto. For the best shots, explain that they should set the camera to extreme wide angle and move it toward the object until they get the image they want. They may find themselves on their hands and knees in the dirt, with the camera two inches from a wildflower, but the picture will be great. Getting close to an object with a wide angle setting will increase the amount of the image that will be in focus.

◆ Be sure to always carry an extra battery. Read the instruction manual so you know, among other things, how to stop the camera from stamping the time and date on the recording. ✳

ACTIVE

C

THEME-BASED

I

V

E

saved in files that do not take up very much disk or memory space. Coloring book images also lend themselves to a more active role for students. Students can label, color, and incorporate parts of the images into their own artwork.

Many teachers may not realize that, among coloring books, there are many theme books published for a variety of audiences. College students enrolled in human anatomy or neuroanatomy frequently use specialized coloring books to study the subject matter of these courses. The students are asked to use colored pencils to indicate certain structures or to differentiate organ systems in a complex line drawing. Other coloring books emphasize specific topics such as butterflies, mammals, plants and animals of Rocky Mountain National Park, or natives of the Northern Plains. Coloring books are frequently published by organizations such as state historical societies, groups with an interest in wildlife management or preservation, the National Park system, and major museums. These coloring books are most easily found by visiting shops run by the organizations. Several publishing companies also offer a variety of publications in coloring book form. These resources are most likely to be found in large bookstores. Often bookstores will have only some of the coloring books available, and you may need to contact the companies directly.

Those producing or sponsoring coloring books have different motives. In many cases, their intent is to make money, and scanning images from the books would be regarded as copyright infringement. Teachers might be surprised to learn that companies have different policies on this matter. A careful reading of the copyright information usually located on the inside of the front cover may yield some surprising information. Many companies simply deny access to the entire contents of the coloring book. However, others will allow a specific number of images to be used for projects. It is also sometimes worth the time to write to organizations sponsoring coloring books. If contacted about the project a teacher has in mind, some organizations will allow images to be used for educational purposes. We discuss this topic in more depth in Chapter 11.

World Wide Web

You know the Web provides access to hypermedia and is rich in high-quality images. Although Web browsers allow you to save any image that strikes your fancy, doing so is a questionable practice (which we will discuss in Chapter 11). If you see an image you would like to use, you should contact the owner of the Web page before taking it.

Search for free clip art

The Web offers an alternative you might consider. Several sites specialize in organizing collections of images for public use. Try using a search engine and the word "clip art" to get started (see search engines in Chapter 6, pages 210 to 213).

Student Art

The second scanning resource that teachers should consider is student artwork. Students can draw or paint images relevant to a particular topic, and these creations can be scanned for inclusion in projects.

Creating multidisciplinary linkages

Two factors particularly recommend this source. First, working with student art provides an opportunity to create a unique multidisciplinary linkage. Art can contribute to other content areas, and the work in content areas can in turn provide opportunities for artistic expression. This relationship may be informal, simply by extending the typical content of a science or history

Engaging student artists actively

| A |
| C |
| **T** | HEME-BASED
| I |
| V |
| E |

course, or it may involve a more formal cooperation between two classes and two instructors.

Second, drawing on student artistic talent showcases the unique abilities of some students who may otherwise receive little attention in a science or history classroom. Artistic talent is far from perfectly correlated with the other academic talents teachers encounter. Providing artistic students an opportunity to contribute may also engage them more actively with the course content.

Clip Art and Sound Clip Collections

Images and sounds can be purchased from a variety of sources. Commercial photos have long been available to those who are willing or able to pay. Advertising agencies or publishers may deal with vendors of **stock photos**, collections of images to use for a fee, rather than attempt to generate their own pictures. If an agency wants a photograph of an Alaskan fishing village, it is certainly less expensive to purchase an image than to send a photographer to Alaska.

CDs containing 100 images

Collections of images have now been organized and offered to computer users. These collections have generally been targeted at desktop publishers, but the collections about places, cultures, land formations, historical events, or biological organisms also have relevance for classrooms. It is possible to purchase CDs containing 100 butterflies, mammals, scenes from Germany, and many similar collections for about $20. CDs containing over 1,000 PICT images are available from another vendor. These resources are often advertised as royalty free. Owning a collection of royalty-free clips would allow use of the resources for classroom projects without concern for copyright restrictions. Collections of sound clips — often sound effects and background music — are also available. Personal computer catalogs are a good source for these CDs.

Finding the educational applications

These resources are not always marketed in ways that emphasize educational applications. Products of this type will eventually become more prevalent for the education market, however, and will be offered through outlets familiar to teachers. A few specific suggestions for locating these resources are included at the end of this chapter.

CAPTURING SOUNDS

Understanding how sounds are captured

The process of capturing sound bears many similarities to the process of capturing a graphic image. The process in both cases requires that an analog signal be converted into a digital signal, which, in both cases, is accomplished using specialized hardware. The hardware may come built into the computer or may require the addition of a special board. A microphone or other source of audio input connected to this hardware brings an audio signal into the computer. The specialized hardware then converts the analog signal into a digital signal that can be stored and used in computer applications. As with the conversion of the analog graphics signal, several variables come into play in converting an analog sound signal.

The first variable concerns the accuracy with which the analog signal is converted to a digital signal. Analog sound is represented as a continuous sound wave. The conversion to a digital form is accomplished by representing this continuous wave in discrete steps. The more steps, the more accurately the original information can be represented. A digital representation allowing 16-bit sound divides the sound wave into 65,536 steps. Hardware allowing 8-bit sound allows 256 steps in the sound wave to be differentiated and to have a lower level of accuracy. This difference is noticeable, but for most applications is not of great importance. As with graphics, the bit depth of the representation influences the size of the file that ends up being stored.

The other variable associated with sound digitizing is the **sampling frequency**, which involves the number of times per second that a digital representation of the analog signal is produced. Sampling frequency is usually described in thousands of samples per second, or kilohertz (kHz). A typical sampling frequency would be 22 kHz. For storage, sounds are often stored at 11 kHz. Both the bit depth and the sampling frequency influence quality and storage requirements. The CD-recorded music that you listen to is probably stored at a bit depth of 16 and a sampling frequency of 44.1 kHz. The sound recorded in the applications described in this chapter would more likely be

Memory required to store sound

recorded at a bit depth of 8 and a sampling frequency of 11 kHz. The difference in sound quality is noticeable, but acceptable for most purposes. A 10-second sound recorded at the lower-quality settings would require about 115 kilobytes of disk space (Murie, 1993). To put this storage requirement in perspective, consider that in the multimedia Ocean Project described in Chapter 1, each student recorded a 30-second report to describe the fish he or she had researched. Although a 30-second report may seem brief, the storage capacity for 25 color pictures and 25 sound clips produced by the entire class would be quite substantial.

The method for recording sounds can be fairly simple. For example,

Built-in sound capabilities

many newer Macintosh computers have sound capabilities built in and do not require the addition of an extra board. Applications that support sound usually open an audio palette when the user selects the menu bar option allowing sound to be recorded. Figure 9.9 shows the audio palette from HyperStudio.

The operation of the sound palette is straightforward. The user clicks the record button with the mouse, speaks into the attached microphone, and clicks the stop button when finished. The play button allows the recorded

Using a sound palette

sound to be played back. A name for the sound is entered in the selection field. When the save button is clicked, the sound is attached to the stack. A sound can be attached to a button (to be played when the button is pushed) or to a card (to be played when the card appears).

FIGURE 9.9 HyperStudio Audio Palette

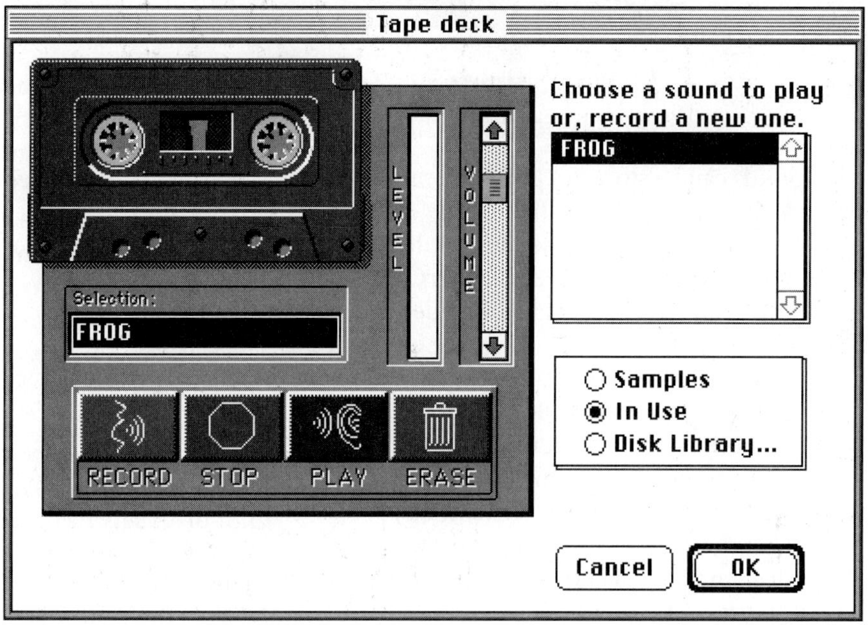

It is easy to become so enamored of sounds that you clutter a presentation with what is actually a lot of useless noise. The skillful use of sound is another of those design-related matters for which there are probably no hard-and-fast rules. Our approach is a little different. Although student projects should be tasteful, our priority is really for the kinds of experiences that motivate students and help them work with information actively. Putting together a 30-second speech about a butterfly or a fish can be a useful experience for a second grader. Agreeing to record a short poem that an elementary school student writes to accompany a drawing can increase her motivation to write the poem. As a teacher, you will need to consider specific situations and determine when working with sounds would meet the criteria of increased motivation or more active involvement with information.

Increasing your students' motivation

LEARNING WITH SOUND AND GRAPHICS TOOLS

Up to this point, the discussion in this chapter has focused mainly on techniques of getting sound and pictures into the computer and manipulating these sources of information once they have been transformed into digital form. These are obviously very practical skills for anyone who wants to work with multimedia. What may not be obvious, though, is what these skills have

Focus

Storing Sounds for Multimedia Productions

Sounds can be stored as independent *files* or as *resources* (a component that is part of a mixed file format). When you create a multimedia program with HyperStudio, HyperCard, or Kid Pix, any sounds that are included are usually incorporated as resources within the stack or the multimedia file. Applications also store sounds as independent files; that is, the file contains nothing but the data necessary to reproduce a sound. Like graphics, sounds can be stored in several different formats. HyperStudio can store a sound as an SND (the native Macintosh sound format) file. The audio interchange file format (AIFF) is used by many software applications that produce files to be loaded by other programs and other hardware platforms. Windows sound applications frequently use the WAV format. There are even generic formats intended to be shared through the World Wide Web. For example, the AU format is commonly used as a component of Web pages because it can be interpreted by Web software running on several different hardware platforms.

We offer educators advice regarding sound file formats similar to that mentioned concerning graphics file formats. First, relevant educational packages that can handle multiple formats are an advantage. For example, HyperStudio, in one way or another, can load AIFF, SND, WAV (Waveform Audio Format), AU (mu-law — the most common Internet format), MOD (music files), and QuickTime sound files (Latess, 1995). This versatility provides HyperStudio users with an advantage when the interest is in incorporating sounds not originally recorded with the host program. A good example would be loading and using sounds recorded within Kid Pix or sounds shared through the Web. Second, it is useful to acquire a utility capable of converting sound files from one format to another (e.g., SoundConverter). This option requires several steps and greater experience. However, a conversion program does increase what you can accomplish when your existing software applications are limited in the file formats they can handle. ✳

Sounds, pictures, and content knowledge

A
C
T
I
V ERSATILE
E

to do with learning more traditional content knowledge. We hope that the background from other chapters has provided some insights into how these skills may facilitate the active manipulation of information. It may also be useful to take a more direct approach and list some of the ways in which working with sound and graphics can contribute to traditional learning.

Two of the more important proposals in Chapter 2 were that certain external tasks or activities increase the probability that students will engage in desirable cognitive behaviors and that those external activities can provide a purpose and meaningful context for important thinking and learning behaviors.

To illustrate these possible links, let's identify some of the actions required when students use sound and graphics tools in projects. Projects can require that students *search for* sounds or graphics that exemplify a particular principle or justify a particular argument. Images students have captured and labeled are more realistic than schematic drawings and are more meaningful because students themselves have collected the examples. To find appropriate examples, they must thoroughly *understand* the principle or argument to be demonstrated and *evaluate* alternative sources of information to find an appropriate illustration. What pictures could be collected at a zoo to provide examples of carnivores, and which would illustrate herbivores? Which poem demonstrates the rhythm of iambic pentameter?

Teachers may also require that students *identify* the features present in visual or auditory information. Students may be required to find the esophagus in a dissected frog or the point at which the oboe begins to play in a piece of music. When a student is asked to use computer tools to label images or to mark the point at which a specific sound is present, identification skills are likely to be engaged.

Images and sounds lend themselves to *comparisons and contrasts* of many types. Illustrate the difference between a moth and a butterfly. Illustrate the difference between a cocoon and a chrysalis. Compare the sounds of an oboe and a bassoon. Discriminate among major thirds, minor thirds, major sevenths, and minor sevenths (musical chords).

Sound and graphics tools and meaningful learning

As we noted at the beginning of this chapter, education continually presents students with information in the form of sounds and graphic images, but students often do not have opportunities to manipulate information in these formats. Students are inundated with graphics and sounds, but they seldom act on this information directly. Sound and graphics tools provide opportunities for manipulation and exploration.

SUMMARY

Students normally play a receptive role when relating to information represented in the form of images or sounds. Tools for manipulating images and sounds allow students to relate to these forms of information more actively.

Technology allows users to create original images or to capture representations of existing images. Software applications that allow images to be created and modified can be categorized as paint and draw programs. These applications differ in their representation of images.

Because a paint program allows the manipulation of images at the individual pixel level, it is probably the most general educational application. Draw programs are used to create and manipulate graphic objects rather than individual pixels. Draw programs may be of special value when precision illustrations are required.

Paint programs differ widely in cost; more expensive programs tend to offer more tools. If a school decides to purchase many copies of a less expensive program, it should also consider making a small number of copies of a more expensive program available.

One very useful feature of more expensive programs is the ability to open and save files in different file formats. Unfortunately, different kinds of computers and different software programs store graphic images in different ways. It is sometimes necessary to convert an image stored in one format to a different format so that other computers or programs will be able to access the image.

Image capture can be accomplished with a scanner or video digitizer. Scanning is used to capture images that already appear on paper. Video digitizers transform the analog signal generated by a camcorder, videocassette player, or television tuner into digital data that can be saved as a graphics file. Short video segments can also be captured using the input from some of these same devices.

Sound capture is similar to video capture. Software and hardware are used to convert an analog signal to a digital signal. The quality of sound resources and the capacity required to store them are influenced by the bit depth and sampling frequency used in the conversion process.

To contemplate the role of graphics and sound tools in content-area instruction, it may be useful to consider the actions these tools allow students to exercise.

REFLECTING ON CHAPTER 9

Activities

◆ Locate an example of a commercial image collection you might use. Describe the properties of this collection, the tools you would use to work with the images, and some projects that might incorporate these images.

◆ Construct a list of criteria you would use in evaluating a graphics tool designed for younger students.

◆ If your students had access to videocapture equipment, what types of graphics collections would you have them compile?

◆ Familiarize yourself with a paint program. Demonstrate the program's capabilities to your classmates.

Key Terms

analog signal *(p. 320)*
bit-mapped *(p. 307)*
charge-coupled device (CCD) *(p. 318)*
clipboard *(p. 306)*
computer-assisted design (CAD) *(p. 307)*
dots per inch (dpi) *(p. 307)*
draw programs *(p. 307)*
graphic user interface (GUI) *(p. 310)*
jaggies *(p. 309)*
line art *(p. 307)*

lossy *(p. 317)*
object-oriented image *(p. 307)*
paint programs *(p. 306)*
pixels *(p. 307)*
QuickTime *(p. 324)*
sampling frequency *(p. 328)*
scanners *(p. 318)*
screen capture *(p. 306)*
stock photos *(p. 327)*
translators *(p. 317)*
video digitizers *(p. 318)*

Resources to Expand Your Knowledge Base

Hardware and Software Resources

Audio and Photo Collections

Applied Optical MediaCorp distributes clip art and sound clips for educational applications. Applied Optical MediaCorp, 1450 Boot Rd., Building 400, West Chester, PA 19380.

Corel distributes a large number of CDs containing royalty-free, photographic-quality images stored in the Kodak Photo-CD format. Software on the CD allows the images to be exported to either Macintosh or Windows machines. Corel, 1600 Carling Ave., Ottawa, Ontario, CANADA K1Z 8R7.

Audio Board

Sound Blaster is an audio board for DOS/Windows platforms. Available from Creative Labs, Inc., 1901 McCarthy Blvd., Malpitas, CA 95035.

Digital Camera

The *Kodak DC40* is manufactured by Eastman Kodak, 343 State St., Rochester, NY 14650. The camera can be used with either Macintosh or Windows systems.

Video Camera

The *QuickCam* and *Color QuickCam* are examples of inexpensive personal video cameras. These products are manufactured by Connectix Corporation, 2655 Campus Drive, San Mateo, CA 94403.

Software

Kid Pix is available for Macintosh and DOS computers from Broderbund Software, 500 Redwood Blvd., P.O. Box 6121, Novato, CA 94948. Sound Blaster is recommended when Kid Pix is used on DOS machines.

Paintbrush comes as one of the tools available in Windows.

QuickTime tools ship with the HyperCard Developer's Kit and many other products.

Photoshop is a product of Adobe Systems, 1585 Chareston Rd., Mountain View, CA 94039.

SoundConverter is a shareware utility designed to convert sounds stored in one file format to other file formats. The best way to locate SoundConverter is to use a World Wide Web search engine.

Chapter 10

Learning from Student Projects: Knowledge as Design and the Design of Hypermedia

ORIENTATION

In this chapter we explore a major concept in both hypermedia and learning: design. It is typical to think of design as the process by which professionals construct useful products. Architects design buildings. Engineers design bridges or new cars. Educational software developers design software to help students learn. It also seems that motivated and active students design their own meaningful representations of their experiences. Design is a general concept that recognizes the importance of skilled behavior applied to the accomplishment of a meaningful goal.

The product of a design process is also called a design. A bridge is a design resulting from a design process. So are buildings, computer programs, and knowledge. Our focus here is on student-designed hypermedia and the learning opportunities when students are involved in such projects. As you read, look for answers to the following questions:

FOCUS QUESTIONS

- ◆ What organizational, graphic, text, and interface design principles should students be aware of as they develop hypermedia projects?
- ◆ What student and teacher activities are typical of the various stages in a cooperative group project?
- ◆ How can the design of hypermedia facilitate the design of knowledge?
- ◆ How does the teacher interact with students to make the creation of projects valuable learning experiences?

334

Discovering the Painted Lady: A Second Grade Adventure in Learning

Two second grade girls sit in the front of the room working on the one computer available to their class. From there you can hear one student ask the other, "But how do I change the font?"

"You need to click in the field and then choose Text Style under Edit."

Near the side of the classroom, two boys are looking at a butterfly distribution chart that has been taped along the length of the chalkboard.

"Do you think the painted lady butterfly lives in places that the monarch butterfly doesn't?"

"You find the monarch on the chart, and I'll find the painted lady, and we'll compare. Look, the monarch doesn't live here. What state do you think this is?"

A butterfly garden has been established in the corner of the classroom. Some painted lady butterflies have already hatched, while others have not emerged from their chrysalises. Pam Carlson, the teacher, is operating the video camera.

"Mrs. Carlson, this would be a good time to get a picture of the butterfly while it rests. See how the wings are straight up?"

In the back of the classroom is a large bookshelf covered with resource books about butterflies.

"Let's see if we can find out what that red liquid is called that's dripping from their wings. Do you think it's blood?"

Two students are standing at a chart reading over the questions: How much does the caterpillar weigh? What does the caterpillar eat? How does the caterpillar move? Will the caterpillar form a chrysalis or a cocoon? How long will it take for the butterfly to hatch out of the chrysalis?

These behaviors are atypical of most second grade classrooms. Students in this classroom are involved in answering science questions that they have posed themselves. You will see shortly that what they do with their answers is even more unusual. Let's follow the project from the beginning.

THE PROJECT BEGINS

In the fall, one of the students brought in a monarch caterpillar, and the second grade class observed its development. The excitement of this event led the teacher to explore other avenues to extend and enhance the experience. She was aware that live caterpillars could be purchased for each student to monitor the development of a larva. She had also experimented with classroom applications of technology and had involved several of her previous classes in the development of simple hypermedia projects. Most recently, she had seen examples of how graphics captured with a video camera could be used in computer applications. Her students could record the development of butterflies on videotape and capture the images for a cooperative class science project.

One morning in April, a box from the scientific supply company arrived. The teacher had decided that the students would not be given any information about the larvae. It would be their job to observe and try to identify which butterfly would emerge. The video camera was readied to capture the experience as each student put some food into a vial and then carefully placed the caterpillar in its new home.

The research began. The students pored over charts and books from the library, hunting for information that might yield the butterfly's identity. They weighed and measured the larvae, all captured on videotape. Each day, a clue was written on the board that might help the students identify the larvae. One of the clues stated that this caterpillar ate the malva plant. Two boys approached the teacher.

"We think it's the painted lady butterfly, but we have one more thing to look up. This book says that the painted lady eats thistles. We need to find out if the malva plant is a thistle."

With the help of the clues and the information gathered from resource books, the class agreed that the developing larvae would hatch into painted lady butterflies. The video camera captured their development as the days progressed. As the students observed the process, they generated a list of questions to help in the research process.

TURNING TO HYPERCARD

The students had previously used the computer to write reports and create slide shows, so the teacher decided HyperCard would be the perfect tool for them to explain this unit to their parents. A question-and-answer format based on the students' research questions was chosen for the HyperCard stacks they would create. Each student would choose a question and create a stack consisting of two cards. On the first card would be a field with the research question, a sound button with the student's recording of the question, and a button that would take the user to the second card. The second card would have a field with the answer to the question, a sound button with a recording of the answer, a button to go back to the question, a button to go to the next stack, and, when possible, a captured picture illustrating the answer.

The students already knew about fonts, font sizes, and styles from their experience with word processing. They were familiar with paint tools and the recording palette from using Kid Pix. They also understood the concept of linking screens and transitions between screens from their work with Kid Pix Companion. So the teacher gave a general introduction of HyperCard to the whole class, focusing on the new elements of cards, buttons, fields, and how to navigate through a stack. She then worked through the individual elements of building the two-card stack with one student. She created the first card in the stack, and the student created the second card minus the captured picture window. After the first stack was created, the experienced student became the teacher for the next student, again modeling the first card and monitoring the creation of the second card. This process continued until all students had created a two-card stack. The students then viewed the videotape and decided on images that would best represent the answers to their questions. Each image was captured, and the teacher keyed in the script necessary for the picture to appear in a window on the card.

Chris decided to find out what the caterpillar eats. In Figure 10.1 you see his answer: "It eats from the Malva plant."

"We think it's some kind of thistle," says Chris.

The completed project provided a chronology of the observed development of the painted lady and consisted of twenty-three two-card stacks connected with buttons and incorporating pictures and full-motion video.

FIGURE 10.1 Chris's Answer to the Question "What does the caterpillar eat?"

THE PAINTED LADY PROJECT
AND MEANINGFUL LEARNING

Active learning, collaboration, and technology

What is going on in this classroom? You probably realize from earlier chapters that these students are working on a hypermedia project as part of a science unit. Why should teachers add hypermedia projects to the more traditional experiences they provide students? How does involvement in such projects help students learn in a generative way? How do students go about putting a project together? In this chapter we provide some answers to these questions by exploring the topic of knowledge as design, by discussing the process and basic principles of multimedia design, and by describing several multimedia projects. We will return to Pam's classroom to follow her and her second grade class as they develop several new projects. One of these projects will be presented in considerable detail so you will have a better understanding of what both a teacher and students do over the course of developing a theme-based project. You will learn how active learning, student collaboration, and technology come together as students prepare for and craft their project.

ACTIVE
COOPERATION
THEME-BASED
INTEGRATED
VERSATILE
EVALUATION

Useful knowledge

As we describe how students can design projects relevant to many content areas, we will try to instill one important perspective: meaningful learning as the result of a student's personal cognitive process of design. *Useful knowledge* can be considered a design (Perkins, 1986). Understanding and developing learning experiences around the concept that useful knowledge is purposefully generated by learners could have important implications for your classroom. The more traditional concept of design may also be important. One way to actively involve students is by challenging them with a design project. Designing a tangible product appears to facilitate the design of personal knowledge. As we proceed, we will explore both the design of products and the design of knowledge as well as possible connections between these two types of tasks.

KNOWLEDGE AS DESIGN

Knowledge as information

How we think about knowledge can strongly influence our behavior as teachers and learners (Perkins, 1986). At least two perspectives are possible. The first views knowledge as information. Information is basically factual knowledge; that is, ideas that are accumulated from various academic and life experiences and that are known for the sake of knowing. Information is stored assuming that it will eventually prove useful. The perspective of knowledge as information is consistent with the metaphor of learning as transmission. A more knowledgeable person passes knowledge on to a less knowledgeable person.

Knowledge as design

In contrast, **knowledge as design** is knowledge adapted to a purpose. In the context of the model of active learning used throughout this book, knowl-

Learning as construction

edge as design is a probable product of meaningful learning. It is information generated by a student as a tool to accomplish some purpose. The perspective of knowledge as design is consistent with the metaphor of learning as construction. The learner with a purpose takes advantage of the information available to build personal understanding. A more knowledgeable person may facilitate the process of knowledge construction in a less knowledgeable person, but the acts of knowledge construction must be performed by the person doing the learning.

It is important to understand that the distinction between knowledge as information and knowledge as design is not inherent in the raw facts and experiences learners encounter, but *in what the learner does with these raw materials.* You can test this position by considering content that most would regard as basic factual information. What about those names and dates we all attempted to learn in history classes? What is the purpose of knowing that Columbus reached the New World in 1492? If you asked a junior high school student this question, you would likely hear that the purpose in knowing this date is to get a question right on the next exam. We might smile at the naiveté of this response, but do we have anything better to offer? Perkins (1986) proposes that even historical dates can represent a design. To understand how this works, think about the work of professional historians and how they might use landmark dates. For the historian, dates become tools of organization. A date can be a way to connect several simultaneous events, perhaps as a precursor to exploring possible cause-and-effect relationships. Dates can also serve to sequence events over time. Students can use dates the same way, but are more likely to think like the junior high school students described here and not like apprentice historians. It is unfair, though, to place the blame totally on the student. The teacher may be as focused on the upcoming test as the student.

A design is a tool

Put in a familiar way, a **design** is a tool developed to accomplish a purpose. Both concrete designs and knowledge as design fit this framework. What is significant here is that a purpose exists and is recognized from the outset. One of Perkins's (1986) favorite examples of a tool is a screwdriver. He suggests the absurdity of someone fashioning an object and then wondering what might be done with it. "Oh, this might be useful for mixing cookie dough. No, I think I'll use it to turn screws." Strange? Yet school learning often proceeds in just this way. A student often learns or memorizes information, feeling that this fact or idea should be useful for something, but at the time the student is often not exactly certain what. In contrast, the introductory example from Pam Carlson's classroom provides some good examples of purpose. The two girls in the example are trying to learn about the features of HyperCard because they want to include some different text styles in the product they are working on. Two of the boys are studying the habitats of the painted lady and monarch butterflies because this information may provide a clue to the identity of the mystery caterpillar they are

Purposes of learning facts

Immediate applications

raising. In these situations, there is an immediate application for what students learn.

These experiences could have been very different. Pam might have asked her class to memorize the names of fifteen different butterflies or the different terms appearing on the HyperCard menu bar. Students would probably have said they were learning because their teacher asked them to learn or because they were preparing for a test. In a way, students always learn with some purpose in mind; even storing information for a test might be considered a purpose. However, storing information has less long-term utility than generating personal knowledge and accumulating at least some experiences in how this knowledge can be used.

Active, purposeful learning

Emphasizing knowledge as design implies that students should spend a good part of their school time in active, purposeful learning. Some activities work particularly well to provide design experiences. For example, what if students designed useful products instead of studying about them? What if they were able to play the roles of engineers, biologists, or historians and had to design a new piece of playground equipment, evaluate the pollution of a local pond, or develop an actual historical account of a past event? What if students designed software—in particular, instructional software?

Student-designed software

LOOKING AT STUDENT-AUTHORED HYPERMEDIA

This chapter emphasizes student-authored hypermedia. Design projects could also be based on the development of databases, projects requiring the analysis of data with a spreadsheet, and various kinds of writing activities. Actually, the idea of learning through design is very versatile and does not require technology, but our focus in this book, of course, is on technology projects and on suggesting productive ways teachers and students can use technology.

Focusing on technology projects

Many possibilities for projects

Possibilities for hypermedia projects abound. Imagine that, on the hundred-and-twenty-fifth anniversary of their state, an eighth grade history class decides to design a World Wide Web account of important aspects of their state's history and to contribute this project to the school and the state by posting this material on the school's server to be viewed during the year-long celebration. Imagine that, as a science project, a second grade class rears painted lady butterflies. The class decides to study different aspects of the butterfly life cycle (form and size at different stages, food consumed at different stages) and presents their observations to their parents in the form of a HyperCard document. As you may have already guessed, this is exactly what was happening in Pam Carlson's classroom.

FOCUSING ON THE DESIGN OF HYPERMEDIA

Now that you have been introduced to the concept of knowledge as design, let's shift our focus to the design of hypermedia. After familiarizing you with some guidelines for the development of hypermedia projects, we will return to the topic of meaningful learning as design and emphasize the opportunities for meaningful learning inherent in hypermedia projects.

PRINCIPLES OF HYPERMEDIA DESIGN: THE PROCESS OF DEVELOPING SOFTWARE

Basic principles

Hypermedia design is the purposeful process of developing a hypermedia product that is informative, interesting, and easy to use and understand. The production of truly professional quality products meeting these standards is both science and art. Certain concrete skills can be learned. There are some standard questions developers should ask of themselves and guidelines that novice developers should follow. In this section, we concentrate on some basic guidelines that apply to HyperStudio and HyperCard creations and other simple development environments likely to be available to students. Many of the principles described here would also be relevant if students have the opportunity to author hypermedia materials for the World Wide Web. The intent of this brief section is to cover some of the basic principles that might be immediately useful in student-generated projects. These principles are (1) content organization, (2) graphic design, (3) text presentation, and (4) development of the user interface (Apple Computer, 1989).

CONTENT ORGANIZATION

An author in any medium exercises a fairly substantial degree of control over the sequence in which the reader or user encounters the various elements of information. For example, in a typical textbook, the author creates a structure so that the reader encounters ideas in a certain order and interrelates them in a certain way. From the textbook author's perspective, ideas flow into each other in a logical way, and the author's intention is to communicate this logical sequence to the reader. In a book, illustrations are placed close to text ideas that they explain or exemplify. Access to ideas or illustrations in other chapters or even earlier in the same chapter can be somewhat cumbersome for the reader. The reader can override the structure imposed by the author, but the reader will then have to search about blindly (thumbing back through a chapter to reread a section) or use a general guide (table of contents) or a specific guide (index) to find related material. The extent to which the author has planned for these alternate ways to interrelate ideas is likely to have been very limited. It is usually not assumed to be the author's responsibility to

Linear organization of books

encourage or expedite nonsequential reading of the book. Books must be organized in a linear style, and the author must commit to a single organizational structure to accommodate this limitation.

Experiencing Content in a Variety of Ways

One of the advantages (and, some might say, curses) of hypermedia is that it allows the author to present content that can be experienced in a variety of ways. The medium does not impose the limits. The user could theoretically move from any unit of information (called a **node**) to any other unit of information. The connections between nodes are called **links** (see Chapter 2).

Nodes are units of information.

Although it is a bit of an exaggeration to claim that all nodes in most hypermedia applications are interconnected, it is fair to claim that multiple linkages among ideas are available. To maximize the effectiveness of the presentation, the hypermedia author designs a structure by allowing some subset of all possible links. The structure the author imposes on the information shapes the environment in which the user can explore. The structure of linkages presented to the user should be based on the author's analysis of the purpose of the software product and the possible logical connections the content expert sees in the material. The extent to which the user is allowed to control access is closely related to the product's intended purpose.

Multiple linkages among ideas

Organizational Structure

Organizational structure concerns the pattern in which nodes are linked (Jonassen and Grabinger, 1990). In the next section we examine some of the common structures. Teachers wishing to help students develop hypermedia products might start with an understanding of the following three basic organizational structures. These models describe "pure" forms. In actual practice, the structure of hypermedia is often some variation on or integration of these structures.

Limited options

Linear Structure. In a **linear design**, as in Figure 10.2, the user's options are very limited. The elements of information are encountered in a specified order. In an extreme version, the user only initiates the display and then simply views the entire presentation. Television programs are viewed this way. Once a viewer selects a channel, the presentation runs until completed or terminated. In a less extreme form, the user can move forward or backward through the sequence of material. The amount of time spent on each node is under the user's control. If you have used a carousel slide projector, you have had some experience displaying information in this way. In addition to allowing the viewer to move ahead and back within the presentation, computer-based linear designs often allow the user to return to the initial or startup screen. This option is useful if the user wants to terminate the session without experiencing the entire sequence and perhaps return to complete the rest of the presentation at a later time.

Simplicity as an advantage

The major advantage of a linear design is simplicity. Users are familiar with this format (from books, television, movies, and so forth) and thus do not have to develop new strategies for interacting with material presented in this manner. What students know about learning from books should transfer and provide all of the background that is necessary. The user interface will also require little experience; even if the user is completely naive, he or she can usually learn the interface very quickly. In the most complex format just described, the user would likely navigate by clicking one of three buttons (forward, backward, or start). Simplicity is also a potential advantage for the hypermedia author. The user interface will require minimal work. The author can concentrate on communicating a specific message logically, informatively, and interestingly.

Tree Structure. A design based on a **tree structure** organizes information hierarchically. As the user interacts with a program of this type, he or she encounters choice points (**branches**). Each branch narrows the user's immediate focus in some way. One purpose of a hierarchical structure is to organize information so users can find what they need without inspecting all the available information.

Hierarchically organized information

A very simple tree structure is illustrated in Figure 10.3. In this example, the user makes a choice in interacting with the initial screen display and then follows one path or the other. The single choice in this case might allow the user to select between two fish to learn about that species. There are many variations on this design. There might be a single level of the hierarchy and several nodes of information associated with each choice (as shown in Figure 10.3); many levels of the hierarchy and a single node of information at the deepest level of the hierarchy; or other combinations within this range.

Some variation on the tree structure is particularly valuable as an efficient way to locate specific information. It will also keep the user from getting lost. This might sound strange if you haven't worked with hypermedia, but getting lost is a real problem when users can jump from node to node in an undisciplined manner. A tree structure allows users to move back up the hierarchy to find their place in the organizational system.

Variations on the tree structure

Learners make distinct choices

Consider a case in which students want to develop a system to organize the artwork contained on a videodisc. A hierarchical system might be created in which the user first selects the period of interest, the artistic style of interest within that period, an artist associated with that style, and finally a

FIGURE 10.2 Linear Design

FIGURE 10.3 Tree Structure

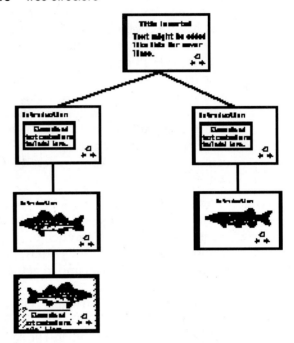

particular work associated with that artist. The final choice would cause the videodisc player to select a single image for display. In this case, the user makes a number of distinct choices to arrive at a single node of information.

A tree structure offers greater user control than a linear structure, but still imposes certain constraints on the user. In a pure application of this style (see Figure 10.3), the user is not allowed to cross between strands at one level of the hierarchy without returning to the choice point that specifically differen-

Organizing information tiated the strands. Structure is important in a second way. Even if the user is intended to process all of the information provided, the structure of the hypermedia can help the user organize what is learned. For example, certain systems for classifying biological organisms (remember phylum, class, order, family, genus, and species from high school biology) have a theoretical rationale. The student may develop an appreciation for such a classification system while navigating the structure to explore individual animals. The biologist's design for classification is integrated into the design of the hypermedia.

Network Structure. A **network structure** links nodes without relying on a strict hierarchical structure. Depending on the complexity of the network, several different pathways might be followed in getting from a given node to another. Figure 10.4 shows how this would be possible. When many of the nodes are linked to several other nodes, alternate pathways are common.

A network structure allows the user the greatest flexibility in examining

Advantages of network structures

the content provided, and it allows the hyperauthor the related opportunity to create more open-ended, exploratory information environments. The World Wide Web is a good example of the power and problems of a network structure. Because the WWW has been created by thousands of different authors who do not have to commit to any given design model and link to other resources as they see fit, the structure of the Web is freeform and complex. The practical value of flexibility depends to some extent on the user's ability to navigate the content effectively. It is quite possible for the user to become lost within the network because the richness of the many interconnections and the lack of a simple organizational structure can be confusing. Even when working within a hypermedia application intended for use on a single computer, the user may be able to move among definitions of key words, alternate documents making a similar point, illustrations, other illustrations providing greater detail of segments of earlier illustrations, selections from speeches or music, and short video pieces. Each of these items might be considered a node, and when it is understood that the user can enter and leave many nodes using different links, the difficulty some users might have in using the network becomes apparent. Once the user is sidetracked, it can be difficult to pick up the initial theme again. The human-factors issue of how to assist the user in navigating complex hypermedia systems has become an interesting area of inquiry (Jonassen and Grabinger, 1990; Nielsen, 1990). Certainly, special features built into the user interface can improve performance (see later section on "Navigation and the User Interface").

GRAPHIC DESIGN

Appearance and content of material

Graphic design concerns the appearance and content of the material appearing on the computer screen. The purpose of careful graphic design is to make

FIGURE 10.4   Network Structure

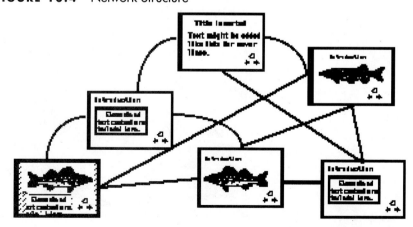

the information displayed on the screen as informative, easy to understand, and interesting as possible. This section provides only an overview of selected topics likely to be applicable to the student developer. While these are sound principles that can guide the graphic design process, truly outstanding products also arise from experience and creative talent.

Screen Layout

Facilitating use

Objects should be placed and grouped in a way that facilitate the user's activities. An object could be a button, picture, or text field. One way to develop a strategy for screens of a certain type is to make use of a **grid** (see Figure 10.5). A grid is a pattern of lines that organizes the placement of objects and maintains consistency across similar screens. A grid does not have to be complicated to be effective—it may be merely a line dividing the screen into two

FIGURE 10.5 Layout Grid

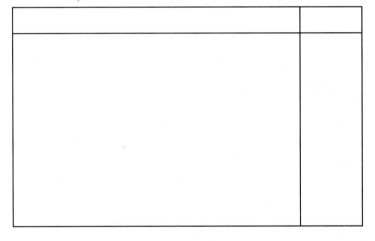

main areas. The layout used in Figure 10.5 might be used to present a series of illustrations. As you can see in the figure, the lines designating key areas of the screen do not actually have to appear on the screen.

Additional Guidelines for Screen Layout

Buttons

◆ Buttons (see pages 350 through 351) should usually appear along the edges of the screen. Make an exception when a button has an impact on just part of the screen. This might be the case when the button would reveal some hidden information such as labels for a diagram. The button should then appear adjacent to the object or area it influences.

Grouping of buttons

◆ Group buttons that serve similar functions together. Buttons that appear on all cards should also be separated from buttons that are card specific.

Size

◆ Use size to control the user's attention. The most important elements should be allocated the most grid space.

Grid concept

◆ Do not abandon the grid concept just because the screen displays only text. A screen of solid text is dull and hard to read. Organizing text elements on the screen can increase both readability and interest (see next section on design principles for text; Apple Computer, 1989).

Try evaluating the principles of screen layout as they apply to the example in Figure 10.6. Could you sketch the grid that was used to organize this screen? Would you organize a set of screens containing a picture, text information,

FIGURE 10.6   Sample Screen Layout

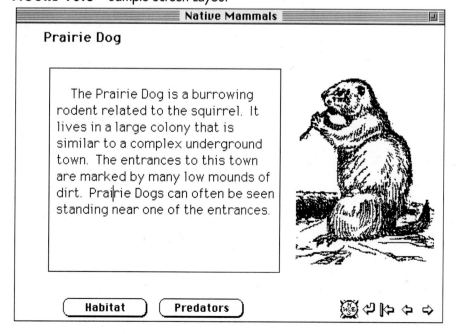

navigation buttons, and buttons establishing topical links in any other way? Have the general guidelines for screen layout been followed?

Text Presentation and Writing Style

Principles for using text in hypermedia emphasize clear communication, legibility, and motivation. In general, hypermedia will not present the user screen after screen of continuous text, for several reasons. First, screens of solid text are difficult to read, so designers are encouraged to present text in chunks surrounded by space for greater legibility. Second, hypermedia is based on the notion of connecting specific idea units in complex ways. Small blocks of text rather than continuous screens of text are best suited to constructing these connections. Usually, the text component of hypermedia prepared for younger readers will read differently than extended text.

Communication, legibility, motivation

Text layout concerns more than writing style and statement length. Text layout also involves the placement of text on the screen and the appearance of the text itself. Briefly summarized, the text on the screen should be easy to read, and special embellishments (special fonts, bold type, size) should be limited to those situations in which it is important to draw the hypermedia user's attention to something unique and specific. Teachers introducing any kind of program allowing text display (word processing, a paint program, HyperCard) are likely to find that students will manipulate text characteristics unnecessarily at first. It is great fun to experiment with the many elements of text appearance, and this process of experimentation is one way for student designers to become familiar with what is possible. However, at some point, the student-as-designer needs to consider how these different options might be used most productively to communicate with the user. The following are some general guidelines for designers of text (Apple Computer, 1989).

Placement and appearance of text on screen

◆ Text messages should be concise. When it is important to communicate complex ideas or large amounts of information, consider identifying the important ideas and presenting the ideas as separate but linked nodes. Avoid the use of scrolling fields except for special circumstances. (*Note:* Scrolling fields allow the user to control the display of a large document using a mouse or the keyboard. The text scrolls, or moves up and down on the screen, as directed by the user. Of course, only part of the total document is visible at any one time.)

Concise text messages

◆ Text should be easy to read. Consider issues such as font size, line spacing, and adequate margins. Line length should be neither too long nor too short. The lines of text should not stretch from one edge of the screen to the other, nor should they be so narrow that they consist of only a couple of words.

Easy to read

◆ Consider presenting text in several different fields within the same screen display. A title or heading can be separated from the main body of text, or distinct ideas can be separated from each other.

Simplicity

◆ Do not overuse multiple fonts, font sizes, or font styles. Use larger fonts, bolding, or underlining to bring attention to titles, important ideas, or key terms. When techniques for distinguishing text are used too frequently, specially designated text is no longer special.

◆ Use special fonts sparingly. For example, script is comparatively difficult to read, but it might be used to designate entries from a special source such as a diary.

◆ Keep in mind that the user of a hypermedia document may interact with the document on a different machine than that on which the document was created. If a particular font is not available on the user's machine, unexpected results may occur.

It is probably fair to argue that the hypermedia author typically does some preprocessing of information for the user. Unless the user is expected to develop an appreciation for original documents or to gain experience in working with primary sources, the author provides a service by identifying and summarizing important ideas, isolating individual ideas as nodes, and providing some appreciation for the structure of the content area through the links among the nodes. Those situations in which the user might be linked to original documents (historic documents, diaries, scientific reports, legal opinions, poems) represent special cases in which the user is expected to gain some unique benefit from interacting with raw materials.

Design principles emphasize using text in a controlled fashion; for example, keeping text segments short and simple. Teachers may want students to write more extensively. Thus, in some situations, the goals of learning from the project and of meeting ideal design guidelines may be in conflict. One solution to this dilemma is to realize that the hypermedia product does not need to contain all of the writing the student has done related to the project.

Students may need to do additional writing.

NAVIGATION AND THE USER INTERFACE

The hypermedia author must give considerable thought to the practical mechanisms by which the potential user will interact with the information provided. Collectively, these mechanisms represent the **user interface**. Careful development of the interface is especially important if the structure of the hypermedia is to allow the user to make choices about what will be experienced. If the user is to exercise a substantial degree of control over interaction with the material, he or she must have some idea what the hypermedia product is about and how the material is organized. At any given point in time, the user must know what actions are possible and what the consequence of each action is likely to be. The user must also have some idea of where he or she is within the total body of information, and how to get from the present location to some other desired location. Finally, it is ideal if the mechanisms by which these goals are accomplished are either intuitively obvious or require

Thinking about the material

very little learning time. The goal is to allow the user to think about the material and not about what must be done to interact with it.

Menus and Maps

It is often helpful to provide a main screen that identifies the major topics covered by a hypermedia product. With World Wide Web projects, this is a common way to use the home page. By identifying the topics, the author gives the user a sense of the scope of the material available and a way to identify *Identifying topics in* what has and has not been covered. A **menu** provides a list of the available *hypermedia* topics. This list might be presented using text or perhaps some form of graphical representation. In contrast, a **map** identifies the components of the presentation, as well as the main links among the components (see Figure 10.7). Maps are of particular value when the hypermedia product has a complex structure and allows the user many choices.

Buttons

In most forms of hypermedia, user actions are usually initiated by clicking a button. **Buttons** are areas of the screen that respond to commands issued by the user, such as clicking with a mouse, touching the screen, or pressing a designated key. Buttons offer a very intuitive method of taking action. This is why buttons and the touch-sensitive screen are used in situations when

FIGURE 10.7   A Graphical Menu Developed by a Junior High School Student

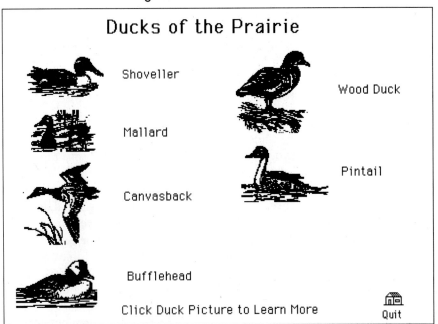

Buttons allow students to control actions

instruction must be minimal and inexperienced users are many (as at kiosks in a museum or shopping mall). Buttons also provide a useful way for both the hypermedia author and the user to exercise control. By programming the allowable actions as buttons, the author can offer the user a specified set of alternative actions and allow the user to control when an action will be initiated and which action will be taken.

Standard Buttons. Authors working in a popular format (e.g., card-based hypermedia systems, Web pages) have developed certain conventions. Some button icons are used consistently to mean certain things. Although using buttons in unconventional ways is perfectly acceptable to the computer, this practice can confuse users and will clearly label the hypermedia author as a novice. For example, novice developers often use the "Home" icon (a picture of a house) to return users to an initial menu. Although this might make some sense, experienced HyperCard or HyperStudio users expect the present application to be exited when the home button is clicked. A little experience with public domain or commercial hypermedia should be sufficient to pick up how the more standard button icons are used. The intended use of a button can also be communicated through an informative label (e.g., Next Card).

Conventional uses of buttons

The home button

These guidelines should acquaint you with basic principles that can guide the creation of hypermedia. Obviously, the guidelines are more concerned with the quality of the hypermedia product than with the learning experience students might have in creating such products. As we have mentioned from time to time, teachers must be sensitive to areas in which product design and learning opportunities may be in conflict and to the amount of time necessary to develop high-quality hypermedia products.

Project design and learning opportunities

In the next sections, we integrate the theoretical ideas of learning through the process of design and concrete suggestions for how to accomplish one type of design project—hypermedia—in classroom applications. For reasons related to practical matters of teacher time and resources and to the design of learning environments likely to encourage active learning, these classroom applications often require that students work together in cooperative groups. We like to think of these groups as design teams. We start with a short general discussion of cooperative learning and eventually move to an example of cross-grade hypermedia design.

Groups of students as design teams

STUDENT COOPERATION: FUNDAMENTALS FOR DESIGN TEAMS

You have encountered cooperative learning a number of times in this book. We have presented cooperative learning as (1) an essential component in many plans for restructuring the mission and methods of schools; (2) a way to make learning more active and meaningful; (3) a partial solution when

A
C OOPERATION
T
I
V
E

Basic principles of cooperative learning

technological resources are in short supply; and (4) a productive way to implement multimedia projects. Cooperative methods can play a very important role in learning with technology. We feel it is worthwhile to consider cooperative learning more directly. Here we want you to consider the basic principles of cooperative learning and to acquire some concrete ideas for using cooperative approaches to student projects. This material should acquaint you with conditions that are essential to productive cooperative environments and leave you with the sense that you would know where to start should you decide to use cooperative methods.

Cooperative learning techniques are hardly new. In elementary school, you probably took turns quizzing a classmate with flash cards. You may have encountered situations in your college experience in which an education instructor broke your class into groups and asked you to discuss a topic, generate possible solutions to a teaching problem, or practice a specific teaching skill. You probably participated in these experiences with little training and with mixed results.

What has changed is that more formal cooperative learning methods have been proposed and carefully evaluated at different grade levels and in different content areas. Details can be important. Not every situation in

Computer-based projects provide many different opportunities for cross-age interaction. (© Michael Zide)

which one student interacts with another is effective. What has come from this research are some concrete and practical learning methods and an understanding of key components that influence student learning. We cannot review this entire body of work or present all of the many successful strategies that have been developed, but if the ideas presented here appeal to you, there are some very helpful sources you might consult to learn more (Johnson, Johnson and Holubec, 1991; Slavin, 1990, 1991). See "Resources to Expand Your Knowledge Base" at the end of the chapter.

Typical cooperative groups

At the most basic level, **cooperative learning** refers to a classroom situation in which students work together to help each other learn. The idea is to create an environment in which students want each other to succeed and work to motivate and teach each other, to accomplish this goal. Typically, cooperative groups consist of two to five students and are often purposely made heterogeneous, or mixed with respect to ability, gender, and ethnic group.

Team success

Research indicates that *team rewards* and *individual accountability* are especially important for success. **Team rewards** are some form of recognition for team success. These rewards can take many different forms: certificates, posting pictures of outstanding teams, and special activities. **Individual accountability** means that team success is based on the individual accomplishments of all team members. For example, each team member may be expected to take a test over the content covered, and team performance is based on all of the scores earned. Sometimes scores are compared with past performance so that each team member has an equal opportunity to contribute to team success (Slavin, 1991).

Considering different learning goals

In considering specific cooperative methods, it is important to recognize that different methods are best suited to different learning goals. Some cooperative methods were designed to help students master content typified by single right answers, and other methods focus on more open-ended problems requiring data acquisition, analysis, and synthesis. Some methods retain a fairly typical role for the teacher; that is, the teacher presents the content. Other methods require the teacher to focus on facilitating the learning process and to allow students to take more responsibility for the content.

GOING BEYOND FACTUAL INFORMATION

The cooperative methods of greatest relevance here are those that have been developed to involve students in group tasks requiring both the acquisition and the application of knowledge and skill. These approaches, referred to as **task specialization methods** (Slavin, 1990), require that individual students contribute in unique ways to the accomplishment of a group task. Task specialization methods require individual accountability and team rewards. In task specialization methods, the quality with which the task is completed determines the team's reward. Individual accountability is accomplished through

Individual accountability

task specialization. Each student must accept unique responsibility for some aspect of the assigned task, and the group's performance thus depends to some extent on the contribution of every group member.

Group investigation is a task specialization method that results in the production of group projects associated with a general theme proposed by the teacher (Sharan and Sharan, 1992). There are several reasons to consider this approach carefully.

First, concrete strategies for group investigations have been worked out in detail, and some very useful guidelines have been established to help teachers implement group projects in their classrooms. Second, the group investigation model can be easily adapted to technology-based projects. Group investigations are intended to result in an informative summary report and presentation, and a multimedia project can serve as the summary report or support the group's presentation to the entire class. Finally, the effectiveness of the group investigation method has been carefully studied. Because the research base in support of technology-based group projects is limited, demonstrations that projects of a similar nature result in effective learning experiences are reassuring. Research demonstrates that group investigations result in significantly better performance than traditional learning activities (Slavin, 1990).

Technology-based projects

The group investigation model has been worked out in detail (Sharan and Shachar, 1988; Slavin, 1990), and you will probably stick close to this model when you implement group projects for the first time. With experience, you will discover what works in your classroom. Substituting a multimedia project for the final report may require some alterations. The system may also require some tweaking to meet the needs of your students, to fit your teaching style, and to be feasible within the amount of time you can allow. When you decide to approach a topic using group investigation, you do not have to limit student learning opportunities to those provided through cooperative group experiences. You might decide to initiate the unit of study in a traditional way. Perhaps students will work with a textbook and whole-group instruction at first. These experiences might be used to establish background and develop some of the issues that might then be pursued through group investigation. You might also decide to jump right in and initiate the study of a new unit with the group investigation process. However, as you think about the topics students have selected, you may feel the need to provide supplemental experiences. As the class moves through the time period allowed for the unit, it is appropriate to mix in other learning experiences and assignments. The group investigation process does not have to be the sole learning experience you use.

Activities and Projects for Your Classroom

Planets

Students study the planets at many grade levels. Let's take a look at how the six stages of group investigation could be applied to this unit using HyperStudio as the presentation tool for the final project.

Stage 1: Identify the Topic and Form Student Groups After viewing an introductory video on the planets, have students submit the name of the planet they would be interested in studying in greater depth. Divide the class into groups based on their choices.

Stage 2: Team Planning Once the group has been formed, the members of the group must decide on a plan for how the group will function. Will each member choose a special area to research, such as the planet's geology or its weather? Or will the team members gather information, come back to the group to share what they have learned, and then divide responsibilities?

Stage 3: Team Members Conduct Inquiry As the group members gather resources, ongoing decisions must be made as to what information should be included in the project. In this phase, it is important that students take detailed notes they will be able to share with group members. They should also keep in mind visual images that might help illustrate the concepts being summarized. For example, students might connect to the Tom Snyder laserdisc *The Great Solar System Rescue* and show clips that give graphical representations of the sizes of the planets.

Stage 4: Prepare the Final Report The students in each group must now map out the project. Each group member can take on a specific role, such as being responsible for the graphics, entering the text, connecting the visuals, or developing the navigation system. Or each student can take responsibility for one planet feature, such as the makeup of the atmosphere, and be responsible for organizing all of the information sources related to that feature. When each group has its planet report put together, the class as a whole can decide how to integrate the different team projects. In what order should the planets be presented? What kind and how many introductory screens are needed? How will the project end?

Stage 5: Present the Final Report The students in the class can view the finished project and question group members about information that may not be clear or that seems of special interest. The project can then be shared with other classes or parents. The project could be recorded on a videotape and saved in the library for future classes to use as a resource.

Stage 6: Evaluation It is important to understand that assessment does not come into play only at the end of the project. The teacher should meet periodically with the groups and discuss what is happening. What kind of resources have been gathered? How was the information organized? How were decisions made as to what information should be included? Who took responsibility for what? What difficulties have been encountered, and how have group members attempted to solve problems? What suggestions do the group members have to improve future projects? ✳

THE HYPERCOMPOSITION DESIGN MODEL

A CTIVE
C OOPERATION
T HEME-BASED
I NTEGRATED
V ERSATILE
E VALUATION

Hypermedia projects as content-area learning experiences

The hypercomposition design model (Lehrer, 1993; Lehrer, Erickson & Connell, 1994) provides a concrete way to integrate many of the themes we have developed. It deals specifically with hypermedia projects as content-area learning experiences and comfortably incorporates meaningful learning, cooperative learning, knowledge as design, and many other themes we have emphasized. The model is intended to guide teachers in the implementation of hypermedia projects. Although we feel it is important to offer concrete ideas that teachers can relate to, we are not suggesting that teachers must implement projects exactly as we have described. Examples and models should provide you with principles, strategies, and ideas. Your own experiences will determine how you integrate these elements into classroom practice.

General framework of this model

The hypercomposition design model was developed by observing and interviewing students as they completed hypermedia projects. The observations were then incorporated into a general framework to help other teachers facilitate hypermedia projects. The general framework for the model was based on a widely accepted model of the writing process (Flower and Hayes, 1981; Hayes and Flower, 1980) and shares many features with the model for group investigations you have just encountered. To create guidelines for hypermedia design, Lehrer extended the writing process model (see writing process, Chapter 5, pages 167 through 169) to include the generation of knowledge (it is not assumed that hypermedia authors have already learned what they will eventually present), attention to the special features of hypermedia, and the requirements of collaborative authorship. Note that hypermedia design is not proposed as a strictly linear process. In general, authors do work from the beginning to the end of a project, but a good deal of looping back occurs as work at later stages reveals the weaknesses of work completed at earlier stages. The model proposes that projects incorporate the major elements of planning, transforming and translating, evaluating, and revising.

PLANNING

Planning format of hypermedia projects

The topics teachers propose to guide their students' hypermedia projects are usually broad. The intent is to allow the members of student groups to explore a bit and then concentrate on what interests them. In the initial planning stage, group members should attempt to define major topics, establish the basic format of the presentation, and work out how the group will function.

It is very possible that students will be so inexperienced with the general topic or with group processes that the group will be unable to make effective decisions. In this case, the teacher must offer advice. You may tell students to

Spotlight on Assessment

Evaluating Projects

For authentic tasks to achieve their potential benefits, student performance must be evaluated in ways that students both find informative and perceive as fair. The information in this box presents two assessment devices you might use to communicate expectations to students, guide your evaluation of projects, and communicate feedback to students. Please understand that the specific components of these assessment devices (some authors have used terms such as the *assessment rubrics* or *analysis guides* in a similar way) will vary with the nature of the project and with what you want to emphasize. What you want to emphasize might also be worked out in the project planning stage through negotiation with your students.

To provide a context for this discussion, let's propose a sample project:

> *Task:* Create a HyperStudio stack that presents your team's analysis and recommendation regarding the problem of beverage container recycling. This stack will be viewed by the general public in the city library and will urge the public to support the recycling plan you propose.

We will gloss over all of the activities required of you to facilitate this project and get right to how you might create useful assessment devices.

Continua of Descriptors Generating continua of descriptors allows you to specify the competence areas to be used in the assessment process and to define specific levels of accomplishment within each competence area (Tierney, Carter, and Desai, 1991). In implementing this approach, it is useful to create a form to clearly present the assessment guidelines and communicate areas of strength and weakness. The form might take the following general structure.

Project Title		
Strong Performance		**Needs Improvement**
	Competency 1	
Descriptor 1A	Descriptor 1B	Descriptor 1C
	Competency 2	
Descriptor 2A	Descriptor 2B	Descriptor 2C
	Competency 3	
Descriptor 3A	Descriptor 3B	Descriptor 3C
	. . .	

Since one of the goals in creating this type of form is to present information concisely, you might feel it is necessary to add material in which the descriptors are laid out in more detail.

Now, let's develop continua of descriptors for our sample project. Again, in practice, we would urge you to develop assessment devices in collaboration with your students.

The project we have taken as an example might require evaluation in several general areas: domain knowledge and procedural skills, design skills, and team skills. Specific competencies could involve content coverage, argument communication, screen layout, graphics, user interface, involvement level of team members, and team support. Each area of competency would then be defined in terms of concrete levels of accomplishment; for example, for content coverage:

exhaustive coverage of multiple issues bearing on local recycling situation;

adequate presentation of main recycling issues; or

incomplete coverage of important issues.

The form built from these continua might look something like this.

Beverage Container Recycling Project

Strong Performance   **Needs Improvement**

Content Coverage

Strong Performance		Needs Improvement
Exhaustive coverage of multiple issues	Adequate coverage of issues	Incomplete coverage of essential issues

Argument Communication

Persuasive use of logic and data	Adequate presentation of position	Unpersuasive or unclear argument

Screen Layout

Interesting display with proper and predictable placement of buttons and graphics; text attractive and easy to read	Understandable positioning of buttons and graphics; text readable	Confusing or disorganized placement of screen elements; text difficult to read

Graphics

Informative and interesting, with proper placement	Adequate information value	Graphics often unrelated to message or improperly placed

User Interface

Easy to understand and functions without error	Error free	Confusing or occasionally fails

Team Involvement Level

All students contribute in meaningful way	All students active	Some students uninvolved

Team Support

Exceptional praise and assistance	Adequate praise for teammates	Inadequate support; bickering

Holistic Scoring Guide The holistic scoring method differs from the continua technique in the assignment of each project to a summary category. In making a holistic judgment, the evaluator could consider the same competency areas used in the continua method, but the descriptive statements associated with the competency areas have been organized to reflect different holistic levels of accomplishment. The evaluator has to determine which cluster of descriptors best describes the project and the process generating the project. The labels assigned to the categories are intended to reflect the nature of the holistic evaluation. Sets of terms—beginning, intermediate, advanced; exceptional, adequate, marginal—that seem suited to the nature of the project and to the type of feedback intended are used as category labels (Tierney, Carter, and Desai, 1991).

A form is useful in guiding evaluators and in providing expectations and feedback to students. A holistic guide for the beverage container recycling project might look something like this:

Beverage Container Recycling Project
Marginal Project

Projects may be classified as marginal because of the quality of the project or the process producing it. Marginal projects might be incomplete or inaccurate or might not function as they should. The process associated with a marginal project might not involve all team members or team members might treat each other poorly. Specific characteristics might include:

Project does not establish sufficient background describing general problem of waste disposal and specific problems associated with the disposal of beverage containers.

The proposed recycling plan is sketchy and difficult to understand.

The arguments supporting the recycling plan are not persuasive.

Placement of buttons is haphazard.

Text segments ramble and make key points difficult to identify.

Message of graphics is frequently unclear.

Unfamiliar user would find it difficult to use this product.

Buttons strand user without a way to move on or do not work at all.

Project was completed by only some of the team members.

Comments of team members were frequently critical or did not provide constructive advice.

Adequate Project

Projects are described as adequate when the projects indicate a reasonable understanding of the problem and propose a logical solution. The entire team should make some contribution to the completion of the project. Specific characteristics might include:

The project presents an overview of the problem of waste disposal and provides specific information on difficulties created by beverage container disposal.

A reasonable plan for beverage container recycling is proposed.

Buttons controlling the presentation appear in a consistent screen location.

Text segments are concise and informative.

Graphics contribute to the message of the presentation.

Use of the project requires little instruction.

Buttons and other control devices function as intended.

All students make a unique contribution to the completion of the project.

Team members are positive in remarks made to other team members.

Exceptional Project

Projects are described as exceptional when the information provided is extensive, the arguments advanced are particularly persuasive, and the proposed problem solution is insightful. The project should be interesting for viewers and exhibit exemplary design principles. Team members should work to bring out the best in each other team member. Specific characteristics might include:

The project provides an extensive overview of the problem of waste disposal and provides specific information on difficulties created by beverage container disposal. An effort has been made to provide information that defines the problem at the local level. The presentation is well organized and interesting.

Multiple suggestions are provided for recycling beverage containers. The argument for recycling is persuasive.

Buttons controlling the presentation appear in a consistent screen location.

Text segments are concise and informative.

Graphics are informative and interesting.

Graphics are used to increase the impact of the basic message.

Use of the project requires little instruction.

Buttons and other control devices function as intended.

All students make a unique contribution to the completion of the project.

Team members go out of their way to encourage and assist each other.

Team members teach each other needed skills.

✳

do some initial research and give them some sample sources of information. More specific decisions about topics and responsibilities may result from this initial investigation. This would be a great opportunity to propose a Web-Quest (see Chapter 6, page 218).

Students also might not function effectively in a group setting. Some students may dominate the decision making and leave others out. Others may not know how to listen, criticize, or accept criticism. The teacher might need to establish some guidelines for group functioning and monitor performance in this area.

The general tasks in planning the group project require the group to do the following:

◆ Develop major goals.
◆ Propose topics and the relationships among topics.
◆ Propose a presentation format to fit this organizational scheme.
◆ Establish team member responsibilities.

TRANSFORMING AND TRANSLATING

The transformation and translation phase consists of two general processes: the collection of information and the generation of knowledge.

Collecting Information

Search strategies

To collect information relevant to project goals, students must identify potentially relevant sources through the use of effective search strategies, locate the actual information relevant to project goals, and employ some process to retain the information for later use. Search strategies could encompass methods as diverse as electronic searches of the card catalog in the school or local library, use of the index in books covering the general area of interest, and asking questions of people who might know something about the topic. Once good sources are located, students might use photocopying, note taking, audio recording, or video recording to collect the information. These skills could be novel and some training might be necessary. Not all students will know how to operate a camcorder, for instance. Students might also need to learn effective note-taking skills.

Creating information

The potential for creating information should not be overlooked. Students can conduct original experiments or replicate established procedures to gather original data, develop questionnaires to give to students from their school or people from the community, or conduct structured interviews.

You will probably want to review samples of student work (notes, sources selected) to provide feedback and offer suggestions. One advantage of a project approach is the opportunity to help students learn to learn. Projects put more responsibility in the hands of students and also require them to engage in diverse self-guided activities. Projects provide great opportunities, but students will need guidance to profit from these opportunities. Students are likely to have the most experience processing information that a textbook author or a teacher has already organized and thought through for them. Be careful that students are not left to drift aimlessly as they encounter new expectations.

Generating Knowledge

Once they have gathered the raw information, students will need to organize, summarize, and interpret it. Some specific academic skills could be introduced at this point. Students might benefit from learning to outline, generate concept maps, or write summaries (Day, 1986). Also, some basic statistical procedures might be applied to quantifiable data. Perhaps these data can then be graphed in informative ways. This might be an opportunity to introduce students to spreadsheets and related data visualization capabilities. Students need to interpret what they have discovered. What are the major ideas? What are the causal factors that appear to be present? What alternative interpretations might be possible?

Organizing, summarizing, interpreting

The other major task of knowledge generation involves the publication of what has been learned. One decision is determining the format for publication. Desktop publishing, electronic slide shows, and hypermedia have been discussed previously and represent alternative formats. The decision you and your students make will depend on the type of information to be conveyed, the equipment and time available, and the students' skills.

To summarize, the stage of transforming and translating includes processes involved in the collection of information and the generation of knowledge. Students working on projects would:

♦ Search and collect information.
♦ Develop new information.
♦ Select and interpret information.
♦ Segment information.
♦ Link information.

EVALUATING AND REVISING

Authoring is not a one-pass process. Sometimes the product does not meet expectations. A variety of difficulties can occur within the product itself or in the way the product conveys information to users. In some cases, a problem is obvious as soon as a button does not take the user to the intended destination. In other cases, problems can be more subtle or even hidden from the author. For example, the author may assume an unrealistic level of background knowledge on the user's part and thus present new information too rapidly or briefly.

Understanding and fixing problems

Evaluation is the process of searching for all of these difficulties and many more. It is really impossible to list all of the things that might go wrong; even very experienced developers continually encounter new problems. We are always amazed when we attend technology demonstrations to see just how frequently experts encounter difficulties demonstrating the products they have created and worked with for hundreds of hours. We have found ourselves in

Focus

Experimenting with Different Structures and Linking Systems

Because students will likely have little experience in browsing or authoring hypermedia, teachers might want to consider the following suggestions for introducing the ideas of nodes and links. It is best to allow students to experiment with ways of partitioning and linking information before investing too much time in software development. Professional instructional designers use a process called **storyboarding**, in which they rough out the sequence of displays and activities to be incorporated in the

software (an example of a storyboard appears in Figure 10.10 on page 377). Students can do the same thing. They can represent nodes with sketches or brief statements entered on notecards. Each node might be thought of as the information the eventual user will view or hear at one time. These notecards can be tacked to a bulletin board and linked with lengths of yarn. It shouldn't be too difficult to imagine representing the different organizational structures presented earlier in this chapter in this manner. One interesting variation is to use Post-It notes instead of notecards. These notes can be easily positioned on a blackboard and connected with chalk lines. ✳

the same situation several times. Since problems seem unavoidable, here are some suggestions for how to make the problems surface so that you or your students can understand and fix them. Note that we use the term *problems* to refer to problems both in the software and in the content the software was developed to present.

Trying out products

◆ *Software developers can learn to test systematically all planned and unplanned actions within programs that have been created.* It is sometimes users' unintended actions that cause problems. It is very easy for a developer to become focused on what he or she thinks should happen and forget that the eventual user does not have this same insight. When confused or without the benefit of knowing exactly what to do, users may do something that was not intended and cause a problem. So test a product for the unanticipated. For example, if the user is asked to type a number into a box, try typing "one" and not just "1." If you developed this product, you probably assumed the user would use a digit and not a word to represent a number.

◆ *Developers can ask naive users to try out products and carefully observe what happens.* Do naive users try to do things that were not intended? Do naive users become confused or say that they cannot understand the ideas presented? Listen carefully to what users have to say. You probably do the same kind of thing with papers you write for college classes. You ask a classmate or a friend to read your paper and tell you what he or she thinks. Consider a hypermedia product as another way to inform or communicate, and ask others what they think.

◆ *Test out products on different equipment* (preferably the exact equipment your target audience will use). Different equipment is the cause of most difficulties experts encounter in novel situations. Programs have a nasty habit of not working exactly the same way on different machines or on machines using different versions of the operating system. Often the equipment used to develop software is more powerful (more memory, larger monitor) than the machines software users work on.

Asking experts' opinions

◆ *Finally, ask a content-area expert to review the product.* Commercial developers of educational software do this all the time. For example, if the product is in the area of history, history teachers and historians not associated with the project are asked to review it. As a classroom teacher, you might end up serving as the content-area expert responsible for this type of review. It might be useful to have several teachers involved in the review of hypermedia projects. One teacher might evaluate how effectively the product meets standards of effective communication (organization, clarity, grammar), and another might evaluate the factual accuracy and logic of arguments. Each of these procedures might identify limitations that the design group will want to take into account in upgrading the product's quality.

THE TEACHER'S ROLE IN THE DESIGN PROCESS

Now that you are familiar with some basic design principles, some of the fundamental ideas of cooperative learning, and at least one general model for student hypermedia projects, let's look at some of the implications of bringing such projects into your classroom. You may have already generated your own implications after considering some of the sample projects.

WORKS OF MIND

Learning by doing

For many teachers, incorporating projects will require adjustments in what they do and, in some cases, in what they teach. Perkins (1986), who advocates the concept of learning as design, justifies the need to engage students in a different type of learning activity this way. His concern is that schools seldom allow students to do "works of mind." Schools teach students about mathematics, history, and biology but do not allow students to *do* mathematics, history, or biology. One of the few exceptions Perkins notes to the principle of "learning about rather than doing" is in art. Students at most grade levels do works of art. Why? It seems that, as educators, we recognize that a design like a picture can exist at a very elementary level. Even kindergarten students draw, paint, and sculpt objects from Play-Doh. Most other content areas seem somehow different. We often cannot think of what an elementary design in biology or history would look like. One reason for this is the assumption that an accumulation of information is required before a work of some form is possible. In many cases, however, the nature of the problem is scalable, and background knowledge can be acquired. Students can design a history of their own families or study the ecology of their classroom aquarium. If second grade students need to know about the malva plant and the identity of marconium (the red liquid Pam Carlson's students observed dripping from the wings of the butterfly emerging from the chrysalis) to understand their observations of butterfly metamorphosis, this information can be acquired and used in the designs they construct to account for their observations.

Coaching small groups of students

Lehrer and his associates (Carver et al., 1992; Lehrer, 1993; Lehrer et al., 1994), as well as others (Brown, 1992; Harel, 1991; Harel and Papert, 1990; Pearlman, 1991; Toomey & Ketterer, 1995), have proposed that projects in which groups of students attempt to explain or teach with technology qualify as works of mind. In a typical classroom activity of this type, the teacher coaches small groups of students as they pursue projects that fall within some general domain. The general domain refers to the topic designated for study by the curriculum: the Civil War, life cycle of the butterfly, and so on. Individual projects prepared by different groups will pursue the general topic in different ways or will emphasize different aspects of the overall theme, depending on the interests and abilities of group members and the information students encounter as they research the general topic. To maintain a student focus, teachers should intervene to redirect students only after careful consideration. Instead of direct intervention, teachers would be more likely to influence students by asking leading questions such as "Why do we have historians? What do they do?" Carver et al. (1992) use Sheingold's (1991) phrase "adventurous teaching" to describe the tolerance teachers must exhibit to allow students the necessary freedom to construct knowledge. Students cannot truly function as junior biologists, historians, writers, or political advocates if teachers make key decisions for them.

Constructing knowledge

APPRENTICESHIP METHOD

If teachers do not transmit information and do not tightly control student activity, what do they do? It is useful to view the teacher's function as initiating students into the community of scholars appropriate to the area or areas being investigated (Lehrer, 1993). To develop domain-appropriate learning and thinking processes, students are engaged in tasks authentic to the domain within an apprenticeship relationship with the teacher and perhaps with other domain experts (people within the community). Students, as a result, experience activities as authentic tasks that might confront domain experts and acquire knowledge and problem-solving skills associated with these tasks. For example, a historian takes primary sources (original maps, diaries, letters, newspaper accounts, legal documents, pictures, personal interviews) and attempts to describe past events and explain past behaviors. The historian must locate sources, analyze the material for important information, integrate ideas into a logical account of behavior, and communicate an effective description and explanation of past events to others. Students can take on similar tasks using similar sources and engaging the same cognitive processes. The issues could resemble the topics covered in traditional textbooks (battles of the Civil War) or could involve something more unique or local in orientation (early education in your community—the first teacher, building, student characteristics). Often, activities are multidisciplinary because scholarship of this type frequently does not confine itself to a single traditional content area, such as reading, mathematics, or science.

Authentic tasks

Multidisciplinary activities

We discussed cognitive apprenticeship in Chapter 2. To review briefly, it concerns the development of cognitive skills and not the transmission of factual information. In developing cognitive skills, the role of the teacher shifts over time from demonstrating (modeling), to coaching the student through early efforts, to a more passive role in which the teacher may observe and intervene only occasionally. The coaching stage is especially critical. A key component of coaching is the provision of support devices, such as reminders,

Developing cognitive skills

conventions, or constraints that help the apprentice to approximate the complex behavior of the expert. When the skills to be learned are cognitive, it is also important to find some way to externalize these behaviors so that the internal cognitive behaviors can be observed and discussed. Often the expert must attempt to explain what he or she is thinking to provide the novice some awareness of internal behavior.

PROJECT QUALITY

The quality that should be expected of student-generated products is the subject of some debate. Some contend that students should develop only prototypes and not strive to produce products of high quality (D'Ignazio, 1990). This position might imply that students should learn only the most basic software design techniques and not spend time on embellishments or refinements. In some respects, it is clear that there is a diminishing return on time spent in polishing a presentation. However, there is also a somewhat different perspective. Much of our rationale for student projects includes the idea of involving students in authentic activities. A student's sense of scholarship and authorship comes with producing something of which he or she can be proud. Students know what a real newspaper, a real video production, and authentic computer software look like. Student designers want to develop projects others would use and appreciate. A realistic classroom goal is probably to familiarize students with some fundamental principles of design that apply to their particular project. These fundamental principles will vary with the nature of the project, the age and experience of the students, whether the project is an individual or a cooperative venture, and the teacher's goals.

Pride in software products

Realistic classroom goals

STUDENT PROJECTS AND RESTRUCTURING

Advocates of engaging students in sophisticated design projects often slip into arguments for restructuring schools (Lehrer et al., 1994; Thomas and Knezek, 1991). When educators talk about restructuring they are, in part, proposing changes in the curriculum, in the roles played by teachers, and in the learning activities provided for students (Thomas and Knezek, 1991). Certainly, design projects engage teachers and students in unique activities, have them play somewhat different roles, and use school time in different ways. Hypermedia design projects change the teacher's role from dispenser to facilitator. In many cases, students are expected to find information themselves and then construct knowledge from it. Students may encounter situations and discover information that teachers have not experienced directly. They may try to do

Changing roles for teachers and students

things that their teachers have not done. The information they use will not always be found in traditional textbooks or even in the school library. Often, it will be found outside the traditional school setting—in the community, biological habitats, work settings, and other nontraditional but content-appropriate settings. The activities of the student focus on gathering, assessing, integrating, and using this information. Projects based on these activities take schools into relatively unfamiliar terrain. More activities will be group based. Activities will have to be graded in different ways. Spending fifty minutes each day in the classroom may not provide the optimal setting for many activities. Traditional school practices are difficult to change, but some very exciting proposals seem to be emerging.

New terrain for schools

Using technology-based projects to explore content you might normally teach in a traditional manner will require flexibility on your part. You cannot expect to approach a project with the same high degree of structure possible with textbook-related instructional materials. Even when a project mimics an activity already implemented by another teacher or when it simply replicates a project you did with last year's class, each project is really an adventure in learning. You will likely find that some uncertainty is desirable and that a degree of flexibility creates a more active learning environment. Uncertainty provides opportunities for students to make decisions and allows you the opportunity to model problem-solving skills. Some degree of spontaneity is necessary. If students run into an idea that fascinates them, they should be encouraged to pursue this opportunity and find a way to integrate their experiences into the project.

Technology-based projects require flexibility

Modeling problem-solving skills

You have had an opportunity to encounter various aspects of project implementation in this textbook. At one point or another, you have been asked to consider how project activities might encourage more active involvement with content, to familiarize yourself with various software and hardware tools that might be used in project activities, to learn basic principles of design relevant to multimedia projects, and to consider planned social processes that might be useful in implementing cooperative projects. As you have progressed through the various topics in this textbook, new ideas may have caused you to recall and reconsider projects you first encountered some time ago. You may have found yourself recalling projects from earlier chapters when we discussed techniques such as scanning, video digitizing, and sound capture or when hypermedia and paint tools were presented. Now you have a better understanding of how those projects were created. The discussions of cooperative learning or design principles may also have encouraged you to reconsider some of these projects. You may already have judged some of the projects against basic standards of design or thought about more effective ways groups of students might have studied the same content areas. Examples represent raw information; we hope you have taken the opportunity to mentally work with these examples to create personal knowledge.

Encouraging more active involvement with content

STUDENT MULTIMEDIA PROJECTS

Practical issues in project implementation

We have devoted the rest of this chapter to some of the practical issues involved in implementing classroom projects. We first discuss the development of World Wide Web pages as an option for student projects. We then discuss an extended example of a hypermedia project developed using HyperCard.

STUDENT PROJECTS ON THE WEB

Web servers are more common

The number of schools capable of serving student Web projects is increasing at a tremendous rate. In early 1997, 1,070 districts encompassing 4,212 U.S. schools had Web servers (Collins, 1997). This does not mean that all of these schools were using their servers to publish student projects, but the capability was there.

The Web offers an alternative outlet for multimedia projects. Most of the projects we have described throughout this book could have been implemented in some form as Web pages. Web projects also offer some powerful and unique opportunities. The capacity to link your multimedia projects with other Internet resources can be useful. The process of searching the Internet for good resources serves as a way to involve students actively with content. The Web also allows an efficient means for collaboration with students from other locations.

Mastery of basics builds confidence

We would like teachers to concentrate on developing stimulating Web projects and on the classroom skills necessary to use such projects to engage students in active learning. These goals are unlikely to be achieved until teachers feel confident they can help their students develop Web materials and get these materials on a Web server. An understanding of some Web basics and the mastery of a couple of basic tools should provide this confidence. Acquiring such knowledge is productive for both teachers and students. As we have suggested in our discussion of other forms of multimedia, the skills necessary to produce Web-based multimedia can be learned in a reasonable amount of time and can be used repeatedly as an efficient and creative way to explore and process course content.

Minimalist approach

In the pages that follow we describe Web materials and the mechanics of Web authoring accurately but simply. The capabilities of the Web are expanding daily and some functions are quite complex. We cannot hope to help you grasp the entire potential of authoring for the Web, but we will give you the background necessary to do useful work. We propose that you adopt a minimalist approach to Web multimedia (D'Ignazio, 1996)—learn as few new software tools and as few new technology skills as possible. If this experience is productive and exciting, there will be plenty of related techniques and ideas you can explore.

Components of Web pages

Think of Web pages as consisting of a combination of (1) multimedia elements (text, graphics, sounds, movies, and such), (2) a special command language called **hypertext markup language (HTML)** that informs the browser how to organize these multimedia elements for display, and (3) links allowing access to other pages. You already have considerable knowledge of multimedia elements from previous chapters. You have also learned that an Internet link can be expressed in the form of a URL (see Chapter 6, page 205). The element of Web authoring you have yet to experience is HTML.

You have already used one type of markup language, perhaps without realizing it. If you have word processing experience, you have probably underlined and bolded text, centered and enlarged a segment of text to serve as the title for a paper, and perhaps inserted a picture at a specific location in your document. You did not type any commands to make text bold (the HTML commands would be <B> text </B>) or to position a graphic (the HTML commands might be <CENTER><IMG SRC="name.GIF" WIDTH="261" HEIGHT="110" ALIGN=bottom NATURALSIZEFLAG="3"><CENTER>), but you did ask the word processing program to perform that function. For example, you probably selected a segment of text and then used a keyboard command (Command-b) or the equivalent menu option to bold text. The commands to create bold text on the screen and on the final printed version of your document were inserted in the word processing file you created. Although the commands are not visible, the results are.

HTML tags

You can now create Web documents in exactly the same way. As you will see, certain Web authoring programs allow you to control the appearance of a Web page by positioning multimedia elements on a blank page and manipulating various aspects of their appearance (e.g., size, justification, and text appearance). The markup language that creates this appearance is not present on the screen, but it is saved in the file that is eventually sent to the machine that serves your Web pages. The commands that are not visible to the user but are interpreted by the browser are called **tags.** You could also create the same file by entering all of the markup tags and the text content of the Web page directly from the computer keyboard. There are some reasons you might want to do this (more options become available or control of screen appearance is more precise), but the time required to learn the unique tags necessary to perform these unique functions is not worthwhile for most individuals.

BASIC FEATURES AND SKILLS

One way to help you understand the possibilities and demands of authoring for the Web is to outline some of the fundamental skills student authors should have. Think of these as the building blocks of Web pages. We propose that by combining these components in different ways, students will be able to create a wide variety of projects. The following is a list of actions and a brief description of how each action is implemented. Several Web authoring programs are listed at the end of this chapter. All of the programs we have included and several more we did not will be capable of doing the following without requiring the user to enter HTML tags:

Essential page construction skills

◆ Set background color—select menu option and then select color from palette to control page color
◆ Add text to page—type or open a text-only file created by some other application
◆ Set size of headings—select text with mouse and then select heading size from menu to create bold page headings of different sizes
◆ Create lists—select lines of text and then select menu option to create hierarchical lists
◆ Add graphic, sounds, and movies to page—drag image file (sound file or Quicktime movie file) to page and drop or open file using menubar option
◆ Link text or graphic to other pages—select text or graphic, then use menu option and select file for link; for pages at other sites—select text or graphic, then use menu option to type in URL for link
◆ Horizontal rule—use menu option to draw horizontal line to separate areas of the page

The techniques described here were used to create the page in Figure 10.8 from two graphics files and a text file. (*Note:* The logo at the top of the page is a graphic image created in another program.) Some comments have been added to the figure to point out noteworthy features. All underlined text and the smaller graphic serve as links to other Web pages. When the Web authoring program saves the page, the resulting HTML file consists of the text, the HTML tags, and information that will allow a browser to load and position the graphics and follow a link to another location. To make this information available to users, the HTML file and the two graphics files would have to be loaded to a server. We won't explain what is necessary to actually operate a server or how to load files to the server—operating the server requires some computer experience and is usually left to someone with special training (see Emerging Technology: Personal Web Servers for a different point of view). Loading files is not difficult, but the technique will vary with the kind of server a school uses.

FIGURE 10.8   A Sample Web Page Showing Common Page Elements

The raw HTML document responsible for what you see in Figure 10.8 looks like this:

```
<HTML>
<HEAD>
    <TITLE>North Dakota Wild</TITLE>
</HEAD>
<BODY>
<CENTER><IMG SRC="pics/ID.GIF"</CENTER>
<BR>
<H1><CENTER>Learning About the Field Biology of North Dakota
</CENTER></H1>
<BR>
Host: <A HREF="/dept/grabe">Mark Grabe</A>
<BR>
<HR>
<H3>Contents</H3>
<UL>
<LI><A HREF="instmat.html">North Dakota Project Wild</A>
<LI>North Dakota Outdoors Media
    <UL>
    <LI><A HREF="media.html#anchor37399">Articles from North Dakota
Outdoors Magazine</A>
    <LI><A HREF="media.html#anchor38708">Features from North Dakota
Outdoors Television</A>
    </UL>
<LI><A HREF="http://www.state.nd.us/gnf/">Official North Dakota Game
and Fish Homepage</A>
<LI><A HREF="others.html">Other Related Web Sites</A>
</UL>
<BR>
<A HREF="keyhead.html"><IMG SRC="pics/rattleS.GIF">North Dakota
Reptile and Amphibian Identification Project</A><BR>
<BR>
<BR>
<A HREF="http://ndwild.psych.und.nodak.edu/owlshome.html">Outdoor
Wildlife Learning Sites (OWLS)</A> - The newest NDWild project focuses
on the development of habitats as service and learning projects. Learn about
this opportunity. This resource is in the early phases of development, but you
are certainly welcome to take a look.<BR>
</BODY>
</HTML>
```

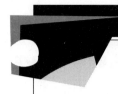

Emerging Technology

Personal Web Servers

Once you or your students have authored Web pages, the final task is to make them available to users of the Internet. Making Web material available requires access to a Web server. It is possible your district may have direct access to the Internet but not be operating a server. It is also possible that a server is available, but creating accounts for individual classrooms is something the Internet administrator does not regard as a high priority. Actually, most individuals responsible for a school's Internet server would probably be very interested in helping you make class projects available. However, there may be something even better than taking advantage of this sophisticated equipment and the expert's willingness to help. What if you and your class could run your own server right in your classroom? If you have a dedicated connection to the Internet running into your classroom, a personal Web server would give you and your class this capability.

Personal Web servers share several attributes:

◆ Low cost: Commercial versions are available for less than $50. There are also free products, but most were designed as dedicated servers.

◆ Limited hardware requirements: Personal Web servers are designed to run in the background on a normally configured computer. The computer can be used for routine applications and will serve Web pages when sufficient memory resources are available.

◆ Limited output: Personal Web servers respond more slowly and can service fewer users. Some of the more sophisticated data-processing options available with dedicated servers and more sophisticated software may not be available.

Personal Web servers were developed for small business applications, often for internal communication within a company (sometimes called an **Intranet**). A personal Web server could be used in exactly the same way within a school building. However, if a machine has a permanent Internet address (a dedicated connection), that machine is part of the Internet and anyone with a browser can access it. The same machine you use to write tests and send notes home to parents can make projects created by your students available over the Internet.

This would seem to be the type of application that will find many uses within educational settings. Imagine the potential of posting assignments, displaying student work, or offering a list of your favorite Web sites from your desktop. It is likely that the basic operating systems for the computers of the future will come with this capability built in. If you can't wait, we list several existing products at the conclusion of the chapter. ✳

THE BUTTERFLY COLLECTION: AN EXTENDED EXAMPLE OF A COLLABORATIVE STUDENT DESIGN PROJECT

How one teacher thinks about integrating technology

A
C
T HEME
I
V
E

We want to use one more classroom example to bring together many of the themes we have considered separately. Implementation of a successful classroom project requires that many issues be considered. We have used many examples from Pam's classroom because we feel the collection will help you better understand how one experienced and creative teacher thinks about integrating technology. The project to be described here came one year after the Ocean Project (see Chapter 1). Again, this project was one of many activities contributing to a multidisciplinary unit, this time developed around the theme of butterflies. At the elementary school level, a theme like this allows the teacher to involve students with a variety of language arts activities, music, visual arts, science activities, problem-solving activities, and social experiences.

GETTING THE PROJECT STARTED

Pam Carlson introduced the class to the idea of a multimedia project by showing them the Ocean Project and describing how last year's class had used the Ocean Project to show their parents what they had learned about ocean life. This year the class was studying butterflies, but maybe they could think of a way to create a similar project. Pam promised to bring in lots of books from the library and find a videotape the class could watch. They would do many different things, not all of them on the computer. They would read a lot, write stories, and draw pictures. Pam said she even knew some songs they could learn. Maybe the class would be able to come up with some ideas of their own. What did they want to know about butterflies? One student did bring in a monarch caterpillar that the class kept in a glass jar and watched as it spun a chrysalis.

To get the class started on their multimedia project, Pam provided scanned pictures. Students were asked to choose a butterfly to work on and learn about. Pam told the students they could color the pictures using Kid Pix and then write something interesting about each butterfly. The students were given the names of the butterfly pictures and then had to use the resources available in the classroom to find a colored picture and learn what they could about each butterfly. Keep in mind that these are second grade students, and research skills at this grade level are quite basic. Students mostly accumulate a list of facts they find interesting. One thing Pam tried to communicate to the students was that they were to try not to copy and were to try to write as much as they could using their own words. She reports an interesting strategy some students used to try to meet her expectations. The students would read a little bit and then close the book while they wrote so they would be less tempted to copy.

Pam wanted to use the basic structure of the Ocean Project but to add some new features that would make the experience more valuable to her students. The Ocean Project was developed in a format we have described as a linear multimedia presentation, or slide show. One of the limitations Pam had encountered with this design was that there was no way to go directly to a specific part of the presentation. If a student wanted to show her parents the work she had done, the only option was to start the presentation and wait. The design of the project also prevented students from exploring the work of classmates. Students seemed to like to show each other what they had done, and the first project Pam's class had completed did not allow students this kind of control. The first project also contained no actual text. Students did write, in the process of preparing the script for their recorded comments, but no text was included in the presentation. Again, because students enjoyed reviewing each other's work, Pam felt it would be valuable to have the text available for them to read. Finally, she wanted the project to include some of the other important things the class had learned from the theme unit. The project could continue to summarize the individual investigations of the students, but also emphasize core ideas the students had learned as a group.

WHILE THE PROJECT IS UNDERWAY

As students investigated individual butterflies and discussed the information they were finding, they made some decisions about what each butterfly report would look like. Each report would include a color image of the butterfly, a brief written summary of student research about the butterfly, and a map showing the butterfly's normal range. Students seemed interested in seeing whether different butterflies might be found where they lived, and including range maps was a way to provide this information. Working with maps added another dimension to the learning experience. Students created their butterfly images by coloring scanned images in Kid Pix. The individual reports were developed in HyperCard. One card was used to display the butterfly, and a second card to present the text information and the range map (Figure 10.9). Students also used the audio record feature in HyperCard to make a recording of their descriptive information.

When most of the butterfly reports were finished and students had completed the other activities associated with the butterfly unit, it was time to work on the final project. Pam talked with the students about what they had learned about butterflies and what they would like to present to their parents. Obviously, the final project would incorporate the individual butterfly reports. What else? Students liked the way the Ocean Project had included the

FIGURE 10.9   Butterfly Information and Range Map

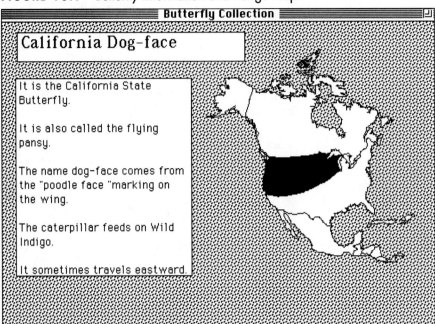

pictures of the students as part of the final presentation. This year's class wanted to see if there was a way to include their pictures, too.

One major thing students had studied was the series of stages in the process by which a butterfly developed. They had even learned a song to help them remember the stages. Thinking about the song gave them an idea. The students could record the song on the computer and show pictures of the different stages of metamorphosis at the same time. They could draw pictures of the egg, caterpillar, chrysalis, and butterfly and then show the pictures using the song as background.

One final question remained: How to create an interesting system allowing users of the class project to view individual butterflies? The answer came from another experience that had been part of the unit: an insect collection. Pam's father is a scientist and trains science teachers at the local university. He brought an insect collection to show the class. Scientists who study insects, entomologists, often mount insects on pins and place the mounted and labeled insects in glass-covered boxes. Later the idea emerged to use an insect collection as a menu allowing access to the individual butterflies in the project. A screen display could be developed that looked like an insect collection, and users could select a butterfly by clicking on the insect.

Now the task was to work these various elements into a presentation. When putting together a presentation, it is often useful to draw a rough sketch

FIGURE 10.10 Butterfly Project Storyboard

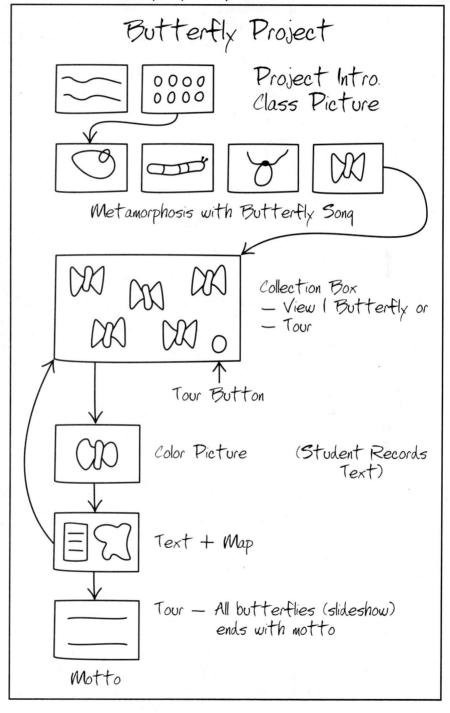

of a project to work out the details of how the parts will fit together and what the individual elements will look like. You will recall that this process is called storyboarding. The storyboard in Figure 10.10 includes sketches and notes that define critical features of the final Butterfly Project.

The Butterfly Project begins with an introductory screen and a digitized copy of the class picture. The introductory images are followed immediately by individual colored pictures of an egg, caterpillar, chrysalis, and butterfly accompanied by the butterfly song. These pictures were scanned from a student drawing and painted with Kid Pix. The composite drawing appears in Figure 10.11.

FIGURE 10.11 Student Drawing of Metamorphosis Stages

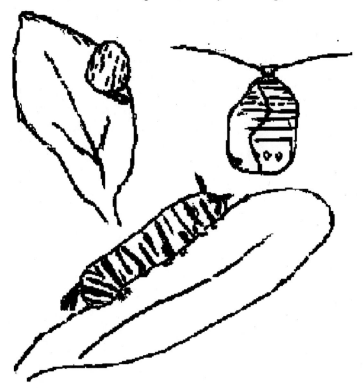

The insect collection box shown in Figure 10.12 serves as a convenient organizational system for users. The butterfly collection can be viewed as a narrated slide show by clicking on the "tour button" (lower right), or the material describing individual butterflies can be viewed by clicking on the small image of a particular butterfly. The small image of each butterfly is covered by an invisible button (see Chapter 8, page 290) and that button is linked (see Chapter 8, page 295) to the other cards providing information about the butterfly.

FIGURE 10.12 User Interface Based on Butterfly Collection Box

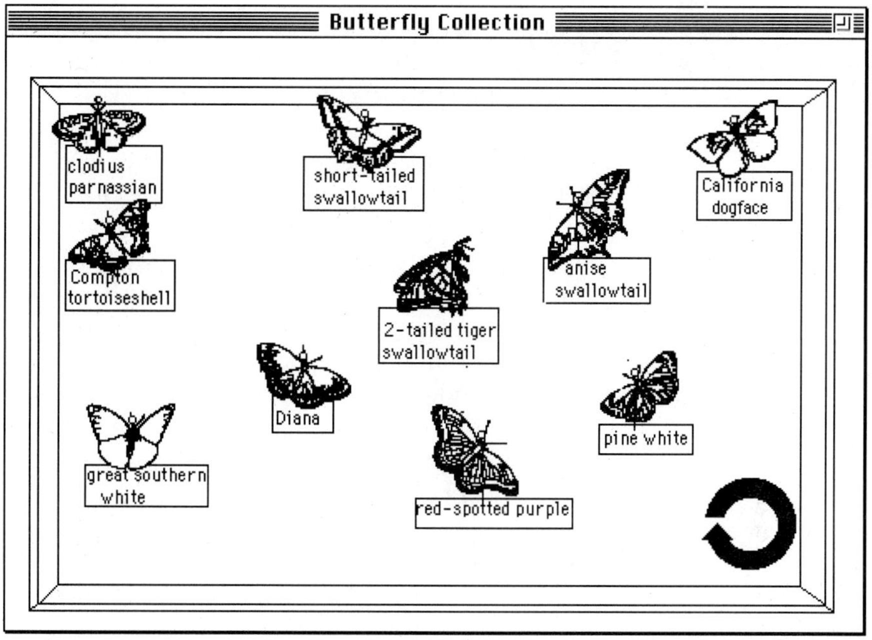

The slide show version of the butterfly tour concludes with a project motto (Figure 10.13) that provides a good message for students of any age: Learning never ends!

FIGURE 10.13 Class Motto and Project Conclusion

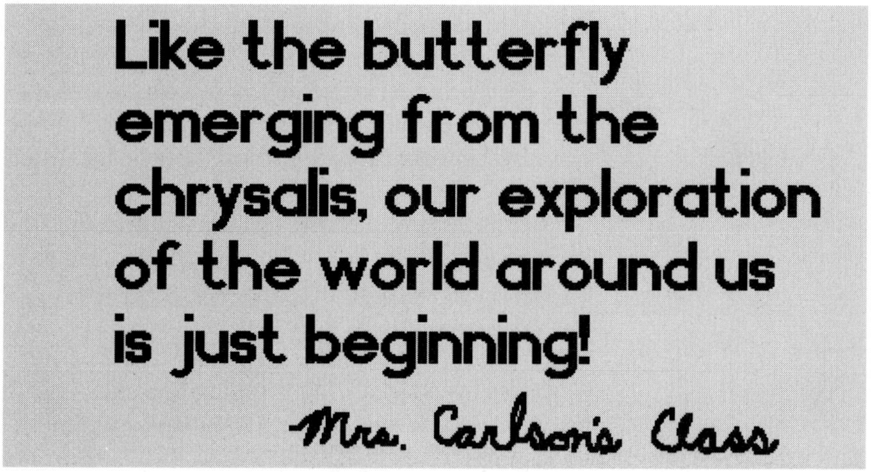

Like the butterfly emerging from the chrysalis, our exploration of the world around us is just beginning!

Mrs. Carlson's Class

SUMMARY

This chapter attempts to integrate two views of design: design of products and design of personal knowledge. Design involves constructing or structuring a product for a purpose. For computer software, the purpose might be to help the user accomplish some task more efficiently, learn something, or have an entertaining experience. The design of knowledge also stresses the connection between structure and function. Knowledge as design helps the learner do something. Without purpose, learning becomes focused on the accumulation of information and not on its application.

Student-authored hypermedia represents a concrete integration of the design of knowledge and the design of a public product. In this unique situation, students are designing knowledge in order to generate a product. The hypermedia product provides a purpose for the hypermedia author's construction of personal knowledge.

To create products that are informative, interesting, and easy to use and understand, hypermedia authors should attend to the organization of content, basic principles of graphic design, clear writing, and the development of an effective user interface.

Hypermedia design projects might be considered a special application of a cooperative learning model called group investigation. In a group investigation, students identify aspects of a general theme that interest them and then join teams to study these individual topics. The teams are expected to determine how they will gather, analyze, and summarize information relevant to their topic. Individual students are expected to assume some independence in contributing to this process. Each team identifies the essence of what they have learned and presents this information to the entire group.

Hypermedia design involves a complex set of processes that can involve young hypermedia authors in the construction of personal knowledge. Learning is situated in a task that provides a purpose for student activities. This design model presented here bears a strong resemblance to a popular model for the writing process. Identifiable components of this model include planning, information collection, knowledge generation, and evaluation/revision.

Within this model, the teacher involves the student as an apprentice and takes responsibility for coaching both the knowledge design and the hypermedia design skills. In the early stages of a project and especially when working with inexperienced designers, the teacher may be required to provide some direct instruction, demonstrate procedural skills, model cognitive processes by externalizing thinking behavior, and stimulate cognitive behavior with leading questions. As students become more experienced and the project takes shape, teachers will play a less direct role. Students will take on a great deal of responsibility for their own learning.

REFLECTING ON CHAPTER 10

Activities

◆ Locate a source for freeware or shareware instructional hypermedia. Critique one of these programs using the organizational, graphic, text, and interface design principles outlined in this chapter.

◆ Briefly outline a potential hypermedia project. Develop a holistic scoring guide and continua of descriptors appropriate to assessing the project and important project-related skills.

◆ Develop a storyboard for a simple hypermedia project appropriate to a content area that interests you.

◆ Use a Web authoring program to create a Web page outlining the requirements and activities of your class. Link to relevant resources on the Internet.

Key Terms

branch   *(p. 343)*
button   *(p. 350)*
cooperative learning   *(p. 353)*
design   *(p. 339)*
graphic design   *(p. 345)*
grid   *(p. 346)*
group investigation   *(p. 354)*
hypertext markup language (HTML)
   (p. 369)
individual accountability   *(p. 353)*
Intranet   *(p. 373)*
knowledge as design   *(p. 338)*

linear design   *(p. 342)*
link   *(p. 342)*
map   *(p. 350)*
menu   *(p. 350)*
network structure   *(p. 344)*
node   *(p. 342)*
storyboarding   *(p. 362)*
tag   *(p. 369)*
task specialization methods   *(p. 353)*
team rewards   *(p. 353)*
tree structure   *(p. 343)*
user interface   *(p. 349)*

Hypermedia Design Principles

Resources to Expand Your Knowledge Base

Apple Computer. (1989). *Hypercard stack design guidelines.* Reading, MA: Addison-Wesley. This source offers concrete advice on all aspects of hypermedia design. The principles are of value no matter what authoring environment you use.

Web Design Principles

Horton, W., Taylor, L., Ignacio, A., & Hoft, N. (1996). *Web page design cookbook.* New York: Wiley.

Wilson, S. (1995). *World wide web design guide.* Indianapolis: Hayden Books.

Resources for Cooperative Learning

Johnson, D., Johnson, R., & Holubec, E. (1991). *Cooperation in the classroom* (rev. ed.). Edina, MN: Interaction Book Company.

Putnam, J. (Ed.). (1993). *Cooperative learning and strategies for inclusion: Celebrating diversity in the classroom.* Baltimore, MD: Brookes Publishing.

Sharan, Y., & Sharan, S. (1992). *Expanding cooperative learning through group investigation* (3rd ed.). New York: Teachers College Press.

Slavin, R. (1991). *Student team learning: A practical guide to cooperative learning.* (3rd ed.). Washington, DC: National Education Association.

Thematic Instruction, the Project Approach, and Project Ideas

Fredericks, A., Meinbach, A., & Rothlein, L. (1993). *Thematic units: An integrated approach to teaching science and social studies.* New York: HarperCollins.

Handler, M., Dana, A., & Moore, J. (1995). *Hypermedia as a student tool.* Englewood, CO: Teachers Idea Press.

Harel, I. (1991). *Children as designers.* Norwood, NJ: Ablex.

Katz, L., & Chard, S. (1989). *Engaging children's minds: The project approach.* Norwood, NJ: Ablex.

Perkins, D. (1986). *Knowledge as design.* Hillsdale, NJ: Erlbaum.

Teachers might review recent copies of *Electronic Learning* and *Learning and Leading with Technology* to find examples of student-generated hypermedia projects.

Web-Authoring Software

The following products allow the creation of Web pages in a manner similar to that described in this chapter.

Adobe PageMill is available for the Macintosh from Adobe Systems Incorporated, P.O. Box 6458, Salinas, CA 93912.

Claris HomePage is available for Macintosh and Windows computers from Claris Corporation, 5201 Patrick Henry Drive, Box 58168, Santa Clara, CA 95052.

Personal Web Servers

Examples of commercial personal Web server software include *Web for One* from RESNOVA, 5011 Argosy Drive, Suite 13, Huntington Beach, CA 92649; and *Personal WebStar* from Quarterdeck's Starnine, 2550 Ninth Street, Suite 112, Berkeley, CA 94710. Both products run on desktop Macintosh computers.

Looking at Issues
and Looking Ahead

In Part Three, *we look at issues and concerns related to using educational technology responsibly. These issues include equity, copyright laws, and computer viruses. Problems can arise in these areas and you will explore ways to create solutions to them. You will also have an opportunity to reflect on what you have learned about educational technology and meaningful learning and to look toward the future and its many promises in education.*

Chapter 11

Being a Responsible User of Technology in Classrooms

ORIENTATION

This chapter discusses three topics related to responsible use of educational technology: equity, copyright law, and computer viruses. Several other topics—harassment, access to inappropriate materials, the invasion of privacy, and the willful destruction of property—are also mentioned to alert you to these additional issues. After you have completed your study of the three major topics, you should be able to explain the basic concerns and list some concrete suggestions for teachers or schools to deal with them. As you read, look for answers to the following questions:

FOCUS QUESTIONS

◆ What inequities exist in student access to technology and in the ways students are allowed to use technology? What factors appear responsible for these inequities?

◆ What adaptations can be implemented to make technology available to students with special needs?

◆ What is copyright law designed to protect? What are key areas in which copyright law should inform teachers using technology? What options are available to teachers who would like to duplicate protected materials?

◆ What can teachers and students do to limit the loss of data and programs to computer viruses and hardware or software malfunctions?

THE EXPERIENCES OF A TECHNOLOGY FACILITATOR

As we mentioned in the Preface, one of us is a technology facilitator for a district of 9,500 students. In other school districts, Cindy Grabe might be called a computer coordinator. A computer coordinator works with administrators, the school board, teachers, and students to see that technology is integrated into the district's curriculum. A coordinator works with others to develop the schools' technology policies and witnesses firsthand how well these policies are implemented. Here are Cindy's comments on situations she has encountered that relate to responsible computer use.

Seeing that technology is integrated into the curriculum

PROTECTING DATA FILES

Protecting files saved on our district network has occasionally been a problem. We have a network security system that establishes a separate folder on the server for each teacher and student, and then protects each folder with a password. The idea of a network security system is to give each user a private place to save his or her work. A very large hard disk that we call a file server is connected to the local network in each building and provides the capacity to save all the files. This system is convenient for students because they don't have to carry their files around on disks and it avoids problems such as misplacing disks or forgetting to bring them to class.

Network security systems

Students always seem to find a way around the security protection. I remember one very upset fifth grade teacher calling me about the projects her students had been working on. The students had been creating a number of Kid Pix pictures for a class project. Someone had found a way to breach the security system. That student then opened some of another student's work, used the mixer tool in Kid Pix to scramble the pictures, and then saved the messed-up picture in place of the originals (see Figure 11.1).

A similar problem occurred with the work of a junior high school English teacher. This teacher was new to computers and very excited after completing some of our basic skills classes. He had used his new skills to develop materials for a unit on Charles Dickens and had the work saved in his folder. Students got into the folder, deleted his work, and replaced it with a note they thought was funny.

Direct access to file folders

One of the students showed us what the problem was. The security system we had purchased prevented direct access to file folders, but did not prevent anyone from starting an application and then accessing the folder through the application. Once you were in a word processing program, you could open all of the folders and any word processing document on the local file server. You might well wonder why the software developer would overlook something as basic as that. The company supplying our security system fixed the problem in their next update.

Most of our problems are not caused by weaknesses in our security system or by student hackers. They are actually caused by students and teachers who allow students to use their passwords. Students tell other students their passwords so that other students can place files in their folders, just like passing notes in class. Teachers sometimes allow a trusted student to perform some work for them. The student must have a password to work on the teacher's files, and the teacher might just give a student the password, which allows entry into all folders, as well as other privileges. If passwords get circulated, it can be very difficult to identify how and where problems originate. Teachers sometimes fail to appreciate the difficulties that seemingly innocent actions can cause. Having to emphasize security is a nuisance and makes everything a little more complicated. Unfortunately, there are always a few kids who will cause problems if they get a chance.

Importance of emphasizing security

FIGURE 11.1   Scrambled Pictures in a Student's Project

DIFFERENTIAL ACCESS TO TECHNOLOGY

Allowing more students access to computers

I'm not sure I've observed a lot of blatant discrimination in the way our teachers use technology, but there is one approach used by a number of teachers that ends up producing the same effect. Some teachers make heavy use of technology either as a reward or as a way to keep some of their more able students occupied. Teachers may have a signup system to determine when students are allowed to work on the classroom computers; students are not allowed to put their names on the list until all of the assigned work has been completed. Some students just don't get to put their names on the list, or when they do finish their work, the day is nearly over, and they seldom get a chance to have some unstructured time on the computers. All students may work on certain expected activities, such as writing, but beyond assigned activities, student time on the computer can vary drastically.

SOFTWARE COPYRIGHT VIOLATIONS

Most students respect copyright policies

We work hard to make sure only legal software is available on our network. We want to maintain a good working relationship with the companies supplying our software. Sometimes copyright violations are malicious. We found one situation in which a middle school student had loaded over 50 megabytes of pirated software to a server. There were games and expensive application programs of every possible type. The student had obtained a privileged password in some way and simply brought disks of programs to the lab. Other students could use the programs or make copies. Students are supervised in the labs, but we do make a large number of programs available and it isn't always possible for the people working in the labs to know when the district owns a program and when it doesn't. But when arcade games start showing up on the lab machines, it's obvious something is up. An incident of this magnitude is rare, however, and most students respect our copyright policy.

Some copyright problems occur because teachers don't have a lot of experience with the law and don't think about what they're doing. I remember one situation in which a group of special education teachers had received a grant. They decided to spend some of their money on software they felt would be beneficial to their students. The teachers wanted to be efficient, so they carefully selected software so that different buildings did not purchase the same packages. The teachers felt they were cooperating to make their money go as far as possible. We had to tell them that they would not be allowed to load the software on each other's machines because that would be a violation of copyright law. Instead we suggested that, to share resources, they might purchase CDs and then develop a system whereby teachers could check the CDs out of the special education office. Since copies of each CD are not saved on multiple machines, this type of sharing would be allowable.

STUDENT ACCESS TO QUESTIONABLE MATERIAL

I remember getting a phone call one morning at breakfast from the education editor of the local newspaper. The district pays for a membership in Sendit, a state telecommunications server and connection to the Internet, and the editor wanted to know about the district's allowing students to access sexually explicit material through the network. Luckily, I was aware of the source the editor had heard about and explained that the state system did not really allow unrestricted student access to the Internet and that students certainly were not downloading pornographic pictures. One of the available services contained a number of electronic publications, one of which did contain explicit stories and poetry. When the article appeared, it discussed the Internet and the educational potential of this resource. It also discussed the issue of free speech and how this issue should be addressed by educational institutions using a resource not specifically intended for students. Since students working through the state system have only controlled access to the Internet, the services available can be restricted. Access to some of the electronic publications was eventually eliminated.

Controlled access to the Internet

With the addition of direct Internet access, issues of responsibility have become even more acute. An initial decision was made to purchase a filtering system so that we could control the material students could access, but we learned that even filtering systems are not perfectly reliable. This led to a legal concern: If we take responsibility for protecting students from objectionable content, are we liable when the protection system fails? The school board sought an opinion from a legal advisor who claimed that the area was still too new to provide a definitive answer. He suggested that we contact our insurance company to see what they would suggest. That is the kind of advice that will really put people at ease. We were eventually told that although we could not guarantee that students wouldn't be exposed to inappropriate material, the district had taken reasonable steps to protect the students and was operating in "good faith."

Filtering is never perfect

RECOGNIZING GRAY AREAS IN RESPONSIBLE USE

Unless you already have some experience working with technology in a school setting, you may be surprised to learn just how frequently problems of the type we just described actually occur. Unfortunately, you occasionally see some of your colleagues and students engaged in these kinds of behaviors. Not all of your experiences will concern activities that are illegal. Perhaps you will just witness behavior that some may regard as being in poor taste or somewhat questionable. You can play some pretty interesting pranks with computers. What if a colleague said that he had rented the movie *When Harry Met Sally* and had digitized several seconds of the soundtrack from the famous restaurant scene? (Just in case you are unfamiliar with this movie, this

Questionable activities

is the scene in which the heroine demonstrates how easy it is to mimic the sounds of sexual pleasure—in the middle of a crowded restaurant.) Your friend's plan is to rig the computer belonging to one of your female colleagues to play the sound he has recorded. Would this be funny, or would it be sexual harassment? Would it be okay if it were a male colleague? Would it matter if you knew the teacher didn't really care, but that there would be a good chance the teacher's class would witness the prank? To make matters even more complicated, would it be a copyright violation?

Rapid pace of change

An interesting conclusion drawn by observers of how the computer and associated technologies have affected society is that the pace of change in this area has outrun the natural process of developing codes of conduct to guide our behavior (Forester and Morrison, 1990). Perhaps we have moved so quickly that we no longer have commonly held beliefs about what is right and what is wrong. This premise supposedly applies both to those who purchase and use the products of the computer revolution and to the companies developing and supplying the products. It is frequently noted that behaviors citizens normally would not even consider are somehow acceptable when the behaviors involve technology. Few people would consider stealing a candy bar from their grocery store, but they would copy a software program worth several hundred dollars without a thought. Similarly, technology companies seem to look at their responsibilities differently. Can you imagine a car manufacturer telling a customer, "If there happens to be a defect in this product and you are injured as a result, we will not consider ourselves responsible"? Read the label on a software program or a box of disks. Here the statement is clear: If something is wrong with this product and you lose your data as a consequence, we will not take responsibility.

EQUITY OF EDUCATIONAL OPPORTUNITY

Preparing students to use technology

We believe that technology already plays an important role in K–12 education and that it will play an increasingly important role in the future. Clearly, technology has become an indispensable part of the way we live and work, and our educational system must accept some responsibility to prepare students for this reality. Students who move through the educational system without acquiring some skills in applying technology will be at a disadvantage when they compete for better opportunities in this kind of environment.

The 1980s were largely a time during which schools became involved with computers and computer-related technologies. Early on, purchasing computers was fairly experimental, and some districts moved ahead more quickly than others. As technology became more commonplace, not providing access to technology soon came to be regarded as a liability. Lack of opportunity was viewed with particular alarm when it perpetuated or exacerbated known group differences. Many descriptive studies sought to determine whether variations in access to technology or how technology was used could be linked to gender, minority or majority group membership, **socioeconomic status (SES),** or student ability.

Here is a quick summary of some of the major conclusions of what is probably the most comprehensive review of the 1980s equity research (Sutton, 1991). Lower-income, minority, and female students had less opportunity to use computers in school. The SES and ethnic differences were somewhat larger than the gender difference. Females were also less involved with school-related computer activities that were not directly connected with classes. Males were more likely to be involved in a computer club and to use computers before and after school. Playing computer games seemed to be a more prevalently male extracurricular activity. In general, group differences were smaller in the upper grades and seemed to decrease somewhat toward the end of the decade. A similar difference has been reported for group differences in ability. More-able students use computers more in school than do less-able students (Becker and Sterling, 1987). Finally, home access to computers tended to increase the magnitude of inequities created by schools. Poor and minority students, as well as females, were less likely to have access to computers at home.

Who has less opportunity to use computers in schools?

Home access

Access to technology does not present the entire picture. Even when students worked with technology, they were not involved in the same kinds of activities. Low-ability, minority, and poorer students tended to be more heavily involved in drill-and-practice activities. Females were less likely to be involved in programming classes and more likely to be involved in word processing classes (Becker and Sterling, 1987; Sutton, 1991).

Schools are addressing some inequities

Schools clearly are addressing some of these inequities. The opportunity to use computers in schools continues to improve. In the most recent of the series of studies conducted by the International Association for the Evaluation of Educational Achievement, the ratio of students to computers showed very little variability associated with the proportion of minority students in schools. It appears that access at the elementary and high school levels is nearly equal (Magnan, 1993). It seems very possible this is one area that federal grant programs have addressed successfully.

Internet use is not equitable

An area in which access differences can still be observed is in the immediate availability of the Internet. Data provided by the National Center for Education Statistics (1996) indicate that 31 percent of schools with a high proportion of students from poor families (71 percent get some reduction in school lunch rates) and 62 percent of schools with a low proportion of students from poor families (less than 11 percent receive reduced lunch rates) had access to the Internet. However, government action has already been initiated in response to this problem. The Telecommunications Act of 1996 stipulates that all elementary and secondary classrooms and public libraries should have access to advanced telecommunications services. With time, it appears, access inequities are being minimized.

Student beliefs about personal abilities and vocational opportunities will influence interest in technology. Students must assume that technology will be an important part of their future. (© Jean-Claude Lejeune)

Gender differences at home

SES differences at home

Nonschool computer use continues to differ. Presently about 39 percent of families with children have a computer, and children are reported to use the computer in 90 percent of these families. Little in the way of gender differences exist through elementary school, but in the middle school years males begin to spend more time using the family computer. Males spend nearly 3 more hours per week than females in the middle school years and 2 more hours per week in the high school years using a computer at home (FIND/SVP, 1995). An even larger difference appears when comparing nonschool access by lower- and upper-SES groups. As you might expect, SES variables such as family income and parental education are strong determinants of whether a computer is found in the home. Families with an income in excess of $75,000 are three times more likely to have a computer than families with an income of $35,000. Parents who are college graduates are nearly three times more likely to own a computer than parents who have gone no further than high school (National Telecommunications and Information Administration, 1995). By the end of high school, students from more affluent families work on computers an additional 3 hours per week in comparison to students from low-SES families. More affluent students spend more time using computers for schoolwork, word processing, draw or paint programs, and games (Beebe, 1993). One potential consequence of these differences in access and experience may be seen in differences in general knowledge of computers and how to solve common computer problems. As part of the study, students were tested on their general computer knowledge with questions such as "Interpret the menu of a word processing program to save your work," and "What is the cursor?" Minority groups, with the exception of Asian Americans, scored lower than white students on this examination. A partial explanation for these differences in computer knowledge may be home computer use. In spite of differences in nonclassroom and nonschool use of computers, no gender differences in computer knowledge were apparent (Anderson, 1993b).

Using computers for remediation

Using computers to develop higher-order thinking skills

Other equity concerns still exist, focused mainly on how teachers use technology in content-area instruction (George, Malcolm, and Jeffers, 1993; McAdoo, 1994). Less able and lower-SES students are more likely to use technology for drill and practice of isolated skills (math facts, phonics, and grammar rules, for example) or tutorials. Technology is viewed as an effective way to provide remediation when it is assumed that basic skills and knowledge are missing. Students in more affluent schools and more able students tend to have more frequent opportunities to use computers in ways that require higher-order thinking skills and in ways that place control of learning and the technology in the students' hands. Many of the tool applications and student projects covered in this book fall into this latter category.

POSSIBLE CAUSES OF INEQUITIES

Moving beyond describing problem areas

In concluding her review of equity issues in the application of technology, Sutton (1991) suggests that it is important to move beyond a descriptive treatment of problem areas. Descriptive data can tell you only that problems exist. Understanding why inequities exist is essential to proposing responsible solutions. In some cases we can make good guesses about the causes of inequities. Does it surprise you that schools in wealthy neighborhoods or wealthy districts would forge ahead in introducing technology or that the homes of higher-income families would be more likely to own computers students could use? One solution to a lack of money is obviously to find money. Government grants have been used successfully to make technology more readily available.

Explanations for inequities

Explanations for some of the other inequities are less apparent, and therefore possible solutions are less obvious. Why do you think female students make less optional use of computers? Why would teachers assign computer activities that are probably less motivating to less-able students? Where is the focus of the problem? Is it something about the student, something about the belief system of the teacher, or something about the social group to which the student belongs? Although the answers to these questions are still somewhat speculative, experts have proposed explanations for inequities and have offered solutions related to these explanations. The discussion that follows presents some of these explanations and possible remedies.

Resources

Costs associated with technology in schools

Resource issues have influenced and continue to influence student access to and experiences with technology. Equipment costs probably come most immediately to mind because most people understand that computers, videodisc players, and other hardware items are expensive. However, it is important to recognize that there are many other costs associated with using technology in instruction. Schools must purchase software and train teachers to use the equipment and software. Federal support can cover some of these costs, but it is difficult to create exactly the same total environment that wealthy schools can provide.

Because teachers in inner-city and rural settings are often inexperienced and frequently professionally isolated, training is a very important issue and represents a need that is often inadequately met (McAdoo, 1994). Training is important in developing teachers who are confident and enthusiastic in working with technology. Confidence and enthusiasm are essential for presenting computer experiences to students in a positive way.

Importance of training and confidence

Training is also likely to heavily influence the way teachers use technology. For example, drill and tutorial applications are easier to implement— once the student gets started, the computer is pretty much in control of the learning experience. Tool and project applications require that students be taught how to use tool programs and also require that teachers facilitate more open-ended learning experiences. Teachers who lack training and confidence are more likely to rely on drill and tutorial programs.

One approach to helping practicing teachers learn new skills is through brief workshops or training sessions. Such training might take place over a weekend or after school. Often, special funds can be secured to provide this type of training. However, a weekend workshop is much less effective in developing teacher skills than access to a full-time computer coordinator. Workshops are limited in that they usually require a lot of information to be taught in a brief period of time. Teachers seldom have the opportunity to spend more than a few minutes trying out applications themselves. Of even greater concern, teachers rarely have the opportunity to seek assistance when applying technology with their own students. Teachers often return in September after a summer workshop and find that they no longer can remember how a particular program works. When students do not respond to an instructional activity as expected, there is no longer an experienced technology user to offer advice. Districts able to afford a staff member dedicated to technology and its applications are going to be able to provide teachers with an entirely different level of training and support. Without continual training and support, many teachers will give up on technology or resort to the activities that are easiest to implement.

When parents are poor, the reason students do not have access to technology in the home is different. Teachers and school administrators have limited opportunities to do something about this type of difficulty. One proposed solution (George, Malcolm, and Jeffers, 1993; McAdoo, 1994) has been to involve the community and businesses in making technology available in more settings. Many community-based technology centers have been established to involve undereducated adults, women, the disadvantaged, the disabled, and minorities with math, science, and technology. These programs might be affiliated with museums, libraries, boys' or girls' clubs, or churches, or they might be freestanding programs. Such programs offer a variety of workshops for all age levels but also just make technology available to anyone who is interested. Often, such programs run with the support (that is, equipment) and using the expertise (volunteer instructors) of local businesses. In some cases, programs of this type are run after hours in schools. Sometimes businesses will donate resources to the schools to facilitate programs aimed at benefiting the entire community, and the schools can then use this same equipment with students during the day. The Telecommunications Act of 1996 proposes to provide universal Internet access not only in schools, but also in public libraries.

Community-based technology centers

Role Models and Stereotypes

Student, parent, and teacher decisions can be influenced by stereotypes. Some stereotypes are based on assumptions about what a certain group of students is interested in, what kind of jobs they will likely get, or what academic skills or deficiencies they are likely to have. We have already noted that parents are more likely to encourage the computer interests of sons than daughters and that teachers are more likely to use drills and tutorials with low-income and less-able students. These decisions may reflect assumptions about vocational opportunities and academic needs. Student beliefs about their own abilities and vocational opportunities also influence decisions. If women or members of minority groups do not feel certain careers involving technology are open to them, spending time learning about technology will not be a high priority.

Stereotypes develop in many ways. Many researchers have been concerned about subtle biases communicated by the media. One frequent example of such bias is the way in which women and minorities are represented in magazine advertisements and in the photographs used to illustrate magazine articles. For example, in one survey of computer advertisements, the most common photograph was of an individual male, and 90 percent of the males shown were white (Demetrulias and Rosenthal, 1985). When women are included, it has been claimed they are more likely to be in passive and supportive roles (Ware and Struck, 1985). Perhaps a woman is shown watching a male working at the computer terminal rather than working at the terminal herself.

Subtle biases

These are relatively easy data to gather. Check out several issues of a computer magazine from your library and conduct your own survey. The data cited here are a little old, and you may find a more equitable representation of the actual population.

Role models

Schools are in a position to provide positive role models. Schools can hire women and minorities for computer staff positions. Each teacher is also a role model. Therefore, it is important that teachers develop their own computer skills, use technology with confidence, and be enthusiastic about computer applications used in the classroom. Teachers must also be careful when they label their own students. Teachers often identify certain students as classroom "experts" and allow these students to work with others who are having difficulty. It may be very productive to have more knowledgeable students help their classmates. Teachers might want to allow several students to fill this role,

Students as role models

be careful how these students are described to the class, and make certain that women and minority students are allowed to function in this role. Finally, schools can link with community businesses to connect students with female and minority role models who use technology in their occupations (George, Malcolm, and Jeffers, 1993). Some businesses have been willing to have their employees conduct computer training sessions and to discuss the kind of work they do.

There is one final way in which technology has been stereotyped. Technology has been linked in many people's minds with math and science (Hawkins, 1987). This association may stem from the long-time perception that computers are machines for manipulating numbers. This connection has been problematic for women, who in general seem to be somewhat less inter-

Problematic association of technology with math and science

ested in math and science. This perception may also influence the areas in which parents are willing to support their daughters' interests. Although it is truly unfortunate that any group would feel less suited to math and science careers, teachers may be able to encourage more interest in technology by emphasizing its versatility. Efforts to encourage general use of word processing, database, spreadsheet, graphic, and multimedia tools in content-area instruction are consistent with the goal of a more general role for technology.

There is some reason to believe that the middle-school years are critical for addressing gender differences. Differences in student interest at home and school do not seem to appear until this age (FIND/SVP, 1995; Silverman & Pritchard, 1996). Two issues seem to be involved. First, middle school females begin to experience an emerging sexism related to their academic interests among peers. Second, female students begin to consider vocational issues, and traditional stereotypes about male/female occupations work against interests they might have in technology.

Changing stereotypes

Educators are in a key position to change stereotypes. Left unchallenged, stereotypes can easily become self-perpetuating. If women or minorities accept the low frequency of women and minorities in the computer industry as an indication that technology-related careers are not appropriate for them, the industry will never change. Teachers are in a position to provide alternate explanations for the perceptions students might have and to expose students to experiences and information allowing students to evaluate their own strengths and interests.

Learning Styles and Social and Motivational Preferences

Several experts have suggested that what might be described as student personality differences interact with the social situation in which computers are made available and the nature of common computer tasks to account for group differences in computer use. For example, there are often fewer computers available than there are students interested in using them. Computers are often made available in settings such as laboratories or school libraries, which are loosely supervised. Males, who tend to be somewhat more aggressive and assertive, may gain more than their fair share of opportunities in these kinds of situations, and females may end up losing interest (Cully, 1988).

Possible group differences

It has also been claimed that the nature of certain computer tasks appeals more to males than to females. Independence, the strict structure required in computer programming, and the clear success or failure in accomplishing a programming task may make programming more appealing to males (Hawkins, 1987). Females are described as preferring a verbal task that can be evaluated more interpretively. Creative writing represents an example of this type of task. There may be group differences in what students enjoy.

In proposing solutions to these difficulties, it is hard to know whether it is more appropriate to address the basic group difference or to accept the group difference and find practical ways to make certain the difference does not limit opportunities with technology. Put somewhat differently, should a teacher's goal be to teach females to be more assertive or to create an environment that is more structured and does not reward more aggressive students with easier access? Both goals are important. The emphasis here is on interventions that can have an immediate impact on student involvement with technology.

Accommodating individual differences

Individual differences can be accommodated in a number of ways. Teachers can monitor student use and create a system that requires equal access. For example, students wanting to use classroom computers might be asked to add their names at the end of a list posted on the blackboard. Once a student's "turn" ends, the student must again add her name to the end of the list to have another turn. If a student is busy when she reaches the top of the list, she can allow the next student on the list to work and still retain her position (Sanders and McGinnis, 1991a). Different kinds of computer activities can be encouraged in a laboratory setting by offering certain programs on certain computers. In this way, students interested in a particular activity will not be able to dominate the laboratory (McAdoo, 1994).

Finally, it is also possible to allow students some flexibility in the social setting in which they use technology. Provide students with the option of working on assignments alone or with someone else (Sanders and McGinnis, 1991a). Different students find different arrangements to be most comfortable, and occasionally allowing them to determine how they will work will increase their enjoyment of technology.

Perceptions of Student Needs

Educational reform has generated two rather different approaches. One theme has encouraged a renewed commitment to basic skills and the other, an emphasis on critical thinking and problem solving. It appears that schools with high and low minority populations have applied these approaches unevenly. Schools with a large proportion of minority students place a heavier emphasis on developing basic skills, and schools with small minority enrollments tend to place greater emphasis on critical thinking and problem solving.

These two approaches result in the application of technology in very different ways. In schools with many minority students, technology is used to deliver tutorials and drills focused on basic skills. Schools with fewer minority students place a greater emphasis on putting students in charge of technology through programming and the application of computer tools to more open-ended tasks (Simmons, 1987). A similar emphasis on using technology to emphasize the basics has been noted for lower-SES students (Simonson and Thompson, 1994) and low-ability students (Cosden, 1988).

Making the mastery of basic skills a priority assumes a hierarchical relationship between fundamental skills and knowledge (word identification, phonics, math facts) and the application of higher-order skills in context (reading for meaning, solving math problems). The instructional approach that results from this model often makes the additional assumption that students can learn basic skills and fundamental knowledge most efficiently by isolating these components for focused instruction and practice. When this bottom-up model is implemented with technology, students spend most of their computer time working on tutorials and drills that develop basic skills (Laboratory of Comparative Human Cognition, 1989).

The focus on basic skills instruction has been challenged in three ways. First, it is claimed that using technology in this way with low-SES children duplicates the style of instruction students would receive without technology. Because access to technology is limited, students using technology to duplicate common instructional strategies learn less about technology and do not experience some of the unique ways technology can be applied in content-area instruction. Second, a strict bottom-up model of instruction is frequently challenged. It is not clear that the isolation and rehearsal of lower-level skills is most productive. The alternative is to embed practice of individual skills within more meaningful activities. Using technology as a way to facilitate activity-centered projects in other content areas is another way to

Embedding basic skills in meaningful activities

embed exposure to basic skills and facts within a meaningful context (Laboratory of Comparative Human Cognition, 1989). Finally, students can be inspired by the opportunity to use technology in interesting and challenging ways. It would be a shame to limit the involvement of any student who could profit from this source of motivation. Even if low-ability and low-SES students profit from drill and computer tutorials, this should not imply that computer experiences should be limited to these kinds of activities (Sutton, 1991).

Increasing Personal Sensitivity

Ways to involve all students equitably

The fact that certain stereotypes exist and may influence how computers are used does not mean that the stereotypes hold in all schools (Sutton, 1991). Some schools have found ways to involve all students equitably. Part of the solution may be a matter of sensitivity or awareness.

It can be quite informative for individual schools and perhaps individual teachers to evaluate equity at the local level. Sanders and McGinnis (1991b) offer some simple ways to generate data that may be helpful in stimulating discussion and initiating change. Their suggestions were intended to point out gender inequities, but the techniques might be altered to search for other inequities as well. Here are a few of their ideas:

◆ Observe computer use during free-access times (before and after school, free periods). Who uses the computers and what do they work on?
◆ If your school has a computer club, which students participate?
◆ Which students take elective computer courses?
◆ Circulate a questionnaire to determine how much and how students use computers at home. Do they have access to a computer?

Asking questions to develop new approaches

Teachers might become more sensitive to their own assumptions by conducting a similar kind of audit. Do I allow certain students to use the computers as a reward, and does this mean that certain students have few opportunities to use technology in a way they might choose? Are the students I would label less able allowed to control the technology—in writing, creating graphics, telecommunications, and similar kinds of open-ended activities? If I request a student for personal assistance or to help out another student, is the student most likely to be a white male from an affluent home? Thinking about these questions may help teachers develop new approaches.

ADAPTING TECHNOLOGY FOR EQUAL ACCESS

This book is based on the premise that the computer and related technologies can provide powerful tools and meaningful learning experiences for the benefit of *all* students. However, more than 50 million Americans have some type

Many citizens require some form of adaptation

of disability that requires adaptations be made to commonly available hardware and software for them to take advantage of what technology can offer (Kamp, 1996). In this section we will identify barriers to the use of technology and related adaptations that improve accessibility (based on suggestions from Apple Computer, 1996; Burgstahler and Disabilities, Opportunities, Internetworking & Technology [DO-IT],1996).

Adapting for mobility impairments

Mobility impairments make it difficult for learners to interact with technology. The problems may involve difficulties in manipulating input devices (keyboard, mouse), performing basic physical tasks associated with the operation of a computer or peripheral (turning the computer on, inserting a diskette or CD), or even positioning equipment so that the learner can interact with it. Here are some ways to respond to mobility impairments:

◆ Flexible work environments can be created to allow repositioning of keyboard, monitor, and work materials.
◆ A power strip can be used to turn all equipment on and off with a single switch.
◆ Alternative keyboards position the keys farther apart and disable repeat keys so users with slower and less precise movements have less difficulty.
◆ Special software adaptations allow shift and control keys to be latched as a substitute for simultaneous key combinations (used to capitalize letters and issue keyboard commands to programs).
◆ Special software causes the cursor to scan across a screen representation of the keyboard or across program choice buttons, allowing individuals with the capacity to control a switch (using knee, mouth, head) to make selections.
◆ Computer actions can be controlled by voice input.

Adapting for visual impairments

Visual impairment should not hinder learners from taking advantage of technology. Some of the following adaptations can be made:

◆ Blind individuals can use a standard keyboard—Braille key labels may be helpful to some.
◆ Special software "reads" the screen to the learner (earphones can be used to reduce the distraction to others). Basic speech synthesis from text is fairly standard, but screen reader software can also "describe" menus, windows, and screen icons (e.g., *outSPOKEN* from Berkeley Systems).
◆ Special software can allow magnification of the screen image for learners with limited vision (e.g., *CloseView* allows magnification of the screen image up to 16 times).
◆ A scanner and OCR (optical character recognition) software allow the conversion of paper documents to computer files so that they can be "read" by a speech synthesizer.

Adapting for learning disabilities

Learning disabled students benefit from adaptations that compensate for communication difficulties.

◆ Spell-check programs improve use of the computer for communications.

CONTROLLING STUDENT ACCESS TO THE INTERNET

Educators must recognize that the Internet does not exist specifically to support educational goals. Cable television has the capacity to bring sporting events, congressional testimony, educational programming, and sexually explicit content into our living rooms. The telephone can be used to chat with grandma about Thanksgiving dinner or a psychic about our future. For adults, all are acceptable forms of "information." Like the telephone or cable TV systems, the Internet supports the needs of government, the business community, and individual citizens. If we want to benefit from powerful

Focus

Web Design for Equal Access

The World Wide Web offers exciting opportunities for all learners. Web designers have a penchant for using the newest features to make their Web sites more exciting. Some of these enhancements may present barriers that are not obvious. To make material available to the widest audience possible, Web authors should either avoid known difficulties or offer alternative pages. The following are some issues to consider (Adaptive Computer Technology Centre, 1996):

◆ Use a consistent design pattern across all Web pages to increase ease of use—for example, place common navigation buttons across the bottom of all pages.

◆ Information presented in multiple columns can be confusing when "read" by a screen-reader program—for example, use a list

of links rather than presenting multiple links in a line; avoid the use of tables (information presented in cells).

◆ Use punctuation—items in lists often do not end with punctuation marks. Screen readers identify punctuation marks for learners with visual difficulties and the lack of punctuation can make content more difficult to interpret.

◆ Avoid blinking text, which causes difficulties for screen readers.

◆ Consider offering alternative sources of information—for example, streaming audio is an effective way to convey information to learners with visual problems; graphical navigation icons (arrows, icons representing information categories) and text can be presented as alternatives, the graphical representations are useful to individuals with learning or intellectual difficulties, and the text can be interpreted by screen readers. ✳

communication systems, we have to tolerate those systems that recognize individual freedoms and even those that can be abused.

The general public and educators are justifiably concerned about the potential dangers of the Internet. However, proper caution and paranoia are two different reactions. There is some level of potential danger involved in any means of communication. Pornography, hate literature, descriptions of how to create explosive devices, and the open discussion of drug use certainly exist. Educators cannot guarantee that students won't find such material on the Internet. Educators also cannot guarantee that such materials are not stashed in some student's locker and being passed around during school. There is also a small number of individuals seeking to manipulate or take advantage of individuals through Internet conversations. Schools need to take reasonable measures to prevent access to inappropriate material and to protect children from being taken advantage of through chat room and e-mail conversations.

Communication systems can be abused

What constitute reasonable measures? Consider this parallel situation. We have always allowed our children to answer the telephone even when we are not at home—the telephone is a valuable communications tool. We recognize that our children have friends they want to talk to and in some cases we want them to answer the phone when we're calling. What happens when a stranger calls and asks to talk to us? Our daughter does not say that her parents are not home—she says that they can't come to the phone right now and asks that the caller leave a phone number or call back in a little while. Just as parents teach their children what to say and what not to say over the phone, students can also be educated as to what information about themselves they should share with others over the Internet.

Reasonable protective measures

There are several reasonable protective measures schools can employ in response to concerns about educational use of the Internet. First, students need to know that inappropriate material exists on the Internet, and that it is possible someone might attempt to exploit them through Internet conversations. Second, schools need to establish clear standards for appropriate use of the Internet. It is useful to formalize such guidelines in written form and to include the guidelines with other standards of behavior in a student handbook. Some schools require students to sign a form indicating they will abide by these guidelines before they will be given a computer account. Educators also need to be willing to monitor student use of school computers. We have frequently argued that teachers should participate actively when students work with technology. Supervision is yet another reason to remain involved and not sit at a desk while students work. The combination of honest concern, clear standards, and appropriate supervision is how schools customarily maintain appropriate behavior.

Be willing to monitor

Special *filtering software* offers another mechanism for protecting students. This software works primarily by refusing to accept material sent from certain targeted sites. The companies selling this software continually update

Filtering software

their lists of sites providing offensive material and make these lists available to those who have purchased their software. These systems do not offer perfect protection because offensive material can be added to an existing site at any time and new computers are always being connected to the Internet. However, this software does provide a reasonable means of protection from established sites providing material not appropriate in a school environment.

There are some other interesting strategies for controlling access. Several companies offer those who purchase their filtering software lists of disapproved and approved sites. The use of a list of approved sites would offer protection against inappropriate material contained on new servers. It is also very unlikely that sites selected for the approved list would suddenly decide to add inappropriate material. Some software can also keep track of which sites students have visited. The intent is not so much to punish those students who ignore school policies (actually, it is the identity of the computer that is stored, not that of the user), but to make school personnel aware of which sites have been visited. If necessary, the school can use this information to add sites to the disapproved list.

Cyber Patrol provides some protection against another concern—young students revealing personal information to strangers during chat sessions. School personnel or parents can enter protected words (names, phone numbers, addresses, credit card numbers) into a file and a series of *X*s will be substituted, should a student type one of the protected words during a chat conversation.

Not every protective method is desirable

Do not assume that every possible method of control should be imposed. For example, a mechanism allowing access only to certain sites might restrict a student's ability to search and do original research. Schools will have to weigh the advantages and disadvantages of such protection schemes and decide which options meet their needs.

COPYRIGHT LAW AND RESPECT FOR INTELLECTUAL PROPERTY

Teachers, whether or not they are heavily involved in the educational applications of technology, need to be aware of their responsibilities regarding copyrighted materials. Teachers also need to teach their students to avoid personal violations of copyright law and to respect the intellectual property of others. A powerful way to develop any behavior in your students is to model this behavior yourself.

The need to appreciate intellectual property

Copyright is such an important issue in education because the process of education relies heavily on instructional materials (textbooks, films, computer software) and on other resources that can serve an educational purpose (newspapers, television broadcasts, reference books). In a way, instructional resources are the necessary raw material for the process of education. These resources contain information that learners can process into personal knowledge. These resources were also purposefully created through the intellectual efforts of others and often were created as a way for these individuals to make a living. Intellectual property represents a potential product.

We have accepted the fact that we cannot fill our cars with gas for free or walk out of a shoe store without paying for our new pair of shoes. In contrast, making a personal copy of the word processing program that a friend has purchased or taping a musical CD is fairly common. Taping an informative television program on the Civil War and using it each year as part of the same history unit might be regarded as "creative teaching." In fact, these activities are illegal.

Copyright infringements

Since teachers are not, as a rule, prone to breaking the law, it may be useful to speculate on why they sometimes violate copyright laws. The reasons may vary, but there are a number of contributing factors. First, teachers may feel obligated to provide students with certain experiences, yet not have the resources to actually provide these experiences. For example, to provide your class access to a specific program that your school owns, it may seem most practical to copy the program to each computer in your school's computer lab and then take your class to the lab so that every student can work on the program at the same time. Unless your school has purchased the software under a special agreement, however, the **multiple loading** of a single copy of a program is illegal. Good intentions can result in clouded judgment.

Second, it seems possible that there is a general lack of appreciation for intellectual property that may influence some teachers' decision making. It may be difficult to appreciate how any computer program that can be copied to an 80-cent disk can be worth $120. Values in this case are probably based on a personal perspective that does not include awareness of the development time, skill, and experience that were required to produce a product that is so easily copied.

A final contributing factor may result from a combination of easy access to the means for making copies and sketchy knowledge of when copying is appropriate. Most people are aware of copyright laws, but most teachers are also aware that there are some situations in which copying is allowed. Photocopy machines, scanners, audiotape recorders, videotape recorders, and computer disk drives are readily available in most educational environments. Schools are likely to make blank materials (paper, tapes, disks) available as well. Copying is obviously an activity that occurs frequently and is encouraged in a school environment, but teachers and students need a better understanding of when it is appropriate.

Countermeasures

Assuming that this is an accurate analysis of some of the basic reasons why teachers and students end up violating copyright laws, it is appropriate to propose countermeasures. One need is surely to develop a better and more general understanding of copyright law, particularly as it relates to educational settings. One concrete step schools can take is to establish a clear district policy on software copyright issues (see "Focus: A Model District Policy . . ."). However, knowledge of the law is unlikely to provide a complete solution. People must also value what the law protects. Because the odds of actually being prosecuted for a copyright violation are small, a change in behavior will often require a change in values. Finally, it may be possible to make copyright issues seem less adversarial and to help teachers deal with personal pressures by identifying some specific alternatives to copyright violations. Teachers may find that there are several ways to accomplish the goal they have in mind. After completing your study of the material that follows, you should be familiar with copyright law as it applies in educational settings and be aware of what copyright law is designed to protect.

THE COPYRIGHT LAW

The government's authority to develop copyright law is established in the Constitution of the United States in Article I, Section 8, which grants Congress the authority "to promote the progress of science and useful arts, by securing for a limited time to authors and inventors the exclusive right to their respective writings and discoveries." This section of the Constitution is responsible for what we know as copyrights and patents. The current copyright law was written in 1976 and has since been amended to make the law more specific. Congress has also formed committees to offer suggestions on such topics as copying from books and periodicals, copying of music, off-air videotaping, and, more recently, multimedia. This collected body of information does not address every possible situation, but the original law was written to

The open-ended law

be very open-ended and defines as copyrightable "original works of authorship fixed in any tangible medium of expression, now known or later developed" (Copyright Act of 1976, Title 17 of the U.S. Code, Section 102, included in Salpeter, 1992). As you can see, copyright law is intended to protect creative people when they are exploring some new area of expression. Nearly any type of instructional material you can think of is probably included: print materi-

Protection for all created works

als, software, pictures, drawings, recorded music, musical scores, television broadcasts, movies, works of art. The law clearly states that created works not listed as part of the law are also protected.

It is easy for educators to see only one side of copyright law: copyright law just tells teachers what they cannot do. However, if you read and think carefully about the statement from the Constitution authorizing copyright laws, you may gain a different perspective. Copyright law is intended to encourage "the progress of science and useful arts." In other words, if educators expect others to create and improve instructional materials, educators should also expect that mechanisms have to be put in place allowing these creative individuals to make a fair profit on their work. If education is perceived as a

Focus

A Model District Policy on Software Copyright

It is the intent of [district] to adhere to the provisions of copyright laws in the area of microcomputer software. It is also the intent of the district to comply with the license agreements and/or policy statements contained in the software packages used in the district. In circumstances where the interpretation of the copyright law is ambiguous, the district shall look to the applicable license agreement to determine appropriate use.

We recognize that computer software piracy is a major problem for the industry and that violations of copyright laws contribute to higher costs and greater efforts to prevent copying and/or lessen incentives for the development of effective uses of microcomputers. Therefore, in an effort to discourage violation of copyright laws and to prevent such illegal activities:

1. The ethical and practical implications of software piracy will be taught to educators and school children in all schools in the district (e.g., covered in the fifth grade social studies classes).

2. District employees will be informed that they are expected to adhere to section 117 of the 1976 Copyright Act, as amended in 1980, governing the use of software (e.g., each building principal will devote one faculty meeting to the subject each year).

3. When permission is obtained from the copyright holder to use software on a disk-sharing system, efforts will be made to secure this software from copying.

4. Under no circumstances shall illegal copies of copyrighted software be made or used on school equipment.

5. [Name or job title] of this school district is designated as the only individual who may sign license agreements for software for schools in the district. Each school using licensed software should have a signed copy of the software agreement.

6. The principal at each school site is responsible for establishing practices which will enforce this district copyright policy at the school level. ✳

From Library of Congress, *Reproduction of Copyrighted Works by Educators and Librarians,* Copyright Office circ. 27, 1988, 27.

market prone to frequent copyright violations, commercial developers will not put effort into creating high-quality products for that market.

ESTABLISHING A COPYRIGHT

An author can provide notice of copyright with the following notation: © *year name*; for example, © 1997 Cindy Grabe. The word *copyright* can also be used in place of the copyright symbol. You are probably aware that there is a Copyright Office and that authors can register their work with this office. The fact that a "work" has not been registered or even that it does not carry a notice of copyright should not be interpreted as a waiver of copyright. Any author's work is protected from the time it is created.

Copyright law grants authors or owners five basic rights:

Five basic rights for authors or owners

1. ***The right to make copies*** If you are the creator of the work, you can make as many copies as you want.
2. ***The right to create derivations*** A derivation is an adaptation of the original. For example, a painter might also create prints from an original painting, or an author might create a movie script based on a book.
3. ***The right to sell or distribute copies*** The author can make a profit by copying and selling works to others.
4. ***The right to perform a work in public***
5. ***The right to display a work in public*** The author of a work controls the presentation of the work to the public. These rights cover performance (live performances of music, the presentation of a play) and display (visual arts).

Transferring rights

The author or creator of a work can transfer some or all of these rights to others. In the assignment of copyright, all rights are transferred. For example, a large software company may pay an independent developer a large sum of money to be assigned the copyright for a computer program written by the developer. From that point on, the company can do whatever it wants with the program. In the granting of a license, only some rights are transferred (Fritz, 1992). Although the term *license* may not always be used, this is a common type of alternative arrangement educators and authors commit to. The agreement may involve money or it may not.

License agreements in education

Examples of license agreements in education are common. You may have heard of a software **site license**, which allows a school or other organization to make copies of software it has purchased. The license may limit the number of copies or allow unlimited copying as long as the software is used on a machine owned by the school. A site license offers some advantages to both parties. The school is allowed to purchase the software for less money per copy. The company selling the software usually saves on packaging and manuals. The site license allows the school the right to make copies within established limits but does not allow the license holder to distribute copies outside the site.

Educators may be involved in other situations involving the granting of licenses. When teachers ask for permission to scan images for a classroom project, the request is for a license to copy and perhaps display an artist's work. The purchase of royalty-free artwork allows someone to copy and display a photographer's work without even seeking written permission. However, only some of the rights are granted in these agreements. For example, the images cannot be sold to someone else.

Educational publishers use license agreements to gain a competitive advantage by making their products more attractive to schools. Publishers and

Does Anyone Understand Copyright Law?

We noticed an interesting phenomenon when reviewing the material various copyright experts have written for educators. Nearly every expert was careful to state that the article he or she had written should not be accepted as legal advice. Everyone included some type of disclaimer, and it was usually suggested that schools should contact a lawyer if they had questions about a particular activity. First, let us say that teachers are very unlikely to contact lawyers on a frequent basis. That would be unreasonable. Let us also say as a preview to what follows that contacting a lawyer would often not be the best course of action anyway. Lawyers can only offer an opinion. When considering a questionable practice, the single best source of advice is the owner of the copyright or an official representative of this party. The copyright holder can even suggest that what you want to do would be illegal, but the copyright holder might be willing to let you do it anyway.

The reasons experts want readers to treat their articles as sources of information and not as advice provide some useful insights into why copyright issues can be confusing. Copyright law is very likely to lag behind practice. This means that people have the ability to do things before there are specific laws to govern their behavior.

Laws are established through the political process, and the interests of many groups must often be considered. It sometimes takes some time before pressure builds to the point at which additions to the law are written. This does not mean you can do what you feel like doing until a law is written to forbid it. You are obliged to follow general principles established in existing law. However, what is or is not allowed is likely to depend on several criteria that are open to interpretation. All citizens are entitled to their interpretations of existing principles, but so is the owner of the copyright. The final ruling may end up being rendered in court. A judge may have to consider both interpretations and offer a decision. What the expert has to offer is an expert's opinion. While an expert's analysis of a complex issue would be more likely to accurately predict a judge's decision than your interpretation or our interpretation, there are no guarantees, and the expert wants you to know that. In fact, major companies consult lawyers with the understanding that there is no certainty that the opinions provided will be correct. Instead, seeking an opinion is one way the company can show it has made an effort to determine whether what it wants to do is illegal. This action may later reduce the damages if a judge determines that the company's decision was wrong.

So we hope you are not disappointed that we offer the following disclaimer. The information on copyright law provided here is intended to acquaint you with what the copyright law states. You should be aware that personal interpretation of copyright law can result in violations. The safest approach is to contact the copyright holder and request permission before you copy anything. ✳

authors may also be willing to grant a license that does not result in a loss of income simply as a contribution to the educational process. There are many situations in which materials are not intended for sale or for a particular use and yet are protected by copyright law. If approached with a worthy application, the creators of these materials may allow their work to be used. A later section of this chapter describes some of the key items to include in a letter seeking permission to copy material.

Copying Computer Software

Copying computer software

The copyright law was amended in 1980 to specifically address the copying of computer software (Section 117). Illegal copying of computer software—often called software **piracy**, is rampant, and the Software Publishers Association estimates that software authors lose $2 billion annually in U.S. sales (Levy, 1993). Section 117 of the copyright law states that legitimate owners of software can copy the software in two situations. First, they can copy the software when making a copy that is essential in allowing the software to run on their own computers. What this usually means is that the owner of the software will have a copy of the program on the disks he or she purchased and also on the hard drive of a computer. Section 117 also allows the individual purchasing software to make a backup or archival copy. The backup is a safeguard against the loss or corruption of the original program. The backup legally should not be used on a second computer while the original is still in use.

The owners of a software copyright can also grant a license allowing software to be copied under an agreement called a site license (see page 408). This agreement allows the purchaser to make a specified number of copies or to allow a specified number of copies to be active on a **local area network (LAN)** of interconnected computers. Copying software to multiple machines (multiple loading) and allowing several users to simultaneously use a program over a network without a site license are violations of copyright law. Sometimes violations of this type are quite purposeful, as when a business purchases one copy of a spreadsheet and loads it on every employee's computer. In other cases, violations are more innocent. A teacher may purchase a program for her home computer and then decide to take the program to school so that her students can use it. If there is only one original, two individuals should not be using a program at the same time.

Copying shareware and freeware

As a computer user, you may encounter software described as shareware, freeware, or public domain. You might download this type of material from a telecommunications service, obtain it through a computer users' group, or purchase a disk containing such programs or files from a catalog. Copyright law applies to these resources as well. Both shareware and freeware resources are copyrighted, but both can be copied under certain circumstances.

A **shareware** product is usually developed by an individual not working through a major company. The author allows copies of his or her work to be distributed in order to make the public aware of the product. After you have had an opportunity to try a shareware product and decide to use it on a regular basis, the author expects to be paid for the product. Documentation provided with the product will describe this arrangement and tell you where your payment should be sent. Upon receiving payment, the author will often provide you with the most recent and fully functioning version of the software and any documentation that is available. **Freeware** does not require that you pay for the product, but the author wants the work to remain intact and to continue to display the author's copyright notice. **Public domain** software carries no restrictions. Examine software carefully to determine the category to which it belongs. You are not free to assume a product is in the public domain if you see no message to the contrary. Your rights in using the software should be clearly stated, and you should assume that a product is protected by copyright unless you find a statement explicitly granting you different privileges.

Public domain software

FAIR USE

As a student or a library patron, you have probably noticed that libraries provide easy access to photocopy machines. The library seems to be making it very easy for you to copy material from books, journals, and magazines. Since it can be assumed that libraries are not going to promote copyright violations, there would seem to be some situations in which material can be copied without seeking permission from the author or creator. You are allowed to make photocopies in the library because of a provision of copyright law called **fair use** guidelines. These guidelines can be confusing, and it is important for you as a teacher to understand what is and is not likely to be considered fair use.

The copyright law allows educators and researchers to make use of intellectual property for scholarly purposes. Guidelines for determining fair use vary with the medium (Martin, 1994; Salpeter, 1992), but consider the following:

Guidelines for fair use vary.

Purpose

◆ Copying should be intended for nonprofit purposes.

Nature of the original

◆ Copying of nonfiction material is more likely to be considered fair than the copying of original poetry or prose.

Amount and substantiality

◆ Copying a small part of the original is more likely to be tolerated than copying the entire work.

Impact on commercial value

◆ Copying of workbooks is not considered fair use because workbooks are intended to be purchased and used once.

The fair use guidelines that apply to copying material for your own professional use differ from those concerning the preparation of multiple copies for your students. This distinction probably results in one of the most frequent unintentional violations of copyright law. For example, consider the guidelines for copying books and periodicals. In general, as an individual, you are allowed to copy more extensively in preparing for your classes or in conducting general scholarly work. For example, your college or university library will likely allow you to copy an entire journal article or book chapter as part of your research for a paper. Fair use guidelines for individual scholarship are quite liberal. This does not mean, however, that there are no limits. For example, when my university library honors my request to copy a chapter from a book, the library records my name and the title of the book. The library will not allow me to copy a second chapter from the same book. This is the point at which the library feels copying might be perceived as a substitute for purchasing the book.

Conservative guidelines for making multiple copies

Guidelines describing when multiple copies can be made for class use are much more conservative than those controlling personal use. The fair use guidelines for books and periodicals include:

Brevity

Guidelines for books and periodicals

◆ The standards for brevity have been carefully delineated for different types of print materials. For poetry, multiple copies can be made of an entire poem if the poem is less than 250 words. A section of up to 250 words can be taken from a longer poem. For articles, stories, or essays, copies can be made of a complete work if the work is less than 2,500 words. For longer prose works, it is possible to copy 10 percent of any work up to a maximum of 1,000 words. For pictures and illustrations, one chart, drawing, or picture may be taken from a book or from an individual issue of a periodical. Special works such as literature for young children represent a distinct case. Because these works have few words, copies are limited to not more than two pages from the work.

Spontaneity

◆ Copying a particular work must be the "inspiration" of the teacher wanting to use the work. The decision to use the work must occur so close in time to its actual use that it would not be practical to obtain permission.

Cumulative effect

◆ Material is to be copied for a single course, and no more than nine items may be copied for that course. Works copied in their entirety must be from different authors. No more than two excerpts can be taken from works of the same author.

GUIDELINES FOR CREATING MULTIMEDIA AND FAIR USE

Although Section 117 provides clear guidelines on duplicating software, and although guidelines from congressional committees have provided specific

Focus

Taping Television Programs for Classroom Use

Television programs offered free of charge for viewing by the general public can be recorded and used for nonprofit instructional purposes. However, a number of conditions must be met. Some of the key conditions are described below.

◆ Recorded material must be used within the first ten school days of the forty-five calendar days following the actual broadcast. Material recorded in June could not be used in October because the time period extends beyond forty-five calendar days. A program recorded on December 27 might legally be used with a class on January 12 because consecutive school days do not include weekends or holidays. Recordings are to be erased by the end of the forty-five day calendar period.

◆ Schools cannot record a variety of programs and then make them available to teachers. Recordings can be made only by or at the request of an individual teacher, to be used by

that teacher. A teacher cannot request that the same program be re-recorded no matter how many times the program is broadcast.

◆ Teachers do not have to show entire programs, but the content of the programs as broadcast is not to be altered. For example, combining small segments from several programs is not allowed. Any copy of a broadcast program must contain the broadcast copyright notice.

◆ Educational institutions are to accept responsibility for implementing adequate control measures to see that recorded material is used within the established guidelines. Schools allowing teachers to use recorded television programs in their classrooms are expected to take a proactive role in guaranteeing compliance with copyright law.

The companies responsible for some television programs have adopted a more lenient set of guidelines related to instructional use of their programs. See the description of *Cable in the Classroom* in the Resources to Expand Your Knowledge Base section at the conclusion of this chapter. ✷

Guidelines for student projects and teacher presentations

recommendations regarding educational use of photocopying, music copying, and off-air taping, no suggested guidelines for teacher- or student-created multimedia were available until late 1996. The following list is a summary of some of the important points from the report of the Educational Multimedia Fair Use Guidelines Development Committee. (*Note:* This committee has no actual authority in law and the following guidelines have yet to be accepted by Congress.) The full text of the document prepared by this committee is widely available on the Internet. You may find it by searching for the guidelines committee listed above.

The 1996 Fair Use Committee outlined the circumstances in which students might use portions of lawfully acquired copyrighted material in educational projects created for a specific course and instructors might use portions of copyrighted materials in support of instructional activities at educational institutions. It is important to note that such materials are intended for carefully prescribed purposes. Student work is to be developed for a specific course, but may also be included in a portfolio of academic work saved for later personal applications, such as a job interview. Works prepared by an educator are intended for use in direct instruction or for the use of students in classes taught by the educator. The educator cannot make multiple copies of the material for student use, but may place a copy on reserve in a library or make the material available over a *secure network* for the exclusive use of his or her students. These guidelines *do not* cover the posting of educational material to the Internet for the general public. An instructor can also retain a copy of a project as part of a professional portfolio.

Internet publication not covered

The 1996 Guidelines include portion limitations for material taken from motion media (10 percent, or fewer than 3 minutes from a source), text (10 percent, or fewer than 1,000 words from a source), music (10 percent, or fewer than 30 seconds from a source), and illustrations/photographs (no more than five images by one artist; 10 percent, or fifteen images from any collection). The correct interpretation of multiple criteria is to use the most conservative value. For example, the allowable selection from a 1,000-word news article would be 100 words (10 percent of 1,000 is less than 1,000).

Finally, the 1996 Guidelines provide specific requirements for acknowledging the original sources and for the length of time products containing elements obtained under fair use provisions can be used in instruction. For images, credit and copyright notice must be visible on the screen when the image is displayed. For other sources, credit and copyright information can be organized and presented as a different part of the multimedia presentation. Materials prepared for instructional use can be utilized for two years.

Although the 1996 Guidelines are helpful in clearly addressing many of the kinds of projects we have discussed in this book, certain issues regarding the Internet are still unclear. The Guidelines clearly indicate that all material made available to the general public on the World Wide Web must either be original or be offered with the permission of the original author or artist. Educational materials made available for such purposes as distance learning must be offered in such a way that only those students involved in a formal course have access. The issue of what can be taken *from* a Web site is still a little unclear and a conservative approach is thus recommended (Martin, 1994). The fair use *portion limitation* would prevent the copying of complete Web pages even for educational use. Because Web pages are linked, it is not always clear when different pages should be treated as part of the same work (as in the chapters in a book) or as different works by the same author (as in different books). Teachers, administrators, and school librarians should make the effort to stay current with the latest opinions on these matters. Although it was carefully done so that all points of view would be considered, the 1996 committee report may yet end up being modified in unpredictable ways. Professional journals and the Internet offer reasonable opportunities to follow new developments (several Web resources are listed at the end of the chapter).

ALTERNATIVES TO THE VIOLATION OF COPYRIGHT LAW

We feel it is important to do more than tell teachers what they are not allowed to do. A completely negative approach leads only to frustration and resentment. We believe a more positive perspective is one that helps teachers see multiple alternatives for how the study of a content area may be approached. Even when teachers want to involve students with technology in the study of a very specific topic, there is no reason to assume that the topic can be studied only by using one specific program or approach. Teachers should never feel that violating copyright law is the only way to provide productive learning experiences.

Recognizing instructional alternatives

Recognizing instructional alternatives depends on flexibility and knowledge. By flexibility, we mean that teachers should resist becoming fixated on a single option. There are often similar computer programs, instructional techniques, and instructional resources. Flexibility implies a willingness to move on when the first preference is not available. If your principal informs you that the word processing program you have used all your life is too expensive to purchase for your classroom, it may be necessary to learn to use a less expensive word processing program. If you would really like to scan some images from a coloring book for your students, but the company publishing the book considers this a copyright violation, perhaps you should modify the project you have in mind and ask students to draw their own images.

Becoming aware of the options

In some cases, alternatives are not considered because teachers are not aware that certain options are available to them. These are the kinds of suggestions that generate an "Oh, I didn't know I could do that" response. In the suggestions that follow, we hope to provide some options that may be unfamiliar to you.

Alternative Ways to Obtain Image Collections

This book is nontraditional in its emphasis on student-generated multimedia projects. Because of the resources used in the construction of multimedia, the discussion of copyright in this textbook has been extended to consider other resources. Our discussion of alternatives must be extended to these resources as well.

Stock photographs and collections

Scanning images or photographs from publications can be an efficient way to gather material for a classroom project. However, if you are unable to obtain permission for the material you want in this form, there are other ways to generate image collections. First, consider purchasing royalty-free art (see Chapter 9). Companies have long made a business of selling stock photographs, and collections have now been digitized for sale on CDs. These images are of high quality and often have been organized by topic into collections that teachers may find very useful. Line art collections are also available. You might begin your search for this type of material in catalogs selling computer hardware and software.

Creating a collection of captured images

If you are interested in pictures, consider using a camcorder and video-capture images to create your own collection. If the images you want can be found locally, this can be a very productive and educational experience. Consider having your students do the work themselves. Students will benefit from searching for the desired images and will also directly experience the environment in which the images are captured.

Hiring an artist

How about hiring your own artist? This suggestion is more reasonable than it might seem. Many of the wildlife line drawings used as examples in this textbook were generated in this manner. These are the property of a state organization called Project WILD and were drawn by an artist for $5 per image (see Figure 11.2). The collection was sold to schools for a site license fee of $10 per building, and this revenue was used to expand the collection. The unique collection now consists of over 130 images of native plants, animals, and fish. (*Note:* A source for this collection is included at the end of this chapter.)

Have students create material

Finally, consider having student artists create material for projects. You may find several variations of this approach useful. Perhaps the theme for a unit in biology or history can also serve as the unit theme for an art class. Through the coordination of the instructors from both classes, students from the classes might team up and learn some of the knowledge and skills from the other area of study as an additional benefit. In those elementary school classrooms with an art curriculum, a similar multidisciplinary approach can be used. Skilled student artists can also be hired for a small amount of money.

FIGURE 11.2 Clip Art from Project WILD Collection

Squirrel
Property of Project Wild
- 1992

Paying a student for work is also a nice way to recognize his or her special talent. Remember, though, that student work represents a creative product, and copyright protection may apply.

Negotiate a License

Suggesting that schools or teachers approach copyright holders and propose a special agreement may strike you as odd. Under normal circumstances we tend to follow the posted rules without question and assume we should pay the going rate when making a purchase. Why should instructional materials be any different? If we read a copyright notice in the front of a coloring book and it says "Reproduction of any illustration is strictly prohibited," we would probably just put the book aside and look for another source. If a software company indicates that the price for a five-user site license is $320, we probably assume we must either pay that amount or forget about that product.

Consider approaching publishers and authors

Here are some reasons to consider approaching the publishers or authors. For materials such as coloring books, videodiscs, and videotapes, the developer or publisher might not have considered the potential use you have in mind. You probably could not purchase a set of image files from these publishers if you wanted to. What you are proposing to the publisher (see "Focus: Obtaining Permission to Copy," page 419, which describes key elements to include in a request for permission) is a way to make their product a more useful resource for your classroom. You want to provide your students with a way to work with the verbal and visual information provided in their product. If it is a videotape, your students are not going to just view the tape, but view it intensively and develop reports using images captured from the tape. The same suggestion can be made for coloring books. If your proposal sounds reasonable, publishers may be willing to allow you to do what you have proposed.

The other reason why publishers may be willing to consider your request is that honoring the request may increase the likelihood they will make a sale. If you feel that viewing videotapes without followup activities is significantly less productive for your students, the opportunity to develop projects involving images from the videotape may be an important factor in your decision to purchase the videotape. A similar issue may be involved in making computer software purchases. In our local district, the philosophy has been to make certain standard tools available on every computer at particular grade levels. This means that the district is often seeking a site license for hundreds of machines, and the money involved can be substantial. The people in the district who are involved in making such purchases do not just look up the prices and send in an order. They contact the companies and attempt to negotiate a volume discount. They have also begun requesting permission to load the software on home computers owned by any teacher using the software in his or her classroom. This is a very reasonable request. Teachers learn software more quickly when they can work with it at home. Teachers can also be more productive when work started at school can be continued at home. The attractiveness of the software to the district is drastically enhanced by the companies' granting a license of this type. Some companies will accept this request as reasonable, and some will not.

All teachers must function continually as problem solvers. The situation is no different when finding effective ways to involve students with technology. Financial limitations may sometimes mean that an approach that seems ideal may not be possible. Making unauthorized copies of software or other resources is not an acceptable solution to this situation. There are alternatives. Teachers may need to use technology in a different way, involve students in creating resources, or seek special permission from copyright holders. Dealing with copyright issues presents an opportunity in working with students. They can be involved in the creative process of searching for alternative ways to learn, and they can learn to respect the hard work of others as well.

Focus

Obtaining Permission to Copy

The first step in obtaining permission is to determine who owns the copyright. With books, journals, and documents, the copyright notice usually appears very near the front of the publication. Also check the acknowledgments page. Pay special attention to information about multiple copyrights. With music, the lyrics and musical score may be protected separately. This is also frequently the case with the text and illustrations in documents.

If dealing with a major publishing company, it is suggested that the request for permission be sent to the publisher's Copyright and Permissions Department at the company address.

A list of items to include in your request for permission follows. This list assumes that you want to copy material from a document, and some of these items may need to be modified slightly if another type of material is involved. Circumstances may also require that the form of the letter be modified. If you are contemplating making a purchase based on whether permission to copy material will be granted, you probably cannot provide the specific information we suggest, because you may not have had the opportunity to examine the product. In this case, a more general description of the type of project you would like to develop should be offered. Be sure to include:

◆ The full name of the author or artist responsible for the work you propose to copy.
◆ The exact reference for the source material.
◆ Page number(s) for the material you want to copy.

◆ The number of copies you propose to make.
◆ A full description of how the copied material will be used, including:
  —The nature of the project.
  —Whether the material will be used alone or combined with materials to be obtained from other companies.
  —Who will assemble the project.
  —Who will view the finished project.
  —How long the materials will be kept and what will happen to the project after the intended academic task has been completed.
◆ A description of the course in which the material is to be used.
◆ Your name, position, institutional affiliation, full address, and telephone number.

Some companies may expect you to pay a royalty fee for using their material. You may feel it is appropriate to acknowledge that this is a possibility and ask what the fee will be. For example, you might say, "If a royalty fee applies to copying the material that has been described, please notify me so that I can determine if funds are available."

It is important to allow several weeks for your request to be considered. It may take a month to process your request, and you will want to allow time to develop an alternate plan in case your request is denied.

Remember to be courteous. What you are requesting is a privilege. Based on suggestions provided by D. Long, C. Risher, and G. Shapiro, *Questions and answers on copyright for the campus community* (Oberlin, Ohio: National Association of College Stores, 1993). We have added other suggestions based on our own experiences. ✳

PROTECTING SOFTWARE AGAINST VIRUSES

Viruses may proliferate themselves

A **virus** is a small, uninvited program that modifies other programs to include an executable copy of itself (Levin, 1990). This means that a virus is capable of making copies of itself and attaching these copies to other programs active on your computer. A very likely target is the **operating system**—the software that starts your computer and performs other basic tasks essential to support any other program you use. Any time unintended modifications occur, things can go wrong and programs may stop working as expected. The additional activity may slow your computer down noticeably, and the proliferation of the virus may take up valuable space on your hard drive. The virus program may also have been written to do more than proliferate itself. The program may contain additional code that performs pranks: the text you see may fall into a heap at the bottom of the screen, derisive comments may be displayed on the screen, or files on your disks may be purposely damaged or erased. As you can see, viruses can be a nuisance, ruin your programs and require that you load them to the hard drive again, or cause serious damage to work it has taken you or others many hours to create. Teachers need to be aware of the potential problems caused by viruses. Even relatively harmless viruses can pose problems for novice users who need the computer to operate in a predictable fashion. Checking for viruses is a reasonable action to take when unusual things start happening.

Check for viruses when unusual things happen

Viruses can run rampant in schools

Once a virus is active, it can spread to programs on any disks you might insert in your computer and across a network to other computers connected to your computer. Viruses often run rampant in laboratory settings in which students bring in their own disks and work on programs stored on the laboratory computers. Once a virus is introduced, it is quickly spread to the other computers in the laboratory and to any disks used in those computers. Soon, upset parents may be calling to complain that the virus is now causing problems on their home computers.

INDICATORS THAT A VIRUS IS ACTIVE ON YOUR SYSTEM

Here are some symptoms that may indicate the presence of a virus.

- System functions, such as starting up the computer, or program functions seem unusually slow.
- The size of some files has grown dramatically.
- You begin experiencing unpredictable system crashes or printing difficulties.

◆ Files may disappear, or file icons (the small Windows or Macintosh symbols representing files) may change in appearance.
◆ The computer may begin displaying strange error messages.
◆ Obvious pranks may begin displaying messages or sounds.

Rules for "Safe Computing"

Sources of viruses

It is important to be aware of common sources of viruses and to be careful when working with files obtained from such sources. Common sources of viruses are disks that have been used on "public computers" and files downloaded from noncommercial Internet sources. Disks used on other computers or used to store downloaded programs should be scanned with a virus detection program. We discuss virus protection programs later.

Write-protection

Write-protect any important disks that you do not intend to use to store new files before using them in your computer. Write protection locks the disk and prevents any file on the disk from being modified. You write-protect a 3.5-inch disk by sliding open the small write-protect tab located in the upper right-hand corner of the disk. When the disk is write-protected, a small hole behind the write-protect tab will be visible. Examples of such disks would include an emergency system disk you can use to start your computer if you are encountering some kind of difficulty, a disk containing a virus disinfectant program to be used when you know your computer has already been infected with a virus, and disks containing any original programs you will need to copy back to your hard drive.

Backup copies

Make backup copies of essential programs and data. If you encounter a problem, carefully rule out the presence of a virus before inserting your backup disks in the computer. It is very easy to panic when encountering a frustrating problem. Immediately using your backup disks to reload files or programs that have become corrupted may leave you with no clean copies of important material.

It is probably impractical for schools to completely eliminate exposure to viruses. Unlike a home computer, which can be used by a single individual for very specific purposes, school computers should be used by many people for many different things. It is even preferable that school computers be networked, connected to Internet services, and equipped to allow students and teachers to load data from their personal disks. Given these realities, there are several things schools can do to combat viruses.

Virus Protection

Purchasing virus protection programs

Virus protection programs can be purchased from major companies but can also be obtained as shareware and freeware (see list of products at the end of this chapter). One of the reasons to consider purchasing virus protection programs is that it is in the best interest of the companies developing these programs to keep their products current. These companies commonly send out updates and make updates available through the Internet. Some products, such as SAM 4.5, now come with communications software that will automatically call the company's bulletin board and download the newest virus antidotes. Most companies also maintain a Web or FTP site that can be contacted for updates. Freeware products can be very effective, but the lag in adjusting the products to new viruses will often be greater. By the way, information about new viruses is one of the very useful resources provided by the Internet. When new viruses are identified, you can be certain that information about the viruses will be posted almost immediately.

Freeware products

There are several kinds of virus protection. **Virus prevention programs** run in the background and identify certain actions that are potentially problematic. The prevention program temporarily blocks these actions, alerts the computer user of the action that was attempted, and asks the user if the action should be allowed. For example, a virus prevention program would probably alert the user when one computer program tries to alter the computer code in another computer program. If the user were installing an upgrade to an old program, this type of reaction would be expected and the user would allow the alteration to occur. However, under most circumstances, one computer program does not alter another program, and the user would want to prevent the alteration from occurring.

Virus detection programs check program code before programs are run, searching for sequences of code that have been identified as part of known viruses. These key sections of code are called **signatures**. Because the programs containing the viruses are never actually run, the viruses are prevented from carrying out their actions. Some detection programs function automatically and will scan key parts of the computer's operating system every time the computer is started and will scan any new disk inserted in the disk drive. As soon as suspect programs are located, the user is notified. In some cases, the antivirus software will take care of the problem, and in other cases, the user will be expected to delete and replace the offending program.

Detection and antidote programs

Finally, **antidotes** are programs that attempt to remove already-attached viruses. As you might expect, detection and antidote programs often work together. The antidote program requires that a virus first be detected and identified so that the proper remedial action can be taken. Commercial antivirus packages can contain prevention, detection, and antidote programs. Each program adds a unique level of protection. For example, the prevention program will identify some potentially damaging actions attempted by viruses whose signatures have yet to be identified.

Taking additional precautions

Experts (Levin, 1990) suggest that users not assume that antivirus programs provide complete protection. Programmers who find some pleasure in creating viruses are completely capable of understanding how virus protection measures work and of developing new viruses to circumvent the protection schemes. It becomes a constant race between the good guys (or gals) and the bad guys. There is always a time lag between the time a new virus is introduced and the time new countermeasures can be developed. During this time lag, everyone is vulnerable. Those who develop viruses realize that if they can find a way to circumvent commercial virus protection software, the users who rely heavily on these programs for protection will be very vulnerable.

SOFTWARE BACKUP

Responsible computer users never assume that information contained on a disk or hard drive is completely secure. Computer viruses represent only one of the possible dangers. Computers and computer disks can fail for many different reasons: the disk may wear out, the power may fail, or user error or malicious behavior may result in files being corrupted.

Copy all important files

The solution to the inevitable failure of storage devices is to make copies of essential files. This is generally referred to as creating a **backup**. Which files should be backed up? The best answer to this question is "Everything." However, this may require more work or equipment than you would like. A second answer to the question may be obtained by considering the consequence of losing each item from your hard drive. If your drive failed, you would lose all the programs stored on it. However, you should still have the original disks containing your word processing program, paint program, instructional software, and other commercial programs, so these programs could simply be reinstalled. Any files you have created with these application programs would be lost, however. Any text documents, multimedia documents, and graphics files would be gone. If these files are important to you or your students, you should copy them to a second storage device.

SUMMARY

This chapter examines several issues under the general heading of the responsible use of technology. Accepting responsibility is a matter of acknowledging, understanding, and meeting obligations to the laws of our society, to parents and students, and to our colleagues. Educational equity defines responsibilities educators have in providing fair and equal experiences for all students. Recognizing the potential dangers of Internet access and taking steps to protect students against such dangers is another responsibility educators must accept. Copyright law defines responsibilities in using products developed by others. Precautionary practices to guard against the introduction of computer viruses and to protect valuable data from accidental loss are responsibilities computer users must accept in order to share expensive computer resources. This chapter identifies problems associated with each type of responsibility and offers suggestions for how teachers and students might resolve these problems.

REFLECTING ON CHAPTER 11

Activities

◆ When women are included in computer ads, it has been claimed that they are more likely to be in passive or supportive roles (Ware and Struck, 1985). A woman may be shown watching a male working at a computer terminal rather than working at the terminal herself. These are relatively easy data to gather. Check out several issues of a computer magazine from your library and conduct your own survey. The data cited here are a little old; you may find a more equitable representation.

◆ Write a "Responsible User" contract that students must sign before they will be allowed to use a school's computer facililities without instructor supervision.

◆ A software product is sold that allows users to duplicate a set of distant Web pages and store them on a local server. The advertisement suggests that this is a way schools can control the material students can access. Write an argument for or against the legality of what is suggested based on your understanding of fair use.

◆ Contact personnel from your local computer center about computer viruses they have encountered. What viruses have been detected recently, and what measures does the computer center recommend to guard against them?

◆ Locate "theme" coloring books in a local bookstore. Read the copyright notices in these books. What is the typical policy on reproducing illustrations? What variations did you find across products offered by different companies?

Key Terms

antidotes *(p. 422)*
backup *(p. 423)*
fair use *(p. 411)*
freeware *(p. 411)*
local area network (LAN) *(p. 410)*
multiple loading *(p. 405)*
operating system *(p. 420)*
piracy *(p. 410)*
public domain *(p. 411)*

shareware *(p. 410)*
signatures *(p. 422)*
site license *(p. 408)*
socioeconomic status (SES) *(p. 392)*
virus *(p. 420)*
virus detection programs *(p. 422)*
virus prevention programs *(p. 422)*
write-protect *(p. 421)*

Resources to Expand Your Knowledge Base

Sources of Copyright Information

McKenzie, J. (1996). Keeping it legal: Questions arising out of web site management. *From Now On, 5*(7). [On-Line Journal]. Available: http://www.pacificrim.net/~mckenzie/jun96/legal.html (November, 1996).

O'Mahoney, B. (1996). *The copyright website.* [On-Line]. Available: http://www.benedict.com (November, 1996).

Smedinghoff, T. (Ed.). (1996). *On-Line Law.* Reading, MA: Addison-Wesley.

Association for Educational Communications and Technology (AECT), 1025 Vermont Ave., NW, Suite 820, Washington, DC 20005. The AECT makes available documents related to copyright issues, including a model policy manual for schools.

The National School Boards Association publishes a number of resources dealing with copyright issues.

The Software Publishers Association is heavily involved in preventing software piracy. This organization publishes *The K–12 Guide to Legal Software Use.* This manual helps schools understand copyright law and different types of licenses and offers relevant sample forms and policies that schools can adapt for local use. National School Board Association 1680 Duke St., Alexandria, VA 22314.

Copying Television Programs for Classroom Use

Cable in the Classroom is a massive public service venture supported by a large number of national cable companies. This organization provides information on cable programming with educational relevance, supplemental materials to accompany selected programs, and information on programming made available with liberalized provisions for copying. Cable in the Classroom has an informative Web site (http://www.ciconline.com) and a magazine. The address is Cable in the Classroom, 86 Elm St., Peterborough, NH, 03458.

Internet Filtering and Control Products

Cyber Patrol is available for Macintosh and Windows computers from Microsystems Software, 600 Worcester Road, STE 4, Framingham, MA, 01702-9544. http://www.cyberpatrol.com

SurfWatch is available for Macintosh and Windows computers from Spyglass, Inc., 1240 E. Diehl Road, Naperville, IL 60563. http://www.surfwatch.com/

Software for Adaptive Access

CloseView allows screen magnification up to 16 times. This software comes as part of the standard Macintosh system software.

outSPOKEN reads the screen (including a description of nontext screen features) to learners. This software is available for the Macintosh from Berkeley Systems, Inc., 2095 Rose St., Berkeley, CA 94709.

Virus Utilities

Central Point Anti-Virus (Macintosh) is a commercial set of virus protection programs available as part of Central Point's Mactools. Available from Central Point Software, Inc., 15220 NW Greenbrier Parkway, Suite 200, Beaverton, OR 97007, and from catalog sources carrying Macintosh products.

Disinfectant is a Macintosh freeware product developed by John Norstad of Northwestern University. It is designed to detect and remove viruses. Download this program from an online service.

F-Prot is an MS-DOS shareware product developed by Fridrik Skulason, designed to detect and remove known viruses and to protect against unusual program activities. Download this program from an online service and, if you use it, pay the shareware fee.

Gatekeeper is a Macintosh freeware product developed by Chris Johnson. It is designed to protect files from becoming infected. Download this program from an online service.

Norton Antivirus is a commercial set of virus protection programs for computers running the Windows and MS-DOS operating systems. The program is available from Symantec Corporation, 10201 Torre Avenue, Cupertino, CA 95014, and from catalog sources carrying MS-DOS and Windows products.

SAM (Symantec Antivirus for the Macintosh) is a commercial set of virus protection programs. The program is available from Symantec Corporation, 10201 Torre Avenue, Cupertino, CA 95014, and from catalog sources carrying Macintosh products.

Clip Art

The *Project Wild* clip art collection described in this chapter is available from Project Wild, Attention: Dave Jensen, Game and Fish, 100 North Bismarck Expressway, Bismarck, ND 58501-5095.

Glossary

access speed   The average time it takes a CD player to locate the information desired.

accommodation   Modification of existing strategies or existing knowledge as a result of a new experience.

analog format   Variations in a signal represented as continuous; a sweep second hand in contrast to a digital clock.

analog modem   A device that transforms a digital signal into an analog signal for transmission via telephone wires.

analog signal   A signal having the capability of being represented by continuous values. For example, there is no set number of colors in the visible spectrum. One shade blends gradually into the next.

antidote   Program that attempts to remove an attached computer virus.

ASCII   American standard code for information interchange; usually plain text files.

assimilation   Using existing strategies or existing knowledge to relate to a new experience.

authentic activities   The activities of people in their daily lives.

automaticity   Process by which well-learned skills are executed with minimal mental effort.

automatization   Mastery of a behavior to such a high degree that the behavior can function without detracting from other behaviors occurring at the same time.

background   The surface of a HyperStudio card.

backup   Copy of a file as a safeguard against loss.

binary   Communication in which information must be coded as 1s and 0s.

binary file   Computer files stored using the binary number system (1s and 0s) to represent information.

bit-mapped   Representation of an image as rows and columns of pixels in which each pixel is represented by a number to indicate color or shade.

Boolean search   Search based on Boolean logic. In an AND search, all search terms must be located for a successful search. In an OR search, locating any one of the search terms results in a successful search.

branch   A choice point that narrows and focuses the information available to the user.

branching tutorial   Tutorial in which the sequence of content a learner encounters is determined by the quality of performance on the previous step.

browser   Software used to connect to Web servers and to display information on the local (client) computer.

bug   Error in a computer program.

build   A presentation technique in which related items are revealed in succession to emphasize the significance of each idea.

bullet chart   A series of text statements often preceded by a bullet (•) for easy reading.

button   A card "hot spot" that initiates an action when clicked.

card   The basic unit of information within HyperStudio and HyperCard. A card consists of the set of text, graphics, sounds, and buttons meant to be presented simultaneously.

CAV (constant angular velocity)   Videodisc format in which each frame takes exactly one track.

CD-ROM   Compact disc read only memory. While the method used to store data on a CD uses a different technology, the data stored on a CD-ROM are in digital form and can be brought into the computer much like data stored on a floppy disk or hard drive.

cell   Intersection of a row and column in a spreadsheet; the point at which a number or formula is entered in the spreadsheet.

charge-coupled device (CCD)   An arrangement of tightly packed photoelectric cells, each of which produces a voltage in proportion to the amount of light received. In scanners these voltages are converted to digital values to generate the information a computer saves as a graphics file.

chat mode   Form of telecommunications in which messages are exchanged in real time rather than stored for later reading.

clean pause   Videocassette player pause that generates an image with no flicker.

clip art   Prepackaged images, often a collection of simple pictures isolated from any background, prepared to be pasted into documents.

clipboard   Computer memory buffer that can hold images and other information for convenient exchange among programs.

CLV (constant linear velocity)   Videodisc format in which each track may contain parts of several frames. Each track is read at a constant speed.

cognitive apprenticeship   Learning within a relationship with a more expert practitioner of the skill to be learned.

collaborative learning   A category of methods in which students learn in some form of group setting.

computer simulation   A computer program that imitates the key elements of realistic experiences.

computer-assisted design (CAD)   Technique for creating engineering drawings and similar images on a computer.

computer-assisted instruction (CAI)   Computer program intended to provide instructional experiences directly to the student.

computer-based instruction (CBI)   *See* computer-assisted instruction (CAI).

computer simulation   A computer-based instructional activity intended to model real-life phenomena.

conditional   A programming control structure in which an action will be taken only when certain conditions exist.

conference   On-line discussion group.

constructionism   Papert's proposal that students learn most effectively by finding and generating their own knowledge and that teachers should find ways to assist students in these activities.

cooperative learning   Situation in which students work together to accomplish an instructional goal.

copy   To copy data from the active document to be temporarily stored in computer memory.

copy and paste   Process available within an application program allowing data to be copied to the memory of the computer and then inserted at another location in the present document or in a different document. In many cases data can also be transferred across application programs.

courseware   Generic term for instructional software.

cursor   Symbol, usually a line or square, displayed on the computer screen indicating where the next symbol entered will appear.

cut   To remove data from the active document for temporary storage in computer memory.

database   Application program allowing the organization, storage, and search of information.

declarative knowledge   Stored verbal information and facts.

delete (in word processing)   To remove text at the location of the cursor.

deselecting   Clicking on a selected option, often a box associated with the description of an option to be applied, causing the option not to be applied.

design   A tool developed to accomplish a purpose.

desktop publishing   Programs that facilitate the entry and positioning of text and graphics to control precisely the appearance of printed documents.

dialog box   A program event in which a box appears on top of the information already appearing on the screen and requests the user to provide input by entering text or clicking on a button.

digital format   Recording format in which information is stored as a series of numbers, allowing exact duplication of the original information.

direct mode   Programming commands are executed as soon as they are entered.

discovery learning   Students discover important principles on their own.

dots per inch (dpi)   Term describing the resolution of printers, monitors, and scanners. The use of the term *dot* can be confusing because the smallest elements a scanner can detect or a monitor can display are called pixels.

double speed drive   CD-ROM drive capable of transferring data at 300 kilobytes per second.

download   To transfer a file from a remote computer to your computer.

dragging   Moving the mouse while holding the mouse button down.

draw program   A graphics program using object-oriented images rather than bit maps. Mathematical descriptions are used to represent these objects.

drill   Computer application designed to facilitate factual memorization.

dual-coding theory   Theory proposing that imagery and verbal information are stored in different ways and that information stored in both forms will be easier to retrieve.

edutainment   Term for game-like software that offers educational benefits.

electronic mail (e-mail)   Personal message sent by the user of one computer to the user of another.

embellished document   A text document enhanced with graphics, video segments, or sound.

episodic memory   Memory for an event usually connected with a specific time and place.

exploratory environments   Setting providing elements for the learner to manipulate and learn as the result of this manipulation.

fair use   Guidelines describing the conditions under which the copying of intellectual property is appropriate.

fidelity   Extent to which a simulation mimics reality.

field (database)   Category defined by the user of a database to contain a specified type of information, such as age, name, zip code.

field (HyperCard)   A container into which you type text.

file (database)   Complete collection of related database records.

fill tool   Paint tool used to fill an enclosed area with a designated color or a pattern.

filtering software   Special software that allows a measure of control over the Internet sites which a student can browse.

font   Standardized design of characters that determines the appearance of text (e.g. Helvetica, Geneva).

formatting   Determining the physical appearance of a document.

forum   On-line discussion group in which participants contribute comments to be read by all participants; *see also* conference.

freeware   Software made available at no cost with the expectation that the software will not be modified and will retain the author's copyright notice.

FTP   File transfer protocol; standards allowing the transfer of files to and from a host computer.

game   Program that emphasizes competition and enjoyment. Certain games have educational benefits as well.

generative learning   A theory emphasizing the student's active search for meaning through the integration of new experiences with existing knowledge structures or the generation of inferences.

gigabyte drive   Hard drive with 1,000-megabyte capacity.

graphic design   Concerns issues of the appearance of information on the computer screen as appearance is related to informativeness, interpretability, and interest.

graphic user interface (GUI)   System for interacting with a computer based on the manipulation of icons rather than the input of typed commands.

gray scale   Picture presented only in shades of gray.

grid   Method for organizing the computer screen using patterns of lines.

group investigation   Cooperative learning method in which group members develop a project related to a general theme proposed by the teacher.

hand-held scanner   Small device intended to be rolled over pictures or text for the purpose of generating and storing a digital representation of the original information.

handler   A block of hypertext statements beginning with the word "on" and ending with the word "end" that are executed in response to a specific message. The word "on" is followed by the name of the message the handler is to respond to; e.g., on MouseUp.

hardware   Computer or media equipment; not the media itself, which is considered software.

home page   Initial display when connecting to a World Wide Web site.

hypermedia   Multimedia that a user can examine in a flexible, nonlinear fashion. The user can typically move from one information source to several others and can control which of these options to take.

hypertext   Text that can be examined in a nonlinear manner. The user can typically move from one segment of text to several others by responding to options made available by the computer program controlling the text presentation.

hypertext markup language (HTML)   The special codes and tags inserted in an HTML document that inform a Web browser how to display hypermedia elements (e.g., text, graphics) and how to take specific actions (e.g., branch to another WWW document).

icon   A small image often used consistently to represent a specific program action or category of information.

imagery   (Memory component) Stored representations of smells, sounds, and sights.

incremental advantage   Improvement due to increased efficiency.

indirect mode   Programming commands are first stored and then executed at a later time.

individual accountability   Requirement of cooperative learning demanding that individuals must achieve for the team to achieve.

inert knowledge   Knowledge that students have acquired but fail to use.

insert (in word processing)   To enter text at the position of the cursor.

instructionism   Orientation emphasizing the improvement of student performance through the development of better instructional methods.

integrated learning system (ILS)   Comprehensive computer-based approach to instruction, including multiple learning activities, possibly in several content areas, and a comprehensive assessment and management system.

integrated teaching system (ITS)   *See* integrated learning system (ILS).

interactive hypermedia   Linked elements of sound, text, graphics, and video that can be examined in an order largely determined by the user.

Internet   International web of computer networks.

Internet service provider   Company providing individuals with modem access to the Internet.

interspersed questions   Questions embedded in the material to be studied as a study aid.

Intranet   A web designed for use within an institution rather than for general access.

jaggies   Staircase effect in the production of lines that are not perfectly horizontal or vertical. Jaggies appear when the individual units used to construct lines are large enough to be visible.

jigsaw cooperation   Form of cooperative learning in which each member of the cooperative group makes a unique and essential contribution to the accomplishment of the group task.

justification (of text)   Alignment of lines of text against the left margin (left-justified), against the right margin (right-justified), or centered on the page.

knowledge as design   Knowledge that has been applied or adapted to a purpose.

laserdisc   Term sometimes used to refer to a videodisc.

LCD projection panel   A special liquid crystal display panel that connects to a computer and sits on an overhead projector to project an image onto a display screen.

line art   Images in which the individual pixels are either black or white. Files of this type are the smallest in size because only two values are needed to describe each pixel. This is called a 1-bit image.

line mode   Software providing World Wide Web access at a minimal level, displaying only text.

linear design   Information is presented in a single fixed sequence.

linear multimedia presentation   Multimedia information presented in a standard sequence; a slide show.

linear tutorial   Form of instruction in which all learners go through the same material in the same sequence.

link   Connection between nodes.

list server   Computer server hosting a mailing list.

load   To bring data stored on a disk into the memory of the computer.

local area network (LAN)   Interconnected computers in one location, such as a school building or office.

long-term memory (LTM)   Memory store allowing virtually permanent storage.

lossy   Implies a form of compression in which data and thus some quality are lost during the compression process.

mailing lists (*see also* list server)   Telecommunications process in which an e-mail message is sent to a designated address and then resent to every member subscribing to receive messages from that address.

map   Device that identifies the components of a hypermedia presentation and shows the main links among components.

margins   Distance between the edge of text and the edge of the paper.

master slide   The common color and visual elements held constant across all slides of a presentation.

meaningful learning   Learning in which new experiences are linked with information already stored in long-term memory.

mediated instruction   Instructional approach in which the teacher works to directly assist the student in acquiring the underlying cognitive skills associated with performing a complex behavior. The teacher's efforts are directed, not just at the ability of the student to generate appropriate outcomes or products, but at the thinking and reasoning processes leading to these products.

megabytes   Approximately one million bytes. The capacity of a high-density floppy disk is between 1 and 1.5 megabytes.

menu   List of available options.

message   A specific word sent through the levels of the HyperCard hierarchy by the occurrence of a specific event.

metacognition   Knowledge about your own thinking and learning.

metacognitive control functions Behaviors involved in planning, regulating, and evaluating mental behaviors.

metacognitive knowledge Knowledge about how tasks are performed, what makes tasks easy or difficult, and personal skills and limitations.

microworld Learning environment allowing the exploration of an academic domain in an experiential way.

mindtool The idea that the use of powerful computer tools may encourage problem-solving and learning by freeing the learner from tasks that require attention or significant storage capacity.

mirror An Internet distribution system designed to provide more widespread access to the original resource.

modem Computer peripheral device allowing information to be exchanged over a telephone line between computers.

multimedia Communication format integrating several media (text, audio, visual), most commonly implemented with a computer.

multimedia library An organized collection of still images, video clips, sounds, text, and simple graphics focused on a theme.

multiple loading Loading a program to several computers from a single original. This practice is a copyright infringement unless covered by a provision of the license.

multisession CD CD player capable of reading all the data stored on CDs that have been recorded in multiple sessions (e.g., Kodak Photo-CD).

naive theories Personal theories fashioned from daily experiences.

net modem Modem attached to a network rather than to a single computer. Any user on the network can access the modem.

network models A model of human memory representing the contexts of memory as interconnected nodes of information.

network server Computer connected to other computers through a network holding programs to be run on the computers or storing files created on the other computers.

network structure Method of information organization in which multiple nodes are interconnected without relying on a strict hierarchical structure.

newsgroup Topical discussion group supported by the Usenet system for collecting and forwarding messages among subscriber sites. Presently over 4,000 topics are available. Messages are searched and read with a special reader.

node Unit of information; an idea, picture, or sound.

object-oriented image Image in which objects are represented using mathematical equations rather than as maps of pixel colors.

operating system Software that controls the computer and allows the computer to perform basic functions.

paint program Computer program designed to create and manipulate graphic information.

paste To insert data stored in the memory of the computer into an active document.

path-based animation The movement of an object along a preplanned path.

performance assessment The demonstration of understanding of a skill through the creation of an authentic product or the performance of an authentic task.

peripheral device Device, such as a printer or CD-ROM drive, that is external to the computer. Usually data are passed between the computer and peripheral through a physical connection in the form of an electrical cable.

photo CD Process allowing photographs to be transferred to a CD.

piracy Illegal copying of software.

pixel The smallest element a scanner can detect or a monitor can display.

practice Computer application designed to facilitate the development of skill fluency.

primitive Individual command built into a programming language.

private speech The external speech of young children that helps guide their actions when completing difficult tasks.

procedural knowledge Memory for how to do something.

procedure Section of code, defined and named by the programmer, capable of accomplishing a specific task.

programming Process of instructing a computer to perform some desired action.

public domain Bearing no copyright restrictions.

QuickTime Format allowing digital movies and sounds to be compressed, edited, and played on a computer.

read only A property of a text field set to prevent users from modifying the text appearing in the field.

reception learning Concepts, principles, and rules to be learned are presented directly to the students.

record Meaningful collection of database fields representing one unit of storage.

recursion Process or procedure that contains itself as a subprocess.

reflector site An Internet site specifically adapted to allow multiple users to simultaneously receive the same CU-SeeMe transmission.

report maker A software program allowing the organization and presentation of existing information resources.

repurposing Controlling the presentation of information from a videodisc to give viewers a different type of experience than was originally intended.

resource interdependence Situation in which members of a cooperative group must combine resources to achieve success.

reward interdependence Situation in which the success or failure experienced by all members of a cooperative group depends on the cumulative accomplishments of all members of the group.

rote learning Learning with little attention to meaning.

sampling frequency Number of times per second, in kilohertz (kHz), that digitized sound is produced. Frequencies used in microcomputer applications are likely to be in the 7 to 22 kHz range. More frequent sampling provides more realistic reproduction of original sound.

scaffolding External support for learning or problem-solving.

scanner A device that captures a bit-mapped representation of an image.

screen capture The process of saving the image appearing on the computer monitor as a graphics file.

screen-reader software Software that reads the text and other screen information (e.g., menu options) for visually impaired users.

script The HyperCard program attached to a HyperCard object.

select To identify material to which some action (such as underlining or deletion) is to be applied.

shareware Software available on "try it before you buy it" basis. If you continue to use the software, you are expected to pay the author.

short-term memory (STM) The limited capacity and duration store containing the thoughts, ideas, and images of which a person is aware; *see also* working memory.

signature Section of computer code that identifies a virus.

simulation Computer program that imitates the key elements of realistic experiences.

site license License offering certain privileges to users at a designated site; for instance, allowing a school district to make a number of copies of software from a single original.

slide show Linear multimedia; a fixed sequence of images, text segments, sounds, or video segments.

socioeconomic status (SES) A measure of prestige based on income, education, and occupation.

software Media stored as computer files, recorded music, videotaped programs, containing the information presented with hardware.

spell checker Word processing feature that checks for spelling errors.

spreadsheet Application program resembling a ledger sheet, allowing numerical data to be entered into cells arranged as rows and columns. Calculations can be performed on these data by attaching formula to cells.

stack A collection of cards; a complete HyperCard document.

stock photos Collections of images that are available for purchase and use.

storyboarding Process of roughing out the sequence of displays and activities to be incorporated into new instructional software.

student teams–achievement divisions (STAD) Form of cooperative learning in which team members are individually tested over course content and contribute to a team score based on a comparison of present score and past performance.

style (of characters) Standardized modification in the appearance of text, such as underlining or italicizing.

subprocedure Procedure representing a component process of the main program.

superprocedure Main program; perhaps organizing several subprocedures.

syntax Rules for combining commands, punctuation, and arguments to produce valid program statements.

tabs Predefined insertion point established in word processing. Setting a tab stop allows the user to move the insertion point to a specified column.

tag An HTML command.

task specialization methods Cooperative learning method in which the goal is cooperative accomplishment of a task requiring the application of what group members have learned.

TCP/IP (Transmission control protocol/Internet protocol) standards that allow different computers to transfer data over the Internet.

team rewards Requirement of cooperative learning that demands the team achievement result in some form of team recognition.

tear-off palette A set of icons allowing the selection of options, for example tools or colors, that can be positioned anywhere on the screen the user desires.

telecommunications Application in which information is transferred over some distance from one computer to another.

template Organizational plan for a database or spreadsheet.

template (programming) Outline for a solution strategy that can be applied to problems of an identifiable type.

terminal server A device allowing remote access to a network.

text object A framed segment of text treated as a unit by certain functions of word processing or desktop publishing programs.

transfer Application of skills or knowledge learned in one situation to a different situation.

transfer speed Time required to load information from the disc to the computer.

transformational advantage Improvement due to a qualitatively superior method.

translator A small utility added to an application that allows the conversion of files created with another program for use in the host application.

tree structure Hypermedia structure that is hierarchically organized.

turtlegraphics Graphics mode in which drawings are created by executing commands that move a shape around the screen. This approach is emphasized in LOGO but is also available in other languages.

tutorial A learning activity in which the computer primarily presents new information to the student and provides opportunities for the student to become proficient with this information.

user interface Methods by which the user interacts with the contents of a computer application.

variable Labeled storage container in a program, set aside to hold data on a temporary basis.

video digitizer Device used to convert an analog video signal to a digital representation of that signal.

videocapture Process of taking a video signal from a camcorder, videocassette player, or related source and trans-forming the signal into a digital format that can be stored, displayed, and manipulated using a computer.

videocapture card Card added to a computer for the purpose of converting video signal into a digital form for storage or display.

videodisc Medium for storing analog video and audio on a disc in a form that is read by bouncing a laser beam off the disc's surface.

video projector Special hardware that projects a screen image onto a large screen.

virus Uninvited program capable of duplicating itself and possibly causing other problems.

virus detection program Program capable of locating the codes associated with known viruses in stored programs and files.

virus prevention program Program running in the background that detects when the computer attempts unexpected actions and notifies the user before those actions are executed.

visual database A collection of images focused on a topic.

wide area network (WAN) A network connecting computers in several different locations (e.g., buildings).

word processing Application program allowing the entry, manipulation, and storage of text and sometimes graphics.

word processor program Computer program designed primarily to input, manipulate, store, and print text documents. More powerful word processing programs allow the same functions to be applied to documents combining text with other types of information, such as pictures and sounds.

word wrap Characteristic of word processing programs allowing text that would extend beyond the right margin of a page to automatically move to the beginning of a new line.

working memory *See* short-term memory.

World Wide Web (WWW) System providing access to Internet resources based on hypertextlike documents.

write-protect Disk adjustment preventing files on disk from being modified.

writing process approach Method of writing instruction emphasizing planning, drafting, editing, revising, and publishing. This method emphasizes rewriting with guidance from the teacher and peers.

zone of proximal development Skills an individual can perform with some assistance.

References

Abelson, H., & diSessa, A. (1981). *Turtle geometry: The computer as a medium for exploring mathematics.* Cambridge, Massachusetts: MIT Press.

Adaptive Computer Technology Centre (1996). *Accessible web page design.* [On-Line]. Available: http://www.igs.net/~starling/acc/ (November, 1996).

Alessi, S. (1988). Fidelity in the design of instructional simulations. *Journal of Computer-Based Instruction, 15*(2), 40–47.

Alessi, S., & Trollip S. (1991). *Computer-based instruction: Methods and development* (2nd ed.). Englewood Cliffs, NJ: Prentice-Hall.

Anderson, J. (1976). *Language, memory, and thought.* Hillsdale, NJ: Erlbaum.

Anderson, J. (1983). *The architecture of cognition.* Cambridge, MA: Harvard University Press.

Anderson, R. (1993). The technology infrastructure of U.S. schools. *Communications of the ACM, 36*(5), 72–73.

Anderson, R. (1993b). Opportunity to learn about computers. In R. Anderson (Ed.), *Computers in American schools 1992: An overview* (pp. 71–82). Minneapolis, MN: University of Minnesota Press.

Andre, T. (1979). Does answering higher-level questions while reading facilitate productive learning? *Review of Educational Research, 49*, 280–318.

Andres, Y. (1996). Elements of an effective CU-SeeMe videoconference. *Connections: Special Interest Group of Technology Coordinators. 12*(4), 28–29.

Apple Computer (1989). *Hypercard stack design guidelines.* Reading, MA: Addison-Wesley.

Apple Computer (1996). *Disability connection—Macintosh Access.* [On-Line]. Available: http://www2.apple.com/disability/macaccess.html (November, 1996).

Au, W., Horton, J., & Ryba, K. (1987). Logo, teacher intervention, and the development of thinking skills. *Computing Teacher, 15*(3), 12–15.

Ausubel, D. (1963). *The psychology of meaningful learning.* New York: Grune and Stratton.

Baird, W. (1989). Status of use: Microcomputers and science teaching. In J. Ellis (Ed.), *1988 AETS yearbook: Information technology and science education.* Columbus, OH: ERIC Clearinghouse for Science, Mathematics and Environmental Education, 85–104.

Baker, L. (1985). Differences in the standards used by college students to evaluate their comprehension of expository prose. *Reading Research Quarterly, 20,* 297–313.

Balajthy, E. (1988). Keyboarding, language arts, and the elementary school child. *The Computing Teacher, 15*(5), 40–43.

Bangert-Drowns, R. (1993). The word processor as an instructional tool: A meta-analysis of word processing in writing instruction. *Review of Educational Research, 63*(1), 69–93.

Barksdale, J. (1996). Why schools of education are still sending you staff you'll have to train in technology. *Electronic Learning, 15*(5), 39–45.

Barrett, H. (1994). Technology-supported assessment portfolios. *The Computing Teacher, 21*(6), 9–12.

Barron, A., Breit, F., Boulware, A., & Bullock, J. (1994). *Videodiscs in education: Overview, evaluation, activities* (2nd ed.). Tampa, FL: University of South Florida.

Battista, M., & Clements, D. (1988). Logo-based elementary school geometry curriculum. *Arithmetic Teacher, 36*(3), 11–17.

Becker, H. (1991). How computers are used in United States schools: Basic data from the 1989 I.E.A. computers in education survey. *Journal of Educational Computing Research, 7*(4), 385–406.

Becker, H., & Sterling, C. (1987). Equity in school computer use: National data and neglected considerations. *Journal of Educational Computing Research, 3,* 289–311.

Becker, J. (1993). Teaching with and about computers in secondary schools. *Communications of the ACM, 36*(5), 69–72.

Beebe, T. (1993). Nonschool computer experiences. In R. Anderson (Ed.), *Computers in American schools 1992: An overview* (pp. 83–98). Minneapolis, MN: University of Minnesota Press.

Beekman, G. (1995). *HyperCard 2.3 in a hurry: The fast track to multimedia.* San Francisco, CA: Peachpit Press.

Bennett, S., & Bennett, R. (1993). *The official Kid Pix activity book.* New York: Random House.

Bernhard, J., & Siegel, L. (1994). Increasing internal locus of control for a disadvantaged group: A computer intervention. *Computers in the Schools, 11*(1), 59–77.

Bitter, G., Camuse, R., & Durbin, V. (1993). *Using a microcomputer in the classroom* (3rd ed.). Boston: Allyn & Bacon.

Bosco, J. (1986, May). An analysis of evaluations of interactive video. *Educational Technology,* 7-17.

Bransford, J., & Stein, B. (1984). *The IDEAL problem solver.* New York: Freeman.

Bransford, J., Sherwood, R., Hasselbring, T., Kinzer, C., & Williams, S. (1990). Anchored instruction: Why we need it and how technology can help. In D. Nix & R. Spiro (Eds.), *Cognition, education and multimedia: Exploring ideas in high technology* (pp. 115-141). Hillsdale, NJ: Erlbaum.

Brant, G., Hooper, E., & Sugrue, B. (1991). Which comes first-the simulation or the lecture? *Journal of Educational Computing Research, 7*(4), 469–481.

Brown (1992). Design experiments: Theoretical and methodological challenges in creating complex interventions in classroom settings. *Journal of the Learning Sciences, 2*(2), 141–178.

Brown, A. (1981). Metacognition: The development of selective attention strategies for learning from texts. In M. Kamil (Ed.), *Directions in reading: Research and instruction* (pp. 21–43). Washington, DC: National Reading Conference.

Brown, A. (1987). Metacognition, executive control, self-rejection and other more mysterious mechanisms. In F. Weinert & R. Kluwe, (Eds.), *Metacognition, motivation, and understanding* (pp. 65–116). Hillsdale, NJ: Erlbaum.

Brown, A. (1992). Design experiments: Theoretical and methodological challenges in creating complex interventions in classroom settings. *Journal of the Learning Sciences, 2*(2), 141-178.

Brown, C. (1989–90). Taking some of the "hype" out of HyperCard. *The Computing Teacher, 17*(4), 50–52.

Brown, J., Collins, A., & Duguid, P. (1989). Situated cognition and the culture of learning. *Educational Researcher, 18, 32–42.*

Brownell, G. (Ed.). (1996). *A Mac for the teacher: Claris-Works version.* Minneapolis, MN: West Publishing.

Burgstahler, S. Disabilities, Opportunities, Internetworking & Technology (DO-IT). (1996). *Adaptive technology that provides access to computers.* [On-Line]. Available: http://weber.u.washington.edu/~doit/Brochures/adap.html (November, 1996).

Bush, V. (1945, August). *As we may think.* The Atlantic Monthly, 101-108.

Carlsen, D., & Andre, T. (1992). Use of a microcomputer simulation and conceptual change text to overcome student preconceptions about electric circuits. *Journal of Computer-Based Instruction, 19,* 105–109.

Carver, S., Lehrer, R., Connell, T., & Erickson, J. (1992). Learning by hypermedia design: Issues of assessment and implementation. *Educational Psychologist, 27*(3), 385–404.

Champagne, A., Gunstone, F., & Klopfer, L. (1985). Instructional consequences of students' knowledge about physical phenomena. In L. West & A. Pines (Eds.), *Cognitive structure and conceptual change* (pp. 163–188). Orlando, FL: Academic Press.

Champagne, A., Klopfer, L., & Anderson, J. (1980), Factors influencing the learning of classical mechanics. *American Journal of Physics, 48,* 1074–1079.

Chan, B. (1993). *Kid Pix around the world: A computer and activities book.* Reading, MA: Addison-Wesley.

Chan, B. (1994). *Kid Pix around the world. A multicultural computer activity book.* International Society for Technology in Education.

Chomsky, C. (1990). Books on videodisc: Computers, video, and reading aloud to children. In D. Nix & R. Spiro (Eds.), *Cognition, education and multimedia: Exploring ideas in high technology* (pp. 31-47). Hillsdale, NJ: Erlbaum.

Clark, R. (1985). Confounding in educational computing research. *Journal of Educational Computing Research, 1,* 137–148.

Clement, J. (1983). A conceptual model discussed by Galileo and used intuitively by physics students. In D. Gentner & A. Stevens (Eds.), *Mental models* (pp. 206–251). Hillsdale, NJ: Erlbaum.

Clements, D., & Gullo, D. (1984). Effects of computer programming on young children's cognition. *Journal of Educational Psychology, 76,* 1051–1058.

Clements, D., & Merriman, S. (1988). Componential developments in LOGO programming environments. In R. Mayer (Ed.), *Teaching and learning computer programming* (pp. 13–54). Hillsdale, NJ: Erlbaum.

Clements, D., & Sarama, J. (1996). Turtle math: Redesigning Logo for elementary mathematics. *Learning and Leading with Technology, 23*(7), 10–15.

Cochran-Smith, M. (1991). Word processing and writing in elementary classrooms: A critical review of related literature. *Review of Educational Research, 61*(1), 107–155.

Cochran-Smith, M., Paris, C., & Kahn, J. (1991). *Learning to write differently: Beginning writers and word processing.* Norwood, NJ: Ablex.

Cognition and Technology Group (1990). Anchored instruction and its relationship to situated cognition. *Educational Researcher, 19*(6), 2–10.

Cognition and Technology Group (1991, May). Technology and the design of generative learning environments. *Educational Technology, 32,* 34–40.

Cognition and Technology Group (1992). The Jasper Series as an example of anchored instruction: Theory, program description and assessment data. *Educational Psychologist, 27*(3), 291–315.

Cognition and Technology Group (1996). Multimedia environments for enhanced learning in mathematics. In S. Vosniadou, E. De Corte, and R. Glaser (Eds.), *International perspectives on the design of technology supported learning environments* (pp. 285–305). Hillsdale, NJ: Erlbaum.

Cohen, M., & Riel, M. (1989). The effect of distant audiences on students' writing. *American Educational Research Journal, 26*(2), 143–150.

Collins, A., & Quillian, M. (1969). Retrieval time from semantic memory. *Journal of Verbal Learning and Verbal Behavior, 8,* 240–247.

Collins, A., Hawkins, J., & Carver, S. (1991). A cognitive apprenticeship for disadvantaged students. In B. Means, C. Chelemer, & M. Knapp (Eds.), *Teaching advanced skills to at-risk students: Views from research and practice* (pp. 216–243). San Francisco, CA: Jossey-Bass.

Collins, S. (1997). Web66 international WWW school registry. [On-line]. Available: http://web66.coled.umn.edu/schools/stats/stats.html (February 1997).

Cosden, M. (1988). Microcomputer instruction and perceptions of effectiveness by special and regular elementary school teachers. *Journal of Special Education, 22*(2), 242–253.

Covey, P. (1990). *A right to die? The case of Dax Cowart.* Paper presented at the annual meeting of the AERA, Boston, MA.

Crooks, T. (1988). The impact of classroom evaluation practices on students. *Review of Educational Research 58,* 438–481.

Cully, L. (1988). Girls, boys and computers. *Educational Studies, 14*(1), 3–8.

Culp, G., & Watkins, G. (1995). *The educator's guide to HyperCard and hypertalk.* Boston, MA: Allyn & Bacon.

D'Ignazio, F. (1990). Restructuring knowledge: Opportunities for classroom learning in the 1990s. *Computing Teacher, 18*(1), 22–25.

D'Ignazio, F. (1996). Minimalist multimedia: Authoring on the world wide web. *Learning and Leading with Technology, 23*(8), 49–51.

Daiute, C. (1983). The computer as stylus and audience. *College Composition and Communication, 34,* 134–145.

Daiute, C., & Taylor, R. (1981). Computers and the improvement of writing. *Association for Computing Machinery Proceedings* (pp. 83–88).

Day, J. (1986). Teaching summarization skills. *Cognition and Instruction, 3,* 193–210.

Demetrulias, D., & Rosenthal, N. (1985). Discrimination against females and minorities in microcomputer advertising. *Computers and the Social Sciences, 1,* 91–95.

Dodge, B. (1995). *Some thoughts about WebQuests.* Available: http://edweb.sdsu.edu/courses/edtec596/about_webquests.html (6/23/96)

Duffy, T., & Bednar, A. (1991, September). Attempting to come to grips with alternative perspectives. *Educational Technology, 32,* 12–15.

Durkin, D. (1978–1979). What classroom observations reveal about reading comprehension instruction. *Reading Research Quarterly, 14,* 481–533.

Eisenberg, M., & Berkowitz, R. (1990). *Information problem-solving: The big six skills approach to library and information skills instruction.* Norwood, NJ: Ablex Publishing Company.

Elton, L., and Laurillard, D. (1979). Trends in research on student learning. *Studies in Higher Education 4,* 87–102.

Emihovich, C., & Miller, G. (1988). Talking to the turtle: A discourse analysis of Logo instruction. *Discourse Processes, 11,* 183–201.

Fay, A., & Mayer, R. (1988). Learning LOGO: A cognitive analysis. In R. Mayer (Ed), *Teaching and learning computer programming* (pp. 55–74). Hillsdale, NJ: Erlbaum.

FIND/SVP Inc. (1995). *1995 American learning household survey—Girls' and boys' use of PCs at home.* [On-Line]. Available: http://etrg.findsvp.com (November, 1996).

Flavell, J. (1987). Speculations about the nature and development of metacognition. In F. Weinert & R. Kluwe (Eds.), *Metacognition, motivation, and understanding* (pp. 21–30). Hillsdale, NJ: Erlbaum.

Fletcher, J. (1990). *Effectiveness and cost of interactive videodisc instruction in defense training and education.* ERIC Document ED 326 194.

Fletcher-Flinn, C. & Gravatt, B. (1995). The efficacy of computer-assisted instruction (CAI): A meta-analysis. *Journal of Educational Computing Research, 12*(3), 219–242.

Flower, L., & Hayes, J. (1981). A cognitive process theory of writing. *College Composition and Communication, 32,* 365–387.

Forester, T., & Morrison, P. (1990). *Computer ethics: Cautionary tales and ethical dilemmas in computing.* Cambridge, MA: The MIT Press.

Fraase, M. (1990). *Macintosh hypermedia: Vol. I. Reference guide.* Glenview, IL: Scott, Foresman and Co.

Fredericks, A., Meinbach, A., & Rothlein, L. (1993). *Thematic units: An integrated approach to teaching science and social studies.* New York: HarperCollins.

Fritz, M. (1992). Be juris-prudent. *CBT Directions, 5*(2), 6,8–10.

Gagne, E. (1985). *The cognitive psychology of school learning.* Boston: Little, Brown.

Gagne, E., Yekovich, C., & Yekovich, F. (1993). *The cognitive psychology of school learning* (2nd ed.). New York: Harper-Collins.

Gagne, R., & Glaser, R. (1987) Foundations in learning research. In R. Gagne (Ed.) , *Instructional technology: Foundations* (pp. 49–83). Hillsdale, NJ: Erlbaum.

Garner, R. (1987). *Metacognition and reading comprehension.* Norwood, NJ: Ablex.

Gates, B. (1995). *The road ahead.* New York: Viking Books.

George, Y., Malcolm, S., & Jeffers, L. (1993). Computer equity for the future. *Communications of the ACM, 36*(5), 78–81.

Glover, J., Ronning, R., & Bruning, R. (1990). *Cognitive psychology for teachers.* New York: Macmillan.

Goldman, S., Petrosino, A., Sherwood, R., Garrison, S., Hickey, D., Bransford, J., & Pellegrino, J. (1996). Anchored science instruction in multimedia learning. In S. Vosniadou, E. De Corte, & R. Glaser (Eds.), *International perspectives on the design of technology supported learning environments.* (pp. 257–284). Hillsdale, NJ: Erlbaum.

Goldman, S., Petrosino, A., Sherwood, R., Garrison, S., Hickey, D., Bransford, J., & Pellegrino, J. (1996). Anchoring science instruction in multimedia learning environments. In S. Vosniadou, E. De Corte, and R. Glaser (Eds.), *International perspectives on the design of technology supported learning environments* (pp. 257–284). Hillsdale, NJ: Erlbaum.

Goodman, D. (1994). *The complete HyperCard 2.2 handbook.* New York: Random House.

Grabe, M. (1985). Evaluating the educational value of computers in the schools. In S. Harlow (Ed.), *Humanistic perspectives on computers in the schools* (pp. 35–44). New York: Haworth Press.

Grabe, M. (1986). A positive comment on drill and practice. *Electronic Learning, 5,* 22–23.

Grabe, M. (1992). Learning in technology enriched study environments: Will students study effectively? *Reading and Writing Quarterly, 8,* 321–336.

Graves, D. (1983). *Writing: Teachers and children at work.* Exeter, NH: Heinemann.

Gray, M. (1996). *Web growth data.* World Wide Web. Available: http://www.mit.edu/people/mkgray/net/web-growth-summary.html (December, 1996)

Hannafin, R., & Freeman, D. (1995). An exploratory study of teachers' view of knowledge acquisition. *Educational Technology, 35*(1), 49–56.

Harel, I. (1991). *Children as designers.* Norwood, NJ: Ablex.

Harel, I., & Papert, S. (1990). Software design as a learning environment. *Interactive Learning Environments, 1,* 1–32.

Harley, S. (1996). Situated learning and classroom instruction. In H. McLellan (Ed.), *Situated learning perspectives* (pp. 113–122). Englewood Cliffs, NJ: Educational Technology Publications.

Harris, J. (1995). Curricularly infused telecomputing: A structural approach to activity design. *Computers in the Schools, 11*(3), 49–59.

Hartson, T. (1993). Kid-appeal science projects. *Computers in Education, 20*(6), 33–36.

Havice, B. (1994). Learning HyperCard through story writing. *Computing Teacher, 22*(1), 23–26.

Hawkins, J. (1987). Computers and girls: Rethinking the issues. In R. Pea & K. Sheingold (Eds.), *Mirrors of minds: Patterns of excellence in educational computing* (pp. 242–257). Norwood, NJ: Ablex.

Hawn, M. (1996). Top search engines. *MacWorld, 13*(8), 114–115.

Hayes, J., & Flower, L. (1980). Writing as problem solving. *Visible Language, 14,* 388–399.

Hayes, J., & Simon, H. (1974). Understanding written problem instructions. In L. Gregg (Ed.), *Knowledge and cognition.* Hillsdale, NJ: Erlbaum.

Henry, M., & Southerly, T. (1994). A comparison of the language features of BASIC and Hypercard. *Computers in the Schools, 10*(1&2), 141–153.

Hill, M. (1993). Chapter 1 revisited: Technology's second chance. *Electronic Learning, 13*(1), 27–32.

Howe, M. (1972). *Understanding school learning.* New York: Harper & Row.

Hsu, J., Chapelle, C., & Thompson, A. (1993). Exploratory learning environments: What are they and do students explore? *Journal of Educational Computing Research, 9*(1), 1–15.

Hutchinson, E., & Whalen, M. (1994–95). Female students and LEGO TC logo. *The Computing Teacher, 22*(4), 22–25.

IITF/CAT (Information Infrastructure Task Force Committee on Applications and Technology). (1994). "A transformation of learning: Use of the NII for education and lifelong learning." Report of the Information Infrastructure Task Force Committee on Applications and Technology, National Institute of Standards and Technology Special Publication No. 857, U.S. Department of Commerce, Washington, DC: Government Printing Office.

Ito, R. (1988, December). Video disc-o-tech. *MacUser,* 209–220.

James, W. (1912). *Talks to teachers on psychology.* New York: Henry Holt.

Jansen, B., & Culpepper, S. (1996). Using the big six research process. *Multimedia Schools, 3*(5), 32–38.

Johnson, D., & Johnson, R. (1989). Social skills for successful group work. *Educational Leadership, 47*(4), 29–33.

Johnson, D., Johnson, R., & Holubec, E. (1991). *Cooperation in the classroom* (rev. ed.). Edina, MN: Interaction Book Company.

Jonassen, D. (1986). Hypertext principles for text and courseware design. *Educational Psychologist, 21,* 269–292.

Jonassen, D. (1991, September). Evaluating constructivistic learning. *Educational Technology, 32,* 28–33.

Jonassen, D. (1995). Supporting communities of learners with technology: A vision for integrating technology with learning in schools. *Educational Technology, 35*(4), 60–63.

Jonassen, D. (1996). *Computers in the classroom: Mindtools for critical thinking.* Englewood, NJ: Prentice-Hall.

Jonassen, D., & Grabinger, R. (1990). Problems and issues in designing hypertext/hypermedia for learning. In D. Jonassen & H. Mandl (Eds.), *Designing hypermedia for learning* (pp. 3–25). New York: Springer-Verlag.

Joyce, J. (1988, November). Siren shapes: Exploratory and constructive hypertexts. *Academic Computing, 3*(4), 10–14, 37–42.

Kafai, Y., & Harel, I. (1991). Children learning through consulting. In I. Harel & S. Papert (Eds.), *Constructionism* (pp. 111–140). Norwood, NJ: Ablex.

Kamp, S. (1996). *Creating software accessible to students and teachers with disabilities.* [On-Line]. Available: http://www.spa.org/project/j.html (November, 1996).

Karoly, F. (1996). Robot games and turtle roses: Teaching LOGO in Hungary. *Learning and Leading with Technology, 23*(7), 62–64.

Katz, L., & Chard, S. (1989). *Engaging children's minds: The project approach.* Norwood, NJ: Ablex.

Keller, J. (1990). Characteristics of Logo instruction promoting transfer of learning: A research review. *Journal of Research on Computing in Education, 23,* 55–71.

Kinzie, M., Larsen, V., Burch, J., & Boker, S. (1996). Frog dissection via the world-wide web: Implications for the widespread delivery of instruction. *Educational Technology Research and Development, 44,* 59–69.

Kovalik, S. (1993). *Integrated thematic instruction: The model* (2nd ed.). Village of Oak Creek, AZ: Books for Educators.

Kozma, R. (1991). Learning with media. *Review of Educational Research, 61*(2), 179-211.

Kurland, D., Clement, C., Mawby, R., & Pea, R. (1987). Mapping the cognitive demands of learning to program. In R. Pea & K. Sheingold (Eds.), *Mirrors of minds: Patterns of experience in educational computer* (pp. 103–127). Norwood, NJ: Ablex.

Laboratory of Comparative Human Cognition. (1989). Kids and computers: A positive vision of the future. *Harvard Educational Review, 59,* 73–86.

Lafer, S., & Markert, A. (1994). Authentic learning situations and the potential of Lego TC Logo. *Computers in the Schools, 11*(1), 79–93.

Lai, K. (1991). Integrating database activities into a primary school curriculum: Instructional procedures and outcomes. *Computers in the Schools, 8*(4), 55–63.

Latess, T. (1995). *HyperStudio reference guide.* El Cajon, CA: Roger Wagner Publishing Company.

Lehrer, R. (1993). Authors of knowledge: Patterns of hypermedia design. In S. Lajoie & S. Derry (Eds.), *Computers as cognitive tools* (pp. 197–227). Hillsdale, NJ: Erlbaum.

Lehrer, R., Erickson, J., & Connell, T. (1994). Learning by designing hypermedia documents. *Computers in the Schools, 10*(1/2), 227–254.

Lepper, M., & Gurtner, J. (1989). Children and computers: Approaching the twenty first century. *American Psychologist, 44*(2), 170–178.

Lepper, M., & Malone, T. (1987). Intrinsic motivation and instructional effectiveness in computer based education. In R. Snow & M. Farr (Eds.), *Aptitude, learning and instruction* (Vol. 3). *Cognitive and affective analysis* (pp. 255–286). Hillsdale, NJ: Erlbaum.

Levin, R. (1990). *The computer virus handbook.* Berkeley, CA: Osborne McGraw-Hill.

Levin, S. (1991). The effects of interactive video enhanced earthquake lessons on achievement of seventh grade earth science students. *Journal of Computer Based Instruction, 18*(4), 125-129.

Levy, S. (1993). The rap on software piracy. *Macworld, 10*(1), 57.

Li, X. (1996) *Electronic Sources: APA style of citation* [Online]. Available:

http://www.uvm.edu/~xli/reference/apa.html. [1996, June 22]

Liao, Y. (1992). Effects of computer-assisted instruction on cognitive outcomes: A meta-analysis. *Journal of Research on Computing in Education, 24*(3), 367–380.

Littlefield, J., Delclos, V., Lever, S., Clayton, K., Bransford, J., & Franks, J. (1988). Learning LOGO: Method of teaching, transfer of general skill, and attitudes toward school and computers. In R. Mayer (Ed.), *Teaching and learning computer programming* (pp. 111–135). Hillsdale, NJ: Erlbaum.

Locatis, C., Letourneau, G., & Banvard, R. (1990). Hypermedia and instruction. *Educational Technology, Research and Development, 37*(4), 65-77.

Loveless, T. (1996). Why aren't computers used more in education? ERIC Document ED 392131. Syracuse, NY: ERIC Clearinghouse for Information Resources.

Magnan, S. (1993). The educational computing infrastructure. In R. Anderson (Ed.), *Computers in American schools 1992: An overview.* Minneapolis, MN: University of Minnesota Press.

Malone, T. (1981). Towards a theory of intrinsically motivating instruction. *Cognitive Science, 5,* 333–369.

Marchionini, G. (1988). Hypermedia and learning: Freedom and chaos. *Educational Technology, 28*(11), 8-12.

Markman, E., & Gorin, L. (1981). Children's ability to adjust their standards for evaluating comprehension. *Journal of Educational Psychology, 73,* 320–325.

Martin, J. (1994). Are you breaking the law? *MacWorld, 11*(5), 125–129.

Mayer, R., & Anderson, R. (1991). Animations need narrations: An experimental test of a dual-coding hypothesis. *Journal of Educational Psychology 83* (4), 484-490.

McAdoo, M. (1994). Equity: Has technology bridged the gap? *Electronic Learning, 13*(7), 24–34.

McCloskey, M. (1983). Naive theories of motion. In D. Gentner & A. Stevens (Eds.), *Mental models* (pp. 71–94). Hillsdale, NJ: Erlbaum.

McGinley, W. (1992). The role of reading and writing while composing from sources. *Reading Research Quarterly, 27,* 227–248.

McLellan, H. (1996). Situated learning: Multiple perspectives. In H. McLellan (Ed.), *Situated learning perspectives* (pp. 5–17). Englewood Cliffs, NJ: Educational Technology Publications.

McLuhan, M. (1964). *Understanding media: The extensions of man.* New York: McGraw-Hill.

McNeil, B., & Nelson, K. (1990). *Meta-analysis of interactive video instruction: A 10-year review of achievement effects.* ERIC Document ED 321 761.

Means, B., Blando, J., Olson, K., Middleton, T., Morocco, C., Remz, A., & Zorfass, J. (1993). *Using technology to support education reform.* Washington, DC: Office of Educational Research and Improvement.

Mehlinger, H. (1996). School reform in the information age. *Phi Delta Kappan, 77*(6), 400–407.

Milheim, W., & Martin, B. (1991). Theoretical bases for the use of learner control: Three different perspectives. *Journal of Computer-Based Instruction, 18,* 99–105.

Montague, M. (1990). Computers and writing process instruction. *Computers in the Schools, 7*(3), 5–20.

Murie, M. (1993). *Macintosh multimedia workshop.* Carmel, IN: Hayden Books.

Naisbitt, J. (1984). *Megatrends: Ten new directions transforming our lives.* New York: Warner Books.

National Center for Education Statistics. (1996). *Advanced Telecommunications in U.S. Public Elementary and Secondary Schools, 1995* (NCES 96–854). Washington, DC: U.S. Department of Education.

National Telecommunications and Information Administration (1995). *Falling through the net: A survey of the "have nots" in rural and urban America.* [On-Line]. Available: http://www.ntia.doc.gov/reports.html (November, 1996).

Nelson, C., Watson, J., & Busch, J. (1989, Summer). The interactive videodisc as an educational tool. *Journal of Interactive Instruction Development,* 11-16.

Newell, F. (1996). Effects of cross-age tutoring program on computer literacy learning of second grade students. *Journal of Research on Computing in Education, 28*(3), 346–358.

Nielsen, J. (1990). *Hypertext and hypermedia.* Boston, MA: Academic Press.

Niemiec, R., Samson, G., Weinstein, T., & Walberg, H. (1989). The effect of computer-based instruction in elementary school: A quantitative synthesis. *Journal of Research on Computing in Education, 20,* 85–103.

Niemiec, R., & Walberg, H. (1987). Comparative effects of computer-assisted instruction: A synthesis of reviews. *Journal of Educational Computing Research, 3*(1), 19–37.

Office of Technology Assessment. (1992). *Testing in American schools: Asking the right questions.* Washington, DC: U.S. Government Printing Office.

Office of Technology Assessment. (1995). *Teachers and technology: Making the connection.* Washington, DC: U.S. Government Printing Office.

Osborne, R., & Freyberg, P. (1985). *Learning in science.* Portsmouth, NH: Heinemann.

Owston, R., Murphy, S., & Wideman, H. (1992). The effects of word processing on students' writing quality and revision strategies. *Research in the Teaching of English, 26*(3), 249–276.

Paivio, A. (1986). *Mental representations: A dual coding approach.* New York: Oxford University Press.

Palincsar, A., & Brown, A. (1984). Reciprocal teaching of comprehension-fostering and comprehension-monitoring activities. *Cognition and Instruction, 1,* 117–175.

Papert, S. (1980). *Mindstorms: Children, computers and powerful ideas.* New York: Basic Books.

Papert, S. (1993). *The children's machine: Rethinking school in the age of the computer.* New York: Basic Books.

Paris, S., & Lindauer, B. (1982). The development of cognitive skills during childhood. In B. Wolman (Ed.), *Handbook of developmental psychology* (pp. 333–349). Englewood Cliffs, NJ: Prentice-Hall.

Paris, S., & Winograd, P. (1990). How metacognition can promote academic learning and instruction. In B. Jones & L. Idol (Eds.), *Dimensions of thinking and cognitive instruction* (pp. 15–51). Hillsdale, NJ: Erlbaum.

Paulson, F., Paulson, P., & Meyer, C. (1991). What makes a portfolio a portfolio? *Educational Leadership, 48*(5), 60–63.

Pea, R., & Kurland, D. (1987a). Cognitive technologies in writing. In E. Rothkopf (Ed.), *Review of research in education #14* (pp. 277–326). Washington, DC: American Educational Research Association.

Pea, R., & Kurland, D. (1987b). On the cognitive effects of learning computer programming. In R. Pea & K. Sheingold (Eds.), *Mirrors of minds: Patterns of experience in educational computer* (pp. 147–177). Norwood, NJ: Ablex.

Pearlman, R. (1991, January). Restructuring with technology: A tour of schools where it's happening. *Technology and Learning,* 30–37.

Perkins, D. (1985). The fingertip effect: How information-processing technology shapes thinking. *Educational Researcher, 14,* 11–17.

Perkins, D. (1986). *Knowledge as design.* Hillsdale, NJ: Erlbaum.

Pon, K. (1988, March). Process writing in the one-computer classroom. *The Computing Teacher, 15* (6), 33–37.

Porter, C., & Cleland, J. (1995). *The portfolio as a learning strategy.* Portsmouth, NH: Heinemann.

Pressley, M., Snyder, B., Levin, J., Murray, H., & Ghatala, E. (1987). Perceived readiness for examination performance (PREP) produced by initial reading of text and text containing adjunct questions. *Reading Research Quarterly, 22,* 219–236.

Price, R. (1991). *Computer-aided instruction: A guide for authors.* Pacific Grove, CA: Brooks/Cole Publishing.

Quality Educational Data (1996). *School technology research results* [On-Line]. Available: http://qeddata.com/results.html [1996, October].

Quality Educational Data (1996). Quality Educational Data National Education Database. [On-line]. Available http://www.qeddata.com. Selections from the database at this on-line site.

Rathje, L. (1996). *ClarisWorks for students* (2nd ed.). Eugene, OR: HRS Publications.

Read, J., & Barnsley, R. (1977). Remember Dick and Jane. *Canadian Journal of Behavioral Science, 9,* 361–370.

Rieber, L. (1996). Seriously considering play: Designing interactive learning environments based on the blending of microworlds, simulations and games. *Educational Technology Research and Development, 44*(2), 43–58.

Ring, G. (1993). The effects of instruction in courseware preview methodology on the predictive validity of teacher preview ratings. *Journal of Educational Computing Research, 9*(2), 197–218.

Robinette, M. (1996). *The ClarisWorks reference for teachers.* Indianapolis, IN: IDG Book Co.

Rosen, M. (1993). Lego meets LOGO. In T. Cannings & L. Finkel (Eds.), *The technology age classroom* (pp. 226–230). Wilsonville, OR: Franklin, Beedle & Associates.

Rothkopf, E. (1970). The concept of mathemagenic activities. *Review of Educational Research, 40,* 325–335.

Salisbury, D. (1990). Cognitive psychology and its implication for designing drill and practice programs for computers. *Journal of Computer-Based Instruction, 17,* 23–30.

Salomon, G., & Perkins, D. (1987). Transfer of cognitive skills from programming: When and how? *Journal of Educational Computing Research, 3*(2), 149–169.

Salpeter, J. (1992). Are you obeying copyright law? *Technology and Learning, 12*(8), 14–23.

Sanders, J., & McGinnis, M. (1991a). *Computer equity in math and science: A trainer's workshop guide.* Metuchen, NJ: Scarecrow Press.

Sanders, J., & McGinnis, M. (1991b). *Counting on computer equity: A quick and easy guide for finding out if your school has a computer gender gap.* Metuchen, NJ: Scarecrow Press.

Scardamalia, B., Bereiter, C., McLean, R., Swallow, J., & Woodruff, E. (1989). Computer-supported intentional learning environments. *Journal of Educational Computing Research, 5*(1), 51–68.

Schallert, D. (1980). The role of illustrations in reading comprehension. In R. Spiro, B. Bruce, & W. Brewer (Eds.), *Theoretical issues in reading comprehension* (pp. 503-524). Hillsdale, NJ: Erlbaum.

Schurman, K. (1994). Today's schools? Three Rs . . . and one T (technology). *PC Novice, 5*(9), 28–32.

Seiter, C. (1996). Better, faster web searching. *MacWorld, 13*(12), 159–162.

Sharan, S., & Shachar, H. (1988). *Language and learning in the cooperative classroom.* New York: Springer-Verlag.

Sharan, Y., & Sharan, S. (1992). *Expanding cooperative learning through group investigation.* New York: Teachers College Press.

Sharp, V. (1994). *Hyperstudio in one hour.* International Society for Technology in Education.

Sheingold, K. (1991, September). Restructuring for learning with technology: The potential for synergy. *Phi Delta Kappan,* 28–36.

Shimabukuro, G. (1989). A class act: Junior high students, LEGO and LOGO. *The Computing Teacher, 16*(5), 37–39.

Shipstone, D. (1988). Pupils' understanding of simple electrical circuits. *Physics Education, 23,* 92–96.

Silverman, S., & Pritchard, A. (1996). Building their future: Girls and technology education in Connecticut. *Journal of Technology Education, 7*(2). [On-Line]. Available: http://scholar.lib.vt.edu/ejournals/JTE/jte-v7n2/silverman.jte-v7n2.html (November, 1996).

Simmons, W. (1987). Beyond basic skills: Literacy and technology for minority schools. In R. Pea & K. Sheingold (Eds.), *Mirrors of minds: Patterns of excellence in educational computing* (pp. 86–102). Norwood, NJ: Ablex.

Simonson, M., & Thompson, A. (1994). *Educational computing foundations* (2nd Ed.). New York: Merrill.

Slavin, R. (1990). *Cooperative learning: Theory, research, and practice.* Englewood Cliffs, NJ: Prentice-Hall.

Slavin, R. (1991). *Student team learning: A practical guide to cooperative learning* (3rd ed.). Washington, DC: National Education Association.

Smagorinsky, P. (1995). Constructing meaning in the disciplines: Reconceptualizing writing across the curriculum as composing across the curriculum. *American Journal of Education, 103,* 160–184.

Snyder, B. (1971). *The hidden curriculum.* Cambridge, MA: MIT Press.

Snyder, I. (1993). Writing with word processors: A research overview. *Educational Research, 35*(1), 49–68.

Spiro, R., Feltovich, P., Jacobson, M., & Coulson, R. (1991, May). Cognitive flexibility, constructivism, and hypertext: Random access instruction for advanced knowledge acquisition in ill-structured domains. *Educational Technology, 3(5),* 24–33.

Spotts, T. & Bowman, M. (1995). Faculty use of instructional technologies in higher education. *Educational Technology, 35*(2), 56–64.

Steinberg, S. (1989). Cognition and learner control: A literature review, 1977–1988. *Journal of Computer-Based Instruction, 16,* 117–121.

Striley, J. (1988). Physics for the rest of us. *Educational Researcher, 17(6),* 7–10.

Sutton, R. (1991). Equity and computers in the schools: A decade of research. *Review of Educational Research, 61*(4), 475–503.

Talmage, H., Pascarella, E., & Ford, S. (1984). The influence of cooperative learning strategies on teacher practices, student perceptions of the learning environment, and academic achievement. *American Educational Research Journal, 21*(1), 163–179.

Taylor, R. (1980). *The computer in the school: Tutor, tool, tutee.* New York: Teachers College Press.

Tennyson, R. (1980). Instructional control strategies and content structure as design variables in concept acquisition using computer-assisted instruction. *Journal of Educational Psychology, 72,* 525–532.

Tennyson, R., & Buttrey, T. (1980). Advisement and management strategies as design variables in computer-assisted instruction. *Educational Communication and Technology Journal, 28,* 169–176.

Thomas, J., & Rohwer, W. (1986). Academic studying: The role of learning strategies. *Educational Psychologist, 21,* 19–41.

Thomas, L., & Knezek, D. (1991). Facilitating restructured learning experiences with technology. *Computing Teacher, 18*(6), 49–53.

Thomas, R., & Hooper, E. (1991). Simulation: An opportunity we are missing. *Journal of Research on Computing in Education, 23*(4), 497–513.

Tierney, R., Carter, M., & Desai, L. (1991). *Portfolio assessment in the reading-writing classroom.* Norwood, MA: Christopher-Gordon Publishers.

Toffler, A. (1980). *The third wave.* New York: Morrow.

Tolhurst, D. (1995). Hypertext, hypermedia, multimedia defined. *Educational Technology, 35*(2), 21-26.

Toomey, R., & Ketterer, K. (1995). Using multimedia as a cognitive tool. *Journal of Research on Computing in Education, 27*(4), 472–482.

Tulving, E. (1972). Episodic and semantic memory. In E. Tulving & W. Donaldson (Eds.), *Organization of memory.* New York: Academic Press.

Turkle, S. (1984). *The second self: Computers and the human spirit.* New York: Simon and Schuster.

Turner, S., & Land, M. (1994). *HyperCard: A tool for learning.* Belmont, CA: Wadsworth.

Ventura, F. (1992). *HyperCard projects for kids.* Newbury Park, CA: Ventura Educational Systems.

Vygotsky, L. (1978). *Mind in society: The development of higher mental processes.* Cambridge, MA: Harvard University Press.

Ware, M., & Struck, M. (1985). Sex-role messages vis-a-vis microcomputer use: A look at the pictures. *Sex Roles, 13*(3/4), 205–214.

Webb, N., & Lewis, S. (1988). The social context of learning computer programming. In R. Mayer (Ed.), *Teaching and learning computer programming* (pp. 179–206). Hillsdale, NJ: Erlbaum.

WebCrawler (1996). WebCrawler's web size. [On-line]. Available http://webcrawler.com/WebCrawler/Facts/Size.html. [1997, March]

Wetzel, K. (1990). Keyboarding. In S. Franklin (Ed.), *The best of the writing notebook* (2nd ed., pp. 46–48). Eugene, OR: The Writing Notebook.

Wheatley, G. (1991). Constructivist perspectives on science and mathematics learning. *Science Education, 75,* 9–21.

Whitehead, A. (1929). *The aims of education.* Cambridge, UK: Cambridge University Press.

Wittrock, M. (1974a). Learning as a generative process. *Educational Psychologist, 11,* 87–95.

Wittrock, M. (1974b). A generative model of mathematics learning. *Journal for Research in Mathematics Education, 5,* 181–197.

Wittrock, M. (1992). Generative learning processes of the brain. *Educational Psychologist, 27,* 531–541.

Yoder, S. (1992, March). 1/3+1/3+1/3=1 . . . Right? *Computing Teacher,* 38–40.

Yoder, S. (1994). *Introduction to programming in Logo using LogoWriter* (3rd ed.). Eugene, OR: International Society for Technology in Education.

Yoder, S., & Smith, I. (1996). *HyperTalk 2.3 for educators.* Eugene, OR: International Society for Technology in Education.

Yusuf, M. (1995). The effects of LOGO-based instruction. *Journal of Educational Computing Research, 12*(4), 335–362.

Zinsser, W. (1988). *Writing to learn.* New York: Harper & Row.

Index

Activities and Projects for Your Classroom

- Telecommunications
- Introducing Students to Computer Programs
- Ideas for Content-Area Projects
- Word Processing Activities for All Grade Levels
- Spreadsheet Activities
- Slide Show Activities
- Images to Capture
- Planets
- Cross-Grade Activities

> Content-area or age-specific variations of applications described in the text

Spotlight on Assessment

- Relating Learning and Assessment
- Performance Assessment
- Electronic Portfolios
- Using Peer Comments
- Evaluating Projects

> Explorations of ways to try to broaden awareness of assessment alternatives

Keeping Current

- Journals for K–12 Teachers
- Locating Appropriate Software
- Finding Useful Lists
- Company Mailing Lists
- General-Purpose Computer Magazines
- Trade Books

> Sources of information that address educational issues and provide reviews of software, hardware, and applications

Focus Boxes

- The Big Six Research Process
- Alternative Methods of Language Learning—The Power of Constructivism
- The Emerging Importance of the Computer Coordinator
- Lev Vygotsky
- Instructional Software on the Web
- Seymour Papert and LOGO
- The Original Bug
- Computer Play— Action Without Cognitive Processing?
- A Process-Oriented Checklist for LOGO
- Learning Word Processing Features
- Publication on the Internet
- Joining a List Maintained by a Server
- Levels of Internet Connection
- Web Excitement
- Citing Internet Sources
- A Brief History of Hypermedia
- What Can You Do with 600 Megabytes of Storage?
- Presentation Tools
- New Button Actions (NBAs)
- Screen Capture
- Sound Resources
- Camcorder Tips
- Storing Sounds for Multimedia Productions
- Web Design for Equal Access
- A Model District Policy on Software Copyright
- Does Anyone Understand Copyright Law?
- Taping Television Programs for Classroom Use
- Obtaining Permission to Copy

> Extended discussions of important people, instructional issues, and instructional strategies

Emerging Technology

- Using Computers and Calculators as Laboratory Tools
- Inexpensive "Keyboard" Computers
- Video Conferencing with CU-SeeMe
- Digital Video Discs
- The Evolution of Multimedia Encyclopedias
- Personal Digital Video Cameras
- Personal Web Servers

The emphasis in this book is on learners' *meaningful* use of technology. The special features above support and help activate key learning goals.